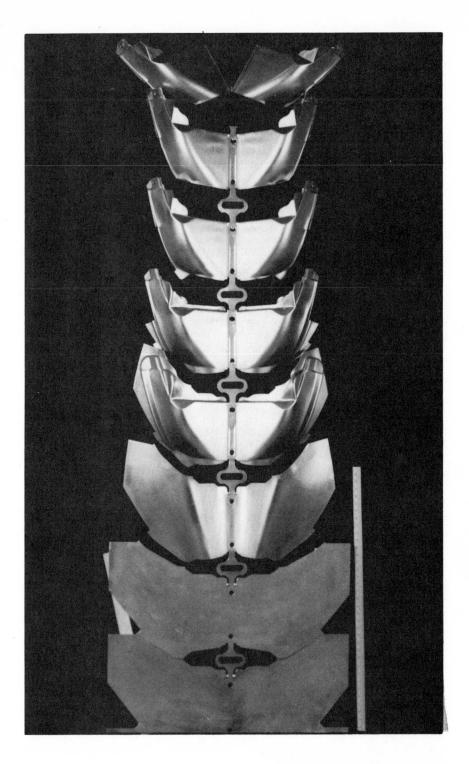

Photo courtesy Capitol Engineering Co.

PRESSWORKING AIDS FOR DESIGNERS AND DIEMAKERS

By Daniel B. Dallas
Editorial Director
Manufacturing Engineering

Library of Congress Catalog Card Number 77-90988
International Standard Book Number 0-87263-042-0

The Society of Manufacturing Engineers
20501 Ford Road
P.O. Box 930
Dearborn, Michigan 48128

Preface

As the die engineer's art grows increasingly scientific, the time-honored use of intuition is increasingly superseded by formulas and tabular data. No longer can the die engineer at the board and the diemaker at the bench make assumptions as to the forces they are working with and attempting to contain. Arithmetic exactitude is mandatory.

Compounding the problem of increasingly tight design requirements is the fact that the world is slowly but surely going metric.

This book is an attempt to provide assistance to the die engineer and diemaker who now—and increasingly in the future—must design and manufacture precision tooling in a mathematical language that is essentially foreign to them.

The author acknowledges his indebtedness for assistance in this endeavor to his many friends in industry and to his colleagues at the Society of Manufacturing Engineers, the editorial staff of MANUFACTURING ENGINEERING in particular.

Finally, the author would be most remiss if he failed to express a word of gratitude to the officers and directors of the Society for their patience in awaiting the long overdue publication of this book.

Daniel B. Dallas
Society of Manufacturing Engineers
Dearborn, Michigan
January, 1978

iii

Contents

Blanking Operations

BLANKING AND PIERCING OPERATIONS

The force required to cut through metal is a function of the following factors:

1. The length of the cut
2. The thickness of the material
3. The material's shear strength.

These factors can be expressed as an equation:

$$F = LtS$$

in which F = force, t = thickness, and S = shear strength.

In this equation, Lt is the *area in shear*. Accordingly, the equation can also be expressed as

$$F = AS$$

in which F = force, A = area in shear, and S = shear strength.

This relationship is shown graphically in *Figure* 1–1. To use this nomogram, it is necessary to determine the length of the cut in inches on Scale B. Next, *area in shear (Lt)* is located on Scale C by finding *thickness t* on Scale D, and connecting this point with *length of cut* on Scale B.

Next, the *shear strength* of the workpiece material is located on Scale A. A line drawn from this point through *area in shear* and extended to Scale E provides a value for the *shearing force* in tons.

Precisely the same nomogram, in metric, is provided in *Figure* 1–1A.

Tables 1–1 through 1–55 provide specific answers to the force equations in tons and kilonewtons. Additionally, a shear strength value for each material (in psi) is also provided. While it would be possible to interpolate tonnage requirements for metal thicknesses other than those specified, the shear strength value will enable the user to obtain a precise value should he prefer to use the equation.

FIG. 1-1. BLANKING

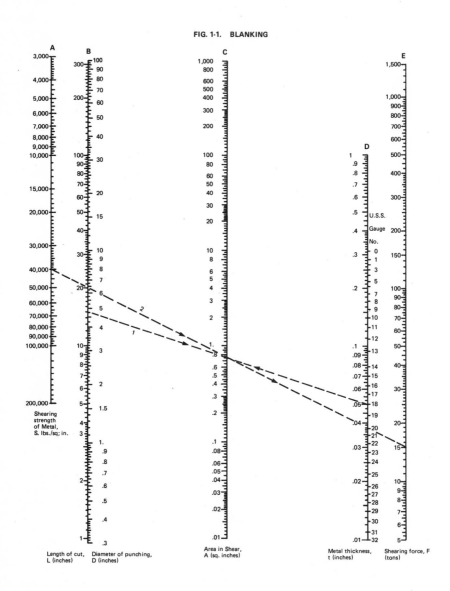

A	B	C	D	E
Shearing strength of Metal, S. lbs./sq; in.	Length of cut, L (inches) · Diameter of punching, D (inches)	Area in Shear, A (sq. inches)	Metal thickness, t (inches) · U.S.S. Gauge No.	Shearing force, F (tons)

FIG. 1-1A
2. BLANKING PRESSURE EQUATION

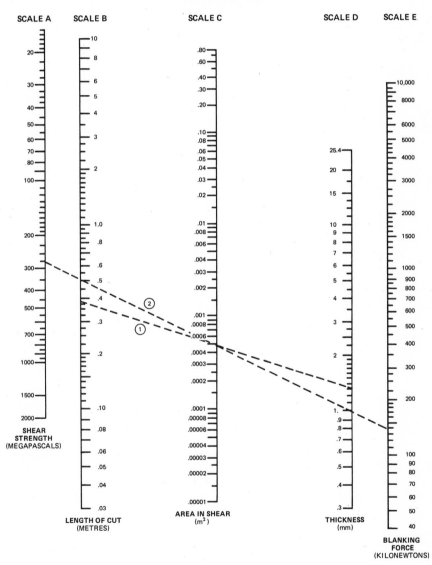

Blanking Force Requirements—Asbestos and Aluminum

Stock Thickness		1-1. Asbestos Board S.S. = 5000 psi				1-2. Aluminum (Cast) S.S. = 12,000 psi				1-3. Aluminum (Soft) S.S. = 15,000 psi			
		1 in Length Cut		1 cm Length Cut		1 in Length Cut		1 cm Length Cut		1 in Length Cut		1 cm Length Cut	
inch	mm	ton	kN	ton	kN	ton	kN	ton	kN	ton	kN	ton	kN
0.0120	0.304 80	0.030	0.267	0.012	0.107	0.072	0.641	0.028	0.249	0.090	0.801	0.035	0.311
0.0135	0.342 90	0.034	0.302	0.013	0.116	0.081	0.721	0.032	0.285	0.101	0.898	0.040	0.356
0.0149	0.378 46	0.037	0.329	0.015	0.133	0.089	0.792	0.035	0.311	0.112	0.996	0.044	0.391
0.0164	0.416 56	0.041	0.365	0.016	0.142	0.098	0.872	0.039	0.347	0.123	1.094	0.048	0.427
0.0179	0.454 66	0.045	0.400	0.018	0.160	0.107	0.952	0.042	0.374	0.134	1.192	0.053	0.471
0.0209	0.530 86	0.052	0.463	0.021	0.187	0.125	1.112	0.049	0.436	0.157	1.397	0.062	0.199
0.0239	0.607 06	0.060	0.534	0.024	0.214	0.143	1.272	0.056	0.498	0.179	1.592	0.071	0.632
0.0269	0.683 26	0.067	0.596	0.026	0.231	0.161	1.432	0.064	0.569	0.202	1.797	0.079	0.703
0.0299	0.759 46	0.075	0.667	0.029	0.258	0.179	1.592	0.071	0.632	0.224	1.993	0.088	0.783
0.0329	0.835 65	0.082	0.729	0.032	0.285	0.197	1.753	0.078	0.694	0.247	2.197	0.097	0.863
0.0359	0.922 86	0.090	0.801	0.035	0.311	0.215	1.913	0.085	0.756	0.269	2.393	0.106	0.943
0.0418	1.061 72	0.105	0.934	0.041	0.365	0.251	2.233	0.099	0.881	0.314	2.793	0.123	1.094
0.0478	1.214 12	0.120	1.068	0.047	0.418	0.287	2.553	0.113	1.005	0.359	3.194	0.141	1.254
0.0538	1.366 52	0.135	1.201	0.053	0.471	0.323	2.873	0.127	1.130	0.404	3.594	0.159	1.414
0.0598	1.518 92	0.150	1.334	0.059	0.525	0.359	3.194	0.141	1.254	0.449	3.994	0.177	1.575
0.0673	1.709 42	0.168	1.495	0.066	0.587	0.404	3.594	0.159	1.414	0.505	4.492	0.199	1.770
0.0747	1.897 38	0.187	1.664	0.074	0.658	0.448	3.985	0.176	1.566	0.560	4.982	0.221	1.966
0.0897	2.278 38	0.224	1.993	0.088	0.783	0.538	4.786	0.212	1.886	0.673	5.987	0.265	2.357
0.1046	2.656 84	0.262	2.331	0.103	0.916	0.628	5.587	0.247	2.197	0.785	6.983	0.309	2.749
0.1196	3.037 84	0.299	2.660	0.118	1.050	0.718	6.387	0.283	2.518	0.897	7.980	0.353	3.140
0.1345	3.416 30	0.336	2.989	0.132	1.174	0.807	7.179	0.318	2.829	1.009	8.976	0.397	3.532
0.1494	3.794 76	0.374	3.327	0.147	1.308	0.896	7.971	0.353	3.140	1.121	9.972	0.441	3.923
0.1644	4.175 76	0.411	3.656	0.162	1.441	0.986	8.771	0.388	3.452	1.233	10.969	0.485	4.315
0.1793	4.554 22	0.448	3.985	0.176	1.566	1.076	9.572	0.424	3.772	1.345	11.965	0.529	4.706
0.1943	4.935 22	0.486	4.323	0.191	1.699	1.166	10.373	0.459	4.083	1.457	12.961	0.574	5.106

Blanking Force Requirements—Aluminum and Brass

Stock Thickness		1-4. Aluminum (Half Hard) S.S. = 19,000 psi				1-5. Aluminum (Hard) S.S. = 25,000 psi				1-6. Brass (Soft) S.S. = 30,000 psi			
		1 in Length Cut		1 cm Length Cut		1 in Length Cut		1 cm Length Cut		1 in Length Cut		1 cm Length Cut	
inch	mm	ton	kN	ton	kN	ton	kN	ton	kN	ton	kN	ton	kN
0.0120	0.304 80	0.144	1.014	0.045	0.400	0.150	1.334	0.059	0.525	0.180	1.601	0.071	0.632
0.0135	0.342 90	0.128	1.139	0.050	0.445	0.169	1.503	0.066	0.587	0.203	1.806	0.080	0.712
0.0149	0.378 46	0.142	1.263	0.056	0.498	0.186	1.655	0.073	0.649	0.224	1.993	0.088	0.782
0.0164	0.416 56	0.156	1.388	0.061	0.543	0.205	1.824	0.081	0.721	0.246	2.188	0.097	0.863
0.0179	0.454 66	0.170	1.512	0.067	0.596	0.224	1.993	0.088	0.783	0.269	2.393	0.106	0.943
0.0209	0.530 86	0.199	1.770	0.078	0.694	0.261	2.322	0.103	0.916	0.314	2.793	0.123	1.094
0.0239	0.607 06	0.227	2.019	0.089	0.792	0.299	2.660	0.118	1.050	0.359	3.194	0.141	1.254
0.0269	0.683 26	0.256	2.277	0.101	0.898	0.336	2.989	0.132	1.174	0.404	3.594	0.159	1.414
0.0299	0.759 46	0.284	2.526	0.112	0.996	0.374	3.327	0.147	1.308	0.449	3.994	0.177	1.575
0.0329	0.835 65	0.313	2.784	0.123	1.094	0.411	3.656	0.162	1.441	0.494	4.395	0.194	1.726
0.0359	0.922 86	0.341	3.036	0.134	1.192	0.449	3.994	0.177	1.575	0.539	4.795	0.212	1.886
0.0418	1.061 72	0.397	3.532	0.156	1.388	0.523	4.653	0.206	1.833	0.627	5.578	0.247	2.197
0.0478	1.214 12	0.454	4.039	0.179	1.592	0.598	5.320	0.235	2.091	0.717	6.378	0.282	2.509
0.0538	1.366 52	0.511	4.546	0.201	1.788	0.673	5.987	0.265	2.357	0.807	7.179	0.318	2.829
0.0598	1.518 92	0.568	5.053	0.224	1.993	0.748	6.654	0.294	2.615	0.897	7.980	0.353	3.140
0.0673	1.709 42	0.639	5.685	0.252	2.242	0.841	7.482	0.331	2.945	1.010	8.985	0.397	3.532
0.0747	1.897 38	0.710	6.316	0.279	2.482	0.934	8.309	0.368	3.274	1.121	9.972	0.441	3.923
0.0897	2.278 38	0.852	7.579	0.335	2.980	1.121	9.972	0.441	3.923	1.346	11.974	0.530	4.715
0.1046	2.656 84	0.994	8.843	0.391	3.478	1.308	11.636	0.515	4.581	1.569	13.958	0.618	5.498
0.1196	3.037 84	1.136	10.106	0.447	3.977	1.495	13.300	0.589	5.240	1.794	15.959	0.706	6.281
0.1345	3.416 30	1.278	11.369	0.503	4.475	1.681	14.954	0.662	5.889	2.018	17.952	0.794	7.063
0.1494	3.794 76	1.419	12.623	0.559	4.973	1.868	16.618	0.735	6.539	2.241	19.936	0.882	7.846
0.1644	4.175 76	1.562	13.896	0.615	5.471	2.055	18.281	0.809	7.197	2.466	21.938	0.971	8.638
0.1793	4.554 22	1.703	15.150	0.671	5.962	2.241	19.936	0.882	7.846	2.690	23.930	1.059	9.421
0.1943	4.935 22	1.846	16.422	0.727	6.467	2.429	21.608	0.956	8.505	2.915	25.932	1.147	10.204

Blanking Force Requirements—Brass and Bronze

Stock Thickness		1–7. Brass (Half Hard) S.S. = 35,000 psi				1–8. Brass (Hard) S.S. = 40,000 psi				1–9. Bronze (Gun Metal) S.S. = 32,000 psi			
		1 in Length Cut		1 cm Length Cut		1 in Length Cut		1 cm Length Cut		1 in Length Cut		1 cm Length Cut	
inch	mm	ton	kN	ton	kN	ton	kN	ton	kN	ton	kN	ton	kN
0.0120	0.304 80	0.210	1.868	0.083	0.738	0.240	2.135	0.094	0.836	0.192	1.708	0.076	0.676
0.0135	0.342 90	0.236	2.099	0.093	0.827	0.270	2.402	0.106	0.943	0.216	1.922	0.085	0.756
0.0149	0.378 46	0.261	2.322	0.103	0.916	0.298	2.651	0.117	1.041	0.238	2.117	0.094	0.836
0.0164	0.416 56	0.287	2.553	0.113	1.005	0.328	2.918	0.129	1.148	0.262	2.331	0.103	0.916
0.0179	0.454 66	0.313	2.784	0.123	1.094	0.358	3.185	0.141	1.254	0.286	2.544	0.113	1.005
0.0209	0.530 86	0.366	3.256	0.144	1.281	0.418	3.719	0.165	1.468	0.334	2.971	0.132	1.174
0.0239	0.607 06	0.418	3.719	0.165	1.468	0.478	4.252	0.188	1.672	0.382	3.398	0.151	1.343
0.0269	0.683 26	0.471	4.190	0.185	1.646	0.538	4.786	0.212	1.886	0.430	3.825	0.169	1.503
0.0299	0.759 46	0.523	4.653	0.206	1.833	0.598	5.320	0.235	2.091	0.478	4.252	0.188	1.672
0.0329	0.835 65	0.576	5.124	0.227	2.019	0.658	5.854	0.259	2.304	0.526	4.679	0.207	1.841
0.0359	0.922 86	0.628	5.587	0.247	2.197	0.718	6.387	0.283	2.518	0.574	5.106	0.226	2.010
0.0418	1.061 72	0.732	6.512	0.288	2.562	0.836	7.437	0.329	2.927	0.669	5.951	0.263	2.340
0.0478	1.214 12	0.837	7.446	0.329	2.927	0.956	8.505	0.376	3.345	0.765	6.806	0.301	2.678
0.0538	1.366 52	0.942	8.380	0.371	3.300	1.076	9.572	0.424	3.772	0.861	7.659	0.339	3.016
0.0598	1.518 92	1.047	9.314	0.412	3.665	1.196	10.640	0.471	4.190	0.957	8.513	0.377	3.354
0.0673	1.709 42	1.178	10.479	0.464	4.128	1.346	11.970	0.530	4.715	1.077	9.581	0.424	3.772
0.0747	1.897 38	1.307	11.627	0.515	4.581	1.494	13.291	0.588	5.231	1.195	10.631	0.471	4.190
0.0897	2.278 38	1.570	13.967	0.618	5.498	1.794	15.959	0.706	6.281	1.435	12.766	0.565	5.026
0.1046	2.656 84	1.831	16.289	0.721	6.414	2.092	18.610	0.824	7.330	1.674	14.892	0.659	5.862
0.1196	3.037 84	2.093	18.619	0.824	7.330	2.392	21.279	0.942	8.380	1.914	17.027	0.754	6.708
0.1345	3.416 30	2.354	20.941	0.927	8.247	2.690	23.930	1.059	9.421	2.152	19.144	0.847	7.535
0.1494	3.794 76	2.615	23.263	1.029	9.154	2.988	26.581	1.176	10.462	2.390	21.261	0.941	8.371
0.1644	4.175 76	2.877	25.594	1.133	10.079	3.288	29.250	1.294	11.511	2.630	23.396	1.036	9.216
0.1793	4.554 22	3.138	27.916	1.235	10.987	3.586	31.901	1.412	12.561	2.869	25.523	1.129	10.044
0.1943	4.935 22	3.400	30.246	1.339	11.918	3.886	34.570	1.530	13.611	3.109	27.658	1.224	10.889

Blanking Force Requirements—Bronze, Cellulose Acetate, and Cloth

Stock Thickness		1-10. Bronze (Phosphor) S.S. = 40,000 psi				1-11. Cellulose Acetate S.S. = 10,000 psi				1-12. Cloth S.S. = 8,000 psi			
		1 in Length Cut		1 cm Length Cut		1 in Length Cut		1 cm Length Cut		1 in Length Cut		1 cm Length Cut	
inch	mm	ton	kN	ton	kN	ton	kN	ton	kN	ton	kN	ton	kN
0.0120	0.304 80	0.240	2.135	0.094	0.836	0.060	0.534	0.024	0.214	0.048	0.427	0.019	0.169
0.0135	0.342 90	0.270	2.402	0.106	0.943	0.068	0.605	0.027	0.240	0.054	0.480	0.021	0.187
0.0149	0.378 46	0.298	2.651	0.117	1.041	0.075	0.667	0.029	0.258	0.060	0.534	0.023	0.205
0.0164	0.416 56	0.328	2.918	0.129	1.148	0.082	0.729	0.032	0.285	0.066	0.587	0.026	0.231
0.0179	0.454 66	0.358	3.185	0.141	1.254	0.090	0.801	0.035	0.311	0.072	0.641	0.028	0.249
0.0209	0.530 86	0.418	3.719	0.165	1.468	0.105	0.934	0.041	0.365	0.084	0.747	0.033	0.294
0.0239	0.607 06	0.478	4.252	0.188	1.672	0.120	1.068	0.047	0.418	0.096	0.854	0.038	0.338
0.0269	0.683 26	0.538	4.786	0.212	1.886	0.135	1.201	0.053	0.471	0.108	0.961	0.042	0.374
0.0299	0.759 46	0.598	5.320	0.235	2.091	0.150	1.334	0.059	0.525	0.120	1.068	0.047	0.418
0.0329	0.835 65	0.658	5.854	0.259	2.304	0.165	1.468	0.064	0.569	0.132	1.174	0.052	0.463
0.0359	0.922 86	0.718	6.387	0.283	2.518	0.180	1.601	0.071	0.632	0.144	1.281	0.057	0.507
0.0418	1.061 72	0.836	7.437	0.329	2.927	0.209	1.859	0.082	0.729	0.167	1.486	0.066	0.487
0.0478	1.214 12	0.956	8.505	0.376	3.345	0.239	2.126	0.094	0.836	0.191	1.699	0.075	0.667
0.0538	1.366 52	1.076	9.572	0.424	3.772	0.269	2.393	0.106	0.943	0.215	1.913	0.085	0.756
0.0598	1.518 92	1.196	10.640	0.471	4.190	0.299	2.660	0.118	1.050	0.239	2.126	0.094	0.836
0.0673	1.709 42	1.346	11.974	0.530	4.715	0.337	2.998	0.132	1.174	0.269	2.393	0.106	0.943
0.0747	1.897 38	1.494	13.291	0.588	5.231	0.374	3.327	0.147	1.308	0.299	2.660	0.118	1.050
0.0897	2.278 38	1.794	15.959	0.706	6.281	0.449	3.994	0.177	1.575	0.359	3.194	0.141	1.254
0.1046	2.656 84	2.092	18.610	0.824	7.330	0.523	4.653	0.206	1.833	0.418	3.719	0.165	1.468
0.1196	3.037 84	2.392	21.279	0.942	8.380	0.598	5.320	0.235	2.091	0.478	4.252	0.188	1.672
0.1345	3.416 30	2.690	23.930	1.059	9.421	0.673	5.987	0.265	2.357	0.538	4.786	0.212	1.886
0.1494	3.794 76	2.988	26.581	1.176	10.462	0.747	6.645	0.294	2.615	0.598	5.320	0.235	2.091
0.1644	4.175 76	3.288	29.250	1.294	11.511	0.822	7.313	0.324	2.882	0.658	5.854	0.259	2.304
0.1793	4.554 22	3.586	31.901	1.412	12.561	0.897	7.980	0.353	3.140	0.717	6.378	0.282	2.509
0.1943	4.935 22	3.886	34.570	1.530	13.611	0.972	8.647	0.382	3.398	0.777	6.912	0.306	2.722

Blanking Force Requirements—Copper and Duralumin

| Stock Thickness | | 1-13. Copper S.S. = 22,000 psi | | | | 1-14. Duralumin (Treated) S.S. = 35,000 psi | | | | 1-15. Duralumin (Treated & Rolled) S.S. = 40,000 psi | | | |
| | | 1 in Length Cut | | 1 cm Length Cut | | 1 in Length Cut | | 1 cm Length Cut | | 1 in Length Cut | | 1 cm Length Cut | |
inch	mm	ton	kN	ton	kN	ton	kN	ton	kN	ton	kN	ton	kN
0.0120	0.304 80	0.132	1.174	0.052	0.463	0.210	1.868	0.083	0.738	0.240	2.135	0.094	0.836
0.0135	0.342 90	0.149	1.326	0.058	0.516	0.236	2.099	0.093	0.827	0.270	2.402	0.106	0.943
0.0149	0.378 46	0.164	1.459	0.065	0.578	0.261	2.322	0.103	0.916	0.298	2.651	0.117	1.041
0.0164	0.416 56	0.180	1.601	0.071	0.632	0.287	2.553	0.113	1.005	0.328	2.918	0.129	1.148
0.0179	0.454 66	0.197	1.753	0.076	0.676	0.313	2.784	0.123	1.094	0.358	3.185	0.141	1.254
0.0209	0.530 86	0.230	2.046	0.091	0.810	0.366	3.256	0.144	1.281	0.418	3.719	0.165	1.468
0.0239	0.607 06	0.263	2.340	0.104	0.925	0.418	3.719	0.165	1.468	0.478	4.252	0.188	1.672
0.0269	0.683 26	0.296	2.633	0.116	1.032	0.471	4.190	0.185	1.646	0.538	4.786	0.212	1.886
0.0299	0.759 46	0.329	2.927	0.129	1.148	0.523	4.653	0.206	1.833	0.598	5.320	0.235	2.091
0.0329	0.835 65	0.362	3.220	0.142	1.263	0.576	5.124	0.226	2.010	0.658	5.854	0.259	2.304
0.0359	0.922 86	0.395	3.514	0.155	1.379	0.628	5.587	0.248	2.206	0.718	6.387	0.283	2.518
0.0418	1.061 72	0.460	4.092	0.181	1.610	0.732	6.512	0.288	2.562	0.836	7.437	0.329	2.927
0.0478	1.214 12	0.526	4.679	0.207	1.841	0.837	7.446	0.329	2.927	0.956	8.505	0.376	3.345
0.0538	1.366 52	0.592	5.266	0.233	2.073	0.942	8.380	0.371	3.300	1.076	9.572	0.424	3.772
0.0598	1.518 92	0.658	5.854	0.259	2.304	1.047	9.314	0.412	3.665	1.196	10.640	0.471	4.190
0.0673	1.709 42	0.740	6.583	0.291	2.589	1.178	10.749	0.464	4.128	1.346	11.974	0.530	4.715
0.0747	1.897 38	0.822	7.313	0.324	2.882	1.307	11.627	0.515	4.581	1.494	13.291	0.588	5.231
0.0897	2.278 38	0.987	8.780	0.388	3.452	1.570	13.967	0.618	5.498	1.794	15.959	0.706	6.281
0.1046	2.656 84	1.151	10.239	0.453	4.030	1.831	16.289	0.721	6.414	2.092	18.610	0.824	7.330
0.1196	3.037 84	1.316	11.707	0.518	4.608	2.093	18.619	0.824	7.330	2.392	21.279	0.942	8.380
0.1345	3.416 30	1.480	13.166	0.582	5.177	2.354	20.941	0.927	8.247	2.690	23.930	1.059	9.421
0.1494	3.794 76	1.643	14.616	0.647	5.756	2.615	23.263	1.029	9.154	2.988	26.581	1.176	10.462
0.1644	4.175 76	1.808	16.084	0.712	6.334	2.877	25.594	1.133	10.079	3.288	29.250	1.294	11.511
0.1793	4.554 22	1.972	17.543	0.776	6.903	3.138	27.916	1.235	10.987	3.586	31.901	1.412	12.561
0.1943	4.935 22	2.137	19.011	0.841	7.482	3.400	30.246	1.339	11.918	3.886	34.570	1.530	13.611

Blanking Force Requirements—Fiber and Inconel

Stock Thickness		1-16. Fiber (Hard) S.S. = 24,000 psi				1-17. Inconel (80,000 UTS) S.S. = 59,000 psi				1-18. Inconel (90,000 UTS) S.S. = 63,000 psi			
		1 in Length Cut		1 cm Length Cut		1 in Length Cut		1 cm Length Cut		1 in Length Cut		1 cm Length Cut	
inch	mm	ton	kN	ton	kN	ton	kN	ton	kN	ton	kN	ton	kN
0.0120	0.304 80	0.144	1.281	0.057	0.507	0.354	3.149	0.139	1.237	0.378	3.363	0.149	1.326
0.0135	0.342 90	0.162	1.441	0.064	0.569	0.398	3.541	0.157	1.397	0.425	3.781	0.167	1.486
0.0149	0.378 46	0.179	1.592	0.070	0.623	0.440	3.914	0.173	1.539	0.469	4.172	0.185	1.646
0.0164	0.416 56	0.197	1.753	0.077	0.685	0.484	4.306	0.190	1.690	0.517	4.599	0.203	1.809
0.0179	0.454 66	0.215	1.913	0.085	0.756	0.528	4.697	0.208	1.850	0.564	5.017	0.222	1.975
0.0209	0.530 86	0.251	2.233	0.099	0.881	0.617	5.489	0.243	2.162	0.658	5.854	0.259	2.304
0.0239	0.607 06	0.287	2.553	0.113	1.005	0.705	6.272	0.278	2.473	0.753	6.699	0.296	2.633
0.0269	0.683 26	0.323	2.873	0.127	1.130	0.794	7.063	0.312	2.776	0.847	7.535	0.334	2.971
0.0299	0.759 46	0.359	3.194	0.141	1.254	0.882	7.846	0.347	3.087	0.942	8.380	0.371	3.300
0.0329	0.835 65	0.395	3.514	0.155	1.379	0.971	8.638	0.382	3.398	1.036	9.216	0.408	3.630
0.0359	0.922 86	0.431	3.834	0.170	1.512	1.059	9.421	0.417	3.710	1.131	10.061	0.445	3.959
0.0418	1.061 72	0.502	4.466	0.197	1.753	1.233	10.969	0.485	4.315	1.317	11.716	0.518	4.608
0.0478	1.214 12	0.574	5.106	0.226	2.010	1.410	12.543	0.555	4.937	1.506	13.397	0.593	5.275
0.0538	1.366 52	0.646	5.747	0.254	2.260	1.587	14.118	0.623	5.560	1.695	15.079	0.667	5.934
0.0598	1.518 92	0.718	6.387	0.283	2.518	1.764	15.693	0.695	6.183	1.884	16.760	0.742	6.601
0.0673	1.709 42	0.808	7.188	0.318	2.829	1.985	17.659	0.782	6.957	2.120	18.860	0.835	7.428
0.0747	1.897 38	0.896	7.971	0.353	3.140	2.204	19.607	0.868	7.722	2.353	20.932	0.926	8.238
0.0897	2.278 38	1.076	9.572	0.424	3.772	2.646	23.539	1.042	9.270	2.826	25.140	1.112	9.892
0.1046	2.656 84	1.255	11.164	0.494	4.395	3.086	27.453	1.215	10.809	3.295	29.312	1.297	11.538
0.1196	3.037 84	1.435	12.766	0.565	5.026	3.528	31.385	1.389	12.357	3.767	33.511	1.483	13.193
0.1345	3.416 30	1.614	14.358	0.635	5.649	3.968	35.299	1.562	13.896	4.237	37.692	1.668	14.839
0.1494	3.794 76	1.793	15.951	0.706	6.281	4.407	39.205	1.735	15.435	4.706	41.865	1.853	16.484
0.1644	4.175 76	1.973	17.552	0.777	6.912	4.850	43.146	1.909	16.982	5.179	46.072	2.039	18.139
0.1793	4.554 22	2.152	19.144	0.847	7.535	5.289	47.051	2.082	18.521	5.648	50.245	2.224	19.785
0.1943	4.935 22	2.332	20.745	0.918	8.167	5.732	50.992	2.257	20.078	6.120	54.444	2.410	21.439

Blanking Force Requirements—Inconel

Stock Thickness		1-19. Inconel (100,000 UTS) S.S. = 66,000 psi				1-20. Inconel (115,000 UTS) S.S. = 71,000 psi				1-21. Inconel (140,000 UTS) S.S. = 78,000 psi			
		1 in Length Cut		1 cm Length Cut		1 in Length Cut		1 cm Length Cut		1 in Length Cut		1 cm Length Cut	
inch	mm	ton	kN	ton	kN	ton	kN	ton	kN	ton	kN	ton	kN
0.0120	0.304 80	0.396	3.523	0.156	1.388	0.426	3.790	0.168	1.495	0.468	4.163	0.184	1.637
0.0135	0.342 90	0.446	3.968	0.175	1.557	0.479	4.261	0.187	1.664	0.527	4.688	0.207	1.841
0.0149	0.378 46	0.492	4.377	0.194	1.726	0.529	4.706	0.208	1.850	0.581	5.169	0.229	2.037
0.0164	0.416 56	0.541	4.813	0.213	1.895	0.582	5.177	0.229	2.037	0.640	5.693	0.252	2.242
0.0179	0.454 66	0.591	5.258	0.233	2.073	0.635	5.649	0.250	2.224	0.698	6.209	0.275	2.446
0.0209	0.530 86	0.690	6.138	0.272	2.420	0.742	6.601	0.292	2.598	0.815	7.250	0.321	2.856
0.0239	0.607 06	0.789	7.019	0.311	2.767	0.848	7.544	0.334	2.971	0.932	8.291	0.367	3.265
0.0269	0.683 26	0.888	7.900	0.349	3.105	0.955	8.496	0.376	3.345	1.049	9.332	0.413	3.674
0.0299	0.759 46	0.987	8.780	0.388	3.452	1.061	9.439	0.418	3.719	1.166	10.373	0.459	4.083
0.0329	0.835 65	1.086	9.661	0.427	3.799	1.168	10.391	0.460	4.092	1.283	11.414	0.505	4.492
0.0359	0.922 86	1.185	10.542	0.466	4.146	1.274	11.334	0.502	4.466	1.400	12.454	0.551	4.902
0.0418	1.061 72	1.379	12.268	0.543	4.831	1.484	13.202	0.584	5.195	1.630	14.500	0.642	5.711
0.0478	1.214 12	1.577	14.029	0.621	5.524	1.697	15.097	0.668	5.943	1.864	16.582	0.734	6.530
0.0538	1.366 52	1.775	15.790	0.699	6.218	1.910	16.991	0.752	6.690	2.098	18.664	0.826	7.348
0.0598	1.518 92	1.973	17.552	0.777	6.912	2.123	18.886	0.836	7.437	2.332	20.745	0.918	8.167
0.0673	1.709 42	2.221	19.758	0.874	7.775	2.389	21.253	0.941	8.371	2.625	23.352	1.033	9.190
0.0747	1.897 38	2.465	21.929	0.971	8.638	2.652	23.592	1.044	9.287	2.913	25.914	1.147	10.204
0.0897	2.278 38	2.960	26.332	1.165	10.364	3.184	28.325	1.254	11.156	3.498	31.118	1.377	12.250
0.1046	2.656 84	3.452	30.709	1.359	12.090	3.713	33.031	1.462	13.006	4.079	36.287	1.606	14.287
0.1196	3.037 84	3.947	35.113	1.554	13.824	4.246	37.772	1.672	14.874	4.664	41.491	1.836	16.333
0.1345	3.416 30	4.439	39.489	1.747	15.541	4.793	42.639	1.887	16.787	5.246	46.668	2.065	18.370
0.1494	3.794 76	4.930	43.857	1.941	17.267	5.304	47.184	2.088	18.575	5.827	51.837	2.294	20.407
0.1644	4.175 76	5.424	48.261	2.136	19.002	5.836	51.917	2.298	20.443	6.412	57.041	2.524	22.454
0.1793	4.554 22	5.917	52.638	2.329	20.719	6.365	56.623	2.506	22.293	6.993	62.210	2.730	24.286
0.1943	4.935 22	6.412	57.041	2.524	22.454	6.898	61.365	2.716	24.162	7.578	67.414	2.983	26.537

Blanking Force Requirements—Inconel and Lead

Stock Thickness		1-22. Inconel (160,000 UTS) S.S. = 84,000 psi				1-23. Inconel (175,000 UTS) S.S. = 87,000 psi				1-24. Lead S.S. = 4,000 psi			
		1 in Length Cut		1 cm Length Cut		1 in Length Cut		1 cm Length Cut		1 in Length Cut		1 cm Length Cut	
inch	mm	ton	kN	ton	kN	ton	kN	ton	kN	ton	kN	ton	kN
0.0120	0.304 80	0.504	4.484	0.198	1.761	0.522	4.644	0.206	1.833	0.024	0.214	0.009	0.080
0.0135	0.342 90	0.567	5.044	0.223	1.984	0.587	5.222	0.231	2.055	0.027	0.240	0.011	0.098
0.0149	0.378 46	0.626	5.569	0.246	2.188	0.648	5.765	0.255	2.268	0.030	0.267	0.012	0.107
0.0164	0.416 56	0.689	6.129	0.271	2.411	0.713	6.343	0.281	2.500	0.033	0.294	0.013	0.116
0.0179	0.454 66	0.752	6.690	0.296	2.633	0.779	6.930	0.307	2.731	0.036	0.320	0.014	0.125
0.0209	0.530 86	0.878	7.811	0.346	3.078	0.909	8.086	0.358	3.185	0.042	0.374	0.016	0.142
0.0239	0.607 06	1.004	8.932	0.395	3.514	1.040	9.252	0.409	3.638	0.048	0.427	0.019	0.169
0.0269	0.683 26	1.130	10.052	0.445	3.959	1.170	10.408	0.461	4.101	0.054	0.480	0.021	0.187
0.0299	0.759 46	1.256	11.173	0.494	4.395	1.301	11.574	0.512	4.555	0.060	0.534	0.024	0.214
0.0329	0.835 65	1.382	12.294	0.544	4.839	1.431	12.730	0.563	5.008	0.066	0.587	0.026	0.231
0.0359	0.922 86	1.508	13.415	0.594	5.284	1.562	13.896	0.615	5.471	0.072	0.641	0.028	0.249
0.0418	1.061 72	1.756	15.621	0.691	6.147	1.818	16.713	0.716	6.370	0.084	0.747	0.033	0.294
0.0478	1.214 12	2.008	17.863	0.790	7.028	2.079	18.495	0.819	7.286	0.096	0.854	0.038	0.338
0.0538	1.366 52	2.260	20.105	0.890	7.917	2.340	20.817	0.921	8.193	0.108	0.961	0.042	0.374
0.0598	1.518 92	2.512	22.347	0.989	8.798	2.601	23.138	1.024	9.110	0.120	1.068	0.047	0.418
0.0673	1.709 42	2.827	25.149	1.113	9.901	2.928	26.047	1.153	10.257	0.135	1.201	0.053	0.471
0.0747	1.897 38	3.137	27.907	1.235	10.987	3.249	28.903	1.279	11.378	0.149	1.326	0.059	0.525
0.0897	2.278 38	3.767	33.511	1.483	13.193	3.902	34.712	1.536	13.664	0.179	1.592	0.071	0.632
0.1046	2.656 84	4.393	39.080	1.730	15.390	4.550	40.477	1.791	15.933	0.209	1.859	0.082	0.729
0.1196	3.037 84	5.023	44.685	1.978	17.596	5.203	46.286	2.048	18.219	0.239	2.126	0.094	0.836
0.1345	3.416 30	5.649	50.254	2.224	19.785	5.851	52.050	2.303	20.487	0.269	2.393	0.106	0.943
0.1494	3.794 76	6.275	55.822	2.470	21.973	6.499	57.815	2.559	22.765	0.299	2.660	0.118	1.050
0.1644	4.175 76	6.905	61.427	2.718	24.179	7.151	63.615	2.816	25.051	0.329	2.927	0.129	1.148
0.1793	4.554 22	7.531	66.996	2.965	26.377	7.800	69.389	3.071	27.320	0.359	3.194	0.141	1.254
0.1943	4.935 22	8.161	72.600	3.213	28.583	8.452	75.189	3.328	29.606	0.389	3.461	0.153	1.361

Blanking Force Requirements—Leather and Monel

Stock Thickness		1-25. Leather (Rawhide) S.S. = 13,000 psi				1-26. Leather (Tanned) S.S. = 7,000 psi				1-27. Monel (Rolled) S.S. = 65,000 psi			
		1 in Length Cut		1 cm Length Cut		1 in Length Cut		1 cm Length Cut		1 in Length Cut		1 cm Length Cut	
inch	mm	ton	kN	ton	kN	ton	kN	ton	kN	ton	kN	ton	kN
0.0120	0.304 80	0.078	0.694	0.031	0.276	0.042	0.374	0.017	0.151	0.390	3.469	0.154	1.370
0.0135	0.342 90	0.088	0.783	0.035	0.311	0.047	0.418	0.019	0.169	0.439	3.905	0.173	1.539
0.0149	0.378 46	0.097	0.863	0.038	0.338	0.052	0.463	0.021	0.187	0.484	4.306	0.191	1.699
0.0164	0.416 56	0.107	0.952	0.042	0.374	0.057	0.507	0.023	0.205	0.533	4.742	0.210	1.868
0.0179	0.454 66	0.116	1.032	0.046	0.409	0.063	0.560	0.025	0.222	0.582	5.177	0.229	2.037
0.0209	0.530 86	0.136	1.210	0.053	0.471	0.073	0.649	0.029	0.258	0.679	6.040	0.267	2.375
0.0239	0.607 06	0.155	1.379	0.061	0.543	0.084	0.747	0.033	0.294	0.777	6.912	0.306	2.722
0.0269	0.683 26	0.175	1.557	0.069	0.614	0.094	0.836	0.037	0.329	0.874	7.775	0.344	3.060
0.0299	0.759 46	0.194	1.726	0.077	0.685	0.105	0.934	0.041	0.365	0.972	8.647	0.383	3.407
0.0329	0.835 65	0.214	1.904	0.084	0.747	0.115	1.023	0.045	0.400	1.069	9.510	0.421	3.745
0.0359	0.922 86	0.233	2.073	0.092	0.818	0.126	1.121	0.049	0.436	1.167	10.382	0.459	4.083
0.0418	1.061 72	0.272	2.420	0.107	0.952	0.146	1.299	0.058	0.516	1.359	12.090	0.535	4.759
0.0478	1.214 12	0.311	2.767	0.122	1.085	0.167	1.486	0.066	0.587	1.554	13.824	0.612	5.444
0.0538	1.366 52	0.350	3.114	0.138	1.228	0.188	1.672	0.074	0.658	1.749	15.559	0.688	6.120
0.0598	1.518 92	0.389	3.461	0.153	1.361	0.209	1.859	0.082	0.729	1.944	17.294	0.765	6.805
0.0673	1.709 42	0.437	3.888	0.172	1.530	0.236	2.099	0.093	0.827	2.187	19.456	0.861	7.659
0.0747	1.897 38	0.486	4.323	0.191	1.699	0.261	2.322	0.103	0.916	2.428	21.599	0.956	8.505
0.0897	2.278 38	0.583	5.186	0.230	2.046	0.314	2.793	0.124	1.103	2.915	25.931	1.148	10.213
0.1046	2.656 84	0.680	6.049	0.268	2.384	0.366	3.256	0.144	1.281	3.400	30.246	1.338	11.903
0.1196	3.037 84	0.777	6.912	0.306	2.722	0.419	3.727	0.165	1.468	3.887	34.579	1.530	13.611
0.1345	3.416 30	0.874	7.775	0.344	3.060	0.471	4.190	0.185	1.646	4.371	38.884	1.721	15.310
0.1494	3.794 76	0.971	8.638	0.382	3.398	0.523	4.653	0.206	1.833	4.856	43.199	1.912	17.009
0.1644	4.175 76	1.069	9.510	0.421	3.745	0.575	5.115	0.227	2.019	5.343	47.531	2.104	18.717
0.1793	4.554 22	1.165	10.364	0.459	4.083	0.628	5.586	0.247	2.197	5.827	51.837	2.294	20.407
0.1943	4.935 22	1.263	11.236	0.497	4.421	0.680	6.049	0.268	2.393	6.315	56.178	2.486	22.115

Blanking Force Requirements—Nickel Silver, Paper, and Phenol Fiber

Stock Thickness		1-28. Nickel Silver (Half Hard) S.S. = 32,000 psi				1-29. Paper S.S. = 6,400 psi				1-30. Phenol Fiber S.S. = 26,000 psi			
		1 in Length Cut		1 cm Length Cut		1 in Length Cut		1 cm Length Cut		1 in Length Cut		1 cm Length Cut	
inch	mm	ton	kN	ton	kN	ton	kN	ton	kN	ton	kN	ton	kN
0.0120	0.304 80	0.192	1.708	0.076	0.676	0.038	0.338	0.015	0.133	0.156	1.388	0.061	0.543
0.0135	0.342 90	0.216	1.922	0.085	0.756	0.043	0.383	0.017	0.151	0.175	1.566	0.069	0.614
0.0149	0.378 46	0.238	2.117	0.094	0.836	0.048	0.427	0.019	0.169	0.194	1.726	0.076	0.676
0.0164	0.416 56	0.262	2.331	0.103	0.916	0.052	0.463	0.021	0.187	0.213	1.895	0.084	0.747
0.0179	0.454 66	0.286	2.544	0.113	1.005	0.057	0.507	0.023	0.205	0.233	2.073	0.092	0.818
0.0209	0.530 86	0.334	2.971	0.132	1.174	0.067	0.596	0.026	0.231	0.272	2.420	0.107	0.952
0.0239	0.607 06	0.382	3.398	0.151	1.343	0.076	0.676	0.030	0.267	0.311	2.767	0.122	1.085
0.0269	0.683 26	0.430	3.825	0.169	1.503	0.086	0.765	0.034	0.302	0.350	3.114	0.138	1.228
0.0299	0.759 46	0.478	4.252	0.188	1.672	0.096	0.854	0.038	0.338	0.389	3.461	0.153	1.361
0.0329	0.835 65	0.526	4.679	0.207	1.841	0.105	0.934	0.041	0.365	0.428	3.807	0.168	1.495
0.0359	0.922 86	0.574	5.106	0.226	2.010	0.115	1.023	0.045	0.400	0.467	4.154	0.184	1.637
0.0418	1.061 72	0.669	5.951	0.263	2.340	0.134	1.192	0.053	0.471	0.543	4.831	0.214	1.904
0.0478	1.214 12	0.765	6.805	0.301	2.678	0.153	1.361	0.060	0.534	0.621	5.524	0.245	2.180
0.0538	1.366 52	0.861	7.659	0.339	3.016	0.172	1.530	0.068	0.605	0.699	6.218	0.275	2.446
0.0598	1.518 92	0.957	8.513	0.377	3.354	0.191	1.699	0.075	0.667	0.777	6.912	0.306	2.722
0.0673	1.709 42	1.077	9.581	0.424	3.772	0.215	1.913	0.085	0.756	0.875	7.784	0.344	3.060
0.0747	1.897 38	1.195	10.631	0.471	4.190	0.239	2.126	0.094	0.836	0.971	8.638	0.382	3.398
0.0897	2.278 38	1.435	12.766	0.565	5.026	0.287	2.553	0.113	1.005	1.166	10.373	0.459	4.083
0.1046	2.656 84	1.674	14.892	0.659	5.862	0.335	2.980	0.132	1.174	1.360	12.099	0.535	4.759
0.1196	3.037 84	1.914	17.027	0.753	6.699	0.383	3.407	0.151	1.343	1.555	13.833	0.612	5.444
0.1345	3.416 30	2.152	19.144	0.847	7.535	0.430	3.825	0.169	1.503	1.749	15.559	0.688	6.120
0.1494	3.794 76	2.390	21.261	0.941	8.371	0.478	4.252	0.188	1.672	1.942	17.276	0.765	6.805
0.1644	4.175 76	2.630	23.396	1.036	9.216	0.526	4.679	0.207	1.841	2.137	19.011	0.841	7.482
0.1793	4.554 22	2.869	25.523	1.129	10.044	0.574	5.106	0.226	2.010	2.331	20.737	0.918	8.167
0.1943	4.935 22	3.109	27.658	1.224	10.889	0.622	5.533	0.245	2.180	2.526	22.471	0.994	8.843

Blanking Force Requirements—Rubber and Nickel

Stock Thickness		1-31. Rubber (Hard) S.S. = 20,000 psi				1-32. SAE 2320 (Nickel) S.S. = 98,000 psi				1-33. SAE 2330 (Nickel) S.S. = 110,000 psi			
		1 in Length Cut		1 cm Length Cut		1 in Length Cut		1 cm Length Cut		1 in Length Cut		1 cm Length Cut	
inch	mm	ton	kN	ton	kN	ton	kN	ton	kN	ton	kN	ton	kN
0.0120	0.304 80	0.120	1.068	0.047	0.418	0.588	5.231	0.231	2.055	0.660	5.871	0.260	2.313
0.0135	0.342 90	0.135	1.201	0.053	0.471	0.662	5.889	0.260	2.313	0.743	6.610	0.292	2.598
0.0149	0.378 46	0.149	1.326	0.059	0.525	0.730	6.494	0.287	2.553	0.820	7.295	0.323	2.873
0.0164	0.416 56	0.164	1.459	0.065	0.578	0.804	7.152	0.316	2.811	0.902	8.024	0.355	3.158
0.0179	0.454 66	0.179	1.592	0.070	0.623	0.877	7.802	0.345	3.069	0.985	8.763	0.388	3.452
0.0209	0.530 86	0.209	1.859	0.082	0.729	1.024	9.110	0.403	3.585	1.150	10.230	0.453	4.030
0.0239	0.607 06	0.239	2.126	0.094	0.836	1.171	10.417	0.461	4.101	1.315	11.698	0.518	4.608
0.0269	0.683 26	0.269	2.393	0.106	0.943	1.318	11.725	0.519	4.617	1.480	13.166	0.582	5.177
0.0299	0.759 46	0.299	2.660	0.118	1.050	1.465	13.033	0.577	5.133	1.645	14.634	0.647	5.756
0.0329	0.835 65	0.329	2.927	0.130	1.156	1.612	14.340	0.635	5.649	1.810	16.102	0.712	6.334
0.0359	0.922 86	0.359	3.194	0.141	1.254	1.759	15.648	0.693	6.165	1.975	17.570	0.777	6.912
0.0418	1.061 72	0.418	3.719	0.165	1.468	2.048	18.219	0.806	7.170	2.299	20.452	0.905	8.051
0.0478	1.214 12	0.478	4.252	0.188	1.672	2.342	20.834	0.922	8.202	2.629	23.388	1.035	9.207
0.0538	1.366 52	0.538	4.786	0.212	1.886	2.636	23.450	1.038	9.234	2.959	26.323	1.165	10.364
0.0598	1.518 92	0.598	5.320	0.235	2.091	2.930	26.065	1.154	10.266	3.289	29.259	1.295	11.520
0.0673	1.709 42	0.673	5.987	0.265	2.357	3.298	29.339	1.298	11.547	3.702	32.933	1.457	12.961
0.0747	1.897 38	0.747	6.645	0.294	2.615	3.660	32.559	1.441	12.819	4.109	36.554	1.618	14.394
0.0897	2.278 38	0.897	7.980	0.353	3.140	4.395	39.098	1.730	15.390	4.934	43.893	1.942	17.276
0.1046	2.656 84	1.046	9.305	0.412	3.665	5.125	45.592	2.018	17.952	5.753	51.179	2.265	20.149
0.1196	3.037 84	1.196	10.640	0.471	4.190	5.860	52.131	2.307	20.523	6.578	58.518	2.590	23.041
0.1345	3.416 30	1.345	11.965	0.530	4.715	6.591	58.634	2.595	23.085	7.398	65.813	2.912	25.905
0.1494	3.794 76	1.494	13.291	0.588	5.231	7.321	65.128	2.882	25.635	8.217	73.098	3.235	28.779
0.1644	4.175 76	1.644	14.625	0.647	5.756	8.056	71.666	3.171	28.209	9.042	80.438	3.560	31.670
0.1793	4.554 22	1.793	15.951	0.706	6.281	8.786	78.160	3.459	30.771	9.862	87.732	3.882	34.534
0.1943	4.935 22	1.943	17.285	0.765	6.805	9.521	84.699	3.748	33.342	10.687	95.072	4.207	37.425

Blanking Force Requirements—SAE 2340, SAE 3120, and SAE 3130

Stock Thickness		1-34. SAE 2340 (Nickel) S.S. = 125,000 psi				1-35. SAE 3120 S.S. = 95,000 psi				1-36. SAE 3130 S.S. = 110,000 psi			
		1 in Length Cut		1 cm Length Cut		1 in Length Cut		1 cm Length Cut		1 in Length Cut		1 cm Length Cut	
inch	mm	ton	kN	ton	kN	ton	kN	ton	kN	ton	kN	ton	kN
0.0120	0.304 80	0.750	6.672	0.295	2.624	0.570	5.070	0.224	1.993	0.660	5.871	0.260	2.313
0.0135	0.342 90	0.844	7.508	0.332	2.953	0.641	5.702	0.252	2.242	0.743	6.610	0.292	2.598
0.0149	0.378 46	0.931	8.282	0.367	3.265	0.708	6.298	0.279	2.482	0.820	7.295	0.323	2.873
0.0164	0.416 56	1.025	9.118	0.404	3.594	0.779	6.930	0.307	2.731	0.902	8.024	0.355	3.158
0.0179	0.454 66	1.119	9.955	0.440	3.914	0.850	7.562	0.335	2.980	0.985	8.763	0.388	3.452
0.0209	0.530 86	1.306	11.618	0.514	4.573	0.993	8.834	0.391	3.478	1.150	10.230	0.453	4.030
0.0239	0.607 06	1.494	13.291	0.588	5.231	1.135	10.097	0.447	3.977	1.315	11.698	0.518	4.608
0.0269	0.683 26	1.681	14.954	0.662	5.889	1.278	11.369	0.503	4.475	1.480	13.166	0.582	5.177
0.0299	0.759 46	1.869	16.627	0.736	6.547	1.420	12.632	0.559	4.973	1.645	14.634	0.647	5.756
0.0329	0.835 65	2.056	18.290	0.810	7.206	1.563	13.904	0.615	5.471	1.810	16.102	0.712	6.334
0.0359	0.922 86	2.244	19.963	0.883	7.855	1.705	15.168	0.671	5.969	1.975	17.570	0.777	6.912
0.0418	1.061 72	2.613	23.245	1.029	9.154	1.986	17.667	0.782	6.957	2.299	20.452	0.905	8.051
0.0478	1.214 12	2.988	26.581	1.176	10.462	2.271	20.203	0.894	7.953	2.629	23.388	1.035	9.207
0.0538	1.366 52	3.363	29.917	1.324	11.778	2.556	22.738	1.006	8.949	2.959	26.323	1.165	10.364
0.0598	1.518 92	3.738	33.253	1.471	13.086	2.841	25.274	1.118	9.946	3.289	29.259	1.295	11.520
0.0673	1.709 42	4.206	37.417	1.656	14.732	3.197	28.441	1.259	11.200	3.702	32.933	1.457	12.961
0.0747	1.897 38	4.669	41.535	1.838	16.351	3.548	31.563	1.397	12.428	4.109	36.554	1.618	14.394
0.0897	2.278 38	5.606	49.871	2.207	19.633	4.261	37.906	1.677	14.919	4.934	43.893	1.942	17.276
0.1046	2.656 84	6.538	58.161	2.574	22.898	4.696	44.204	1.956	17.401	5.753	51.179	2.265	20.149
0.1196	3.037 84	7.476	66.506	2.943	26.181	5.681	50.538	2.237	19.900	6.578	58.518	2.590	23.041
0.1345	3.416 30	8.406	74.780	3.310	29.446	6.389	56.837	2.515	22.373	7.398	65.813	2.912	25.905
0.1494	3.794 76	9.338	83.071	3.676	32.702	7.097	63.135	2.794	24.855	8.217	73.098	3.235	28.779
0.1644	4.175 76	10.275	91.406	4.045	35.984	7.809	69.469	3.074	27.346	9.042	80.438	3.560	31.670
0.1793	4.554 22	11.206	99.689	4.412	39.249	8.517	75.767	3.353	29.828	9.862	87.733	3.882	34.534
0.1943	4.935 22	12.144	108.033	4.781	42.532	9.229	82.101	3.634	32.328	10.687	95.072	4.207	37.425

Blanking Force Requirements—SAE 3140, SAE 3280, and SAE 3240

| Stock Thickness | | 1-37. SAE 3140 S.S. = 130,000 psi | | | | 1-38. SAE 3280 S.S. = 135,000 psi | | | | 1-39. SAE 3240 S.S. = 150,000 psi | | | |
| | | 1 in Length Cut | | 1 cm Length Cut | | 1 in Length Cut | | 1 cm Length Cut | | 1 in Length Cut | | 1 cm Length Cut | |
inch	mm	ton	kN	ton	kN	ton	kN	ton	kN	ton	kN	ton	kN
0.0120	0.304 80	0.780	6.939	0.307	2.731	0.810	7.206	0.319	2.838	0.900	8.006	0.354	3.149
0.0135	0.342 90	0.878	7.811	0.345	3.069	0.911	8.104	0.359	3.194	1.013	9.012	0.398	3.541
0.0149	0.378 46	0.969	8.620	0.381	3.389	1.006	8.949	0.396	3.523	1.118	9.946	0.440	3.914
0.0164	0.416 56	1.066	9.483	0.420	3.736	1.107	9.848	0.436	3.879	1.230	10.942	0.484	4.306
0.0179	0.454 66	1.164	10.355	0.458	4.074	1.208	10.746	0.476	4.234	1.343	11.947	0.529	4.706
0.0209	0.530 86	1.359	12.090	0.535	4.759	1.411	12.552	0.555	4.937	1.568	13.949	0.617	5.489
0.0239	0.607 06	1.554	13.824	0.612	5.444	1.613	14.348	0.635	5.649	1.793	15.951	0.706	6.281
0.0269	0.683 26	1.749	15.559	0.688	6.120	1.816	16.155	0.715	6.361	2.018	17.952	0.794	7.063
0.0299	0.759 46	1.944	17.294	0.765	6.805	2.018	17.952	0.795	7.072	2.243	19.954	0.883	7.855
0.0329	0.835 65	2.139	19.029	0.842	7.490	2.221	19.759	0.874	7.775	2.468	21.955	0.971	8.638
0.0359	0.922 86	2.334	20.763	0.919	8.175	2.423	21.555	0.954	8.487	2.693	23.947	1.060	9.430
0.0418	1.061 72	2.718	24.179	1.070	9.519	2.822	25.105	1.111	9.883	3.135	27.889	1.234	10.978
0.0478	1.214 12	3.108	27.649	1.223	10.880	3.227	28.707	1.270	11.298	3.585	31.892	1.411	12.552
0.0538	1.366 52	3.497	31.109	1.377	12.250	3.632	32.310	1.430	12.721	4.035	35.895	1.589	14.136
0.0598	1.518 92	3.887	34.579	1.530	13.611	4.037	35.913	1.589	14.136	4.485	39.899	1.766	15.710
0.0673	1.709 42	4.375	38.920	1.722	15.319	4.543	40.415	1.788	15.906	5.048	44.907	1.987	17.676
0.0747	1.897 38	4.856	43.199	1.912	17.009	5.042	44.854	1.985	17.659	5.603	49.844	2.206	19.625
0.0897	2.278 38	5.831	51.873	2.295	20.416	6.055	53.865	2.384	21.208	6.728	59.852	2.649	23.566
0.1046	2.656 84	6.799	60.484	2.677	23.815	7.061	62.815	2.780	24.731	7.845	69.789	3.089	27.480
0.1196	3.037 84	7.774	69.158	3.061	27.231	8.073	71.817	3.178	28.271	8.970	79.797	3.531	31.412
0.1345	3.416 30	8.743	77.778	3.442	30.620	9.079	80.767	3.574	31.794	10.088	89.743	3.971	35.326
0.1494	3.794 76	9.711	86.389	3.823	34.009	10.085	89.716	3.970	35.317	11.205	99.680	4.411	39.240
0.1644	4.175 76	10.686	95.063	4.207	37.425	11.097	98.719	4.369	38.867	12.330	109.688	4.854	43.181
0.1793	4.554 22	11.655	103.683	4.588	40.815	12.103	107.668	4.765	42.389	13.448	119.633	5.294	47.095
0.1943	4.935 22	12.630	112.356	4.972	44.231	13.115	116.671	5.163	45.930	14.573	129.641	5.737	51.036

16

Blanking Force Requirements—SAE 3250, SAE 4130, and SAE 4130

Stock Thickness		1-40. SAE 3250 S.S. = 165,000 psi				1-41. SAE 4130 (90,000 UTS) S.S. = 55,000 psi				1-42. SAE 4130 (100,000 UTS) S.S. = 65,000 psi			
		1 in Length Cut		1 cm Length Cut		1 in Length Cut		1 cm Length Cut		1 in Length Cut		1 cm Length Cut	
inch	mm	ton	kN	ton	kN	ton	kN	ton	kN	ton	kN	ton	kN
0.0120	0.304 80	0.990	8.807	0.390	3.469	0.330	2.936	0.130	1.156	0.390	3.469	0.154	1.370
0.0135	0.342 90	1.114	9.910	0.438	3.896	0.371	3.300	0.146	1.299	0.439	3.905	0.173	1.539
0.0149	0.378 46	1.229	10.993	0.484	4.306	0.410	3.647	0.161	1.432	0.484	4.306	0.191	1.699
0.0164	0.416 56	1.353	12.036	0.533	4.742	0.451	4.012	0.176	1.566	0.533	4.742	0.210	1.868
0.0179	0.454 66	1.477	13.139	0.581	5.169	0.492	4.377	0.194	1.726	0.582	5.177	0.229	2.037
0.0209	0.530 86	1.724	15.337	0.679	6.040	0.575	5.115	0.226	2.010	0.679	6.040	0.267	2.375
0.0239	0.607 06	1.972	17.543	0.776	6.903	0.657	5.845	0.259	2.304	0.777	6.912	0.306	2.722
0.0269	0.683 26	2.219	19.740	0.874	7.775	0.740	6.583	0.291	2.589	0.874	7.775	0.344	3.060
0.0299	0.759 46	2.467	21.946	0.971	8.638	0.822	7.313	0.324	2.882	0.972	8.647	0.383	3.407
0.0329	0.835 65	2.714	24.144	1.069	9.510	0.905	8.051	0.356	3.167	1.069	9.510	0.421	3.745
0.0359	0.922 86	2.962	26.350	1.166	10.373	0.987	8.780	0.389	3.461	1.167	10.382	0.459	4.083
0.0418	1.061 72	3.449	30.682	1.358	12.801	1.150	10.230	0.453	4.030	1.359	12.090	0.535	4.759
0.0478	1.214 12	3.944	35.086	1.553	13.815	1.314	11.698	0.518	4.608	1.554	13.824	0.612	5.444
0.0538	1.366 52	4.439	39.489	1.747	15.541	1.480	13.166	0.582	5.177	1.749	15.559	0.688	6.120
0.0598	1.518 92	4.934	43.893	1.942	17.276	1.645	14.634	0.647	5.756	1.944	17.294	0.765	6.805
0.0673	1.709 42	5.552	49.391	2.186	19.447	1.851	16.466	0.729	6.485	2.187	19.456	0.861	7.659
0.0747	1.897 38	6.163	54.826	2.426	21.582	2.054	18.272	0.809	7.197	2.428	21.599	0.956	8.505
0.0897	2.278 38	7.400	65.830	2.913	25.914	2.467	21.946	0.971	8.638	2.915	25.932	1.148	10.213
0.1046	2.656 84	8.630	76.772	3.397	30.220	2.877	25.594	1.132	10.070	3.400	30.246	1.338	11.903
0.1196	3.037 84	9.867	87.777	3.885	34.561	3.289	29.259	1.295	11.520	3.887	34.579	1.530	13.611
0.1345	3.416 30	11.096	98.710	4.369	38.867	3.699	32.906	1.456	12.953	4.371	38.884	1.721	15.310
0.1494	3.794 76	12.326	109.652	4.853	43.172	4.109	36.554	1.618	14.394	4.856	43.199	1.912	17.009
0.1644	4.175 76	13.563	120.656	5.340	47.505	4.521	40.219	1.780	15.835	5.343	47.531	2.104	18.717
0.1793	4.554 22	14.792	131.590	5.824	51.810	4.931	43.866	1.941	17.267	5.827	51.837	2.294	20.407
0.1943	4.935 22	16.030	142.603	6.311	56.143	5.343	47.531	2.104	18.717	6.315	56.178	2.486	22.115

Blanking Force Requirements—SAE 4130

Stock Thickness		1-43. SAE 4130 (125,000 UTS) S.S. = 75,000 psi				1-44. SAE 4130 (150,000 UTS) S.S. = 90,000 psi				1-45. SAE 4130 (180,000 UTS) S.S. = 105,000 psi			
		1 in Length Cut		1 cm Length Cut		1 in Length Cut		1 cm Length Cut		1 in Length Cut		1 cm Length Cut	
inch	mm	ton	kN	ton	kN	ton	kN	ton	kN	ton	kN	ton	kN
0.0120	0.304 80	0.450	4.003	0.177	1.575	0.540	4.804	0.213	1.895	0.630	5.604	0.248	2.206
0.0135	0.342 90	0.506	4.501	0.199	1.770	0.608	5.409	0.239	2.126	0.709	6.307	0.279	2.482
0.0149	0.378 46	0.559	4.973	0.220	1.957	0.671	5.969	0.264	2.349	0.782	6.957	0.308	2.740
0.0164	0.416 56	0.615	5.471	0.242	2.153	0.738	6.565	0.291	2.589	0.861	7.659	0.339	3.016
0.0179	0.454 66	0.671	5.969	0.264	2.349	0.806	7.170	0.317	2.820	0.940	8.362	0.370	3.292
0.0209	0.530 86	0.784	6.974	0.309	2.749	0.941	8.371	0.370	3.292	1.097	9.759	0.432	3.843
0.0239	0.607 06	0.896	7.971	0.353	3.140	1.076	9.572	0.423	3.763	1.255	11.164	0.494	4.395
0.0269	0.683 26	1.009	8.976	0.397	3.532	1.211	10.773	0.477	4.243	1.412	12.561	0.556	4.946
0.0299	0.759 46	1.121	9.972	0.441	3.923	1.346	11.974	0.530	4.715	1.570	13.967	0.618	5.498
0.0329	0.835 65	1.234	10.976	0.486	4.324	1.481	13.175	0.583	5.186	1.727	15.363	0.680	6.049
0.0359	0.922 86	1.346	11.974	0.530	4.715	1.616	14.376	0.636	5.658	1.885	16.769	0.742	6.601
0.0418	1.061 72	1.568	13.949	0.617	5.489	1.881	16.733	0.741	6.592	2.195	19.527	0.864	7.686
0.0478	1.214 12	1.793	15.951	0.706	6.761	2.151	19.135	0.847	7.535	2.510	22.329	0.988	8.789
0.0538	1.366 52	2.018	17.952	0.794	7.063	2.421	21.537	0.953	8.478	2.825	25.131	1.112	9.892
0.0598	1.518 92	2.243	19.954	0.883	7.855	2.691	23.939	1.059	9.421	3.140	27.933	1.236	10.995
0.0673	1.709 42	2.524	22.454	0.994	8.843	3.029	26.946	1.192	10.604	3.533	31.430	1.391	12.374
0.0747	1.897 38	2.801	24.918	1.103	9.812	3.362	29.908	1.323	11.769	3.922	34.890	1.544	13.735
0.0897	2.278 38	3.364	29.926	1.324	11.778	4.037	35.913	1.589	14.136	4.709	41.891	1.854	16.493
0.1046	2.656 84	3.923	34.899	1.544	13.735	4.707	41.873	1.853	16.484	5.492	48.857	2.162	19.233
0.1196	3.037 84	4.485	39.899	1.766	15.710	5.382	47.878	2.119	18.851	6.279	55.858	2.472	21.991
0.1345	3.416 30	5.044	44.871	1.986	17.667	6.053	53.847	2.383	21.199	7.061	62.815	2.780	24.731
0.1494	3.794 76	5.603	49.844	2.206	19.625	6.723	59.808	2.647	23.548	7.844	69.780	3.088	27.471
0.1644	4.175 76	6.165	54.843	2.427	21.591	7.398	65.813	2.913	25.914	8.631	76.781	3.398	30.229
0.1793	4.554 22	6.724	59.817	2.647	23.548	8.069	71.782	3.177	28.263	9.413	83.738	3.706	32.969
0.1943	4.935 22	7.286	64.816	2.869	25.523	8.744	77.787	3.442	30.620	10.201	90.748	4.016	35.726

Blanking Force Requirements—Stainless and Steel

Stock Thickness		1-46. Stainless (18-8 Nickel) S.S. = 70,000 psi				1-47. Steel (0.10 Carbon) S.S. = 45,000 psi				1-48. Steel (0.25% Carbon) S.S. = 50,000 psi			
		1 in Length Cut		1 cm Length Cut		1 in Length Cut		1 cm Length Cut		1 in Length Cut		1 cm Length Cut	
inch	mm	ton	kN	ton	kN	ton	kN	ton	kN	ton	kN	ton	kN
0.0120	0.304 80	0.420	3.736	0.165	1.468	0.270	2.402	0.106	0.943	0.300	2.669	0.118	1.050
0.0135	0.342 90	0.473	4.208	0.186	1.655	0.304	2.704	0.120	1.068	0.338	3.007	0.133	1.183
0.0149	0.378 46	0.522	4.644	0.205	1.824	0.335	2.980	0.132	1.174	0.373	3.318	0.147	1.308
0.0164	0.416 56	0.574	5.106	0.226	2.010	0.369	3.283	0.145	1.290	0.410	3.647	0.161	1.432
0.0179	0.454 66	0.627	5.578	0.247	2.197	0.403	3.585	0.159	1.414	0.448	3.985	0.176	1.566
0.0209	0.530 86	0.732	6.512	0.288	2.562	0.470	4.181	0.185	1.646	0.523	4.653	0.206	1.833
0.0239	0.607 06	0.837	7.446	0.329	2.927	0.538	4.786	0.212	1.886	0.598	5.320	0.235	2.091
0.0269	0.683 26	0.942	8.380	0.371	3.300	0.605	5.382	0.238	2.117	0.673	5.987	0.265	2.357
0.0299	0.759 46	1.047	9.314	0.412	3.664	0.673	5.987	0.265	2.357	0.748	6.654	0.294	2.615
0.0329	0.835 65	1.152	10.248	0.453	4.030	0.740	6.583	0.291	2.589	0.823	7.321	0.324	2.882
0.0359	0.922 86	1.257	11.182	0.495	4.404	0.808	7.188	0.318	2.829	0.898	7.989	0.353	3.140
0.0418	1.061 72	1.463	13.015	0.576	5.124	0.941	8.371	0.370	3.292	1.045	9.296	0.411	3.656
0.0478	1.214 12	1.673	14.883	0.659	5.862	1.076	9.572	0.423	3.763	1.195	10.631	0.470	4.181
0.0538	1.366 52	1.883	16.751	0.741	6.592	1.211	10.773	0.477	4.243	1.345	11.965	0.530	4.715
0.0598	1.518 92	2.093	18.619	0.824	7.330	1.346	11.974	0.530	4.715	1.495	13.300	0.589	5.240
0.0673	1.709 42	2.356	20.959	0.927	8.247	1.514	13.469	0.596	5.302	1.683	14.972	0.662	5.889
0.0747	1.897 38	2.615	23.263	1.029	9.154	1.681	14.954	0.663	5.889	1.868	16.618	0.735	6.539
0.0897	2.278 38	3.140	27.933	1.236	10.995	2.018	17.952	0.795	7.072	2.243	19.954	0.883	7.855
0.1046	2.656 84	3.661	32.568	1.441	12.819	2.354	20.941	0.927	8.247	2.615	23.263	1.030	9.163
0.1196	3.037 84	4.186	37.239	1.648	14.661	2.691	23.939	1.059	9.421	2.990	26.599	1.177	10.471
0.1345	3.416 30	4.708	41.882	1.853	16.484	3.026	26.919	1.191	10.595	3.363	29.917	.1324	11.778
0.1494	3.794 76	5.229	46.517	2.059	18.317	3.362	29.908	1.323	11.769	3.735	33.227	1.470	13.077
0.1644	4.175 76	5.754	51.188	2.265	20.149	3.699	32.906	1.456	12.953	4.110	36.563	1.618	14.394
0.1793	4.554 22	6.276	55.831	2.471	21.982	4.034	35.886	1.588	14.127	4.483	39.881	1.765	15.701
0.1943	4.935 22	6.801	60.502	2.677	23.815	4.372	38.893	1.721	15.310	4.858	43.217	1.912	17.009

Blanking Force Requirements—Steel

Stock Thickness		1-49. Steel (0.5% Carbon) S.S. = 70,000 psi				1-50. Steel (0.75% Carbon) S.S. = 80,000 psi				1-51. Steel (1.0% Carbon) S.S. = 85,000 psi			
		1 in Length Cut		1 cm Length Cut		1 in Length Cut		1 cm Length Cut		1 in Length Cut		1 cm Length Cut	
inch	mm	ton	kN	ton	kN	ton	kN	ton	kN	ton	kN	ton	kN
0.0120	0.304 80	0.420	3.736	0.165	1.468	0.048	0.427	0.019	0.169	0.510	4.537	0.201	1.788
0.0135	0.342 90	0.473	4.208	0.186	1.655	0.054	0.480	0.021	0.187	0.574	5.106	0.226	2.010
0.0149	0.378 46	0.522	4.644	0.205	1.824	0.060	0.534	0.023	0.205	0.633	5.631	0.249	2.215
0.0164	0.416 56	0.574	5.106	0.226	2.010	0.066	0.587	0.026	0.231	0.697	6.201	0.274	2.438
0.0179	0.454 66	0.627	5.578	0.247	2.197	0.072	0.641	0.028	0.249	0.761	6.770	0.300	2.669
0.0209	0.530 86	0.732	6.512	0.288	2.562	0.084	0.747	0.033	0.294	0.888	7.900	0.350	3.114
0.0239	0.607 06	0.837	7.446	0.329	2.927	0.096	0.854	0.038	0.338	1.016	9.038	0.400	3.558
0.0269	0.683 26	0.942	8.380	0.371	3.300	0.108	0.961	0.042	0.374	1.143	10.168	0.450	4.003
0.0299	0.759 46	1.047	9.314	0.412	3.665	0.120	1.068	0.047	0.418	1.271	11.307	0.500	4.448
0.0329	0.835 65	1.152	10.248	0.453	4.030	0.132	1.174	0.052	0.463	1.398	12.437	0.550	4.893
0.0359	0.922 86	1.257	11.182	0.495	4.404	0.144	1.281	0.057	0.507	1.526	13.575	0.601	5.346
0.0418	1.061 72	1.463	13.015	0.576	5.124	0.167	1.486	0.066	0.587	1.777	15.808	0.700	6.227
0.0478	1.214 12	1.673	14.883	0.659	5.862	0.191	1.699	0.075	0.667	2.032	18.077	0.800	7.117
0.0538	1.366 52	1.883	16.751	0.741	6.592	0.215	1.913	0.085	0.756	2.287	20.345	0.900	8.006
0.0598	1.518 92	2.093	18.619	0.824	7.330	0.239	2.126	0.094	0.836	2.542	22.614	1.001	8.905
0.0673	1.709 42	2.356	20.959	0.927	8.247	0.269	2.393	0.106	0.943	2.860	25.443	1.126	10.017
0.0747	1.897 38	2.615	23.263	1.029	9.154	0.299	2.660	0.118	1.050	3.175	28.245	1.250	11.120
0.0897	2.278 38	3.140	27.933	1.236	10.995	0.359	3.194	0.141	1.254	3.812	33.912	1.501	13.353
0.1046	2.656 84	3.661	32.568	1.441	12.819	0.418	3.719	0.165	1.468	4.446	39.552	1.750	15.568
0.1196	3.037 84	4.186	37.239	1.648	14.661	0.478	4.252	0.188	1.672	5.083	45.218	2.001	17.801
0.1345	3.416 30	4.708	41.882	1.853	16.484	0.538	4.786	0.212	1.886	5.716	50.850	2.250	20.016
0.1494	3.794 76	5.229	46.517	2.059	18.317	0.598	5.320	0.235	2.091	6.350	56.490	2.500	22.240
0.1644	4.175 76	5.754	51.188	2.265	20.149	0.658	5.854	0.259	2.304	6.987	62.156	2.751	24.473
0.1793	4.554 22	6.276	55.831	2.471	21.982	0.717	6.378	0.282	2.509	7.620	67.788	3.000	26.688
0.1943	4.935 22	6.801	60.502	2.677	23.815	0.777	6.912	0.306	2.722	8.258	73.463	3.251	28.921

Blanking Force Requirements—Steel and Tin

Stock Thickness		1-52. Steel (Silicon) S.S. = 65,000 psi				1-53. Steel (Stainless) S.S. = 57,000 psi				1-54. Tin S.S. = 6,000 psi			
		1 in Length Cut		1 cm Length Cut		1 in Length Cut		1 cm Length Cut		1 in Length Cut		1 cm Length Cut	
inch	mm	ton	kN	ton	kN	ton	kN	ton	kN	ton	kN	ton	kN
0.0120	0.304 80	0.390	3.469	0.154	1.370	0.342	3.042	0.135	1.201	0.036	0.320	0.014	0.125
0.0135	0.342 90	0.439	3.905	0.173	1.539	0.385	3.425	0.151	1.343	0.041	0.365	0.016	0.142
0.0149	0.378 46	0.484	4.306	0.191	1.699	0.425	3.781	0.167	1.486	0.045	0.400	0.018	0.160
0.0164	0.416 56	0.533	4.742	0.210	1.868	0.467	4.154	0.184	1.637	0.049	0.436	0.019	0.169
0.0179	0.454 66	0.582	5.177	0.229	2.037	0.510	4.537	0.201	1.788	0.054	0.480	0.021	0.187
0.0209	0.530 86	0.679	6.040	0.267	2.375	0.596	5.302	0.235	2.091	0.063	0.560	0.025	0.222
0.0239	0.607 06	0.777	6.912	0.306	2.722	0.681	6.058	0.268	2.384	0.072	0.641	0.028	0.249
0.0269	0.683 26	0.874	7.775	0.344	3.060	0.767	6.823	0.302	2.687	0.081	0.721	0.032	0.285
0.0299	0.759 46	0.972	8.647	0.383	3.407	0.852	7.579	0.335	2.980	0.090	0.801	0.035	0.311
0.0329	0.835 65	1.069	9.510	0.421	3.745	0.938	8.344	0.369	3.283	0.099	0.881	0.039	0.347
0.0359	0.922 86	1.167	10.382	0.459	4.083	1.023	9.101	0.403	3.585	0.108	0.961	0.042	0.374
0.0418	1.061 72	1.359	12.090	0.535	4.759	1.191	10.595	0.469	4.172	0.125	1.112	0.049	0.436
0.0478	1.214 12	1.554	13.824	0.612	5.444	1.362	12.116	0.536	4.768	0.143	1.272	0.056	0.498
0.0538	1.366 52	1.749	15.559	0.688	6.120	1.533	13.638	0.604	5.373	0.161	1.432	0.064	0.569
0.0598	1.518 92	1.944	17.294	0.765	6.805	1.704	15.159	0.671	5.969	0.179	1.592	0.071	0.632
0.0673	1.709 42	2.187	19.456	0.861	7.659	1.918	17.063	0.755	6.716	0.202	1.797	0.079	0.703
0.0747	1.897 38	2.428	21.599	0.956	8.505	2.129	18.940	0.838	7.455	0.224	1.992	0.088	0.783
0.0897	2.278 38	2.915	25.932	1.148	10.213	2.556	22.738	1.006	8.949	0.269	2.393	0.106	0.943
0.1046	2.656 84	3.400	30.246	1.338	11.903	2.981	26.519	1.174	10.444	0.314	2.793	0.124	1.103
0.1196	3.037 84	3.887	34.579	1.530	13.611	3.409	30.326	1.342	11.938	0.359	3.194	0.141	1.254
0.1345	3.416 30	4.371	38.884	1.721	15.310	3.833	34.098	1.509	13.424	0.404	3.594	0.159	1.414
0.1494	3.794 76	4.856	43.199	1.912	17.009	4.258	37.879	1.676	14.910	0.448	3.985	0.176	1.566
0.1644	4.175 76	5.343	47.531	2.104	18.717	4.685	41.678	1.845	16.413	0.493	4.386	0.194	1.726
0.1793	4.554 22	5.827	51.837	2.294	20.407	5.110	45.459	2.012	17.899	0.538	4.786	0.212	1.886
0.1943	4.935 22	6.315	56.178	2.486	22.115	5.538	49.266	2.180	19.393	0.538	5.186	0.229	2.037

Blanking Force Requirements—Zinc

1-55. Zinc
S.S. = 20,000 psi

Stock Thickness		1 in Length Cut		1 cm Length Cut	
inch	mm	ton	kN	ton	kN
0.0120	0.304 80	0.120	1.068	0.047	0.418
0.0135	0.342 90	0.135	1.201	0.053	0.471
0.0149	0.378 46	0.149	1.326	0.059	0.525
0.0164	0.416 56	0.164	1.459	0.065	0.578
0.0179	0.454 66	0.179	1.592	0.070	0.623
0.0209	0.530 86	0.209	1.859	0.082	0.729
0.0239	0.607 06	0.239	2.126	0.094	0.836
0.0269	0.683 26	0.269	2.393	0.106	0.943
0.0299	0.759 46	0.299	2.660	0.118	1.050
0.0329	0.835 65	0.329	2.927	0.130	1.156
0.0359	0.922 86	0.359	3.194	0.141	1.254
0.0418	1.061 72	0.418	3.719	0.165	1.468
0.0478	1.214 12	0.478	4.252	0.188	1.672
0.0538	1.366 52	0.538	4.786	0.212	1.886
0.0598	1.518 92	0.598	5.320	0.235	2.091
0.0673	1.709 42	0.673	5.987	0.265	2.357
0.0747	1.897 38	0.747	6.645	0.294	2.615
0.0897	2.278 38	0.897	7.980	0.353	3.140
0.1046	2.656 84	1.046	9.305	0.412	3.665
0.1196	3.037 84	1.196	10.640	0.471	4.190
0.1345	3.416 30	1.345	11.965	0.530	4.715
0.1494	3.794 76	1.494	13.291	0.588	5.231
0.1644	4.175 76	1.644	14.625	0.647	5.756
0.1793	4.554 22	1.793	15.951	0.706	6.281
0.1943	4.935 22	1.943	17.285	0.765	6.805

EFFECT OF SHEAR

Tonnage requirements for cutting through a material can be substantially reduced by adding shear to a punch or die. The formula is as follows:

$$P = \frac{t \times \% \text{ penetration}}{\text{shear}} \times \text{Maximum Pressure}$$

In this formula, P = force required to shear the metal, t = material thickness, shear is the amount of relief given the punch or die, and maximum pressure is the total force requirement as determined by the formula or as obtained from the values in Tables 1–1 through 1–55.

The nomogram in *Figure 1–2* provides a fast way to calculate P, the force required to shear the metal.

Scale A. This is the thickness (t) scale in inches and U.S. Gage numbers.

Scale B. This is the percent penetration scale. Again two scales are given. The upper scale is for dies with insufficient clearance, as evidenced by secondary shearing. The lower scale is for dies with standard clearance.

Scale C. This pivot line represents the product of metal thickness (t) and percent penetration. In the example given, the metal thickness is assumed to be $\frac{1}{8}$ inch, and the percent penetration is assumed to be 40. Connecting these points on Scales A and B respectively gives a value of 0.05 on Scale C.

Scale D. This scale is used to denote the physical dimension of shear, noted in the drawing at Scale D.

Scale E. This line provides a value for

$$\frac{t \times \% \text{ penetration}}{\text{shear}}$$

A line is drawn from the indicated point on Scale C through the designated shear dimension on Scale D. It provides a value for $\frac{1}{8} \times 40\% \div 0.1$.

Scale F. This scale is for maximum force as determined by the formula $F = Lts$ or from the numerical values in Tables 1–1 through 1–55. In this example, the tonnage is assumed to be 60. Thus, a line extended from the pivot point on Scale E through 60 on Scale F provides a value for the corrected shearing force on Scale F.

Scale G. This scale represents the corrected shearing force.

It will be noted that little is given for numerical values on Scales C and E. Since these scales serve as pivot points, no values are necessary.

One final point. Shear is ground on a punch *only* if the part punched out is scrap. If the part punched is the workpiece, the shear must be placed on the die—not on the punch.

ENERGY REQUIRED IN SHEARING

In determining power requirements or flywheel capacities, it is necessary to know the amount of energy consumed in doing the work. In the case of shearing, the energy expended can be determined by the following equation:

$$W = t \times \% \text{ penetration} \times F \times 1.16$$

In this equation,

> W = Work performed in inch-tons
> t = Material thickness
> F = Force required to shear (from *Figure* 1–1)
> 1.16 = Constant to provide for machine friction.

This equation is expressed as the nomogram shown in *Figure* 1–3. In using this nomogram, read *thickness* and *percent penetration* (Scales A and C) to obtain the pivot point on Scale E. Then connect the pivot point to the *maximum force*, Scale B. The intersection of this line with Scale D provides a reading for *work performed* in inch-tons.

It should be remembered, however, that if the punch or die has shear, the value for *maximum force* should be replaced with the value for *corrected shearing force*, as determined by *Figure* 1–2.

PUNCH AND DIE CLEARANCE

The correct amount of clearance is a controversial subject. Therefore, no attempt to specify clearance for a given material will be made.

It should be noted, however, that harder materials generally require a greater degree of clearance than softer materials. Significantly, tonnage requirements generally fall off as clearance increases.

Table 1–56 provides inch and metric values for clearances from 1 to 10 degrees. Stock thicknesses specified range from 0.001 inch (0.0254 mm) to 0.100 inch (2.54 mm). The illustration related to this table is presented as *Figure* 1–4.

As a die is ground for sharpening, its clearance increases as a function of the angle of clearance. Values for the *amount of increase* are given in Table 1–57. The condition referred to is illustrated in *Figure* 1–5. As an example, assume $\frac{1}{2}$ degree clearance per side (which is to say, a total of 1 degree clearance in a round die opening). If 0.001 inch is ground off the face of the die, the *clearance on one side only* will increase 0.0000087 inch (0.00022 mm)—an obviously negligible figure. The *total increase in clearance* when 0.001 inch is ground off this die is 0.0000174 inch (0.00044 mm).

Although these figures are small, they tend to build up as grinding proceeds. When 0.060 inch is removed from the die face, the total clearance will have increased to 0.001047 inch (0.02659 mm).

STRIPPER PLATES

Two basic stripper plate designs are given in *Figure* 1–6. The *positive* stripper design is shown at the left, the *spring* stripper at the right.

FIG. 1-2   EFFECT OF ANGULAR SHEAR

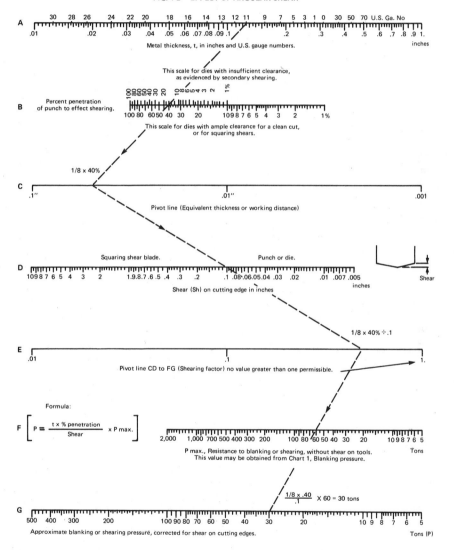

ENERGY REQUIRED IN SHEARING

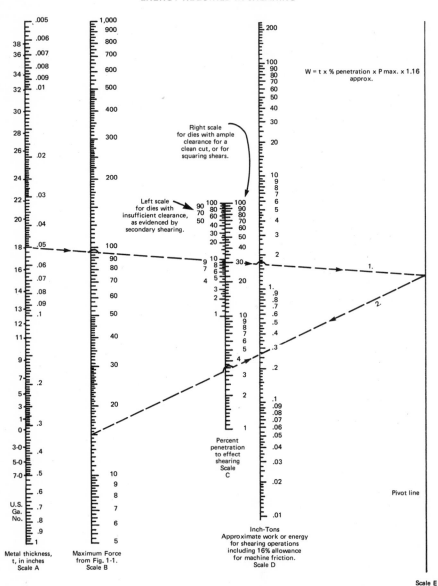

$W = t \times \% \text{ penetration} \times P\,\text{max.} \times 1.16$
approx.

Right scale
for dies with ample
clearance for a
clean cut, or for
squaring shears.

Left scale
for dies with
insufficient clearance,
as evidenced by
secondary shearing.

Percent
penetration
to effect
shearing
Scale
C

Metal thickness,
t, in inches
Scale A

Maximum Force
from Fig. 1-1.
Scale B

Inch-Tons
Approximate work or energy
for shearing operations
including 16% allowance
for machine friction.
Scale D

Pivot line

Scale E

FIG. 1-3

The formula for determining the thickness T of a stripper plate is,

$$T = \frac{W}{30} + 2t$$

In this formula,

  T = *Minimum* stripper thickness
  W = Width of stock
  t = Workpiece metal thickness.

Table 1–58 provides inch and metric solutions to this equation. It must be reiterated, however, that these are *minimum* values, and in many cases actual stripper thickness will be much greater, especially with the workpiece materials of 0.100 inch (2.54 mm) and less.

The formula for calculating *stripping force* is as follows:

$$F = 1.75 \times L \times t$$

In this formula,

  F = Total stripping force
  L = Total length of cut edge
  t = Material thickness

Table 1–59 provides solutions to the stripping force equation for materials ranging in thickness from 0.001 inch (0.0254 mm) to 0.300 inch (7.62 mm). Stripping force is given in tons and kilonewtons for inches and millimetres of cut length.

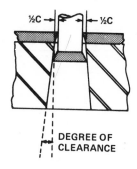

Fig. 1-4

Table 1–56. Percent Clearance for Stock Thicknesses from 0.001 (0.0254 mm) to 0.100 (2.540 mm).

Stock Thickness		1% Clearance		2% Clearance		3% Clearance		4% Clearance		5% Clearance	
inch	mm	inch	mm	inch	mm	inch	mm	inch	mm	inch	mm
0.001	0.0254	0.00001	0.00025	0.00002	0.00051	0.00003	0.00076	0.00004	0.00103	0.00005	0.00127
0.002	0.0508	0.00002	0.00051	0.00004	0.00102	0.00006	0.00152	0.00008	0.00203	0.00010	0.00254
0.003	0.0762	0.00003	0.00076	0.00006	0.00152	0.00009	0.00229	0.00012	0.00305	0.00015	0.00381
0.004	0.1016	0.00004	0.00102	0.00008	0.00203	0.00012	0.00305	0.00016	0.00406	0.00020	0.00508
0.005	0.1270	0.00005	0.00127	0.00010	0.00254	0.00015	0.00381	0.00020	0.00508	0.00025	0.00635
0.010	0.2540	0.00010	0.00254	0.00020	0.00508	0.00030	0.00762	0.00040	0.01016	0.00050	0.01270
0.015	0.3810	0.00015	0.00381	0.00030	0.00762	0.00045	0.01143	0.00060	0.01524	0.00075	0.01905
0.020	0.5080	0.00020	0.00508	0.00040	0.01016	0.00060	0.01524	0.00080	0.02032	0.00100	0.02540
0.025	0.6350	0.00025	0.00635	0.00050	0.01270	0.00075	0.01905	0.00100	0.02540	0.00125	0.03175
0.030	0.7620	0.00030	0.00762	0.00060	0.01524	0.00090	0.02286	0.00120	0.03048	0.00150	0.03810
0.035	0.8890	0.00035	0.00889	0.00070	0.01778	0.00105	0.02667	0.00140	0.03556	0.00175	0.04445
0.040	1.0160	0.00040	0.01016	0.00080	0.02032	0.00120	0.03048	0.00160	0.04064	0.00200	0.05080
0.045	1.1430	0.00045	0.01143	0.00090	0.02286	0.00135	0.03429	0.00180	0.04572	0.00225	0.05715
0.050	1.2700	0.00050	0.01270	0.00100	0.02540	0.00150	0.03810	0.00200	0.05080	0.00250	0.06350
0.055	1.3970	0.00055	0.01397	0.00110	0.02794	0.00165	0.04191	0.00220	0.05588	0.00275	0.06985
0.060	1.5240	0.00060	0.01524	0.00120	0.03048	0.00180	0.04572	0.00240	0.06096	0.00300	0.07620
0.065	1.6510	0.00065	0.01651	0.00130	0.03302	0.00195	0.04953	0.00260	0.06604	0.00325	0.08255
0.070	1.7780	0.00070	0.01778	0.00140	0.03556	0.00210	0.05334	0.00280	0.07112	0.00350	0.08890
0.075	1.9050	0.00075	0.01905	0.00150	0.03810	0.00225	0.05715	0.00300	0.07620	0.00375	0.09525
0.080	2.0320	0.00080	0.02032	0.00160	0.04064	0.00240	0.06096	0.00320	0.08128	0.00400	0.10160
0.085	2.1590	0.00085	0.02159	0.00170	0.04318	0.00255	0.06477	0.00340	0.08636	0.00425	0.10795
0.090	2.2860	0.00090	0.02286	0.00180	0.04572	0.00270	0.06858	0.00360	0.09144	0.00450	0.11430
0.095	2.4130	0.00095	0.02413	0.00190	0.04826	0.00285	0.07239	0.00380	0.09652	0.00475	0.12065
0.100	2.5400	0.00100	0.02540	0.00200	0.05080	0.00300	0.07620	0.00400	0.10160	0.00500	0.12700

Table 1-56. Percent Clearance for Stock Thicknesses from 0.001 (0.0254 mm) to 0.100 (2.540 mm) (Continued).

Stock Thickness		6% Clearance		7% Clearance		8% Clearance		9% Clearance		10% Clearance	
inch	mm	inch	mm	inch	mm	inch	mm	inch	mm	inch	mm
0.001	0.0254	0.00006	0.00152	0.00007	0.00178	0.00008	0.00203	0.00009	0.00229	0.00010	0.00254
0.002	0.0508	0.00012	0.00305	0.00014	0.00356	0.00016	0.00406	0.00018	0.00457	0.00020	0.00508
0.003	0.0762	0.00018	0.00457	0.00021	0.00533	0.00024	0.00610	0.00027	0.00686	0.00030	0.00762
0.004	0.1016	0.00024	0.00610	0.00028	0.00711	0.00032	0.00813	0.00036	0.00914	0.00040	0.01016
0.005	0.1270	0.00030	0.00762	0.00035	0.00889	0.00040	0.01016	0.00045	0.01143	0.00050	0.01270
0.010	0.2540	0.00060	0.01524	0.00070	0.01778	0.00080	0.02032	0.00090	0.02286	0.00100	0.02540
0.015	0.3810	0.00090	0.02286	0.00105	0.02667	0.00120	0.03048	0.00135	0.03429	0.00150	0.03810
0.020	0.5080	0.00120	0.03048	0.00140	0.03556	0.00160	0.04064	0.00180	0.04572	0.00200	0.05080
0.025	0.6350	0.00150	0.03810	0.00175	0.04445	0.00200	0.05080	0.00225	0.05715	0.00250	0.06350
0.030	0.7620	0.00180	0.04572	0.00210	0.05334	0.00240	0.06096	0.00270	0.06858	0.00300	0.07620
0.035	0.8890	0.00210	0.05334	0.00245	0.06223	0.00280	0.07112	0.00315	0.08001	0.00350	0.08890
0.040	1.0160	0.00240	0.06096	0.00280	0.07112	0.00320	0.08128	0.00360	0.09144	0.00400	0.10160
0.045	1.1430	0.00270	0.06858	0.00315	0.08001	0.00360	0.09144	0.00405	0.10287	0.00450	0.11430
0.050	1.2700	0.00300	0.07620	0.00350	0.08890	0.00400	0.10160	0.00450	0.11430	0.00500	0.12700
0.055	1.3970	0.00330	0.08382	0.00385	0.09779	0.00440	0.11176	0.00495	0.12573	0.00550	0.13970
0.060	1.5240	0.00360	0.09144	0.00420	0.10668	0.00480	0.12192	0.00540	0.13716	0.00600	0.15240
0.065	1.6510	0.00390	0.09906	0.00455	0.11557	0.00520	0.13208	0.00585	0.14859	0.00650	0.16510
0.070	1.7780	0.00420	0.10668	0.00490	0.12446	0.00560	0.14224	0.00630	0.16002	0.00700	0.17780
0.075	1.9050	0.00450	0.11430	0.00525	0.13335	0.00600	0.15240	0.00675	0.17145	0.00750	0.19050
0.080	2.0320	0.00480	0.12192	0.00560	0.14224	0.00640	0.16256	0.00720	0.18288	0.00800	0.20320
0.085	2.1590	0.00510	0.12954	0.00595	0.15113	0.00680	0.17272	0.00765	0.19431	0.00850	0.21590
0.090	2.2860	0.00540	0.13716	0.00630	0.16002	0.00720	0.18288	0.00810	0.20574	0.00900	0.22860
0.095	2.4130	0.00570	0.14478	0.00665	0.16891	0.00760	0.19304	0.00855	0.21717	0.00950	0.24130
0.100	2.5400	0.00600	0.15240	0.00700	0.17780	0.00800	0.20320	0.00900	0.22860	0.01000	0.25400

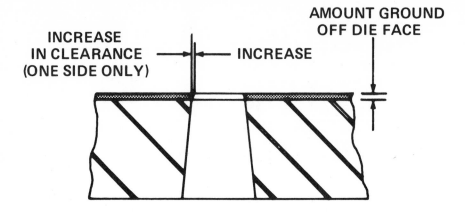

Fig. 1–5

Table 1–57. Increase in Clearance as Die Face is Ground.

| Amount Ground off Die Face | | Increase in Clearance for 1/2° | | | |
| | | One Side Only | | Both Sides | |
inch	mm	inch	mm	inch	mm
0.001	0.0254	0.0000087	0.00022	0.0000174	0.00044
0.002	0.0508	0.0000174	0.00044	0.0000348	0.00088
0.003	0.0762	0.0000261	0.00066	0.0000522	0.00133
0.004	0.1016	0.0000349	0.00089	0.0000698	0.00177
0.005	0.1270	0.0000436	0.00111	0.0000872	0.00221
0.006	0.1524	0.0000523	0.00133	0.0001046	0.00266
0.007	0.1778	0.0000610	0.00155	0.0001220	0.00310
0.008	0.2032	0.0000698	0.00177	0.0001396	0.00355
0.009	0.2286	0.0000785	0.00199	0.000157	0.00399
0.010	0.2540	0.000087	0.00221	0.000174	0.00442
0.015	0.3810	0.000131	0.00333	0.000262	0.00665
0.020	0.5080	0.000175	0.00445	0.000350	0.00889
0.025	0.6350	0.000218	0.00554	0.000436	0.01107
0.030	0.7620	0.000262	0.00665	0.000524	0.01331
0.035	0.8890	0.000305	0.00775	0.000610	0.01549
0.040	1.0160	0.000349	0.00886	0.000698	0.01773
0.045	1.1430	0.000393	0.00998	0.000786	0.01996
0.050	1.2700	0.000436	0.01107	0.000872	0.02215
0.055	1.3970	0.000480	0.01219	0.000960	0.02438
0.060	1.5240	0.0005236	0.01330	0.001047	0.02659

Table 1-57. Increase in Clearance as Die Face is Ground (Continued).

Amount Ground off Die Face		Increase in Clearance for 3/4°				Increase in Clearance for 1°			
		One Side Only		Both Sides		One Side Only		Both Sides	
inch	mm	inch	mm	inch	mm	inch	mm	inch	mm
0.001	0.0254	0.000013	0.00033	0.000026	0.00066	0.0000174	0.00044	0.0000348	0.00088
0.002	0.0508	0.000026	0.00066	0.000052	0.00132	0.0000349	0.00089	0.0000698	0.00177
0.003	0.0762	0.000039	0.00099	0.000078	0.00198	0.0000523	0.00133	0.0001046	0.00266
0.004	0.1016	0.000052	0.00132	0.000104	0.00264	0.0000698	0.00177	0.0001396	0.00355
0.005	0.1270	0.000065	0.00165	0.000130	0.00330	0.0000872	0.00221	0.0001744	0.00443
0.006	0.1524	0.000079	0.00201	0.000158	0.00401	0.0001047	0.00266	0.0002094	0.00532
0.007	0.1778	0.000092	0.00234	0.000184	0.00467	0.0001221	0.00310	0.0002442	0.00620
0.008	0.2032	0.000105	0.00267	0.000210	0.00533	0.0001396	0.00355	0.0002792	0.00709
0.009	0.2286	0.000118	0.00300	0.000236	0.00599	0.0001570	0.00399	0.0003140	0.00798
0.010	0.2540	0.000131	0.00333	0.000262	0.00665	0.0001745	0.00443	0.0003490	0.00886
0.015	0.3810	0.000196	0.00498	0.000392	0.00996	0.0002618	0.00665	0.0005236	0.01330
0.020	0.5080	0.000262	0.00665	0.000524	0.01331	0.0003491	0.00887	0.0006982	0.01773
0.025	0.6350	0.000327	0.00831	0.000654	0.01661	0.0004363	0.01108	0.0008726	0.02216
0.030	0.7620	0.000393	0.00998	0.000786	0.01996	0.0005236	0.01330	0.0010472	0.02660
0.035	0.8890	0.000458	0.01163	0.000916	0.02327	0.0006109	0.01552	0.0012218	0.03103
0.040	1.0160	0.000524	0.01331	0.001048	0.02662	0.0006982	0.01773	0.0013964	0.03547
0.045	1.1430	0.000589	0.01496	0.001178	0.02992	0.0007854	0.01995	0.0015708	0.03990
0.050	1.2700	0.000655	0.01664	0.001310	0.03327	0.0008727	0.02217	0.0017454	0.04433
0.055	1.3970	0.000720	0.01829	0.001440	0.03658	0.0009600	0.02438	0.0019200	0.04877
0.060	1.5240	0.000785	0.01995	0.001570	0.03990	0.0010470	0.02660	0.0020940	0.05319

Table 1-57. Increase in Clearance as Die Face is Ground (Continued).

Amount Ground off Die Face		Increase in Clearance for 1 1/4°				Increase in Clearance for 1 1/2°			
		One Side Only		Both Sides		One Side Only		Both Sides	
inch	mm	inch	mm	inch	mm	inch	mm	inch	mm
0.001	0.0254	0.0000218	0.00055	0.0000436	0.00111	0.0000261	0.00066	0.0000522	0.00133
0.002	0.0508	0.0000436	0.00111	0.0000872	0.00221	0.0000523	0.00133	0.0001046	0.00266
0.003	0.0762	0.0000654	0.00166	0.0001308	0.00332	0.0000785	0.00199	0.0001570	0.00399
0.004	0.1016	0.0000872	0.00221	0.0001744	0.00443	0.0001047	0.00266	0.0002094	0.00532
0.005	0.1270	0.0001091	0.00277	0.0002182	0.00554	0.0001309	0.00332	0.0002618	0.00665
0.006	0.1524	0.0001309	0.00332	0.0002618	0.00665	0.0001571	0.00399	0.0003142	0.00798
0.007	0.1778	0.0001527	0.00388	0.0003054	0.00776	0.0001833	0.00466	0.0003666	0.00931
0.008	0.2032	0.0001745	0.00443	0.0003490	0.00886	0.0002094	0.00532	0.0004188	0.01064
0.009	0.2286	0.0001963	0.00499	0.0003926	0.00997	0.0002356	0.00598	0.0004712	0.01197
0.010	0.2540	0.0002182	0.00554	0.0004364	0.01108	0.0002618	0.00665	0.0005236	0.01330
0.015	0.3810	0.0003273	0.00831	0.0006546	0.01663	0.0003927	0.00997	0.0007854	0.01995
0.020	0.5080	0.0004364	0.01108	0.0008728	0.02217	0.0005237	0.01330	0.0010474	0.02660
0.025	0.6350	0.0005455	0.01386	0.0010910	0.02771	0.0006546	0.01663	0.0013092	0.03325
0.030	0.7620	0.0006546	0.01663	0.0013092	0.03325	0.0007855	0.01995	0.0015710	0.03990
0.035	0.8890	0.0007637	0.01940	0.0015274	0.03880	0.0009165	0.02328	0.0018330	0.04656
0.040	1.0160	0.0008728	0.02217	0.0017456	0.04434	0.0010474	0.02660	0.0020948	0.05321
0.045	1.1430	0.0009819	0.02494	0.0019638	0.04988	0.0011783	0.02993	0.0023566	0.05986
0.050	1.2700	0.0010910	0.02771	0.0021820	0.05542	0.0013093	0.03326	0.0026186	0.06651
0.055	1.3970	0.0012001	0.03048	0.0024002	0.06097	0.0014402	0.03658	0.0028804	0.07316
0.060	1.5240	0.0013092	0.03325	0.0026184	0.06651	0.0015711	0.03991	0.0031422	0.07981

Table 1-57. Increase in Clearance as Die Face is Ground (Continued).

| Amount Ground off Die Face | | Increase in Clearance for 1 3/4° | | | | Increase in Clearance for 2° | | | |
| | | One Side Only | | Both Sides | | One Side Only | | Both Sides | |
inch	mm	inch	mm	inch	mm	inch	mm	inch	mm
0.001	0.0254	0.0000305	0.00077	0.0000610	0.00155	0.0000349	0.00089	0.0000698	0.00177
0.002	0.0508	0.0000611	0.00155	0.0001222	0.00310	0.0000698	0.00177	0.0001396	0.00355
0.003	0.0762	0.0000916	0.00233	0.0001832	0.00465	0.0001047	0.00266	0.0002094	0.00532
0.004	0.1016	0.0001222	0.00310	0.0002444	0.00621	0.0001396	0.00355	0.0002792	0.00709
0.005	0.1270	0.0001527	0.00388	0.0003054	0.00776	0.0001746	0.00443	0.0003492	0.00887
0.006	0.1524	0.0001833	0.00466	0.0003666	0.00931	0.0002095	0.00532	0.0004190	0.01064
0.007	0.1778	0.0002138	0.00543	0.0004276	0.01086	0.0002444	0.00621	0.0004888	0.01242
0.008	0.2032	0.0002444	0.00621	0.0004888	0.01242	0.0002793	0.00709	0.0005586	0.01419
0.009	0.2286	0.0002749	0.00698	0.0005498	0.01396	0.0003142	0.00798	0.0006284	0.01596
0.010	0.2540	0.0003055	0.00776	0.0006110	0.01552	0.0003492	0.00887	0.0006984	0.01774
0.015	0.3810	0.0004582	0.01164	0.0009164	0.02328	0.0005238	0.01330	0.0010476	0.02661
0.020	0.5080	0.0006110	0.01552	0.0012220	0.03104	0.0006984	0.01774	0.0013968	0.03548
0.025	0.6350	0.0007638	0.01940	0.0015276	0.03880	0.0008730	0.02217	0.0017460	0.04435
0.030	0.7620	0.0009165	0.02328	0.0018330	0.04656	0.0010476	0.02661	0.0020952	0.05322
0.035	0.8890	0.0010693	0.02716	0.0021386	0.05432	0.0012222	0.03104	0.0024444	0.06209
0.040	1.0160	0.0012221	0.03104	0.0024442	0.06208	0.0013968	0.03548	0.0027936	0.07096
0.045	1.1430	0.0013748	0.03492	0.0027496	0.06984	0.0015714	0.03991	0.0031428	0.07983
0.050	1.2700	0.0015276	0.03880	0.0030552	0.07760	0.0017460	0.04435	0.0034920	0.08870
0.055	1.3970	0.0016804	0.04268	0.0033608	0.08536	0.0019206	0.04878	0.0038412	0.09757
0.060	1.5240	0.0018331	0.04656	0.0036662	0.09312	0.0020952	0.05322	0.0041904	0.10644

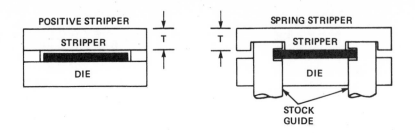

Fig. 1-6   THE TWO BASIC STRIPPERS

Table 1–58.   Minimum Stripper Thickness.

Stock Width	Stock Thickness		Minimum Stripper Thickness	
	inch	*mm*	*inch*	*mm*
1 inch (25.4 mm) and under	0.001 to 0.010	0.0254 to 0.2540	0.053	1.3462
	0.021 to 0.040	0.5334 to 1.016	0.113	2.8702
	0.041 to 0.060	1.0414 to 1.524	0.153	3.8862
	0.061 to 0.080	1.5494 to 2.032	0.193	4.9022
	0.081 to 0.100	2.0574 to 2.540	0.233	5.9182
1 inch (25.4 mm) to 2 inches (50.8 mm)	0.010 to 0.020	0.2540 to 0.5080	0.106	2.6924
	0.021 to 0.040	0.5334 to 1.0160	0.146	3.7084
	0.041 to 0.060	1.0414 to 1.5240	0.186	4.7244
	0.061 to 0.080	1.5494 to 2.0320	0.226	5.7404
	0.081 to 0.100	2.0574 to 2.5400	0.266	6.7564

Table 1–58. Minimum Stripper Thickness *(Continued).*

Stock Width	Stock Thickness		Minimum Stripper Thickness	
	inch	mm	inch	mm
2 inches (50.8 mm) to 3 inches (76.2 mm)	0.000 to 0.040	0.000 to 1.0160	0.090	2.2860
	0.041 to 0.080	0.0414 to 2.032	0.170	4.3180
	0.081 to 0.120	2.0574 to 3.0480	0.250	6.3500
	0.121 to 0.160	3.0734 to 4.0640	0.330	8.3830
	0.161 to 0.200	4.0894 to 5.0800	0.50	12.7000
3 inches (76.2 mm) to 4 inches (101.6 mm)	0.000 to 0.040	0.0000 to 1.0160	0.213	5.4102
	0.041 to 0.080	1.0414 to 2.0320	0.293	7.4422
	0.081 to 0.120	2.0574 to 3.0480	0.373	9.4742
	0.121 to 0.160	3.0734 to 4.064	0.453	11.5062
	0.161 to 0.200	4.0894 to 5.0800	0.533	13.5382
4 inches (101.6 mm) to 5 inches (127.0 mm)	0.030 to 0.070	0.7620 to 1.7780	0.306	7.7724
	0.071 to 0.110	1.8034 to 2.7940	0.386	9.8044
	0.111 to 0.150	2.8194 to 3.8100	0.466	11.8364
	0.151 to 0.190	3.8354 to 4.8260	0.546	13.8684
	0.191 to 0.230	4.8514 to 5.8420	0.626	15.9004

Table 1–58. Minimum Stripper Thickness *(Continued).*

Stock Width	Stock Thickness		Minimum Stripper Thickness	
	inch	*mm*	*inch*	*mm*
	0.030 to 0.070	0.7620 to 1.7780	0.340	8.6360
	0.071 to 0.110	1.8034 to 2.7940	0.420	10.6680
5 inches (127.0 mm) to 6 inches (152.4 mm)	0.111 to 0.150	2.8194 to 3.8100	0.500	12.7000
	0.151 to 0.190	3.8354 to 4.8260	0.580	14.7320
	0.191 to 0.230	4.8514 to 5.8420	0.660	16.7640
	0.040 to 0.090	1.0160 to 2.2860	0.413	10.4902
	0.091 to 0.140	2.3114 to 3.5560	0.513	13.0302
6 inches (152.4 mm) to 7 inches (177.8 mm)	0.141 to 0.190	3.5814 to 4.8260	0.613	15.5702
	0.191 to 0.240	4.8514 to 6.0960	0.713	18.1102
	0.241 to 0.290	6.1214 to 7.3660	0.813	20.6502
	0.040 to 0.100	1.0160 to 2.5400	0.466	11.8364
	0.101 to 0.160	2.5654 to 4.0640	0.586	14.8844
7 inches (152.4 mm) to 8 inches (203.2 mm)	0.161 to 0.220	4.0894 to 5.5880	0.706	17.9324
	0.221 to 0.280	5.6134 to 7.1120	0.826	20.9804
	0.281 to 0.340	7.1374 to 8.6360	0.946	24.0284

Table 1–58.   Minimum Stripper Thickness *(Continued).*

Stock Width	Stock Thickness		Minimum Stripper Thickness	
	inch	*mm*	*inch*	*mm*
8 inches (203.2 mm) to 9 inches (228.6 mm)	0.040 to 0.110	1.0160 to 2.7940	0.520	13.2080
	0.111 to 0.180	2.8194 to 4.5720	0.560	14.2240
	0.181 to 0.250	4.5974 to 6.3500	0.800	20.3200
	0.251 to 0.320	6.3754 to 8.1280	0.940	23.8760
	0.321 to 0.390	8.1534 to 9.9060	1.080	27.4320
9 inches (228.6 mm) to 10 inches (254.0 mm)	0.060 to 0.130	1.5240 to 3.3020	0.593	15.0622
	0.131 to 0.200	3.3274 to 5.0800	0.733	18.6182
	0.201 to 0.270	5.1054 to 6.8580	0.873	22.1742
	0.271 to 0.340	6.8834 to 8.6360	1.013	25.7302
	0.341 to 0.410	8.6614 to 10.4140	1.153	29.2862

Table 1–59. Stripping Force Requirements.

Stock Thickness		Force per Inch of Cut Length		Force per Millimeter of Cut Length	
inch	mm	ton	kN	ton	kN
0.001	0.0254	0.00175	0.1556	0.000068	0.000 612
0.002	0.0508	0.00350	0.3113	0.000137	0.001 225
0.003	0.0762	0.00525	0.4670	0.000206	0.001 838
0.004	0.1016	0.00700	0.6227	0.000275	0.002 451
0.005	0.1270	0.00875	0.7784	0.000344	0.003 064
0.006	0.1524	0.01050	0.093 40	0.000413	0.003 677
0.007	0.1778	0.01225	0.108 97	0.000482	0.004 290
0.008	0.2032	0.01400	0.124 54	0.000551	0.004 903
0.009	0.2286	0.01575	0.140 11	0.000620	0.005 516
0.010	0.2540	0.01750	0.155 68	0.000689	0.006 129
0.015	0.3810	0.02625	0.233 52	0.001033	0.009 193
0.020	0.5080	0.03550	0.311 36	0.001377	0.012 258
0.025	0.6350	0.04375	0.389 20	0.001722	0.015 322
0.030	0.7620	0.05250	0.467 04	0.002066	0.018 387
0.035	0.8890	0.06125	0.544 88	0.002411	0.021 451
0.040	1.0160	0.07000	0.622 72	0.002755	0.024 516
0.045	1.1430	0.07875	0.700 56	0.003100	0.027 581
0.050	1.2700	0.08750	0.778 40	0.003440	0.030 645
0.055	1.3970	0.09625	0.856 24	0.003789	0.033 710
0.060	1.5240	0.10500	0.934 08	0.004133	0.036 774
0.065	1.6510	0.11375	1.011 92	0.004478	0.039 839
0.070	1.7780	0.12250	1.089 76	0.004822	0.042 903
0.075	1.9050	0.13125	1.167 60	0.005167	0.045 968
0.080	2.0320	0.14000	1.245 44	0.005511	0.049 033
0.085	2.1590	0.14875	1.323 28	0.005856	0.052 097
0.090	2.2860	0.15750	1.401 12	0.00620	0.055 162
0.095	2.4130	0.16625	1.478 96	0.006545	0.058 226
0.100	2.5400	0.17500	1.556 80	0.00688	0.061 291
0.110	2.7940	0.19250	1.712 48	0.00757	0.067 420
0.120	3.0480	0.2100	1.868 16	0.00826	0.073 549
0.130	3.3020	0.22750	2.023 84	0.00895	0.079 678
0.140	3.5560	0.245	2.179 52	0.00964	0.085 807
0.150	3.8100	0.2625	2.335 20	0.01033	0.091 937
0.160	4.0640	0.280	2.490 88	0.01102	0.098 066
0.170	4.3180	0.2975	2.646 56	0.01171	0.104 195
0.180	4.5720	0.315	2.802 24	0.01240	0.110 324
0.190	4.8260	0.3325	2.957 92	0.01309	0.116 453
0.200	5.0800	0.350	3.113 60	0.01377	0.122 582
0.210	5.3340	0.3675	3.269 28	0.01446	0.128 711
0.220	5.5880	0.385	3.424 96	0.01515	0.134 840
0.230	5.8420	0.4024	3.580 64	0.01584	0.140 970
0.240	6.0960	0.42	3.736 32	0.01653	0.147 099
0.250	6.3500	0.4375	3.892 00	0.01722	0.153 228
0.260	6.6040	0.455	4.047 68	0.01791	0.159 357
0.270	6.8580	0.4725	4.203 36	0.01860	0.165 486
0.280	7.1120	0.490	4.359 04	0.01929	0.171 615
0.290	7.3660	0.5075	4.514 72	0.01998	0.177 744
0.300	7.6200	0.525	4.670 40	0.02066	0.183 874

Forming Operations

HARD METAL BENDS

A typical bending operation and the die sections that perform it are shown in *Figure* 2–1. Assuming a relatively hard workpiece material, the total length of metal required to form this part is equal to $a + b +$ the length of the metal in the bend.

$$L = a + \text{BL} + b$$

in which

    L = Total length
    a = One leg
    BL = Length of metal in the bend
    b = The other leg

The equation for finding BL in hard metal bends is

$$\text{BL} = (t/2 + R) \times 1.5708$$

in which

    BL = Length of metal in the bend
    t = Metal thickness
    R = Inside radius of bend

Table 2–1 provides inch and metric values for BL in values of 0.012 inch (0.3048 mm) to 0.375 inch (9.525 mm) for thickness t, and 0 to $1\frac{1}{4}$ inch for inside radius R.

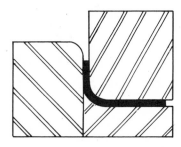

FIG 2-1

39

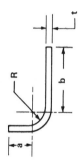

Table 2-1. Length of Metal in Bend when Workpiece is Relatively Hard.

Thickness		BL (R = 0)		BL (R = 1/64)		BL (R = 1/32)		BL (R = 1/16)		BL (R = 3/32)		BL (R = 1/8)		BL (R = 5/32)	
inch	mm	inch	mm	inch	mm	inch	mm	inch	mm	inch	mm	inch	mm	inch	mm
0.012	0.3048	0.009	0.2286	0.034	0.8636	0.058	1.4732	0.108	2.7432	0.157	3.9878	0.206	5.2324	0.255	6.474
0.015	0.3810	0.012	0.3048	0.036	0.9144	0.061	1.5494	0.110	2.7940	0.169	4.040	0.208	5.2832	0.257	6.533
0.018	0.4572	0.014	0.3556	0.039	0.9820	0.063	1.6002	0.112	2.853	0.161	4.0894	0.210	5.334	0.260	6.593
0.021	0.5334	0.016	0.4064	0.041	1.0414	0.066	1.6764	0.115	2.9210	0.164	4.1656	0.213	5.4102	0.262	6.653
0.024	0.6096	0.019	0.4826	0.043	1.0922	0.068	1.7272	0.117	2.9718	0.166	4.2164	0.215	5.466	0.264	6.713
0.030	0.7620	0.024	0.6096	0.048	1.2192	0.073	1.8542	0.122	3.0988	0.171	4.3434	0.220	5.586	0.269	6.833
0.036	0.9144	0.028	0.7112	0.053	1.3462	0.077	1.9558	0.126	3.2004	0.176	4.459	0.225	5.705	0.274	6.952
0.048	1.2192	0.038	0.9652	0.062	1.5748	0.088	2.2352	0.136	3.4544	0.185	4.6990	0.234	5.945	0.283	7.192
0.062	1.5748	0.049	1.2450	0.073	1.860	0.097	2.4638	0.147	3.730	0.196	4.977	0.245	6.224	0.294	7.471
0.075	1.9050	0.059	1.4990	0.083	2.1082	0.108	2.7432	0.157	3.9878	0.206	5.2324	0.255	6.483	0.304	7.730
0.093	2.3622	0.073	1.8542	0.098	2.489	0.122	3.102	0.171	4.349	0.220	5.596	0.269	6.843	0.318	8.089
0.109	2.7686	0.086	2.1740	0.110	2.798	0.135	3.421	0.184	4.668	0.233	5.915	0.282	7.162	0.331	8.409
0.125	3.1750	0.098	2.4934	0.123	3.117	0.147	3.740	0.196	4.987	0.245	6.234	0.295	7.481	0.344	8.728
0.140	3.5560	0.110	2.7940	0.134	3.416	0.159	4.039	0.208	5.287	0.257	6.533	0.306	7.780	0.355	9.027
0.156	3.9624	0.123	3.112	0.147	3.735	0.172	4.359	0.221	5.606	0.270	6.852	0.319	8.099	0.368	9.346
0.187	4.7498	0.147	3.7304	0.171	4.354	0.196	4.977	0.245	6.224	0.294	7.471	0.343	8.718	0.392	9.965
0.203	5.1562	0.159	4.0502	0.184	4.673	0.209	5.297	0.258	6.543	0.307	7.790	0.356	9.037	0.405	10.283
0.218	5.5372	0.171	4.3434	0.196	4.971	0.220	5.596	0.269	6.842	0.318	8.089	0.368	9.336	0.417	10.583
0.234	5.9436	0.184	4.6736	0.208	5.2832	0.233	5.9182	0.282	7.1628	0.331	8.4074	0.380	9.655	0.429	10.902
0.250	6.3500	0.196	4.9784	0.221	5.611	0.245	6.223	0.295	7.481	0.344	8.728	0.393	9.975	0.442	11.221
0.265	6.7310	0.208	5.2832	0.233	5.9182	0.257	6.5278	0.306	7.7724	0.355	9.0170	0.404	10.274	0.454	11.520
0.281	7.1374	0.221	5.6134	0.245	6.2230	0.270	6.8580	0.319	8.1026	0.368	9.3472	0.417	10.593	0.466	11.840
0.312	7.9248	0.245	6.2230	0.270	6.848	0.294	7.471	0.343	8.718	0.392	9.965	0.441	11.211	0.490	12.458
0.375	9.5250	0.295	7.493	0.319	8.104	0.344	8.728	0.393	9.974	0.442	11.221	0.491	12.468	0.540	13.715

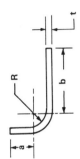

Table 2-1. Length of Metal in Bend when Workpiece is Relatively Hard (Continued).

Thickness		BL (R = 3/16)		BL (R = 7/32)		BL (R = 1/4)		BL (R = 9/32)		BL (R = 5/16)		BL (R = 3/8)		BL (R = 7/16)	
inch	mm	inch	mm	inch	mm	inch	mm	inch	mm	inch	mm	inch	mm	inch	mm
0.012	0.3048	0.304	7.720	0.353	8.967	0.402	10.214	0.451	11.461	0.500	12.708	0.598	15.201	0.697	17.695
0.015	0.3810	0.306	7.780	0.355	9.027	0.404	10.274	0.454	11.521	0.503	12.767	0.601	16.261	0.699	17.755
0.018	0.4572	0.309	7.840	0.358	9.087	0.407	10.338	0.456	11.580	0.505	12.827	0.603	15.321	0.701	17.815
0.021	0.5334	0.311	7.900	0.360	9.144	0.409	10.394	0.458	11.640	0.507	12.887	0.606	15.381	0.704	17.874
0.024	0.6096	0.313	7.960	0.362	9.207	0.412	10.453	0.461	11.700	0.510	12.947	0.608	15.441	0.706	17.934
0.030	0.7620	0.318	8.079	0.367	9.326	0.416	10.573	0.465	11.820	0.514	13.067	0.613	15.560	0.711	18.054
0.036	0.9144	0.323	8.199	0.372	9.446	0.421	10.693	0.470	11.940	0.519	13.186	0.617	15.680	0.715	18.174
0.048	1.2192	0.332	8.438	0.381	9.685	0.430	10.932	0.479	12.179	0.529	13.426	0.627	15.919	0.725	18.413
0.062	1.5748	0.343	8.718	0.392	9.965	0.441	11.211	0.490	12.458	0.540	13.705	0.638	16.199	0.736	18.692
0.075	1.9050	0.353	8.977	0.403	10.224	0.452	11.471	0.501	12.718	0.550	13.964	0.648	16.458	0.746	18.951
0.093	2.3622	0.368	9.336	0.417	10.583	0.466	11.830	0.515	13.077	0.564	14.323	0.662	16.817	0.760	19.311
0.109	2.7686	0.380	9.655	0.429	10.902	0.478	12.149	0.527	13.396	0.576	14.643	0.675	17.136	0.773	19.630
0.125	3.1750	0.393	9.975	0.442	11.221	0.491	12.468	0.540	13.715	0.589	14.961	0.687	17.456	0.785	19.949
0.140	3.5560	0.404	10.274	0.454	11.521	0.503	12.767	0.552	14.014	0.601	15.261	0.699	17.755	0.797	20.248
0.156	3.9624	0.417	10.593	0.466	11.840	0.515	13.087	0.564	14.333	0.613	15.580	0.712	18.074	0.810	20.568
0.187	4.7498	0.441	11.211	0.490	12.458	0.540	13.704	0.589	14.952	0.638	16.199	0.736	18.692	0.834	21.186
0.203	5.1562	0.454	11.531	0.503	12.777	0.552	14.024	0.601	15.271	0.650	16.518	0.748	19.012	0.847	21.505
0.218	5.5372	0.466	11.830	0.515	13.077	0.564	14.323	0.613	15.570	0.662	16.817	0.760	19.311	0.858	21.804
0.234	5.9436	0.478	12.149	0.527	13.396	0.576	14.643	0.626	15.890	0.675	17.136	0.773	19.630	0.871	22.124
0.250	6.3500	0.491	12.468	0.540	13.715	0.589	14.962	0.638	16.209	0.687	17.456	0.785	19.949	0.884	22.443
0.265	6.7310	0.503	12.767	0.552	14.014	0.601	15.261	0.650	16.508	0.699	17.755	0.797	20.248	0.895	22.742
0.281	7.1374	0.515	13.087	0.564	14.333	0.613	15.580	0.662	16.827	0.712	18.074	0.810	20.568	0.908	23.061
0.312	7.9248	0.540	13.705	0.588	14.952	0.638	16.205	0.687	17.446	0.736	18.692	0.834	21.186	0.932	23.680
0.375	9.5250	0.589	14.962	0.634	16.109	0.687	17.456	0.736	18.702	0.785	19.949	0.884	22.443	0.982	24.936

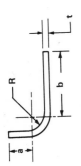

Table 2-1.   Length of Metal in Bend when Workpiece is Relatively Hard (Continued).

Thickness		BL (R = 1/2)		BL (R = 5/8)		BL (R = 3/4)		BL (R = 7/8)		BL (R = 1)		BL (R = 1 1/4)	
inch	mm	inch	mm	inch	mm	inch	mm	inch	mm	inch	mm	inch	mm
0.012	0.3048	0.795	20.189	0.991	25.176	1.188	30.163	1.384	35.150	1.580	40.138	1.973	50.112
0.015	0.3810	0.797	20.248	0.994	25.236	1.190	30.223	1.386	35.210	1.583	40.198	1.975	50.172
0.018	0.4572	0.800	20.308	0.996	25.296	1.192	30.283	1.389	35.270	1.585	40.257	1.978	50.232
0.021	0.5334	0.802	20.368	0.998	25.356	1.195	30.343	1.391	35.330	1.587	40.317	1.980	50.292
0.024	0.6096	0.804	20.428	1.001	25.415	1.197	30.403	1.393	35.390	1.590	40.377	1.982	50.352
0.030	0.7620	0.809	20.548	1.005	25.535	1.202	30.522	1.398	35.510	1.594	40.497	1.987	50.471
0.036	0.9144	0.814	20.667	1.010	25.655	1.206	30.642	1.403	35.629	1.599	40.616	1.992	50.591
0.048	1.2192	0.823	20.907	1.019	25.894	1.216	30.881	1.412	35.865	1.608	40.856	2.001	50.830
0.062	1.5748	0.834	21.186	1.030	26.173	1.227	31.161	1.423	36.148	1.619	41.135	2.012	51.110
0.075	1.9050	0.844	21.445	1.041	26.433	1.237	31.420	1.433	36.407	1.630	41.395	2.022	51.369
0.093	2.3622	0.858	21.804	1.055	26.792	1.251	31.779	1.447	36.766	1.644	41.754	2.037	51.728
0.109	2.7686	0.871	22.124	1.067	27.111	1.264	32.098	1.460	37.085	1.656	42.073	2.049	52.047
0.125	3.1750	0.884	22.443	1.080	27.430	1.276	32.410	1.473	37.405	1.669	42.392	2.062	52.367
0.140	3.5560	0.895	22.742	1.092	27.729	1.288	32.717	1.484	37.704	1.681	42.691	2.073	52.666
0.156	3.9624	0.908	23.061	1.104	28.049	1.301	33.036	1.497	38.023	1.693	43.010	2.086	52.985
0.187	4.7498	0.932	23.680	1.129	28.667	1.325	33.654	1.521	38.642	1.718	43.629	2.110	53.603
0.203	5.1562	0.945	23.999	1.141	28.986	1.338	33.973	1.534	38.961	1.730	43.948	2.123	53.923
0.218	5.5372	0.957	24.298	1.153	29.285	1.349	34.273	1.547	39.260	1.742	44.247	2.135	54.222
0.234	5.9436	0.969	24.617	1.166	29.605	1.362	34.592	1.558	39.579	1.755	44.566	2.147	54.541
0.250	6.3500	0.982	24.936	1.178	29.924	1.374	34.911	1.571	39.898	1.767	44.886	2.160	54.860
0.265	6.7310	0.994	25.236	1.190	30.223	1.386	35.210	1.583	40.198	1.779	45.185	2.172	55.159
0.281	7.1374	1.006	25.555	1.202	30.542	1.399	35.529	1.595	40.517	1.791	45.504	2.184	55.479
0.312	7.9248	1.030	26.173	1.227	31.161	1.423	36.148	1.619	41.135	1.816	46.122	2.209	56.097
0.375	9.5250	1.080	27.430	1.276	32.417	1.473	37.405	1.669	42.392	1.865	47.379	2.258	57.354

V-BENDS FOR MEDIUM STEEL

A typical V-bending operation and the die sections that perform it are shown in *Figure* 2–2. Assuming a medium workpiece material, the total length of metal required to form this part is equal to $a + b +$ the length of metal in the bend.

$$L = a + BL + b$$

in which

L = Total length
a = One leg
BL = Length of metal in the bend
b = The other leg

The equation for finding BL in this case is

$$BL = (t/3 + R) \times 1.5708$$

in which

BL = Length of metal in the bend
t = Metal thickness
R = Inside radius of bend

Table 2–2 provides inch and metric values for BL in values of 0.012 inch (0.3048 mm) to 0.375 inch (9.525 mm) for thickness t, and 0 to $1\frac{1}{4}$ inch for inside radius R.

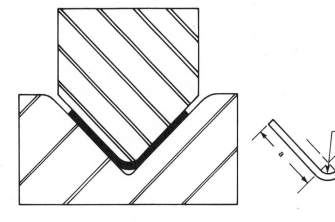

Fig. 2-2

43

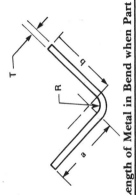

Table 2-2. Length of Metal in Bend when Part is V-Bent.

BL (R = 0)		BL (R = 1/64)		BL (R = 1/32)		BL (R = 1/16)		BL (R = 3/32)		BL (R = 1/8)		BL (R = 5/32)		BL (R = 3/16)	
inch	mm	inch	mm	inch	mm	inch	mm	inch	mm	inch	mm	inch	mm	inch	mm
0.006	0.160	0.031	0.782	0.055	1.404	0.104	2.653	0.153	3.898	0.203	5.147	0.252	6.392	0.300	7.621
0.008	0.199	0.032	0.822	0.057	1.444	0.106	2.693	0.155	3.938	0.204	5.187	0.253	6.431	0.301	7.660
0.009	0.239	0.034	0.862	0.058	1.484	0.108	2.733	0.157	3.978	0.206	5.227	0.255	6.472	0.303	7.700
0.011	0.279	0.036	0.902	0.060	1.524	0.109	2.773	0.158	4.018	0.207	5.267	0.256	6.511	0.305	7.740
0.013	0.319	0.037	0.942	0.062	1.564	0.111	2.813	0.160	4.058	0.209	5.306	0.258	6.551	0.306	7.780
0.016	0.399	0.042	1.021	0.065	1.644	0.114	2.893	0.163	4.137	0.212	5.386	0.261	6.631	0.309	7.860
0.019	0.479	0.043	1.101	0.068	1.724	0.117	2.972	0.166	4.217	0.215	5.466	0.264	6.711	0.313	7.940
0.025	0.638	0.050	1.261	0.074	1.883	0.123	3.132	0.172	4.377	0.221	5.626	0.270	6.870	0.319	8.099
0.032	0.825	0.057	1.447	0.081	2.069	0.131	3.318	0.180	4.563	0.229	5.812	0.278	7.057	0.326	8.286
0.039	0.997	0.064	1.620	0.088	2.242	0.137	3.491	0.186	4.736	0.236	5.985	0.285	7.230	0.333	8.458
0.049	1.237	0.073	1.859	0.098	2.482	0.147	3.730	0.196	4.975	0.245	6.224	0.294	7.469	0.342	8.698
0.057	1.450	0.082	2.072	0.106	2.694	0.155	3.943	0.204	5.188	0.253	6.437	0.302	7.682	0.351	8.911
0.065	1.662	0.090	2.285	0.114	2.907	0.164	4.156	0.213	5.401	0.262	6.650	0.311	7.895	0.359	9.123
0.073	1.862	0.098	2.484	0.122	3.107	0.171	4.356	0.220	5.600	0.270	6.849	0.319	8.094	0.367	9.323
0.082	2.075	0.106	2.697	0.131	3.320	0.180	4.568	0.229	5.813	0.278	7.062	0.327	8.307	0.375	9.536
0.098	2.487	0.122	3.109	0.147	3.732	0.196	4.981	0.245	6.225	0.294	7.474	0.343	8.719	0.392	9.948
0.106	2.700	0.131	3.322	0.155	3.945	0.204	5.193	0.253	6.438	0.303	7.687	0.352	8.932	0.400	10.161
0.114	2.899	0.139	3.522	0.163	4.144	0.212	5.393	0.261	6.638	0.310	7.887	0.360	9.131	0.408	10.360
0.123	3.112	0.147	3.734	0.172	4.357	0.219	5.606	0.270	6.851	0.319	8.099	0.368	9.344	0.416	10.573
0.131	3.325	0.155	3.947	0.180	4.570	0.229	5.819	0.278	7.063	0.327	8.312	0.376	9.557	0.425	10.786
0.139	3.524	0.163	4.147	0.188	4.769	0.237	6.018	0.286	7.263	0.335	8.512	0.384	9.757	0.432	10.985
0.147	3.737	0.172	4.360	0.196	4.982	0.245	6.231	0.294	7.476	0.343	8.724	0.392	9.969	0.440	11.198
0.163	4.149	0.188	4.772	0.212	5.394	0.262	6.643	0.311	7.888	0.360	9.127	0.409	10.382	0.457	11.610
0.196	4.987	0.221	5.610	0.245	6.232	0.295	7.481	0.344	8.726	0.393	3.975	0.442	11.219	0.490	12.448

Table 2-2. Length of Metal in Bend when Part is V-Bent (Continued).

BL (R = 0)		BL (R = 7/32)		BL (R = 1/4)		BL (R = 9/32)		BL (R = 5/16)		BL (R = 3/8)		BL (R = 7/16)		BL (R = 1/2)	
inch	mm	inch	mm	inch	mm	inch	mm	inch	mm	inch	mm	inch	mm	inch	mm
0.006	0.160	0.350	8.885	0.399	10.134	0.448	11.371	0.496	12.608	0.595	15.121	0.694	17.615	0.792	20.109
0.008	0.199	0.351	8.925	0.401	10.174	0.450	11.411	0.498	12.648	0.597	15.161	0.695	17.655	0.793	20.149
0.009	0.239	0.353	8.965	0.402	10.214	0.451	11.451	0.500	12.688	0.598	15.201	0.697	17.695	0.795	20.189
0.011	0.279	0.355	9.005	0.404	10.254	0.452	11.491	0.501	12.728	0.600	15.241	0.698	17.735	0.796	20.228
0.013	0.319	0.356	9.045	0.405	10.294	0.454	11.531	0.503	12.767	0.602	15.281	0.700	17.775	0.798	20.268
0.016	0.399	0.359	9.125	0.408	10.457	0.457	11.610	0.506	12.847	0.605	15.361	0.703	17.854	0.801	20.348
0.019	0.479	0.362	9.205	0.412	10.453	0.460	11.690	0.509	12.927	0.608	15.441	0.706	17.934	0.804	20.428
0.025	0.638	0.369	9.364	0.418	10.613	0.467	11.850	0.515	13.087	0.614	15.600	0.712	18.094	0.811	20.588
0.032	0.825	0.376	9.550	0.425	10.799	0.474	12.036	0.523	13.273	0.622	15.786	0.720	18.280	0.818	20.774
0.039	0.997	0.383	9.723	0.432	10.972	0.481	12.209	0.529	13.446	0.628	15.959	0.726	18.453	0.825	20.947
0.049	1.237	0.392	9.963	0.442	11.211	0.490	12.448	0.539	13.685	0.638	16.199	0.736	18.692	0.834	21.186
0.057	1.450	0.401	10.175	0.450	11.424	0.498	12.661	0.547	13.898	0.646	16.412	0.744	18.905	0.842	21.399
0.065	1.662	0.409	10.388	0.458	11.637	0.507	12.874	0.556	14.111	0.654	16.624	0.753	19.118	0.851	21.612
0.073	1.862	0.417	10.588	0.466	11.836	0.515	13.073	0.563	14.310	0.662	16.824	0.761	19.317	0.859	21.811
0.082	2.075	0.425	10.800	0.474	12.049	0.523	13.286	0.572	14.523	0.671	17.037	0.769	19.530	0.867	22.024
0.098	2.487	0.441	11.213	0.491	12.461	0.539	13.698	0.588	14.935	0.687	17.449	0.785	19.943	0.883	22.436
0.106	2.700	0.450	11.426	0.499	12.674	0.548	13.911	0.596	15.148	0.695	17.662	0.794	20.155	0.892	22.649
0.114	2.899	0.458	11.625	0.507	12.874	0.556	14.111	0.604	15.348	0.703	17.861	0.801	20.356	0.900	22.848
0.123	3.112	0.466	11.838	0.515	13.087	0.564	14.323	0.613	15.560	0.712	18.074	0.810	20.568	0.908	23.061
0.131	3.325	0.474	12.050	0.524	13.299	0.572	14.536	0.621	15.773	0.720	18.287	0.818	20.780	0.916	23.274
0.139	3.524	0.482	12.250	0.531	13.499	0.580	14.736	0.629	15.973	0.728	18.486	0.826	20.980	0.924	23.474
0.147	3.737	0.490	12.463	0.540	13.712	0.589	14.949	0.637	16.185	0.736	18.699	0.834	21.193	0.933	23.686
0.163	4.149	0.507	12.875	0.556	14.124	0.605	15.361	0.653	16.598	0.752	19.111	0.851	21.605	0.949	24.099
0.196	4.987	0.540	13.713	0.589	14.961	0.638	16.199	0.686	17.436	0.785	19.949	0.884	22.443	0.982	24.936

Table 2-2. Length of Metal in Bend When Part is V-Bent (*Continued*).

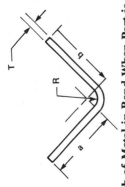

BL (R = 0)		BL (R = 5/8)		BL (R = 3/4)		BL (R = 7/8)		BL (R = 1)		BL (R = 1 1/4)	
inch	mm	inch	mm	inch	mm	inch	mm	inch	mm	inch	mm
0.006	0.160	0.988	25.096	1.184	30.803	1.381	35.071	1.577	40.058	1.970	50.032
0.008	0.199	0.990	25.136	1.186	30.123	1.382	35.111	1.579	40.098	1.971	50.072
0.009	0.239	0.991	25.176	1.188	30.163	1.384	35.150	1.580	40.138	1.973	50.112
0.011	0.279	0.993	25.216	1.189	30.203	1.385	35.190	1.582	40.178	1.974	50.152
0.013	0.319	0.994	25.256	1.191	30.243	1.387	35.230	1.583	40.218	1.976	50.192
0.016	0.399	0.997	25.335	1.194	30.323	1.390	35.310	1.587	40.297	1.979	50.272
0.019	0.479	1.001	25.415	1.197	30.403	1.393	35.390	1.590	40.377	1.982	50.362
0.025	0.638	1.007	25.575	1.203	30.562	1.400	35.550	1.596	40.537	1.989	50.511
0.032	0.825	1.014	25.761	1.211	30.748	1.407	35.736	1.603	40.723	1.996	50.697
0.039	0.997	1.021	25.934	1.217	30.921	1.414	35.908	1.610	40.896	2.003	50.870
0.049	1.237	1.030	26.173	1.227	31.161	1.423	36.148	1.619	41.135	2.012	51.110
0.057	1.450	1.039	26.386	1.235	31.373	1.432	36.361	1.628	41.348	2.021	51.323
0.065	1.662	1.047	26.599	1.244	31.586	1.440	36.573	1.636	41.561	2.029	51.535
0.073	1.862	1.055	26.798	1.251	31.786	1.448	36.773	1.644	41.760	2.037	51.735
0.082	2.075	1.063	27.011	1.260	31.998	1.456	36.986	1.652	41.972	2.045	51.948
0.098	2.487	1.080	27.423	1.276	32.411	1.472	37.398	1.669	42.385	2.061	52.360
0.106	2.700	1.088	27.636	1.284	32.624	1.481	37.611	1.677	42.598	2.070	52.573
0.114	2.899	1.096	27.836	1.292	32.823	1.489	37.810	1.685	42.798	2.078	52.772
0.123	3.112	1.104	28.049	1.301	33.036	1.497	38.023	1.693	43.010	2.086	52.985
0.131	3.325	1.113	28.261	1.309	33.249	1.505	38.236	1.702	43.223	2.094	53.198
0.139	3.524	1.121	28.461	1.317	33.448	1.513	38.435	1.710	43.423	2.102	53.397
0.147	3.737	1.129	28.674	1.325	33.661	1.522	38.648	1.718	43.636	2.111	53.610
0.163	4.149	1.145	29.086	1.341	34.073	1.538	39.060	1.734	44.048	2.127	54.022
0.196	4.987	1.178	29.924	1.374	34.911	1.571	39.899	1.767	44.886	2.160	54.860

U-BENDS FOR MEDIUM STEEL

A typical U-forming operation and the die sections that perform it are shown in *Figure* 2–3. Assuming a medium workpiece material, the total length of metal required to form this part is equal to $a + b + c + 2$ (length of metal in bend).

$$L = a + b + c + 2\text{BL}$$

in which

L = Total length
a = First leg
b = Second leg
c = Third leg
BL = Length of metal in the bend

The equation for finding BL in this case is

$$\text{BL} = (t/4 + R) \times 1.5708$$

in which

BL = Length of metal in the bend
t = Metal thickness
R = Inside radius of bend

Table 2–3 provides inch and metric values for BL in values of 0.012 inch (0.3048 mm) to 0.375 inch (9.525 mm) for thickness t, and 0 to $1\frac{1}{4}$ inch for inside radius R.

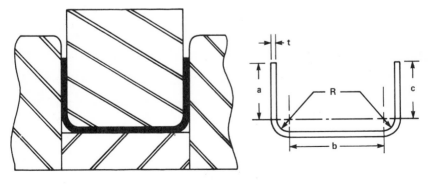

Fig. 2-3

47

Table 2-3. Length of Metal in Bend When Part is U-Bent.

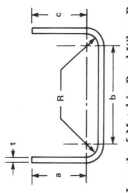

Stock Thickness		BL (R = 0)		BL (R = 1/64)		BL (R = 1/32)		BL (R = 1/16)		BL (R = 3/32)		BL (R = 1/8)		BL (R = 5/32)	
inch	mm	inch	mm	inch	mm	inch	mm	inch	mm	inch	mm	inch	mm	inch	mm
0.012	0.3048	0.005	0.1197	0.029	0.742	0.054	1.365	0.103	2.613	0.152	3.858	0.201	5.107	0.250	6.352
0.015	0.3810	0.006	0.1496	0.030	0.772	0.055	1.394	0.104	2.643	0.153	3.888	0.202	5.137	0.251	6.382
0.018	0.4572	0.007	0.1795	0.032	0.802	0.056	1.424	0.105	2.673	0.154	3.918	0.203	5.167	0.252	6.412
0.021	0.5334	0.008	0.209	0.033	0.832	0.057	1.454	0.106	2.703	0.155	3.948	0.205	5.197	0.254	6.442
0.024	0.6096	0.009	0.239	0.034	0.862	0.058	1.484	0.108	2.733	0.157	3.978	0.206	5.227	0.255	6.472
0.030	0.7620	0.012	0.299	0.036	0.922	0.061	1.544	0.110	2.793	0.159	4.038	0.208	5.287	0.257	6.531
0.036	0.9144	0.014	0.359	0.039	0.981	0.062	1.604	0.112	2.853	0.161	4.098	0.210	5.346	0.259	6.591
0.048	1.2192	0.019	0.479	0.043	1.101	0.068	1.724	0.117	2.972	0.166	4.217	0.215	5.466	0.264	6.711
0.062	1.5748	0.024	0.618	0.049	1.241	0.073	1.863	0.123	3.112	0.172	4.357	0.221	5.606	0.270	6.851
0.075	1.9050	0.029	0.748	0.054	1.371	0.078	1.993	0.128	3.242	0.177	4.487	0.226	5.735	0.275	6.980
0.093	2.3622	0.037	0.928	0.061	1.550	0.086	2.172	0.135	3.421	0.184	4.666	0.233	5.915	0.282	7.160
0.109	2.7686	0.043	1.087	0.067	1.710	0.092	2.332	0.141	3.581	0.190	4.826	0.239	6.075	0.288	7.319
0.125	3.1750	0.049	1.247	0.074	1.870	0.098	2.492	0.147	3.740	0.196	4.985	0.245	6.234	0.294	7.479
0.140	3.5560	0.055	1.396	0.079	2.019	0.104	2.641	0.153	3.890	0.202	5.135	0.251	6.384	0.300	7.629
0.156	3.9624	0.061	1.556	0.086	2.178	0.110	2.801	0.159	4.050	0.208	5.295	0.258	6.543	0.307	7.788
0.187	4.7498	0.073	1.865	0.098	2.488	0.122	3.110	0.172	4.359	0.221	5.604	0.270	6.853	0.319	8.097
0.203	5.1562	0.080	2.025	0.104	2.647	0.129	3.270	0.178	4.518	0.227	5.763	0.276	7.012	0.325	8.257
0.218	5.5372	0.086	2.174	0.110	2.797	0.135	3.419	0.184	4.668	0.233	5.913	0.282	7.162	0.331	8.407
0.234	5.9436	0.092	2.334	0.116	2.956	0.141	3.579	0.190	4.828	0.239	6.073	0.288	7.321	0.337	8.566
0.250	6.3500	0.098	2.494	0.123	3.116	0.147	3.738	0.196	4.987	0.245	6.232	0.295	7.481	0.344	8.726
0.265	6.7310	0.104	2.643	0.129	3.266	0.153	3.888	0.202	5.137	0.251	6.382	0.300	7.631	0.349	8.875
0.281	7.1374	0.110	2.803	0.135	3.425	0.159	4.048	0.209	5.297	0.258	6.541	0.307	7.790	0.356	9.035
0.312	7.9248	0.123	3.112	0.147	3.734	0.172	4.357	0.221	5.606	0.270	6.851	0.319	8.099	0.368	9.345
0.375	9.5250	0.147	3.740	0.172	4.363	0.196	4.985	0.245	6.234	0.294	7.479	0.344	8.728	0.393	9.973

Table 2-3. Length of Metal in Bend When Part is U-Bent (*Continued*).

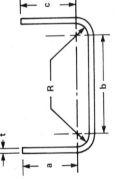

Stock Thickness		BL (R = 3/16)		BL (R = 7/32)		BL (R = 1/4)		BL (R = 9/32)		BL (R = 5/16)		BL (R = 3/8)		BL (R = 7/16)	
inch	mm	inch	mm	inch	mm	inch	mm	inch	mm	inch	mm	inch	mm	inch	mm
0.012	0.3048	0.299	7.601	0.348	8.845	0.397	10.094	0.446	11.339	0.496	12.588	0.594	15.082	0.692	17.575
0.015	0.3810	0.300	7.631	0.349	8.875	0.399	10.124	0.448	11.369	0.497	12.618	0.595	15.111	0.693	17.605
0.018	0.4572	0.302	7.660	0.351	8.905	0.400	10.154	0.449	11.399	0.498	12.648	0.596	15.141	0.694	17.635
0.021	0.5334	0.303	7.690	0.352	8.935	0.401	10.184	0.450	11.429	0.499	12.678	0.597	15.171	0.695	17.665
0.024	0.6096	0.304	7.720	0.353	8.965	0.402	10.214	0.451	11.459	0.500	12.708	0.598	15.201	0.697	17.695
0.030	0.7620	0.306	7.780	0.355	9.025	0.404	10.274	0.453	11.519	0.503	12.767	0.601	15.261	0.699	17.755
0.036	0.9144	0.309	7.840	0.358	9.085	0.407	10.334	0.456	11.578	0.505	12.827	0.603	15.321	0.701	17.815
0.048	1.2192	0.313	7.960	0.362	9.205	0.412	10.453	0.461	11.698	0.510	12.947	0.608	15.441	0.706	17.934
0.062	1.5748	0.319	8.099	0.368	9.344	0.417	10.593	0.466	11.838	0.515	13.087	0.613	15.580	0.712	18.074
0.075	1.9050	0.324	8.229	0.373	9.474	0.422	10.723	0.471	11.967	0.520	13.216	0.619	15.710	0.717	18.204
0.093	2.3622	0.331	8.409	0.380	9.653	0.429	10.902	0.478	12.147	0.527	13.396	0.626	15.890	0.724	18.383
0.109	2.7686	0.337	8.568	0.386	9.813	0.436	11.062	0.485	12.307	0.534	13.555	0.632	16.049	0.730	18.543
0.125	3.1750	0.344	8.728	0.393	9.973	0.442	11.221	0.491	12.466	0.540	13.715	0.638	16.209	0.736	18.702
0.140	3.5560	0.350	8.877	0.399	10.122	0.448	11.371	0.497	12.616	0.546	13.865	0.644	16.358	0.742	18.852
0.156	3.9624	0.356	9.037	0.405	10.282	0.454	11.531	0.503	12.775	0.552	14.024	0.650	16.518	0.748	19.012
0.187	4.7498	0.368	9.346	0.417	10.591	0.466	11.840	0.515	13.085	0.564	14.333	0.662	16.827	0.761	19.321
0.203	5.1562	0.374	9.506	0.423	10.750	0.472	11.999	0.521	13.244	0.571	14.493	0.669	16.987	0.767	19.480
0.218	5.5372	0.380	9.655	0.429	10.900	0.478	12.149	0.527	13.394	0.576	14.643	0.675	17.136	0.773	19.630
0.234	5.9436	0.386	9.815	0.435	11.060	0.485	12.309	0.534	13.553	0.583	14.802	0.681	17.296	0.779	19.790
0.250	6.3500	0.393	9.975	0.442	11.219	0.491	12.468	0.540	13.713	0.589	14.962	0.687	17.456	0.785	19.949
0.265	6.7310	0.399	10.124	0.488	11.369	0.497	12.618	0.546	13.863	0.595	15.111	0.693	17.605	0.791	20.099
0.281	7.1374	0.405	10.284	0.454	11.529	0.503	12.777	0.552	14.022	0.601	15.271	0.699	17.765	0.798	20.259
0.312	7.9248	0.417	10.593	0.466	11.838	0.515	13.087	0.564	14.331	0.613	15.580	0.712	18.074	0.810	20.568
0.375	9.5250	0.442	11.221	0.491	12.466	0.540	13.715	0.589	14.960	0.638	16.209	0.736	18.702	0.834	21.196

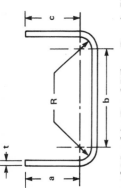

Table 2–3. Length of Metal in Bend When Part is U-Bent (Continued).

Stock Thickness		BL (R = 1/2)		BL (R = 5/8)		BL (R = 3/4)		BL (R = 7/8)		BL (R = 1)		BL (R = 1 1/4)	
inch	mm	inch	mm	inch	mm	inch	mm	inch	mm	inch	mm	inch	mm
0.012	0.3048	0.790	20.069	0.986	25.056	1.183	30.043	1.379	35.031	1.576	40.018	1.968	49.993
0.015	0.3810	0.791	20.099	0.988	25.086	1.184	30.073	1.380	35.061	1.577	40.048	1.969	50.023
0.018	0.4572	0.792	20.129	0.989	25.116	1.185	30.103	1.382	35.091	1.578	40.078	1.971	50.052
0.021	0.5334	0.794	20.159	0.990	25.146	1.186	30.133	1.383	35.120	1.579	40.108	1.972	50.082
0.024	0.6096	0.795	20.189	0.991	25.176	1.188	30.163	1.384	35.150	1.580	40.138	1.973	50.112
0.030	0.7620	0.797	20.248	0.994	25.236	1.190	30.223	1.386	35.210	1.583	40.198	1.975	50.172
0.036	0.9144	0.800	20.308	0.996	25.296	1.192	30.293	1.389	35.270	1.585	40.258	1.978	50.232
0.048	1.2192	0.804	20.428	1.001	25.415	1.197	30.403	1.393	35.390	1.590	40.377	1.982	50.352
0.062	1.5748	0.810	20.568	1.006	25.555	1.202	30.542	1.399	35.529	1.595	40.517	1.988	50.491
0.075	1.9050	0.815	20.697	1.011	25.685	1.208	30.672	1.404	35.659	1.600	40.646	1.993	50.621
0.093	2.3622	0.822	20.877	1.018	25.864	1.215	30.851	1.411	35.839	1.607	40.826	2.000	50.801
0.109	2.7686	0.828	21.036	1.025	26.024	1.221	31.011	1.417	35.998	1.614	40.986	2.006	50.960
0.125	3.1750	0.834	21.196	1.031	26.183	1.227	31.171	1.424	36.158	1.620	41.145	2.013	51.120
0.140	3.5560	0.840	21.346	1.037	26.333	1.233	31.320	1.429	36.307	1.626	41.295	2.018	51.269
0.156	3.9624	0.847	21.505	1.043	26.492	1.239	31.480	1.436	36.467	1.632	41.454	2.025	51.429
0.187	4.7498	0.859	21.814	1.055	26.802	1.252	31.789	1.448	36.776	1.644	41.764	2.037	51.738
0.203	5.1562	0.865	21.974	1.061	26.961	1.258	31.949	1.454	36.936	1.651	41.923	2.043	51.898
0.218	5.5372	0.871	22.124	1.067	27.111	1.264	32.098	1.460	37.085	1.656	42.073	2.049	52.047
0.234	5.9436	0.877	22.283	1.074	27.271	1.270	32.258	1.466	37.245	1.663	42.232	2.055	52.207
0.250	6.3500	0.884	22.443	1.080	27.430	1.276	32.417	1.473	37.405	1.669	42.392	2.062	52.367
0.265	6.7310	0.889	22.592	1.086	27.580	1.282	32.567	1.479	37.554	1.675	42.542	2.068	52.516
0.281	7.1374	0.896	22.752	1.092	27.740	1.288	32.727	1.485	37.714	1.681	42.701	2.074	52.676
0.312	7.9248	0.908	23.061	1.104	28.049	1.301	33.036	1.497	38.023	1.693	43.010	2.086	52.985
0.375	9.5250	0.933	23.690	1.129	28.677	1.325	33.664	1.522	38.651	1.718	43.639	2.111	53.613

WIPES IN MEDIUM STEEL

A typical wipe operation and the die sections that perform it are shown in *Figure* 2–4. Assuming a medium workpiece material, the total length of metal required to form this part is equal to a + length of metal in bend + b.

$$L = a + \mathrm{BL} + b$$

in which

> L = Total length
> a = One leg
> BL = Length of metal in the bend
> b = The other leg

The equation for finding BL in this case is

$$\mathrm{BL} = (t/5 + R) \times 1.5708$$

in which

> BL = Length of metal in the bend
> t = Metal thickness
> R = Inside radius of bend

Table 2–4 provides inch and metric values for BL in values of 0.012 inch (0.3048 mm) to 0.375 inch (9.525 mm) for thickness t, and 0 to $1\frac{1}{4}$ inch for inside radius R.

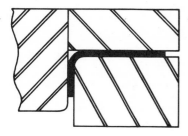
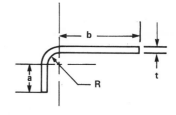

Fig. 2-4

Table 2-4. Length of Metal in Bend when Part is Wiped.

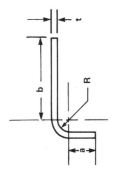

Thickness		BL (R = 0)		BL (R = 1/64)		BL (R = 1/32)		BL (R = 1/16)		BL (R = 3/32)		BL (R = 1/8)		BL (R = 5/32)	
inch	mm	inch	mm	inch	mm	inch	mm	inch	mm	inch	mm	inch	mm	inch	mm
0.012	0.3048	0.004	0.096	0.028	0.718	0.053	1.341	0.102	2.589	0.151	3.834	0.200	5.083	0.249	6.328
0.015	0.3810	0.005	0.120	0.029	0.742	0.054	1.365	0.103	2.613	0.152	3.858	0.201	5.107	0.250	6.352
0.018	0.4572	0.006	0.144	0.030	0.766	0.055	1.388	0.104	2.637	0.153	3.882	0.202	5.131	0.251	6.376
0.021	0.5334	0.007	0.168	0.031	0.790	0.056	1.412	0.105	2.661	0.154	3.906	0.203	5.155	0.252	6.400
0.024	0.6096	0.008	0.192	0.032	0.814	0.057	1.436	0.106	2.685	0.155	3.930	0.204	5.179	0.253	6.424
0.030	0.7620	0.009	0.239	0.034	0.862	0.058	1.484	0.108	2.733	0.157	3.978	0.206	5.227	0.255	6.472
0.036	0.9144	0.011	0.287	0.036	0.910	0.060	1.532	0.109	2.781	0.158	4.026	0.208	5.275	0.257	6.519
0.048	1.2192	0.015	0.383	0.040	1.005	0.064	1.628	0.113	2.877	0.162	4.121	0.211	5.370	0.260	6.615
0.062	1.5748	0.019	0.495	0.044	1.117	0.068	1.740	0.118	2.988	0.167	4.233	0.216	5.482	0.265	6.727
0.075	1.9050	0.024	0.598	0.048	1.221	0.073	1.843	0.122	3.092	0.171	4.337	0.220	5.586	0.269	6.831
0.093	2.3622	0.029	0.742	0.054	1.365	0.078	1.987	0.127	3.236	0.176	4.481	0.226	5.729	0.275	6.974
0.109	2.7686	0.034	0.870	0.059	1.492	0.083	2.115	0.132	3.363	0.181	4.608	0.231	5.857	0.280	7.102
0.125	3.1750	0.039	0.997	0.064	1.620	0.088	2.242	0.137	3.491	0.186	4.736	0.236	5.985	0.285	7.230
0.140	3.5560	0.044	1.117	0.068	1.740	0.093	2.362	0.142	3.611	0.191	4.856	0.240	6.104	0.289	7.349
0.156	3.9624	0.049	1.245	0.074	1.867	0.098	2.490	0.147	3.738	0.196	4.983	0.245	6.232	0.294	7.477
0.187	4.7498	0.059	1.492	0.083	2.115	0.108	2.737	0.157	3.986	0.206	5.231	0.255	6.479	0.304	7.724
0.203	5.1562	0.064	1.620	0.088	2.242	0.113	2.865	0.162	4.114	0.211	5.358	0.260	6.607	0.309	7.852
0.218	5.5372	0.068	1.740	0.093	2.362	0.117	2.984	0.167	4.233	0.216	5.478	0.265	6.727	0.314	7.972
0.234	5.9436	0.074	1.867	0.098	2.490	0.123	3.112	0.172	4.361	0.219	5.606	0.270	6.855	0.319	8.099
0.250	6.3500	0.079	1.995	0.103	2.617	0.128	3.240	0.177	4.489	0.226	5.733	0.275	6.982	0.324	8.227
0.265	6.7310	0.083	2.115	0.108	2.737	0.132	3.359	0.182	4.608	0.230	5.853	0.280	7.102	0.329	8.347
0.281	7.1374	0.088	2.242	0.113	2.865	0.137	3.487	0.186	4.736	0.235	5.981	0.285	7.230	0.334	8.474
0.312	7.9248	0.098	2.490	0.123	3.112	0.147	3.734	0.196	4.983	0.245	6.228	0.294	7.477	0.343	8.722
0.375	9.5250	0.118	2.992	0.142	3.615	0.167	4.237	0.216	5.486	0.265	6.731	0.314	7.980	0.363	9.244

Table 2-4. Length of Metal in Bend When Part is Wiped (Continued).

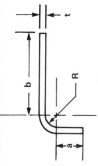

Thickness		BL (R = 3/16)		BL (R = 7/32)		BL (R = 1/4)		BL (R = 9/32)		BL (R = 5/16)		BL (R = 3/8)		BL (R = 7/16)	
inch	mm	inch	mm	inch	mm	inch	mm	inch	mm	inch	mm	inch	mm	inch	mm
0.012	0.3048	0.298	7.577	0.347	8.822	0.396	10.070	0.445	11.315	0.494	12.564	0.593	15.058	0.691	17.551
0.015	0.3810	0.299	7.601	0.348	8.845	0.397	10.094	0.446	11.339	0.495	12.588	0.594	15.082	0.692	17.575
0.018	0.4572	0.300	7.625	0.349	8.869	0.398	10.118	0.447	11.363	0.496	12.612	0.595	15.106	0.693	17.599
0.021	0.5334	0.301	7.649	0.350	8.893	0.399	10.142	0.448	11.387	0.497	12.636	0.596	15.129	0.694	17.623
0.024	0.6096	0.302	7.671	0.351	8.917	0.400	10.166	0.449	11.411	0.498	12.660	0.597	15.153	0.695	17.647
0.030	0.7620	0.304	7.720	0.353	8.965	0.402	10.214	0.451	11.459	0.500	12.708	0.598	15.201	0.697	17.695
0.036	0.9144	0.306	7.768	0.355	9.013	0.404	10.262	0.453	11.507	0.502	12.755	0.600	15.249	0.699	17.743
0.048	1.2192	0.310	7.864	0.359	9.109	0.408	10.358	0.457	11.602	0.506	12.851	0.604	15.345	0.702	17.839
0.062	1.5748	0.314	7.976	0.363	9.220	0.412	10.469	0.461	11.714	0.510	12.963	0.609	15.457	0.707	17.950
0.075	1.9050	0.318	8.079	0.367	9.324	0.416	10.573	0.465	11.818	0.514	13.067	0.613	15.560	0.711	18.054
0.093	2.3622	0.324	8.223	0.373	9.468	0.422	10.717	0.471	11.962	0.520	13.210	0.618	15.704	0.716	18.198
0.109	2.7686	0.329	8.351	0.378	9.596	0.427	10.844	0.476	12.089	0.525	13.338	0.623	15.832	0.721	18.325
0.125	3.1750	0.334	8.478	0.383	9.723	0.432	10.972	0.481	12.217	0.530	13.466	0.628	15.959	0.726	18.453
0.140	3.5560	0.339	8.598	0.388	9.843	0.437	11.092	0.486	12.337	0.535	13.585	0.633	16.079	0.731	18.573
0.156	3.9624	0.344	8.726	0.393	9.971	0.442	11.219	0.491	12.464	0.540	13.713	0.638	16.207	0.736	18.700
0.187	4.7498	0.353	8.973	0.402	10.218	0.451	11.467	0.500	12.712	0.550	13.960	0.648	16.454	0.746	18.948
0.203	5.1562	0.358	9.101	0.407	10.346	0.456	11.594	0.505	12.839	0.555	14.088	0.653	16.582	0.751	19.075
0.218	5.5372	0.363	9.220	0.412	10.465	0.461	11.714	0.510	12.959	0.559	14.208	0.658	16.701	0.756	19.195
0.234	5.9436	0.368	9.348	0.417	10.593	0.466	11.842	0.515	13.087	0.564	14.335	0.663	16.829	0.761	19.323
0.250	6.3500	0.373	9.476	0.422	10.721	0.471	11.969	0.520	13.214	0.569	14.463	0.668	16.957	0.766	19.450
0.265	6.7310	0.378	9.596	0.427	10.840	0.476	12.089	0.525	13.334	0.574	14.583	0.672	17.076	0.770	19.570
0.281	7.1374	0.383	9.723	0.432	10.968	0.481	12.217	0.530	13.462	0.579	14.711	0.677	17.204	0.776	19.698
0.312	7.9248	0.393	9.971	0.442	11.215	0.491	12.464	0.540	13.709	0.589	14.958	0.687	17.452	0.785	19.945
0.375	9.5250	0.412	10.473	0.461	11.718	0.511	12.967	0.560	14.212	0.609	15.461	0.707	17.954	0.805	20.448

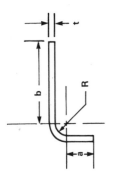

Table 2-4. Length of Metal in Bend When Part is Wiped (Continued).

Thickness		BL (R = 1/2)		BL (R = 5/8)		BL (R = 3/4)		BL (R = 7/8)		BL (R = 1)		BL (R = 1 1/4)	
inch	mm	inch	mm	inch	mm	inch	mm	inch	mm	inch	mm	inch	mm
0.012	0.3048	0.789	20.045	0.985	25.032	1.182	30.019	1.378	35.007	1.574	39.994	1.967	49.969
0.015	0.3810	0.790	20.069	0.986	25.056	1.183	30.044	1.379	35.031	1.575	40.018	1.968	49.993
0.018	0.4572	0.791	20.093	0.987	25.080	1.184	30.067	1.380	35.055	1.576	40.042	1.969	50.017
0.021	0.5334	0.792	20.117	0.988	25.104	1.185	30.091	1.381	35.079	1.577	40.066	1.970	50.040
0.024	0.6096	0.793	20.141	0.989	25.128	1.186	30.115	1.382	35.103	1.578	40.090	1.971	50.064
0.030	0.7620	0.795	20.189	0.991	25.176	1.188	30.163	1.384	35.150	1.580	40.138	1.973	50.112
0.036	0.9144	0.797	20.236	0.993	25.244	1.189	30.211	1.386	35.198	1.582	40.186	1.975	50.160
0.048	1.2192	0.800	20.332	0.997	25.319	1.193	30.307	1.390	35.294	1.586	40.281	1.979	50.256
0.062	1.5748	0.805	20.444	1.001	25.431	1.198	30.418	1.394	35.406	1.590	40.393	1.983	50.368
0.075	1.9050	0.809	20.548	1.005	25.535	1.202	30.522	1.398	35.510	1.594	40.497	1.987	50.471
0.093	2.3622	0.815	20.691	1.011	25.679	1.207	30.666	1.404	35.653	1.600	40.640	1.993	50.615
0.109	2.7686	0.820	20.819	1.016	25.806	1.212	30.794	1.409	35.781	1.605	40.768	1.998	50.743
0.125	3.1750	0.825	20.947	1.021	25.934	1.217	30.921	1.414	35.908	1.610	40.896	2.003	50.870
0.140	3.5560	0.829	21.066	1.026	26.054	1.222	31.041	1.418	36.028	1.615	41.015	2.007	50.990
0.156	3.9624	0.834	21.194	1.031	26.181	1.227	31.169	1.423	36.156	1.620	41.143	2.013	51.118
0.187	4.7498	0.844	21.441	1.040	26.429	1.237	31.416	1.434	36.403	1.630	41.391	2.022	51.365
0.203	5.1562	0.849	21.569	1.046	26.556	1.242	31.544	1.438	36.531	1.635	41.518	2.027	51.493
0.218	5.5372	0.854	21.689	1.050	26.676	1.247	31.663	1.443	36.651	1.639	41.638	2.032	51.612
0.234	5.9436	0.859	21.816	1.055	26.804	1.252	31.791	1.448	36.778	1.644	41.766	2.037	51.740
0.250	6.3500	0.864	21.944	1.060	26.931	1.257	31.919	1.453	36.906	1.649	41.893	2.042	51.868
0.265	6.7310	0.869	22.064	1.065	27.051	1.261	32.038	1.458	37.026	1.654	42.013	2.047	51.988
0.281	7.1374	0.874	22.191	1.070	27.179	1.266	32.166	1.463	37.153	1.659	42.141	2.052	52.115
0.312	7.9248	0.883	22.439	1.080	27.426	1.276	32.413	1.472	37.401	1.669	42.388	2.062	52.363

U-BENDS IN COPPER AND BRASS

A typical U-bending operation and the die sections that perform it are shown in *Figure* 2–5. Assuming a workpiece material of copper or brass, the total length of metal required to form this part is equal to $a + b + c + 2$ (length of metal in bend).

$$L = a + b + c + 2\text{BL}$$

in which

    L = Total length
    a = First leg
    b = Second leg
    c = Third leg
  BL = Length of metal in bend

The equation for finding BL in this case is

$$\text{BL} = 0.55\,t + 1.57\,R$$

in which

  BL = Length of metal in the bend
    t = Metal thickness
    R = Inside radius of bend

Table 2–5 provides inch and metric values for BL in values of 0.012 inch (0.3048 mm) to 0.375 inch (9.525 mm) for thickness t, and 0 to $1\frac{1}{2}$ inch for inside radius R.

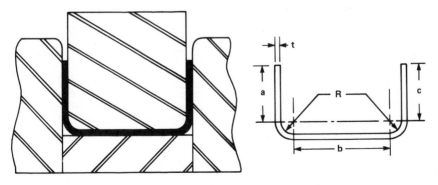

Fig. 2–5

Table 2-5. Length of Metal in Bend when Part is U-Bent (Copper and Brass).

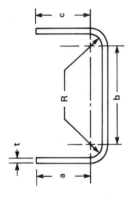

Stock Thickness		BL (R = 1/64)		BL (R = 1/32)		BL (R = 1/16)		BL (R = 3/32)		BL (R = 1/8)		BL (R = 5/32)		BL (R = 3/16)	
inch	mm	inch	mm	inch	mm	inch	mm	inch	mm	inch	mm	inch	mm	inch	mm
0.015	0.381	0.032	0.813	0.057	1.448	0.106	2.692	0.155	3.937	0.204	5.182	0.253	6.426	0.302	7.671
0.025	0.635	0.038	0.965	0.063	1.600	0.112	2.845	0.161	4.089	0.210	5.334	0.259	6.579	0.308	7.823
0.031	0.787	0.041	1.041	0.066	1.676	0.115	2.921	0.164	4.166	0.213	5.410	0.262	6.655	0.311	7.899
0.040	1.016	0.046	1.168	0.071	1.803	0.120	3.048	0.169	4.293	0.218	5.537	0.267	6.782	0.316	8.026
0.046	1.168	0.049	1.245	0.074	1.880	0.123	3.124	0.172	4.369	0.221	5.613	0.270	6.858	0.319	8.103
0.050	1.270	0.051	1.295	0.077	1.956	0.126	3.200	0.175	4.445	0.224	5.690	0.273	6.934	0.322	8.179
0.062	1.575	0.058	1.473	0.083	2.108	0.132	3.353	0.181	4.597	0.230	5.842	0.279	7.087	0.328	8.331
0.070	1.778	0.063	1.600	0.088	2.235	0.137	3.480	0.186	4.724	0.235	5.969	0.284	7.214	0.333	8.458
0.078	1.981	0.067	1.702	0.092	2.337	0.141	3.581	0.190	4.826	0.239	6.071	0.288	7.315	0.337	8.560
0.093	2.362	0.075	1.905	0.100	2.540	0.149	3.785	0.198	5.029	0.247	6.274	0.296	7.518	0.345	8.763
0.109	2.769	0.084	2.134	0.109	2.769	0.158	4.013	0.207	5.258	0.256	6.502	0.305	7.747	0.354	8.992
0.125	3.175	0.093	2.362	0.118	2.997	0.167	4.242	0.216	5.486	0.265	6.731	0.314	7.976	0.363	9.220
0.156	3.962	0.110	2.794	0.135	3.429	0.184	4.674	0.233	5.918	0.282	7.163	0.331	8.407	0.380	9.652
0.187	4.750	0.127	3.226	0.152	3.861	0.201	5.105	0.250	6.350	0.299	7.595	0.348	8.839	0.397	10.084
0.218	5.537	0.144	3.658	0.169	4.293	0.218	5.537	0.267	6.782	0.316	8.026	0.365	9.271	0.414	10.516
0.250	6.350	0.162	4.115	0.187	4.750	0.236	5.994	0.285	7.239	0.334	8.484	0.383	9.728	0.432	10.973
0.281	7.137	0.179	4.547	0.204	5.182	0.253	6.426	0.302	7.671	0.351	8.915	0.400	10.160	0.449	11.405
0.312	7.929	0.196	4.978	0.221	5.613	0.270	6.858	0.319	8.103	0.368	9.347	0.417	10.592	0.466	11.836
0.375	9.525	0.230	5.842	0.256	6.502	0.304	7.722	0.353	8.966	0.402	10.211	0.451	11.455	0.499	12.675

Table 2-5. Length of Metal in Bend when Part is U-Bent (Copper and Brass) (Continued).

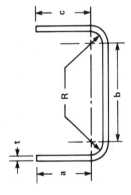

Stock Thickness		BL (R = 7/32)		BL (R = 1/4)		BL (R = 9/32)		BL (R = 5/16)		BL (R = 3/8)		BL (R = 7/16)		BL (R = 1/2)	
inch	mm	inch	mm	inch	mm	inch	mm	inch	mm	inch	mm	inch	mm	inch	mm
0.015	0.381	0.352	8.941	0.401	10.185	0.450	11.430	0.499	12.675	0.597	15.164	0.695	17.653	0.793	20.142
0.025	0.635	0.357	9.068	0.406	10.312	0.455	11.557	0.504	12.802	0.602	15.291	0.701	17.805	0.799	20.295
0.031	0.787	0.360	9.144	0.410	10.414	0.458	11.633	0.508	12.903	0.606	15.392	0.704	17.882	0.802	20.371
0.040	1.016	0.365	9.271	0.415	10.541	0.463	11.760	0.513	13.030	0.611	15.519	0.709	18.009	0.807	20.498
0.046	1.168	0.368	9.347	0.418	10.617	0.467	11.862	0.516	13.106	0.614	15.596	0.712	18.085	0.810	20.574
0.050	1.270	0.371	9.423	0.420	10.668	0.469	11.913	0.518	13.157	0.616	15.646	0.714	18.136	0.813	20.650
0.062	1.575	0.377	9.576	0.427	10.846	0.476	12.090	0.525	13.335	0.623	15.824	0.721	18.313	0.819	20.803
0.070	1.778	0.382	9.703	0.431	10.947	0.480	12.192	0.529	13.437	0.627	15.926	0.725	18.415	0.824	20.930
0.078	1.981	0.386	9.804	0.435	11.049	0.484	12.294	0.534	13.564	0.632	16.053	0.730	18.542	0.828	21.031
0.093	2.362	0.394	10.008	0.444	11.278	0.493	12.522	0.542	13.767	0.640	16.256	0.738	18.745	0.836	21.234
0.109	2.769	0.403	10.236	0.452	11.481	0.501	12.725	0.551	13.995	0.649	16.485	0.747	18.974	0.845	21.463
0.125	3.175	0.412	10.465	0.461	11.709	0.510	12.954	0.559	14.199	0.657	16.688	0.756	19.202	0.854	21.692
0.156	3.962	0.429	10.897	0.478	12.141	0.527	13.386	0.577	14.656	0.675	17.145	0.773	19.634	0.871	22.123
0.187	4.750	0.446	11.328	0.495	12.573	0.544	13.818	0.594	15.088	0.692	17.577	0.790	20.066	0.888	22.555
0.218	5.537	0.463	11.760	0.512	13.005	0.561	14.249	0.611	15.519	0.709	18.009	0.807	20.498	0.905	22.987
0.250	6.350	0.481	12.217	0.530	13.462	0.579	14.707	0.628	15.951	0.726	18.440	0.824	20.930	0.923	23.444
0.281	7.137	0.498	12.649	0.547	13.894	0.596	15.138	0.645	16.383	0.743	18.872	0.841	21.361	0.940	23.876
0.312	7.929	0.515	13.081	0.564	14.326	0.613	15.570	0.662	16.815	0.760	19.304	0.858	21.793	0.957	24.308
0.375	9.525	0.549	13.945	0.599	15.215	0.648	16.459	0.697	17.704	0.795	20.193	0.893	22.682	0.991	25.171

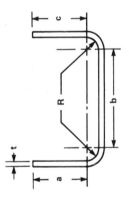

Table 2-5. Length of Metal in Bend when Part is U-Bent (Copper and Brass) *(Continued)*.

Stock Thickness		BL (R = 5/8)		BL (R = 3/4)		BL (R = 7/8)		BL (R = 1)		BL (R = 1 1/4)		BL (R = 1 1/2)	
inch	mm	inch	mm	inch	mm	inch	mm	inch	mm	inch	mm	inch	mm
0.015	0.381	0.989	25.121	1.186	30.124	1.382	35.103	1.578	40.081	1.971	50.063	2.363	60.020
0.025	0.635	0.995	25.273	1.191	30.251	1.387	35.230	1.584	40.234	1.976	50.190	2.369	60.173
0.031	0.787	0.998	25.349	1.195	30.353	1.391	35.331	1.587	40.310	1.980	50.292	2.372	60.249
0.040	1.016	1.003	25.476	1.200	30.480	1.396	35.458	1.592	40.437	1.985	50.419	2.377	60.376
0.046	1.168	1.007	25.578	1.203	30.556	1.399	35.535	1.595	40.513	1.988	50.495	2.380	60.452
0.050	1.270	1.009	25.629	1.205	30.607	1.401	35.585	1.598	40.589	1.990	50.456	2.383	60.528
0.062	1.575	1.015	25.781	1.212	30.785	1.408	35.763	1.604	40.742	1.997	50.724	2.389	60.681
0.070	1.778	1.020	25.908	1.216	30.886	1.412	35.865	1.609	40.869	2.001	50.825	2.394	60.808
0.078	1.981	1.024	26.010	1.220	30.988	1.417	35.992	1.613	40.970	2.005	50.927	2.398	60.909
0.093	2.362	1.032	26.213	1.229	31.217	1.425	36.195	1.621	41.173	2.014	51.156	2.407	61.138
0.109	2.769	1.041	26.441	1.237	31.420	1.434	36.424	1.630	41.402	2.022	51.359	2.415	61.341
0.125	3.175	1.050	26.670	1.246	31.648	1.443	36.652	1.639	41.631	2.031	51.587	2.424	61.570
0.156	3.962	1.067	27.102	1.263	32.080	1.460	37.084	1.656	42.062	2.048	52.019	2.441	62.001
0.187	4.750	1.084	27.534	1.280	32.512	1.477	37.516	1.673	42.494	2.065	52.451	2.458	62.433
0.218	5.537	1.101	27.965	1.297	32.944	1.494	37.948	1.690	42.926	2.082	52.883	2.475	62.865
0.250	6.350	1.119	28.423	1.315	33.401	1.512	38.405	1.708	43.383	2.100	53.340	2.493	63.322
0.281	7.137	1.136	28.854	1.332	33.833	1.528	38.811	1.725	43.815	2.117	53.772	2.510	63.754
0.312	7.929	1.153	29.286	1.349	34.265	1.545	39.243	1.742	44.247	2.134	54.204	2.527	64.186
0.375	9.525	1.187	30.150	1.384	35.154	1.580	40.132	1.776	45.110	2.169	55.093	2.561	65.049

WIPES IN MEDIUM HARD COPPER AND BRASS

A typical wipe operation and the die sections that perform it are shown in *Figure* 2–6. Assuming a medium hard copper or brass workpiece material, the total length of metal required to form this part is equal to a + length of metal in bend + b.

$$L = a + BL + b$$

in which

L = Total length
a = One leg
BL = Length of metal in bend
b = The other leg

The equation for finding BL in this case is

$$BL = 0.64\,t + 1.57\,R$$

in which

BL = Length of metal in the bend
t = Metal thickness
R = Inside radius of bend

Table 2–6 provides inch and metric values for BL in values of 0.012 inch (0.3048 mm) to 0.375 inch (9.525 mm) for thickness t, and 0 to $1\frac{1}{2}$ inch for inside radius R.

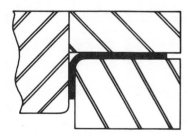
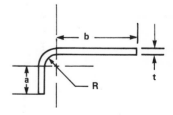

Fig. 2–6

Table 2-6. Length of Metal in Bend when Part is Wiped (Medium Hard Copper and Brass).

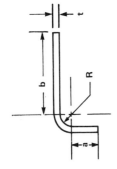

Thickness		BL (R = 1/64)		BL (R = 1/32)		BL (R = 1/16)		BL (R = 3/32)		BL (R = 1/8)		BL (R = 5/32)		BL (R = 3/16)	
inch	mm	inch	mm	inch	mm	inch	mm	inch	mm	inch	mm	inch	mm	inch	mm
0.015	0.381	0.034	0.864	0.059	1.499	0.108	2.743	0.157	3.988	0.206	5.232	0.255	6.477	0.304	7.722
0.025	0.635	0.041	1.041	0.065	1.651	0.114	2.896	0.163	4.140	0.212	5.385	0.261	6.629	0.310	7.874
0.031	0.787	0.044	1.118	0.069	1.753	0.118	2.997	0.167	4.242	0.216	5.486	0.265	6.731	0.314	7.976
0.040	1.016	0.050	1.270	0.075	1.905	0.124	3.150	0.173	4.394	0.222	5.639	0.271	6.883	0.320	8.128
0.046	1.168	0.054	1.372	0.078	1.981	0.128	3.251	0.177	4.496	0.226	5.740	0.275	6.985	0.324	8.230
0.050	1.270	0.057	1.448	0.081	2.057	0.130	3.302	0.179	4.547	0.228	5.791	0.277	7.036	0.326	8.280
0.062	1.575	0.064	1.626	0.089	2.261	0.138	3.505	0.187	4.750	0.236	5.994	0.285	7.239	0.334	8.484
0.070	1.778	0.069	1.753	0.094	2.388	0.143	3.632	0.192	4.877	0.241	6.121	0.290	7.366	0.339	8.611
0.078	1.981	0.074	1.880	0.099	2.515	0.148	3.759	0.197	5.004	0.246	6.248	0.295	7.493	0.344	8.738
0.093	2.362	0.084	2.134	0.109	2.769	0.158	4.013	0.207	5.258	0.256	6.502	0.305	7.747	0.354	8.992
0.109	2.769	0.094	2.388	0.119	3.023	0.168	4.267	0.217	5.512	0.266	6.756	0.315	8.002	0.364	9.246
0.125	3.175	0.105	2.667	0.129	3.277	0.178	4.521	0.227	5.766	0.276	7.010	0.325	8.255	0.374	9.500
0.156	3.962	0.124	3.150	0.149	3.785	0.198	5.029	0.247	6.274	0.296	7.518	0.345	8.763	0.394	10.008
0.187	4.750	0.144	3.658	0.169	4.293	0.218	5.537	0.267	6.782	0.316	8.026	0.365	9.271	0.414	10.516
0.218	5.537	0.164	4.166	0.189	4.801	0.238	6.045	0.287	7.290	0.336	8.534	0.385	9.779	0.434	11.024
0.250	6.350	0.185	4.699	0.209	5.309	0.258	6.553	0.307	7.798	0.356	9.042	0.405	10.287	0.454	11.532
0.281	7.137	0.204	5.182	0.229	5.817	0.278	7.061	0.327	8.306	0.376	9.550	0.425	10.795	0.474	12.040
0.312	7.929	0.224	5.690	0.249	6.325	0.298	7.569	0.347	8.814	0.396	10.058	0.445	11.303	0.494	12.548
0.375	9.525	0.265	6.731	0.289	7.341	0.338	8.585	0.388	9.855	0.436	11.074	0.485	12.319	0.534	13.564

Table 2-6. Length of Metal in Bend when Part is Wiped (Medium Hard Copper and Brass) (Continued).

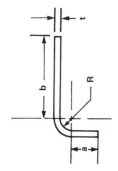

Thickness		BL (R = 7/32)		BL (R = 1/4)		BL (R = 9/32)		BL (R = 5/16)		BL (R = 3/8)		BL (R = 7/16)		BL (R = 1/2)	
inch	mm	inch	mm	inch	mm	inch	mm	inch	mm	inch	mm	inch	mm	inch	mm
0.015	0.381	0.353	8.966	0.402	10.211	0.451	11.455	0.500	12.700	0.598	15.189	0.697	17.704	0.795	20.193
0.025	0.635	0.359	9.119	0.409	10.389	0.458	11.633	0.506	12.852	0.605	15.367	0.703	17.856	0.801	20.345
0.031	0.787	0.363	9.220	0.412	10.465	0.461	11.709	0.510	12.954	0.609	15.469	0.707	17.958	0.805	20.447
0.040	1.016	0.369	9.373	0.418	10.617	0.467	11.862	0.515	13.081	0.614	15.596	0.713	18.110	0.811	20.599
0.046	1.168	0.373	9.474	0.422	10.719	0.471	11.963	0.519	13.183	0.618	15.697	0.716	18.186	0.814	20.676
0.050	1.270	0.375	9.525	0.425	10.795	0.474	12.040	0.522	13.259	0.621	15.773	0.719	18.263	0.817	20.752
0.062	1.575	0.383	9.728	0.432	10.973	0.481	12.217	0.529	13.437	0.628	15.951	0.727	18.466	0.825	20.955
0.070	1.778	0.388	9.855	0.437	11.100	0.486	12.344	0.535	13.589	0.634	16.104	0.732	18.593	0.830	21.082
0.078	1.981	0.393	9.982	0.442	11.227	0.491	12.471	0.540	13.716	0.639	16.231	0.737	18.720	0.835	21.209
0.093	2.362	0.403	10.236	0.452	11.481	0.501	12.725	0.549	13.945	0.648	16.459	0.746	18.948	0.845	21.436
0.109	2.769	0.413	10.490	0.462	11.735	0.511	12.979	0.560	14.224	0.659	16.739	0.757	19.228	0.855	21.717
0.125	3.175	0.423	10.744	0.473	12.014	0.522	13.259	0.570	14.478	0.669	16.993	0.767	19.482	0.865	21.971
0.156	3.962	0.443	11.252	0.492	12.497	0.541	13.741	0.590	14.986	0.689	17.501	0.787	19.990	0.885	22.479
0.187	4.750	0.463	11.760	0.512	13.005	0.561	14.249	0.609	15.469	0.708	17.983	0.807	20.498	0.905	22.987
0.218	5.537	0.483	12.268	0.532	13.513	0.581	14.757	0.629	15.977	0.728	18.491	0.826	20.980	0.925	23.495
0.250	6.350	0.503	12.776	0.553	14.046	0.602	15.291	0.650	16.510	0.749	19.025	0.847	21.514	0.945	24.003
0.281	7.137	0.523	13.284	0.572	14.529	0.621	15.773	0.670	17.018	0.769	19.533	0.867	22.022	0.965	24.511
0.312	7.929	0.543	13.792	0.592	15.037	0.641	16.281	0.689	17.501	0.788	20.015	0.887	22.530	0.985	25.109
0.375	9.525	0.583	14.808	0.633	16.078	0.682	17.329	0.730	18.542	0.829	21.057	0.927	23.546	1.025	26.035

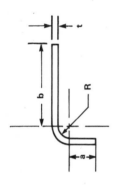

Table 2-6. Length of Metal in Bend when Part is Wiped (Medium Hard Copper and Brass) (Continued).

Thickness		BL (R = 5/8)		BL (R = 3/4)		BL (R = 7/8)		BL (R = 1)		BL (R = 1 1/4)		BL (R = 1 1/2)	
inch	mm	inch	mm	inch	mm	inch	mm	inch	mm	inch	mm	inch	mm
0.015	0.381	0.991	25.171	1.187	30.150	1.383	35.128	1.580	40.132	1.972	50.089	2.365	60.071
0.025	0.635	0.997	25.324	1.194	30.328	1.390	35.306	1.586	40.284	1.979	50.267	2.371	60.223
0.031	0.787	1.001	25.425	1.197	30.404	1.394	35.408	1.590	40.386	1.983	50.368	2.375	60.325
0.040	1.016	1.007	25.578	1.203	30.556	1.400	35.560	1.596	40.538	1.988	50.495	2.381	60.477
0.046	1.168	1.011	25.679	1.207	30.658	1.403	35.636	1.600	40.640	1.992	50.597	2.384	60.554
0.050	1.270	1.013	25.730	1.210	30.734	1.406	35.712	1.602	40.691	1.995	50.673	2.387	60.630
0.062	1.575	1.021	25.933	1.217	30.912	1.415	35.941	1.610	40.894	2.007	50.851	2.395	60.833
0.070	1.778	1.026	26.060	1.222	31.039	1.419	36.043	1.615	41.021	2.007	50.978	2.400	60.960
0.078	1.981	1.031	26.187	1.227	31.166	1.424	36.170	1.620	41.148	2.012	51.150	2.405	61.087
0.093	2.362	1.041	26.441	1.237	31.420	1.433	36.398	1.630	41.402	2.022	51.359	2.415	61.341
0.109	2.769	1.051	26.695	1.247	31.674	1.444	36.678	1.640	41.656	2.032	51.613	2.425	61.595
0.125	3.175	1.061	26.949	1.258	31.953	1.454	36.932	1.650	41.910	2.043	51.892	2.435	61.849
0.156	3.962	1.081	27.457	1.277	32.436	1.474	37.440	1.670	42.418	2.062	52.375	2.455	62.357
0.187	4.750	1.101	27.965	1.297	32.944	1.494	37.948	1.690	42.926	2.082	52.883	2.475	62.865
0.218	5.537	1.121	28.473	1.317	33.452	1.513	38.430	1.710	43.434	2.102	53.391	2.495	63.373
0.250	6.350	1.141	28.981	1.338	33.985	1.534	38.964	1.730	43.942	2.123	53.924	2.515	63.881
0.281	7.137	1.161	29.489	1.357	34.468	1.554	39.472	1.750	44.450	2.142	54.407	2.535	64.389
0.312	7.929	1.181	29.997	1.377	34.976	1.574	39.980	1.770	44.958	2.162	54.915	2.555	64.897
0.375	9.525	1.221	31.013	1.418	36.017	1.614	40.996	1.810	45.974	2.203	55.956	2.595	65.913

BENDS IN HARD COPPER AND CRS

A typical bending operation and the die sections that perform it are shown in *Figure* 2–7. Assuming a workpiece of hard copper or cold rolled steel, the total length of metal required to form this part is equal to $a + b +$ the length of the metal in the bend.

$$L = a + BL + b$$

in which

$\quad L = $ Total length
$\quad a = $ One leg
$\quad b = $ The other leg
$\quad BL = $ Length of metal in the bend

The equation for finding BL in this case is

$$BL = 0.71\ t + 1.57\ R$$

in which

$\quad BL = $ Length of metal in the bend
$\quad t = $ Metal thickness
$\quad R = $ Inside radius of the bend

Table 2–7 provides inch and metric value for BL in values of 0.012 inch (0.3048 mm) to 0.375 inch (9.525 mm) for thickness t, and 0 to $1\frac{1}{2}$ inch for inside radius R.

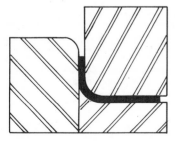
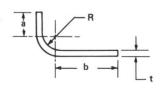

Fig. 2–7

Table 2-7. Length of Metal in Bend when Work is Hard Copper or CRS.

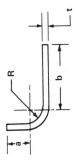

Thickness		BL (R = 1/64)		BL (R = 1/32)		BL (R = 1/16)		BL (R = 3/32)		BL (R = 1/8)		BL (R = 5/32)		BL (R = 3/16)	
inch	mm	inch	mm	inch	mm	inch	mm	inch	mm	inch	mm	inch	mm	inch	mm
0.015	0.381	0.035	0.889	0.060	1.524	0.109	2.769	0.158	4.013	0.207	5.258	0.256	6.502	0.305	7.747
0.025	0.635	0.043	1.092	0.067	1.702	0.116	2.946	0.165	4.191	0.214	5.436	0.263	6.680	0.312	7.925
0.031	0.787	0.047	1.194	0.071	1.803	0.120	3.048	0.169	4.293	0.218	5.537	0.267	6.782	0.316	8.026
0.040	1.016	0.053	1.346	0.077	1.956	0.127	3.226	0.176	4.470	0.225	5.715	0.274	6.960	0.323	8.204
0.046	1.168	0.057	1.448	0.082	2.083	0.131	3.327	0.180	4.572	0.229	5.817	0.278	7.061	0.327	8.306
0.050	1.270	0.060	1.524	0.085	2.159	0.134	3.404	0.183	4.648	0.232	5.893	0.281	7.137	0.330	8.382
0.062	1.575	0.069	1.753	0.093	2.362	0.142	3.607	0.191	4.851	0.240	6.096	0.289	7.341	0.338	8.585
0.070	1.778	0.074	1.880	0.099	2.515	0.148	3.759	0.197	5.004	0.246	6.248	0.295	7.493	0.344	8.738
0.078	1.981	0.080	2.032	0.104	2.642	0.154	3.912	0.203	5.156	0.252	6.401	0.301	7.645	0.350	8.890
0.093	2.362	0.091	2.311	0.115	2.921	0.164	4.166	0.213	5.410	0.262	6.655	0.311	7.899	0.360	9.144
0.109	2.769	0.102	2.591	0.126	3.200	0.176	4.470	0.225	5.715	0.274	6.960	0.323	8.204	0.372	9.449
0.125	3.175	0.113	2.870	0.138	3.505	0.187	4.750	0.236	5.994	0.285	7.239	0.334	8.484	0.383	9.728
0.156	3.962	0.135	3.420	0.160	4.064	0.209	5.309	0.258	6.553	0.307	7.798	0.356	9.042	0.405	10.287
0.187	4.750	0.157	3.988	0.182	4.623	0.231	5.867	0.280	7.112	0.329	8.357	0.378	9.601	0.427	10.846
0.218	5.537	0.179	4.547	0.204	5.182	0.253	6.426	0.302	7.671	0.351	8.915	0.400	10.160	0.449	11.405
0.250	6.350	0.202	5.131	0.227	5.766	0.276	7.010	0.325	8.255	0.374	9.500	0.423	10.744	0.472	11.989
0.281	7.137	0.224	5.690	0.249	6.325	0.298	7.569	0.347	8.814	0.396	10.058	0.445	11.303	0.494	12.548
0.312	7.929	0.246	6.248	0.271	6.883	0.320	8.128	0.369	9.373	0.418	10.617	0.467	11.467	0.516	13.106
0.375	9.525	0.291	7.391	0.315	8.001	0.364	9.247	0.413	10.490	0.463	11.760	0.512	13.005	0.561	14.249

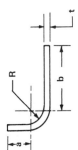

Table 2-7. Length of Metal in Bend when Work is Hard Copper or CRS (Continued).

Thickness		BL (R = 7/32)		BL (R = 1/4)		BL (R = 9/32)		BL (R =5/16)		BL (R = 3/8)		BL (R = 7/16)		BL (R = 1/2)	
inch	mm	inch	mm	inch	mm	inch	mm	inch	mm	inch	mm	inch	mm	inch	mm
0.015	0.381	0.354	8.992	0.403	10.236	0.452	11.481	0.501	12.725	0.600	15.240	0.698	17.729	0.796	20.218
0.025	0.635	0.361	9.169	0.410	10.414	0.459	11.659	0.508	12.903	0.607	15.418	0.705	17.907	0.803	20.396
0.031	0.787	0.365	9.271	0.415	10.451	0.464	11.786	0.512	13.005	0.611	15.519	0.709	18.009	0.807	20.498
0.040	1.016	0.372	9.449	0.421	10.693	0.470	11.938	0.518	13.157	0.617	15.672	0.715	18.161	0.813	20.650
0.046	1.168	0.376	9.550	0.425	10.795	0.474	12.040	0.523	13.284	0.622	15.799	0.720	18.288	0.818	20.777
0.050	1.270	0.379	9.627	0.428	10.871	0.477	12.116	0.525	13.335	0.624	15.850	0.722	18.339	0.821	20.853
0.062	1.575	0.387	9.830	0.437	11.100	0.486	12.344	0.534	13.564	0.633	16.078	0.731	18.567	0.829	21.057
0.070	1.778	0.393	9.982	0.442	11.227	0.491	12.471	0.540	13.716	0.639	16.231	0.737	18.720	0.835	21.209
0.078	1.981	0.399	10.135	0.448	11.379	0.497	12.624	0.545	13.843	0.644	16.358	0.742	18.847	0.840	21.336
0.093	2.362	0.409	10.387	0.459	11.659	0.508	12.903	0.556	14.122	0.655	16.637	0.753	19.126	0.851	21.615
0.109	2.769	0.421	10.693	0.470	11.938	0.519	13.183	0.567	14.402	0.666	16.916	0.764	19.406	0.862	21.895
0.125	3.175	0.432	10.973	0.481	12.217	0.530	13.462	0.579	14.707	0.678	17.221	0.776	19.710	0.874	22.200
0.156	3.962	0.454	11.532	0.503	12.776	0.552	14.021	0.601	15.265	0.700	17.780	0.798	20.269	0.896	22.758
0.187	4.750	0.476	12.090	0.525	13.335	0.574	14.580	0.623	15.824	0.722	18.339	0.820	20.828	0.918	23.317
0.218	5.537	0.498	12.649	0.547	13.894	0.596	15.138	0.645	16.383	0.744	18.898	0.842	21.387	0.940	23.876
0.250	6.350	0.521	13.233	0.570	14.478	0.619	15.723	0.667	16.942	0.766	19.456	0.864	21.946	0.963	24.460
0.281	7.137	0.543	13.792	0.592	15.037	0.641	16.281	0.689	17.501	0.788	20.015	0.886	22.504	0.985	25.019
0.312	7.929	0.565	14.351	0.614	15.596	0.663	16.840	0.712	18.085	0.810	20.574	0.908	23.063	1.007	25.578
0.375	9.525	0.610	15.494	0.659	16.739	0.708	17.983	0.756	19.202	0.855	21.717	0.953	24.206	1.051	26.695

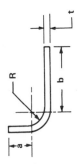

Table 2-7. Length of Metal in Bend when Work is Hard Copper or CRS (Continued).

Thickness		BL (R = 5/8)		BL (R = 3/4)		BL (R = 7/8)		BL (R = 1)		BL (R = 1 1/4)		BL (R = 1 1/2)	
inch	mm	inch	mm	inch	mm	inch	mm	inch	mm	inch	mm	inch	mm
0.015	0.381	0.992	25.197	1.188	30.175	1.385	35.179	1.581	40.157	1.973	50.114	2.366	60.096
0.025	0.635	0.999	25.375	1.195	30.353	1.392	35.357	1.588	40.335	1.980	50.292	2.373	60.274
0.031	0.787	1.003	25.476	1.200	30.480	1.396	35.458	1.592	40.437	1.985	50.419	2.377	60.376
0.040	1.016	1.010	25.654	1.206	30.632	1.402	35.611	1.598	40.589	1.991	50.571	2.383	60.528
0.046	1.168	1.014	25.756	1.210	30.734	1.407	35.738	1.603	40.716	1.995	50.673	2.388	60.655
0.050	1.270	1.017	25.832	1.213	30.810	1.409	35.789	1.606	40.792	1.998	50.749	2.391	60.731
0.062	1.575	1.025	26.035	1.222	31.039	1.418	36.017	1.614	40.996	2.007	50.978	2.399	60.935
0.070	1.778	1.031	26.187	1.227	31.166	1.424	36.170	1.620	41.148	2.012	51.105	2.405	61.087
0.078	1.981	1.037	26.340	1.233	31.318	1.429	36.297	1.625	41.275	2.018	51.257	2.410	61.214
0.093	2.362	1.047	26.594	1.244	31.598	1.440	36.576	1.636	41.554	2.029	51.537	2.421	61.493
0.109	2.769	1.059	26.899	1.255	31.877	1.451	36.855	1.647	41.834	2.040	51.816	2.432	61.773
0.125	3.175	1.070	27.178	1.266	32.156	1.463	37.160	1.659	42.139	2.051	52.095	2.444	62.078
0.156	3.962	1.092	27.737	1.288	32.715	1.485	37.719	1.681	42.697	2.073	52.654	2.466	62.636
0.187	4.750	1.114	28.296	1.310	33.274	1.507	38.278	1.703	43.256	2.095	53.213	2.488	63.195
0.218	5.537	1.136	28.854	1.332	33.833	1.529	38.837	1.725	43.815	2.117	53.772	2.510	63.754
0.250	6.350	1.158	29.413	1.355	34.417	1.551	39.395	1.748	44.399	2.140	54.356	2.533	64.338
0.281	7.137	1.181	29.997	1.377	34.976	1.573	39.954	1.770	44.958	2.162	54.915	2.555	64.897
0.312	7.929	1.203	30.556	1.399	35.535	1.595	40.513	1.792	45.517	2.184	55.474	2.577	65.456
0.375	9.525	1.248	31.669	1.444	36.678	1.640	41.656	1.836	46.634	2.229	56.617	2.621	66.573

Bending Force Factors

V-bends and wipes are two types of forming that receive a great deal of use in modern pressworking. An example of a V-bend is shown in *Figure* 3-1. An example of a wiping operation is seen in *Figure* 3-2. Like blanking, these forming operations require tonnage—and their tonnage requirements must often be calculated prior to press selection.

V-bending. The tonnage requirements for V-bending operations can be found from the equation,

$$F = 1.33 \frac{S \, W \, t^2}{2000 \, L}$$

in which

    F = Tonnage required to perform the operation
    S = The material's tensile strength
    W = The length of the bend
    t = Material thickness
    L = Length between bend radii centers (*Figure* 3-1)

As an example of the use of this equation, let us consider the tonnage calculations for a piece of cast monel. Let us assume that its thickness is 0.060 inch, that its length is 100 inches and that the distance between bend centers is 5 inches. Turning to Table 3-23, we find that cast monel's tensile strength is 75,000 psi. Therefore,

$$F = 1.33 \frac{75,000 \times 100 \times 0.060^2}{2000 \times 5}$$

$$= 1.33 \frac{27,000}{10,000}$$

$$= 3.591 \text{ tons}$$

V-bending Force Factors. To use this equation, it is necessary to first find the tensile strength—a value these tables provide for each metal. But these tables also provide *force factors* which greatly simplify the calculations.

To find an answer by way of the force factors listed in these tables (Tables 3-1 through 3-38), simply take the ratio of the length of the bend (W) to the length between bend radii centers (L), and multiply it by the relevant force factor.

In the preceding example, the W/L ratio is 20; the force factor for 0.0598

67

inch thick cast Monel is 0.178353. Thus, tonnage can be easily calculated as

$$F = 20 \times 0.178353$$
$$= 3.56 \text{ tons}$$

The extremely small discrepancy stems from the fact that the force factor is based on a thickness of 0.0598, but the tonnage calculation by formula uses a value of 0.060 inch.

In any case, it is necessary to look up the tensile strength for insertion in the formula. It is far easier to look up the force factor in the same table and multiply it by the W/L ratio.

Wiping Operations. Tonnage calculations for wiping are based on the following equation:

$$F = 0.333 \frac{SWt^2}{2000\,L}$$

in which

F = Tonnage required
S = The material's tensile strength
L = Distance between centers of bend radii (*Figure* 3-2)
t = Metal thickness
W = The length of the bend

In this instance, let us assume that the material being wiped is 0.10 carbon steel. Turning to Table 3-32, we find that the tensile strength of this steel is 60,000 psi. Let us further assume that metal thickness (t) is 0.1345, that the distance between bend radii (L) is 0.8 inch, and that the length of the bend (W) is 1.73 inch.

Using the equation, the tonnage is calculated as,

$$F = 0.333 \frac{60,000 \times 1.73 \times 0.1345^2}{2000 \times 0.8}$$
$$= 0.390 \text{ ton}$$

Wiping Force Factors. The same result is obtained by using the force factor—in this case 0.179091

$$W/L = 2.1625$$
$$F = W/L \times \text{Force Factor}$$
$$F = 2.1625 \times 0.179091$$
$$F = 0.387 \text{ ton}$$

3–1. ALUMINUM (SOFT) TS = 15,000 psi

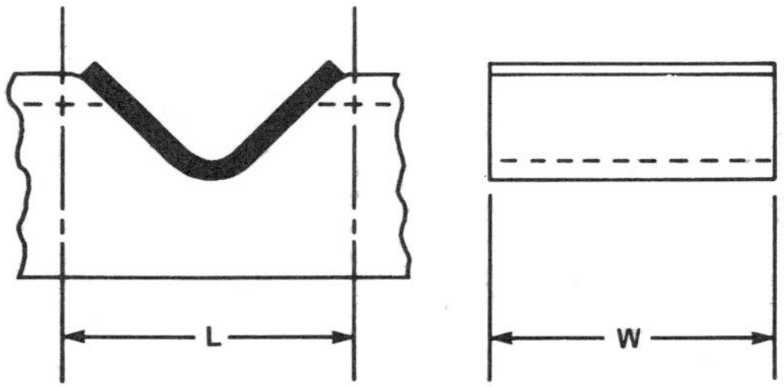

Bend Force = W/L times Force Factor

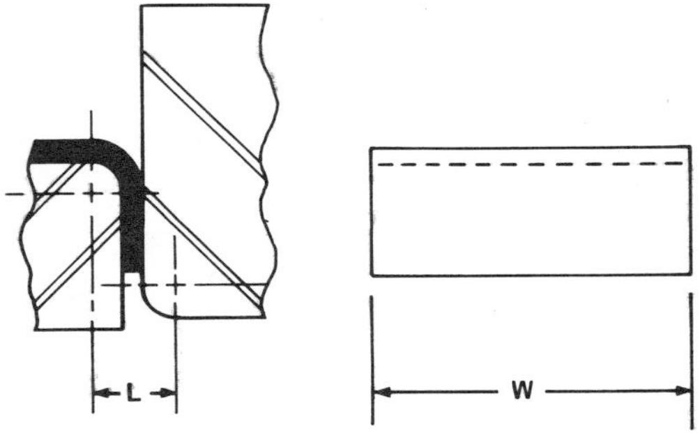

THICKNESS		V-BEND FORCE FACTORS		90° WIPE FORCE FACTORS	
inch	mm	To Obtain Tons	To Obtain kN	To Obtain Tons	To Obtain kN
0.0120	0.3048	0.0014364	0.0127782	0.0003596	0.003199
0.0135	0.3429	0.0018154	0.0161497	0.0004545	0.0040432
0.0149	0.3785	0.0022144	0.0196999	0.0005544	0.0049319
0.0165	0.4166	0.0026733	0.0237816	0.0006693	0.005954
0.0179	0.4547	0.003192	0.028396	0.0007992	0.0071096
0.0209	0.5309	0.0043491	0.0386895	0.0010889	0.0096868
0.0239	0.6071	0.0056957	0.0506689	0.001426	0.0126856
0.0269	0.6833	0.0072219	0.064246	0.0018081	0.0160848
0.0299	0.7595	0.0089176	0.0793309	0.0022327	0.019862
0.0329	0.8357	0.0107929	0.0960136	0.0027022	0.0240387
0.0359	0.9119	0.0128478	0.114294	0.0032167	0.0286157
0.0418	1.0617	0.0174263	0.1550243	0.0043631	0.0388141
0.0478	1.2141	0.0227928	0.2027647	0.0057067	0.0507668
0.0538	1.3665	0.0288676	0.2568061	0.0072277	0.0642976
0.0598	1.5189	0.0356706	0.3173256	0.008931	0.0794501
0.0673	1.7094	0.0451767	0.4018919	0.0113111	0.1006235
0.0747	1.8974	0.0556605	0.4951558	0.013936	0.1239746
0.0897	2.2784	0.0802588	0.7139822	0.0200948	0.1787633
0.1046	2.6568	0.1091364	0.9708774	0.0273251	0.243084
0.1196	3.0378	0.1426824	1.2693026	0.0357242	0.3178024
0.1345	3.4163	0.1804477	1.605267	0.0451797	0.4019186
0.1494	3.7948	0.222642	1.9806232	0.0557442	0.4959004
0.1644	4.1758	0.2695943	2.3983108	0.0674999	0.6004791
0.1793	4.5542	0.3206763	2.8527363	0.0802896	0.7142562
0.1943	4.9352	0.3765562	3.3498439	0.0942806	0.8387202
0.2092	5.3137	0.4365459	3.8835123	0.1093005	0.9723372
0.2242	5.6947	0.5013933	4.4603947	0.1255368	1.1167753
0.2391	6.0731	0.5702607	5.0730391	0.1427795	1.2701664

Fig. 3-1

Fig. 3-2

3-2. ALUMINUM (HALF HARD) TS = 19,000 psi

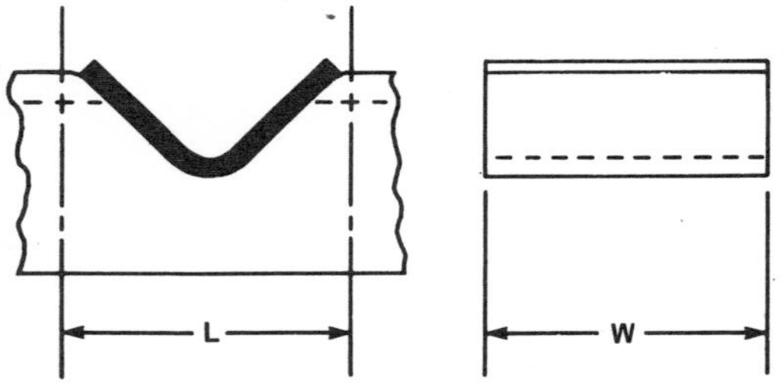

Bend Force = W/L times Force Factor

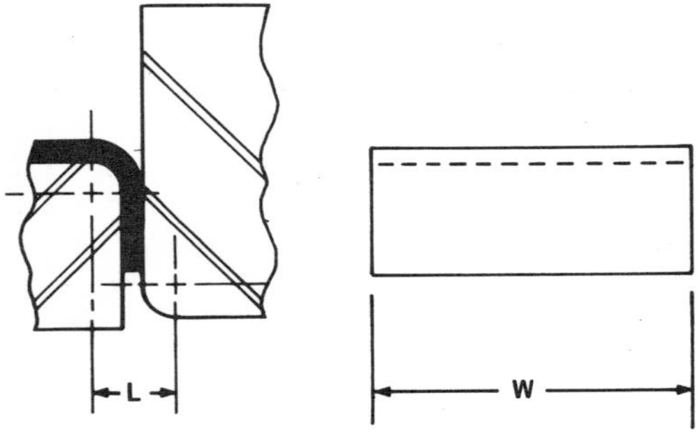

THICKNESS		V-BEND FORCE FACTORS		90° WIPE FORCE FACTORS	
inch	mm	To Obtain Tons	To Obtain kN	To Obtain Tons	To Obtain kN
0.0120	0.3048	0.0018194	0.0161853	0.0004514	0.0040156
0.0135	0.3429	0.0022995	0.0204563	0.0005705	0.0050751
0.0149	0.3785	0.0028049	0.0249523	0.0006959	0.0061907
0.0164	0.4166	0.0033861	0.0301227	0.0008401	0.0074735
0.0179	0.4547	0.0040432	0.0359683	0.0010032	0.0089244
0.0209	0.5309	0.0055088	0.0490062	0.0013668	0.012159
0.0239	0.6071	0.0072145	0.0641801	0.00179	0.0159238
0.0269	0.6833	0.0091477	0.0813779	0.0022697	0.0201912
0.0299	0.7595	0.0112956	0.1004856	0.0028026	0.0249319
0.0329	0.8357	0.013671	0.1216172	0.003392	0.0310752
0.0359	0.9119	0.0162738	0.1447717	0.0040378	0.0359202
0.0418	1.0617	0.0220733	0.196364	0.0054768	0.0487216
0.0478	1.2141	0.0288709	0.2568355	0.0071634	0.0637256
0.0538	1.3665	0.0365656	0.3252875	0.0090726	0.0807098
0.0598	1.5189	0.0451827	0.4019452	0.0112107	0.0997303
0.0673	1.7094	0.0572239	0.5090638	0.0141984	0.1263089
0.0747	1.8974	0.0705033	0.6271973	0.0174933	0.1556209
0.0897	2.2784	0.1016612	0.904378	0.0252242	0.2243944
0.1046	2.6568	0.1382395	1.2297785	0.0343	0.3051328
0.1196	3.0378	0.180731	1.6077829	0.044843	0.3989233
0.1345	3.4163	0.2285671	2.0333329	0.0567121	0.5045108
0.1494	3.7948	0.2820132	2.5087894	0.0699732	0.6224815
0.1644	4.1758	0.3414861	3.0378603	0.0847296	0.7537545
0.1793	4.5542	0.4061899	3.6134653	0.1007839	0.8965735
0.1943	4.9352	0.4769712	4.2431357	0.1183462	1.0528077
0.2092	5.3137	0.5229581	4.9191152	0.1372001	1.220532
0.2242	5.6947	0.6350982	5.6498335	0.1575807	1.4018379
0.2391	6.0731	0.7223303	6.4258503	0.1792248	1.5943838

Fig. 3-1

Fig. 3-2

3-3. ALUMINUM (HARD) TS = 28,000 psi

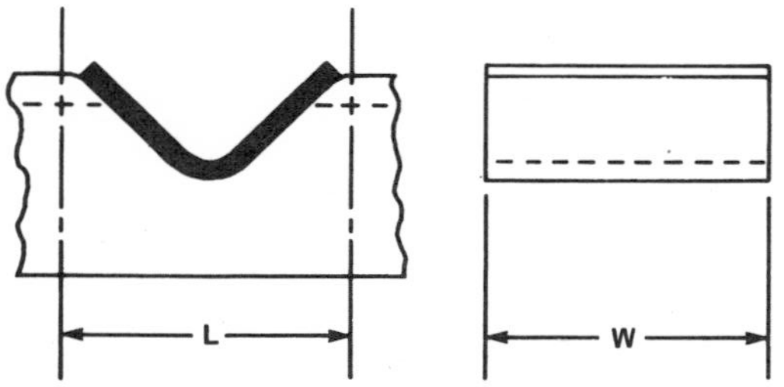

Bend Force = W / L times Force Factor

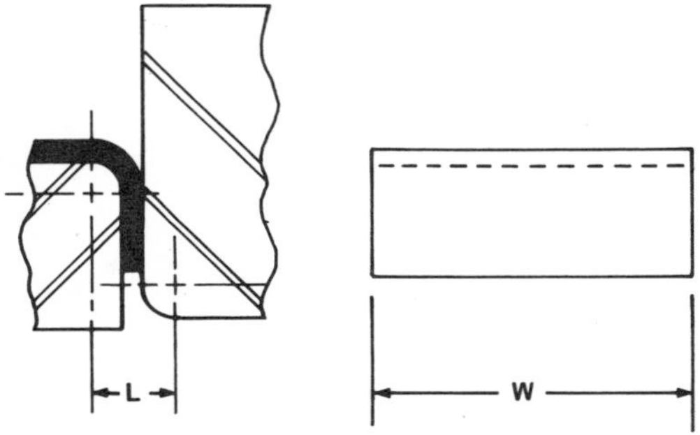

THICKNESS		V-BEND FORCE FACTORS		90° WIPE FORCE FACTORS	
inch	mm	To Obtain Tons	To Obtain kN	To obtain Tons	To Obtain kN
0.0120	0.3048	0.0026812	0.0238519	0.0006652	0.0059176
0.0135	0.3429	0.0033888	0.0301467	0.0008408	0.0074797
0.0149	0.3785	0.0041336	0.0367725	0.0010256	0.0091237
0.0164	0.4166	0.0049901	0.0443919	0.0012381	0.0110141
0.0179	0.4547	0.0059584	0.0530059	0.0014784	0.0131518
0.0209	0.5309	0.0081183	0.0722203	0.0020143	0.0179192
0.0239	0.6071	0.010632	0.0945822	0.002638	0.0234676
0.0269	0.6833	0.0134808	0.1199251	0.0033448	0.0297553
0.0299	0.7595	0.0166462	0.1480845	0.0041302	0.0367422
0.0329	0.8357	0.0201468	0.1792259	0.0049988	0.0444693
0.0359	0.9119	0.0239825	0.2133483	0.0059505	0.0529356
0.0418	1.0617	0.0325291	0.2893788	0.0080711	0.0718005
0.0478	1.2141	0.0425467	0.3784954	0.0105567	0.0939124
0.0538	1.3665	0.0538862	0.4793716	0.0133702	0.1189142
0.0598	1.5189	0.0665851	0.592341	0.0165211	0.1469717
0.0673	1.7094	0.0843299	0.7501987	0.2029239	0.186139
0.0747	1.8974	0.1038996	0.9242908	0.0257796	0.2293353
0.0897	2.2784	0.1498165	1.3327675	0.0371725	0.3306865
0.1046	2.6568	0.2037214	1.8123055	0.0505474	0.4496696
0.1196	3.0378	0.2663404	2.3693641	0.0660844	0.5878869
0.1345	3.4163	0.3368358	2.9964912	0.0835758	0.7434903
0.1494	3.7948	0.4155984	3.6971633	0.1031184	0.9173412
0.1644	4.1758	0.5082427	4.476847	0.1248647	1.1107963
0.1793	4.5542	0.5985957	5.3251073	0.1485237	1.3212668
0.1943	4.9352	0.702905	6.2530428	0.174405	1.5515068
0.2092	5.3137	0.8148856	7.2492222	0.2021896	1.7986786
0.2242	5.6947	0.9359343	8.3260715	0.2322243	2.0655673
0.2391	6.0731	1.0644867	9.4696736	0.2641207	2.3496177

Fig. 3-1

Fig. 3-2

3-4. BRASS (SOFT)
TS = 47,000 psi

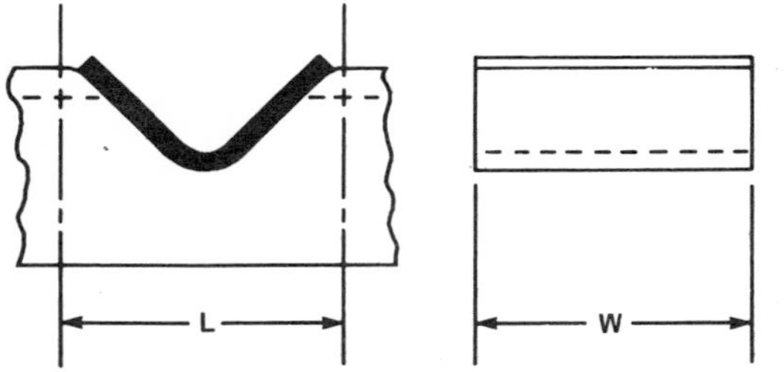

Bend Force = W/L times Force Factor

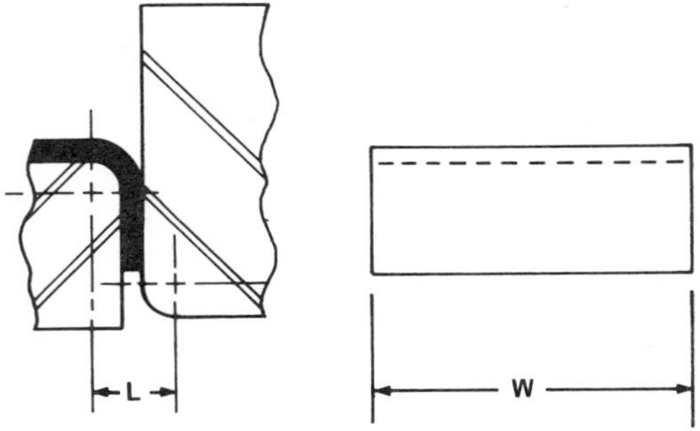

THICKNESS		V-BEND FORCE FACTORS		90° WIPE FORCE FACTORS	
inch	mm	To Obtain Tons	To Obtain kN	To Obtain Tons	To Obtain kN
0.0120	0.3048	0.0045007	0.0400382	0.0011167	0.0099341
0.0135	0.3429	0.0056884	0.050604	0.0014114	0.0125558
0.0149	0.3785	0.0069386	0.0617257	0.0017216	0.0153153
0.0164	0.4166	0.0083763	0.0745155	0.0020783	0.0184885
0.0179	0.4547	0.0100016	0.0889742	0.0024816	0.0220763
0.0209	0.5309	0.0136271	0.121226	0.0033811	0.0300782
0.0239	0.6071	0.0178466	0.1587633	0.0044281	0.0393923
0.0269	0.6833	0.0226286	0.201304	0.0056146	0.0499474
0.0299	0.7595	0.0279419	0.2485711	0.0069329	0.061675
0.0329	0.8357	0.0338179	0.300844	0.0083909	0.0746454
0.0359	0.9119	0.0402564	0.3581209	0.0099884	0.0888568
0.0418	1.0617	0.0546024	0.4857429	0.0135479	0.1205221
0.0478	1.2141	0.0714176	0.6353309	0.0177201	0.157638
0.0538	1.3665	0.0904519	0.8046601	0.0224429	0.199652
0.0598	1.5189	0.1117678	0.9942863	0.0277318	0.246702
0.0673	1.7094	0.1415538	1.2592626	0.0351223	0.3124479
0.0747	1.8974	0.1744029	1.5514881	0.0432729	0.3849557
0.0897	2.2784	0.2514777	2.2371456	0.0623967	0.55508
0.1046	2.6568	0.3419609	3.0420841	0.0848474	0.7548024
0.1196	3.0378	0.4470715	3.977148	0.1109275	0.986811
0.1345	3.4163	0.5654029	5.0298241	0.1402879	1.2480011
0.1494	3.7948	0.6976116	6.2059527	0.1730916	1.5398228
0.1644	4.1758	0.8447288	7.5147074	0.2095943	1.8645508
0.1793	4.5542	1.0047857	8.9385735	0.2493077	2.2178412
0.1943	4.9352	1.1798762	10.496178	0.2927512	2.6043146
0.2092	5.3137	1.3678438	12.168338	0.3393898	3.0192116
0.2242	5.6947	1.5710325	13.975905	0.389805	3.4677052
0.2391	6.0731	1.786917	15.896413	0.433455	3.940015

Fig. 3-1

Fig. 3-2

3–5. BRASS (HALF HARD)
TS = 60,000 psi

Bend Force = W/L times Force Factor

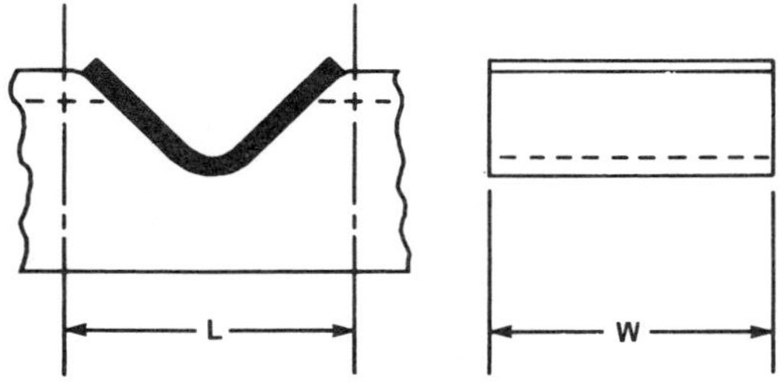

THICKNESS		V-BEND FORCE FACTORS		90° WIPE FORCE FACTORS	
inch	mm	To Obtain Tons	To Obtain kN	To Obtain Tons	To Obtain kN
0.0120	0.3048	0.0057456	0.0511128	0.0014256	0.0126821
0.0135	0.3429	0.0072618	0.0646009	0.0018018	0.0160288
0.0149	0.3785	0.0088578	0.0787989	0.0021978	0.0195516
0.0164	0.4166	0.0106932	0.0951267	0.0026532	0.0236028
0.0179	0.4547	0.012768	0.1135841	0.003168	0.0281825
0.0209	0.5309	0.0173964	0.1547583	0.0043164	0.0383986
0.0239	0.6071	0.0227829	0.2026766	0.0056529	0.0502881
0.0269	0.6833	0.0288876	0.256984	0.0071676	0.0637629
0.0299	0.7595	0.0356706	0.3173256	0.0088506	0.0787349
0.0329	0.8357	0.0431718	0.3840563	0.0107118	0.0952921
0.0359	0.9119	0.0513912	0.4571761	0.0127512	0.1134346
0.0418	1.0617	0.0697053	0.6200983	0.0172953	0.1538589
0.0478	1.2141	0.0911715	0.8110616	0.0226215	0.2012408
0.0538	1.3665	0.1154706	1.0272264	0.0286506	0.2548757
0.0598	1.5189	0.1426824	1.2693026	0.0354024	0.3149397
0.0673	1.7094	0.1807071	1.6075703	0.0448371	0.398708
0.0747	1.8974	0.222642	1.9806232	0.055242	0.4914328
0.0897	2.2784	0.3210354	2.8559309	0.0796554	0.7086144
0.1046	2.6568	0.4365459	3.8835123	0.1083159	0.9635782
0.1196	3.0378	0.5707296	5.0772105	0.1416096	1.259759
0.1345	3.4163	0.721791	6.4210527	0.179091	1.5931935
0.1494	3.7948	0.890568	7.9224929	0.220968	1.9657313
0.1644	4.1758	1.0783773	9.5932444	0.2675673	2.3802787
0.1793	4.5542	1.2827052	11.410945	0.3182652	2.8312872
0.1943	4.9352	1.506225	13.399377	0.373725	3.3246576
0.2092	5.3137	1.7461836	15.534049	0.4332636	3.8543129
0.2242	5.6947	2.0055735	17.841581	0.4976235	4.4268586
0.2391	6.0731	2.2810431	20.292159	0.5659731	5.0348966

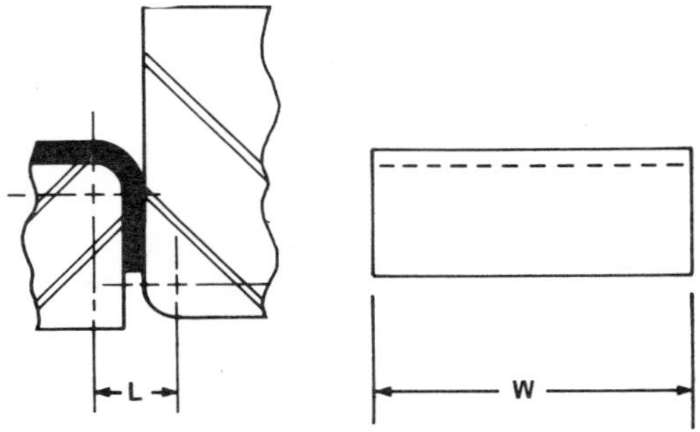

Fig. 3-1

Fig. 3-2

73

3-6. BRASS (HARD)
TS = 85,000 psi

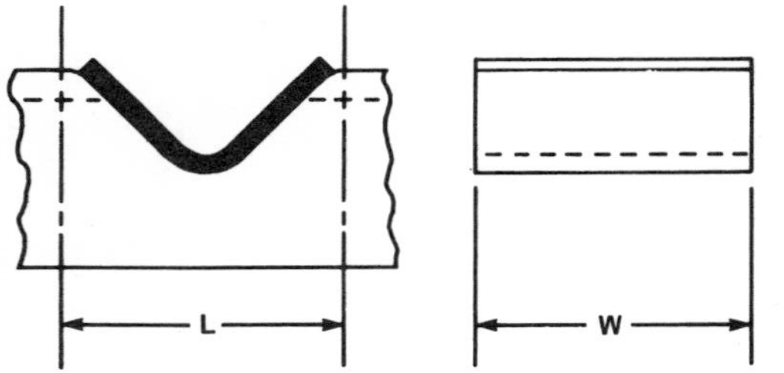

Bend Force = W / L times Force Factor

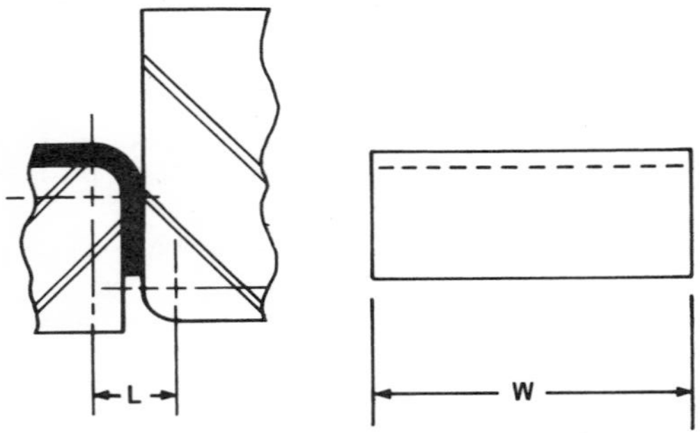

THICKNESS		V-BEND FORCE FACTORS		90° WIPE FORCE FACTORS	
inch	mm	To Obtain Tons	To Obtain kN	To Obtain Tons	To Obtain kN
0.0120	0.3048	0.0081396	0.0724098	0.0020196	0.0179663
0.0135	0.3429	0.0102875	0.915176	0.0025525	0.022707
0.0149	0.3785	0.0125485	0.1116314	0.0031135	0.0276976
0.0164	0.4166	0.0151487	0.1347628	0.0037587	0.0334373
0.0179	0.4547	0.018088	0.1609108	0.004488	0.0399252
0.0209	0.5309	0.0246449	0.219241	0.0061149	0.0543981
0.0239	0.6071	0.0322757	0.2871246	0.0080082	0.0712409
0.0269	0.6833	0.0409941	0.3640607	0.0101541	0.0903309
0.0299	0.7595	0.0505333	0.4495442	0.0125383	0.1115407
0.0329	0.8357	0.06116	0.5440793	0.015175	0.1349968
0.0359	0.9119	0.0728042	0.6476661	0.0180642	0.1606991
0.0418	1.0617	0.0987491	0.8784719	0.0245016	0.2179662
0.0478	1.2141	0.1291596	1.1490038	0.0320471	0.285091
0.0538	1.3665	0.1635833	1.455237	0.0405883	0.3610735
0.0598	1.5189	0.2021334	1.7981787	0.0501534	0.4461646
0.0673	1.7094	0.2560017	2.2773911	0.0635192	0.5650668
0.0747	1.8974	0.3154095	2.8058829	0.0782595	0.6961965
0.0897	2.2784	0.4548001	4.0459016	0.1128451	1.00387
0.1046	2.6568	0.61844	5.5016422	0.1534475	1.3650689
0.1196	3.0378	0.8085336	7.1927149	0.2006136	1.7846585
0.1345	3.4163	1.0025372	9.0964909	0.2537122	2.2570237
0.1494	3.7948	1.261638	11.223531	0.313038	2.784786
0.1644	4.1758	1.5277011	13.590428	0.3790536	3.3720608
0.1793	4.5542	1.8171657	16.165506	0.4508757	4.0109902
0.1943	4.9352	2.1338187	18.982451	0.5294437	4.7099311
0.2092	5.3137	2.4737601	22.006569	0.6137901	5.4602767
0.2242	5.6947	2.8412291	25.275574	0.7049666	6.2718828
0.2391	6.0731	3.2314777	28.747225	0.8017952	7.13277

Fig. 3-1

Fig. 3-2

3-7. BRONZE (GUN METAL) TS = 40,000 psi

Bend Force = W/L times Force Factor

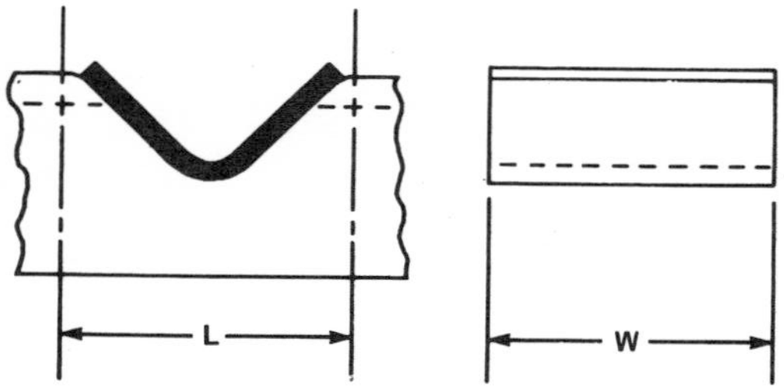

THICKNESS		V-BEND FORCE FACTORS		90° WIPE FORCE FACTORS	
inch	mm	To Obtain Tons	To Obtain kN	To Obtain Tons	To Obtain kN
0.0120	0.3048	0.0038304	0.0340752	0.0009504	0.0084547
0.0135	0.3429	0.0048412	0.0430673	0.0012012	0.0106858
0.0149	0.3785	0.0059052	0.525326	0.0014652	0.0130344
0.0164	0.4166	0.0071288	0.634178	0.0017688	0.0157352
0.0179	0.4547	0.008512	0.0757227	0.0021122	0.0187883
0.0209	0.5309	0.0115976	0.1031722	0.0028776	0.0255991
0.0239	0.6071	0.0151886	0.1351177	0.0037686	0.0335254
0.0269	0.6833	0.0192584	0.1713227	0.0047784	0.0425086
0.0299	0.7595	0.0237804	0.2115504	0.0059004	0.0524899
0.0329	0.8357	0.0287812	0.2560375	0.0071412	0.0635281
0.0359	0.9119	0.0342608	0.304784	0.0085008	0.0756231
0.0418	1.0617	0.0464702	0.4133988	0.0115302	0.1025726
0.0478	1.2141	0.060781	0.5407077	0.015081	0.1341605
0.0538	1.3665	0.0769804	0.6848176	0.0191004	0.1699171
0.0598	1.5189	0.0951216	0.8462017	0.0236016	0.2099598
0.0673	1.7094	0.1204714	1.0717135	0.0298914	0.2659138
0.0747	1.8974	0.148428	1.3204154	0.036828	0.3276218
0.0897	2.2784	0.2140236	1.9039539	0.0531036	0.4724096
0.1046	2.6568	0.2910306	2.5890082	0.0722106	0.6423854
0.1196	3.0378	0.3804864	3.384807	0.0944064	0.8398398
0.1345	3.4163	0.481194	4.2807018	0.119394	1.062129
0.1494	3.7948	0.593712	5.2816619	0.174312	1.3104875
0.1644	4.1758	0.7189181	6.3954963	0.1783782	1.5868524
0.1793	4.5542	0.8551368	7.6072969	0.2121768	1.8875248
0.1943	4.9352	1.00415	8.9329184	0.24915	2.2154384
0.2092	5.3137	1.1641224	10.356032	0.2888424	2.5695419
0.2242	5.6947	1.337049	11.849387	0.331749	2.9512391
0.2391	6.0731	1.5206954	13.528106	0.3773154	3.3565977

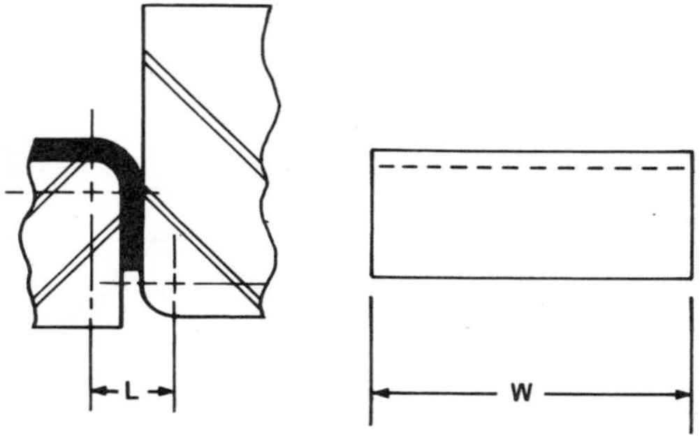

Fig. 3-1

Fig. 3-2

3–8. BRONZE (PHOSPHOR)
TS = 45,000 psi

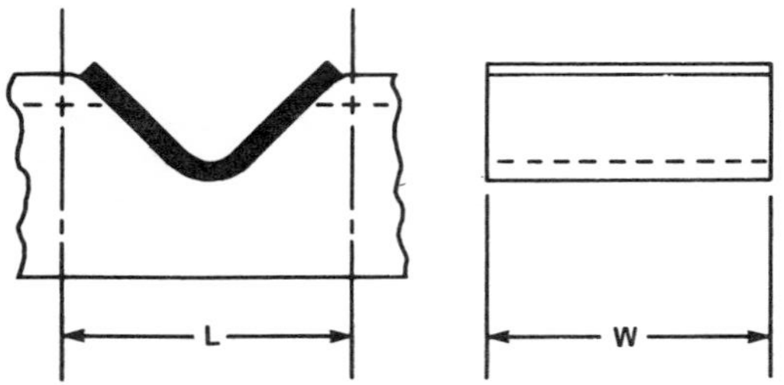

Fig. 3-1

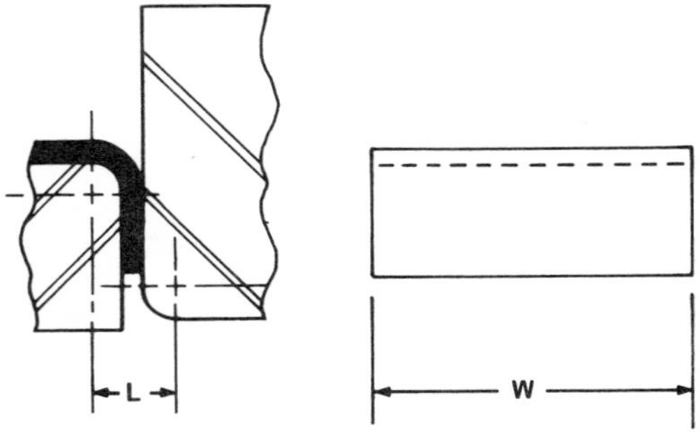

Fig. 3-2

Bend Force = W/L times Force Factor

THICKNESS inch	THICKNESS mm	V-BEND FORCE FACTORS *To Obtain Tons*	V-BEND FORCE FACTORS *To Obtain kN*	90° WIPE FORCE FACTORS *To Obtain Tons*	90° WIPE FORCE FACTORS *To Obtain kN*
0.0120	0.3048	0.0043092	0.0383346	0.0010692	0.0095116
0.0135	0.3429	0.0054463	0.0484502	0.0013513	0.0120211
0.0149	0.3785	0.0066433	0.0590987	0.0016483	0.0146632
0.0164	0.4166	0.0080199	0.071345	0.0019899	0.0177021
0.0179	0.4547	0.009576	0.085188	0.0022376	0.0211368
0.0209	0.5309	0.0130473	0.1160687	0.0032373	0.028799
0.0239	0.6071	0.0170871	0.1520068	0.0042396	0.0377154
0.0269	0.6833	0.0216657	0.192738	0.0053757	0.0478222
0.0299	0.7595	0.0267529	0.2379937	0.0066379	0.0590507
0.0329	0.8357	0.0323783	0.2880373	0.0080338	0.0714686
0.0359	0.9119	0.0385434	0.342882	0.0095634	0.085076
0.0418	1.0617	0.0522789	0.465073	0.0129714	0.1153935
0.0478	1.2141	0.0683786	0.608296	0.0169661	0.1509304
0.0538	1.3665	0.0866029	0.7704193	0.0214879	0.1911563
0.0598	1.5189	0.1070118	0.9519769	0.0265518	0.2362048
0.0673	1.7094	0.1355303	1.2056775	0.0336278	0.2991529
0.0747	1.8974	0.1669815	1.4854674	0.0414315	0.3685746
0.0897	2.2784	0.2407765	2.1419477	0.0597415	0.5314603
0.1046	2.6568	0.3274094	2.912634	0.0812369	0.7226834
0.1196	3.0378	0.4280472	3.8079078	0.1062072	0.9448192
0.1345	3.4163	0.5413432	4.8157891	0.1343182	1.1948947
0.1494	3.7948	0.667926	5.9418696	0.165725	1.4742984
0.1644	4.1758	0.8087829	7.1949326	0.2006754	1.7852083
0.1793	4.5542	0.9620289	8.558209	0.2386989	2.1234654
0.1943	4.9352	1.1296687	10.049532	0.2802937	2.4934927
0.2092	5.3137	0.3096377	11.650536	0.3249477	2.8907347
0.2242	5.6947	1.5041801	13.381186	0.3732176	3.3201437
0.2391	6.0731	1.7107823	15.219119	0.4244798	3.7761723

3–9. BRONZE (TOBIN ALLOY)
TS = 60,000 psi

Bend Force = W/L times Force Factor

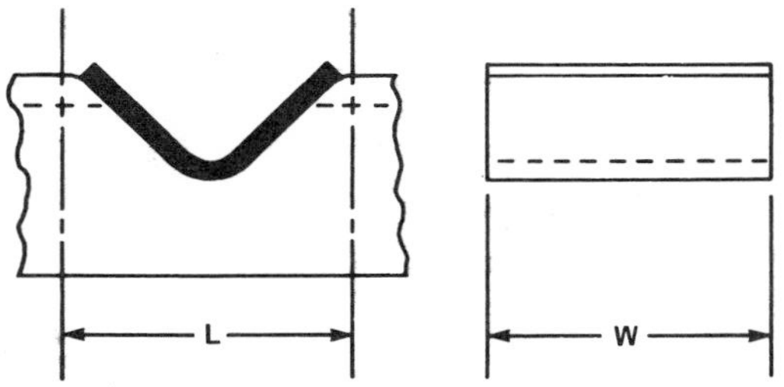

Fig. 3-1

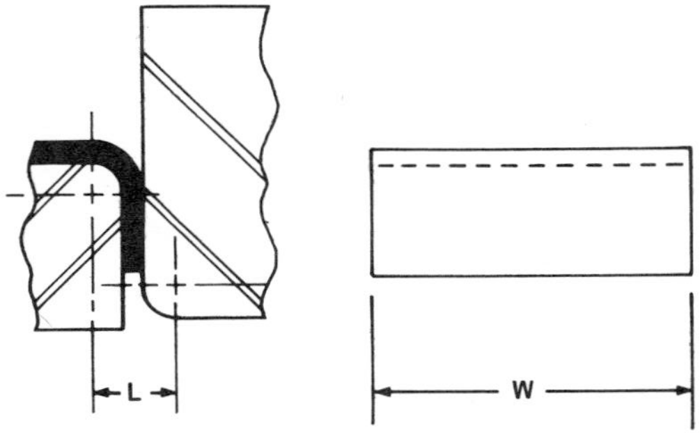

Fig. 3-2

THICKNESS inch	THICKNESS mm	V-BEND FORCE FACTORS To Obtain Tons	V-BEND FORCE FACTORS To Obtain kN	90° WIPE FORCE FACTORS To Obtain Tons	90° WIPE FORCE FACTORS To Obtain kN
0.0120	0.3048	0.0057456	0.0511128	0.0014256	0.0126821
0.0135	0.3429	0.0072618	0.0646009	0.0018018	0.0160288
0.0149	0.3785	0.0088578	0.0787989	0.0021978	0.0195516
0.0164	0.4166	0.0106932	0.0951267	0.0026532	0.0236028
0.0179	0.4547	0.012768	0.1135841	0.003168	0.0281825
0.0209	0.5309	0.0173964	0.1547583	0.0043164	0.0383986
0.0239	0.6071	0.0277829	0.2026766	0.0056529	0.0502881
0.0269	0.6833	0.0288876	0.256984	0.0071676	0.0637629
0.0299	0.7595	0.0356706	0.3173256	0.0088506	0.0787349
0.0329	0.8357	0.0431718	0.3840563	0.0117118	0.0952921
0.0359	0.9119	0.0513912	0.4571761	0.0127512	0.1134356
0.0418	1.0617	0.0697053	0.6200983	0.0172953	0.1538589
0.0478	1.2141	0.0911715	0.8110616	0.0226215	0.2012408
0.0538	1.3665	0.1154706	1.0272264	0.0286506	0.2548757
0.0598	1.5189	0.1426824	1.2693026	0.0354024	0.3149397
0.0673	1.7094	0.1807071	1.6075703	0.0448371	0.3988708
0.0747	1.8974	0.222642	1.9806232	0.055242	0.4914328
0.0897	2.2784	0.3210354	2.8559309	0.0796554	0.7068352
0.1046	2.6568	0.4365459	3.8835129	0.1083159	0.9635782
0.1196	3.0378	0.5707296	5.0772105	0.1416096	1.259759
0.1345	3.4163	0.721791	6.4210527	0.179091	1.5391935
0.1494	3.7948	0.890568	7.9224929	0.220968	1.9657313
0.1644	4.1758	1.0783773	9.5932444	0.2675673	2.3802787
0.1793	4.5542	1.2827052	11.410945	0.3182652	2.8312872
0.1943	4.9352	1.506225	13.399377	0.373725	3.3246576
0.2092	5.3137	1.7461836	15.534049	0.4332636	3.8543129
0.2242	5.6947	2.0055735	17.841481	0.4976235	4.4268586
0.2391	6.0731	2.2810431	20.292159	0.5659731	5.0348966

3-10. BRONZE (MANGANESE)
TS = 70,000 psi

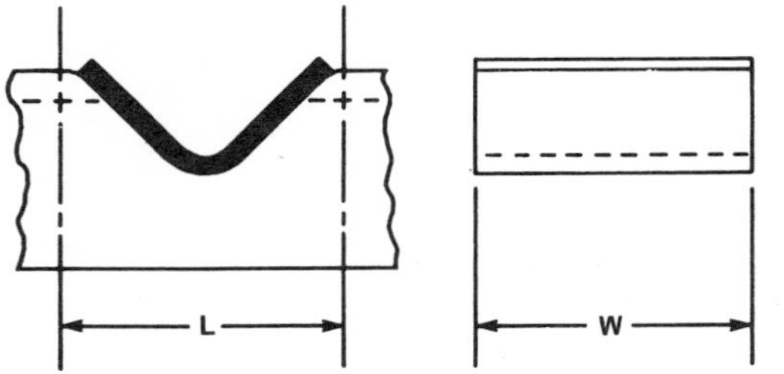

Bend Force = W/L times Force Factor

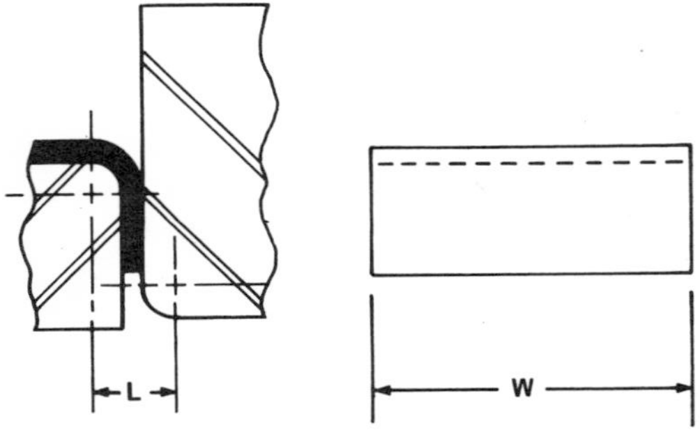

THICKNESS		V-BEND FORCE FACTORS		90° WIPE FORCE FACTORS	
inch	mm	To Obtain Tons	To Obtain kN	To Obtain Tons	To Obtain kN
0.0120	0.3048	0.0067032	0.0596316	0.0016632	0.0147958
0.0135	0.3429	0.0084721	0.0753678	0.0021021	0.0187002
0.0149	0.3785	0.0103341	0.0919321	0.0025641	0.0228102
0.0164	0.4166	0.0124754	0.1109811	0.0030954	0.0275366
0.0179	0.4547	0.014896	0.1325148	0.003696	0.0328796
0.0209	0.5309	0.0202958	0.1805514	0.0050358	0.0447984
0.0239	0.6071	0.02658	0.2364556	0.006595	0.0586691
0.0269	0.6833	0.0337022	0.2998147	0.0083622	0.0743901
0.0299	0.7595	0.0416157	0.3702132	0.0103257	0.0918574
0.0329	0.8357	0.0503671	0.4480657	0.0124971	0.1111742
0.0359	0.9119	0.0599564	0.5333721	0.0148764	0.1323404
0.0418	1.0617	0.0813228	0.7234476	0.0201778	0.1795017
0.0478	1.2141	0.1063667	0.9462381	0.0263917	0.2347805
0.0538	1.3665	0.1347157	1.1984308	0.0334257	0.297355
0.0598	1.5189	0.1664628	1.480853	0.0413028	0.3674297
0.0673	1.7094	0.2108249	1.8754983	0.0523099	0.4653488
0.0747	1.8974	0.259749	2.3107271	0.064449	0.5733383
0.0897	2.2784	0.3745413	3.3319194	0.0929313	0.8267168
0.1046	2.6568	0.5093035	4.5307639	0.1263685	1.1241741
0.1196	3.0378	0.6658512	5.9234122	0.1652112	1.4697188
0.1345	3.4163	0.8420895	7.4912281	0.2089395	1.8587257
0.1494	3.7948	1.038996	9.2429084	0.257796	2.2933532
0.1644	4.1758	1.2581068	11.192118	0.3121618	2.7769913
0.1793	4.5542	1.4964894	13.312769	0.3713094	3.3031684
0.1943	4.9352	1.7572625	15.632607	0.4360125	3.8787672
0.2092	5.3137	2.0372142	18.123057	0.5054742	4.4966984
0.2242	5.6947	2.3398357	20.815178	0.4804607	5.1646679
0.2391	6.0731	2.6612169	23.674185	0.6603019	5.8740457

Fig. 3-1

Fig. 3-2

3-11. COPPER
TS = 37,000 psi

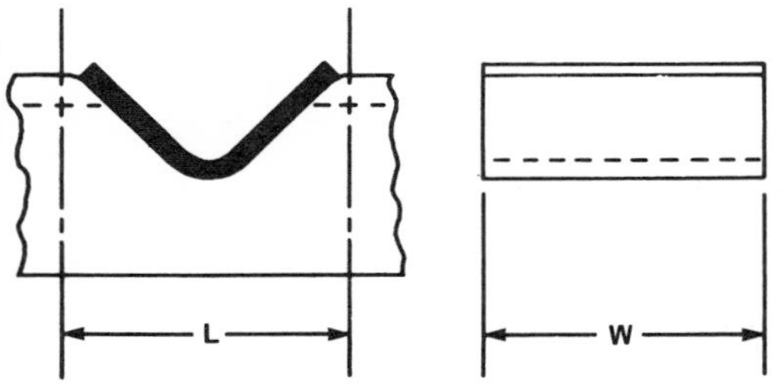

Bend Force = W/L times Force Factor

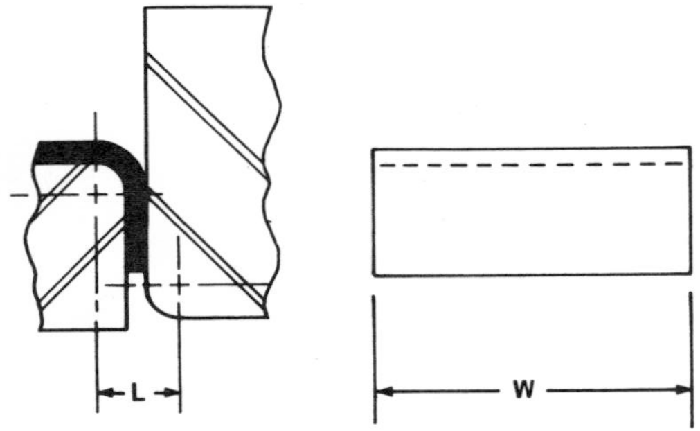

THICKNESS		V-BEND FORCE FACTORS		90° WIPE FORCE FACTORS	
inch	mm	To Obtain Tons	To Obtain kN	To Obtain Tons	To Obtain kN
0.0120	0.3048	0.0035431	0.0315194	0.0008791	0.0078204
0.0135	0.3429	0.0044781	0.0398371	0.0011111	0.0098843
0.0149	0.3785	0.0054623	0.0485926	0.0013553	0.0120567
0.0164	0.4166	0.0065941	0.0586611	0.0016361	0.0145547
0.0179	0.4547	0.0078736	0.0700435	0.0019536	0.0173792
0.0209	0.5309	0.0107277	0.0954336	0.0026617	0.0236784
0.0239	0.6071	0.0140494	0.1249834	0.0034859	0.0310105
0.0269	0.6833	0.017814	0.1584733	0.00442	0.0393203
0.0299	0.7595	0.0219968	0.1956835	0.0054578	0.0485525
0.0329	0.8357	0.0026622	0.0236829	0.0066056	0.0587634
0.0359	0.9119	0.0316912	0.2819249	0.0078632	0.069951
0.0418	1.0617	0.0429849	0.3823936	0.0106654	0.0948793
0.0478	1.2141	0.0562224	0.5001544	0.0139499	0.1240983
0.0538	1.3665	0.0712068	0.6334555	0.0176678	0.1571727
0.0598	1.5189	0.0879874	0.7827359	0.0218314	0.1942121
0.0673	1.7094	0.111436	0.9913346	0.0276495	0.2459699
0.0747	1.8974	0.1372959	1.2213843	0.0340659	0.3030502
0.0897	2.2784	0.1979718	1.7611571	0.0491208	0.3665863
0.1046	2.6568	0.2692033	2.3948325	0.0667948	0.5942065
0.1196	3.0378	0.3519499	3.1309463	0.0873259	0.7768512
0.1345	3.4163	0.4451044	3.9596487	0.1104394	0.9834689
0.1494	3.7948	0.5491836	4.8855373	0.1362636	1.2122009
0.1644	4.1758	0.6649993	5.9158337	0.1649999	1.4678391
0.1793	4.5542	0.7910015	7.0367493	0.1962635	1.74596
0.1943	4.9352	0.9288387	8.262949	0.2345637	2.050205
0.2092	5.3137	1.0768132	9.5793302	0.2671792	2.3768261
0.2242	5.6947	1.2367703	11.002308	0.3068678	2.7298959
0.2391	6.0731	1.4066432	12.513497	0.3490167	3.1048525

Fig. 3-1

Fig. 3-2

3-12. DURALUMIN (SOFT)
TS = 35,000 psi

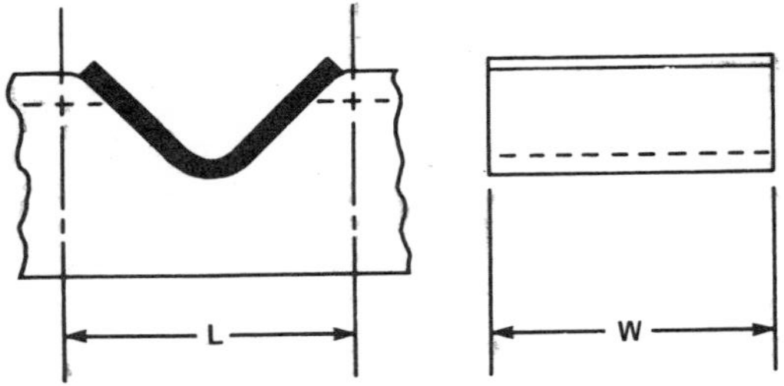

Bend Force = W/L times Force Factor

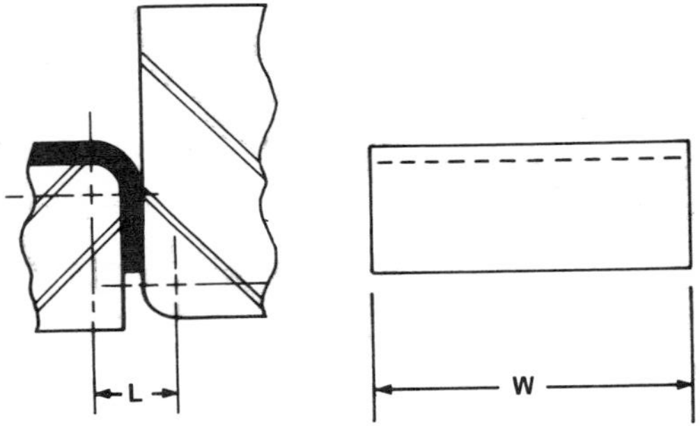

THICKNESS		V-BEND FORCE FACTORS		90° WIPE FORCE FACTORS	
inch	mm	To Obtain Tons	To Obtain kN	To Obtain Tons	To Obtain kN
0.0120	0.3048	0.0033516	0.0298158	0.0008316	0.0073979
0.0135	0.3429	0.004236	0.0376834	0.001051	0.0093496
0.0149	0.3785	0.005167	0.0459656	0.001282	0.0114046
0.0164	0.4166	0.0062377	0.0554905	0.0015477	0.0137683
0.0179	0.4547	0.007448	0.0662574	0.001848	0.0164398
0.0209	0.5309	0.0101479	0.0902757	0.0025179	0.0223992
0.0239	0.6071	0.01329	0.1182278	0.0032975	0.0293345
0.0269	0.6833	0.0168511	0.1499073	0.0041811	0.037195
0.0299	0.7595	0.0208078	0.1851061	0.0051628	0.0459282
0.0329	0.8357	0.0251835	0.2240324	0.0062485	0.0555865
0.0359	0.9119	0.0299782	0.266686	0.0074382	0.0661702
0.0418	1.0617	0.0406614	0.3617238	0.0100889	0.0897508
0.0478	1.2141	0.0531833	0.4731186	0.0131958	0.1173898
0.0538	1.3665	0.0673578	0.5992149	0.0167128	0.148677
0.0598	1.5189	0.0832314	0.7404265	0.0206514	0.1837148
0.0673	1.7094	0.1054124	0.9377487	0.0261549	0.2326739
0.0747	1.8974	0.1298745	1.1553635	0.0322245	0.2866691
0.0897	2.2784	0.1872706	1.6659592	0.0464656	0.4133579
0.1046	2.6568	0.2546517	2.2653815	0.0631842	0.5620866
0.1196	3.0378	0.3329256	2.9617061	0.0826056	0.7348594
0.1345	3.4163	0.4120447	3.7456136	0.1044697	0.9293624
0.1494	3.7948	0.519498	4.6214542	0.128898	1.1466766
0.1644	4.1758	0.6290534	5.596059	0.1560809	1.3884956
0.1793	4.5542	0.7482447	6.6563848	0.1856547	1.6515842
0.1943	4.9352	0.8786312	7.8163031	0.2180062	1.9393831
0.2092	5.3137	1.0186071	9.0615287	0.2427371	2.2483492
0.2242	5.6947	1.1699178	10.407588	0.2902803	2.5823335
0.2391	6.0731	1.3306084	11.837092	0.3301509	2.9370224

Fig. 3-1

Fig. 3-2

3-13. DURALUMIN (TREATED)
TS = 55,000 psi

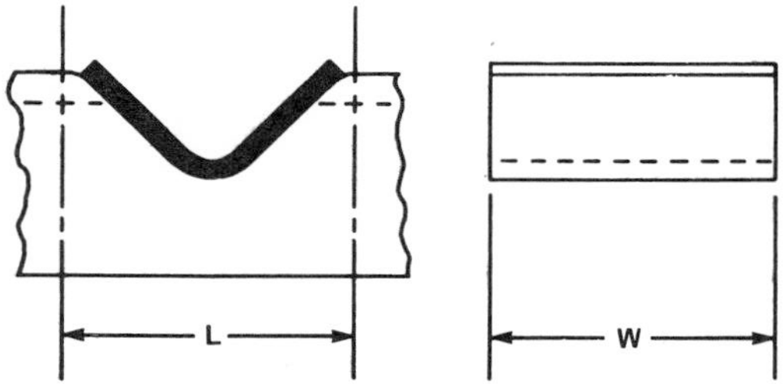

Bend Force = W/L times Force Factor

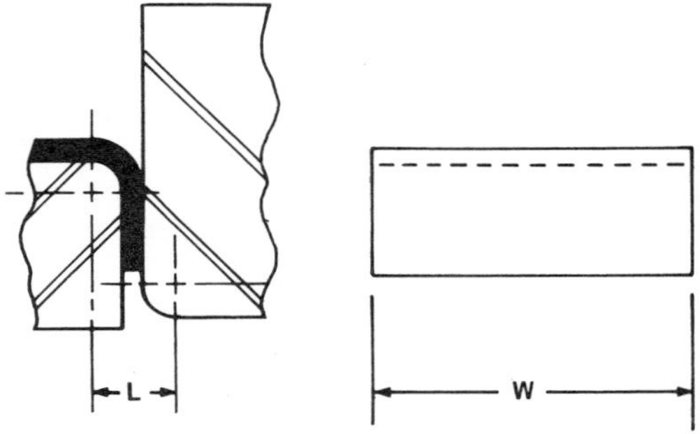

THICKNESS		V-BEND FORCE FACTORS		90° WIPE FORCE FACTORS	
inch	mm	To Obtain Tons	To Obtain kN	To Obtain Tons	To Obtain kN
0.0120	0.3048	0.0052668	0.0468534	0.0013068	0.0116252
0.0135	0.3429	0.0066566	0.0592171	0.0016516	0.0146926
0.0149	0.3785	0.0081196	0.0722319	0.0020146	0.0179218
0.0164	0.4166	0.0098021	0.0871994	0.0024321	0.0216359
0.0179	0.4547	0.011704	0.104187	0.002904	0.0258339
0.0209	0.5309	0.0159467	0.1418618	0.0039567	0.0351988
0.0239	0.6071	0.0208843	0.1857867	0.0058181	0.0460972
0.0269	0.6833	0.0264803	0.2355687	0.0065703	0.0584493
0.0299	0.7595	0.032698	0.2908814	0.008113	0.0721732
0.0329	0.8357	0.0395741	0.3520511	0.0098191	0.0873507
0.0359	0.9119	0.0471086	0.4190781	0.0116886	0.1039817
0.0418	1.0617	0.0638965	0.5684232	0.015854	0.1410371
0.0478	1.2141	0.0835783	0.7434725	0.0207363	0.184701
0.0538	1.3665	0.105848	0.9416238	0.026263	0.2336356
0.0598	1.5189	0.1307922	1.1635274	0.0324522	0.2886947
0.0673	1.7094	0.1656481	1.4736054	0.0511006	0.3656309
0.0747	1.8974	0.2040885	1.8155712	0.0506385	0.45048
0.0897	2.2784	0.2942824	2.6179362	0.0730174	0.6495627
0.1046	2.6568	0.400167	3.5598856	0.0992895	0.8832793
0.1196	3.0378	0.5231688	4.6541096	0.1298088	1.154779
0.1345	3.4163	0.6616417	5.8849645	0.1641667	1.4604269
0.1494	3.7948	0.816354	7.2622851	0.202554	1.8019203
0.1644	4.1758	0.9885125	8.7938072	0.24527	2.1819219
0.1793	4.5542	1.1758131	10.460033	0.2917431	2.5953466
0.1943	4.9352	1.3807062	12.282762	0.3425812	3.0476023
0.2092	5.3137	1.6006683	14.239545	0.3971583	3.5331202
0.2242	5.6947	1.8384423	16.354782	0.4561548	4.0579531
0.2391	6.0731	2.0909561	18.601145	0.5188086	4.6153213

Fig. 3-1

Fig. 3-2

3–14. DURALUMIN (TREATED AND COLD ROLLED) TS = 75,000 psi

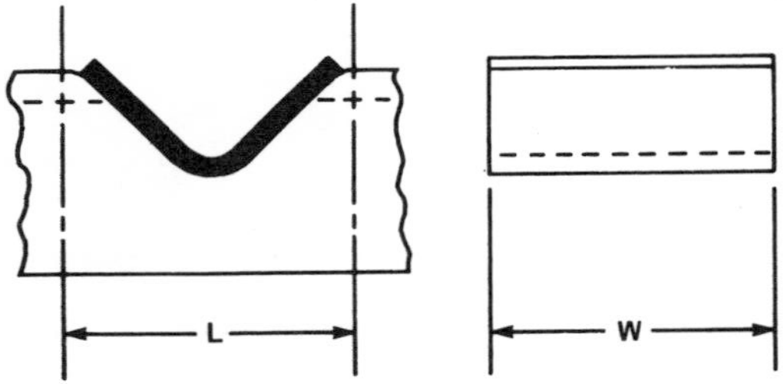

Fig. 3-1

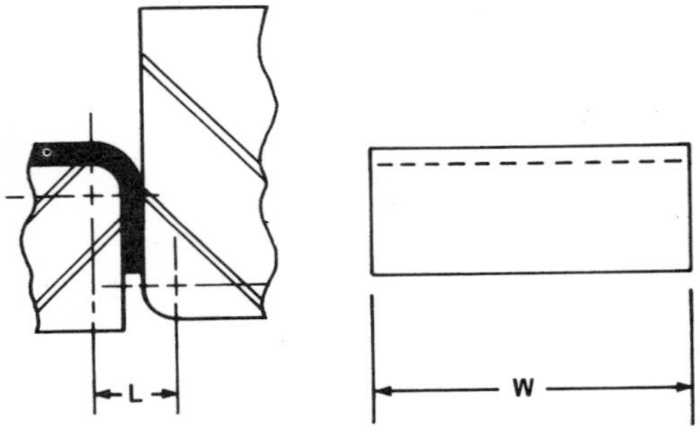

Fig. 3-2

Bend Force = W/L times Force Factor

THICKNESS inch	THICKNESS mm	V-BEND FORCE FACTORS To Obtain Tons	V-BEND FORCE FACTORS To Obtain kN	90° WIPE FORCE FACTORS To Obtain Tons	90° WIPE FORCE FACTORS To Obtain kN
0.0120	0.3048	0.007182	0.063891	0.001782	0.0158526
0.0135	0.3429	0.0090772	0.0807507	0.0022522	0.0200355
0.0149	0.3785	0.0110722	0.0984982	0.0027472	0.024439
0.0164	0.4166	0.0133665	0.1189083	0.0033165	0.0295035
0.0179	0.4547	0.01596	0.1419801	0.00396	0.0352281
0.0209	0.5309	0.0217455	0.1934479	0.0053955	0.0479983
0.0239	0.6071	0.0284785	0.2533447	0.0070661	0.06286
0.0269	0.6833	0.0361095	0.03212301	0.0089595	0.0797037
0.0299	0.7595	0.0445882	0.3966566	0.0110632	0.0984182
0.0329	0.8357	0.0539647	0.4800699	0.0133897	0.1191147
0.0359	0.9119	0.064239	0.5714701	0.015939	0.1417933
0.0418	1.0617	0.0871316	0.7751227	0.0216191	0.1923236
0.0478	1.2141	0.1139643	1.0138264	0.0282768	0.2515504
0.0538	1.3665	0.1443382	1.2840326	0.0358132	0.3185942
0.0598	1.5189	0.178353	1.5866282	0.044253	0.3936746
0.0673	1.7094	0.2258838	2.0094622	0.0560463	0.4985878
0.0747	1.8974	0.2783025	2.475779	0.0690525	0.614291
0.0897	2.2784	0.4012942	3.5699132	0.0995692	0.8857676
0.1046	2.6568	0.5456823	4.8543897	0.1353948	1.2044721
0.1196	3.0378	0.713412	6.3465131	0.177012	1.5746987
0.1345	3.4163	0.9022387	8.0263154	0.2238637	1.9914914
0.1494	3.7948	1.11321	9.9031161	0.27621	2.4571641
0.1644	4.1758	1.3479716	11.991555	0.3344591	2.9753481
0.1793	4.5542	1.6033815	14.263681	0.3978315	3.539109
0.1943	4.9352	1.8827812	16.749221	0.4671562	4.1558215
0.2092	5.3137	2.1827295	19.417561	0.5415795	4.8178912
0.2242	5.6947	2.5069669	22.310977	0.6220293	5.5335726
0.2391	6.0731	2.8513038	25.365198	0.7074663	6.2936202

3-15. INCONEL
TS = 80,000 psi

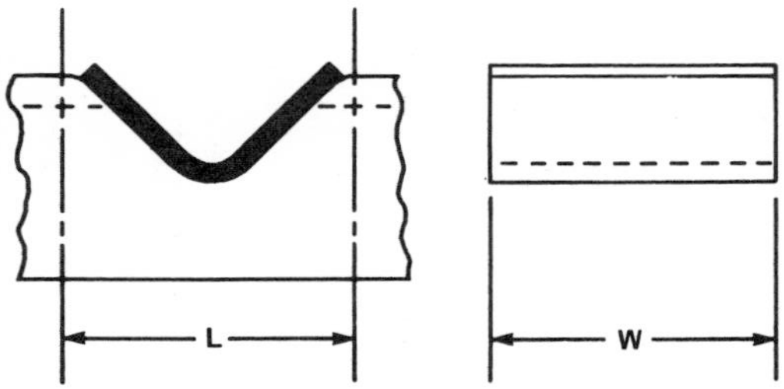

Bend Force = W/L times Force Factor

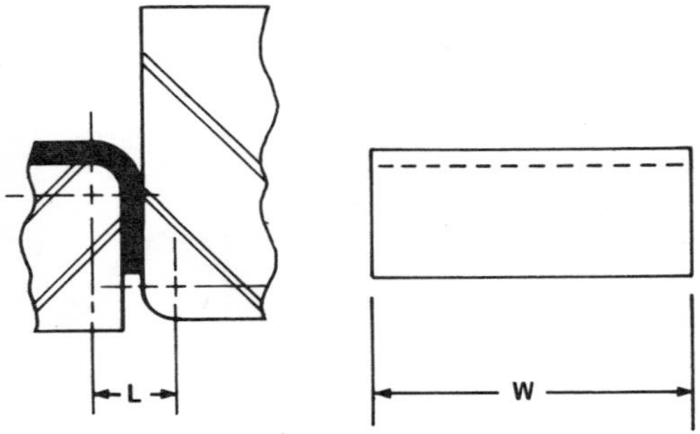

THICKNESS		V-BEND FORCE FACTORS		90° WIPE FORCE FACTORS	
inch	mm	To Obtain Tons	To Obtain kN	To Obtain Tons	To Obtain kN
0.0120	0.3048	0.0076609	0.0681513	0.0019008	0.0169095
0.0135	0.3429	0.0096824	0.0861346	0.0024024	0.0213717
0.0149	0.3785	0.0118104	0.1050653	0.0029304	0.0260688
0.0164	0.4166	0.0142576	0.1268356	0.0035376	0.0314704
0.0179	0.4547	0.017024	0.1514455	0.004224	0.0375767
0.0209	0.5309	0.021952	0.1952849	0.0057552	0.0511982
0.0239	0.6071	0.0303772	0.2702353	0.0075372	0.0670509
0.0269	0.6833	0.0385168	0.3426454	0.0095568	0.0850172
0.0299	0.7595	0.0475608	0.4231008	0.0118008	0.1049799
0.0329	0.8357	0.0575624	0.5120751	0.0142824	0.1270562
0.0359	0.9119	0.0685216	0.6095681	0.0170016	0.1512462
0.0418	1.0617	0.0929404	0.8267977	0.0230604	0.2051453
0.0478	1.2141	0.121562	1.0814155	0.030162	0.2683211
0.0538	1.3665	0.1539608	1.3696352	0.0382008	0.3398343
0.0598	1.5189	0.1902432	1.6924035	0.0472032	0.4199196
0.0673	1.7094	0.2409428	2.1434271	0.0597828	0.5318277
0.0747	1.8974	0.296856	2.6408309	0.073656	0.6552437
0.0897	2.2784	0.4280472	3.8079078	0.1062072	0.9448192
0.1046	2.6568	0.5820612	5.1780164	0.144212	1.2847709
0.1196	3.0378	0.7609728	6.769614	0.1888128	1.6796786
0.1345	3.4163	0.962388	8.5614036	0.238788	2.124258
0.1494	3.7948	1.187424	10.563323	0.294624	2.6209751
0.1644	4.1758	1.4378364	12.790992	0.3567564	3.1737049
0.1793	4.5542	1.7102736	15.214593	0.4243536	3.7750496
0.1943	4.9352	2.0083	17.865836	0.4983	4.4328768
0.2092	5.3137	2.3282448	20.712065	0.5776848	5.1390839
0.2242	5.6947	2.674098	23.788775	0.663498	5.9024782
0.2391	6.0731	3.0413908	27.056212	0.7546308	6.7131955

Fig. 3-1

Fig. 3-2

3-16. INCONEL
TS = 90,000 psi

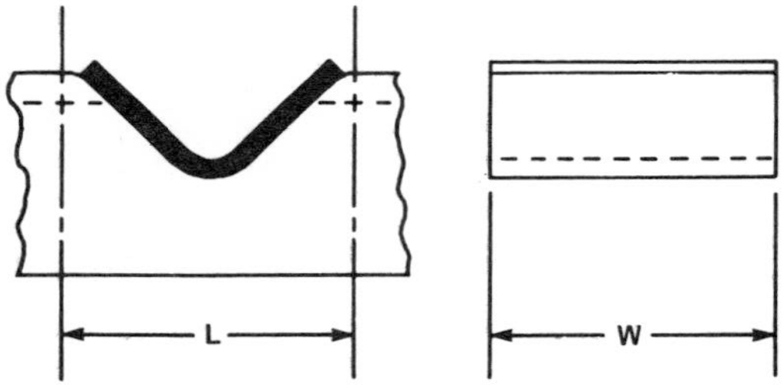

Bend Force = W/L times Force Factor

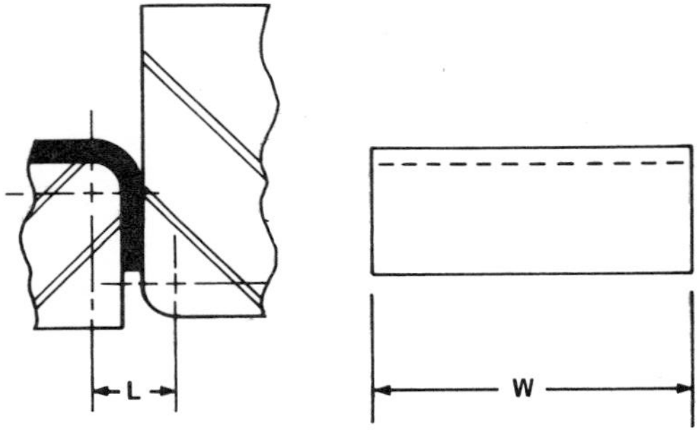

THICKNESS		V-BEND FORCE FACTORS		90° WIPE FORCE FACTORS	
inch	mm	To Obtain Tons	To Obtain kN	To Obtain Tons	To Obtain kN
0.0120	0.3048	0.0086184	0.0766692	0.0021384	0.0190232
0.0135	0.3429	0.0108927	0.0969014	0.0027027	0.0240432
0.0149	0.3785	0.0132867	0.1181984	0.0032967	0.0293274
0.0164	0.4166	0.0160398	0.14269	0.0039798	0.0354043
0.0179	0.4547	0.019152	0.1703761	0.004752	0.0422737
0.0209	0.5309	0.0260946	0.2321375	0.0064746	0.057598
0.0239	0.6071	0.0341743	0.3040145	0.0084793	0.0754318
0.0269	0.6833	0.043314	0.3854761	0.0107514	0.0956444
0.0299	0.7595	0.0535059	0.4759884	0.0132759	0.1181024
0.0329	0.8357	0.0647577	0.5670844	0.0160677	0.1429382
0.0359	0.9119	0.0770868	0.6857641	0.0191268	0.170152
0.0418	1.0617	0.1045579	0.930147	0.0259429	0.230788
0.0478	1.2141	0.1367572	1.216592	0.0339322	0.3018608
0.0538	1.3665	0.1732059	1.5408396	0.0429759	0.3823136
0.0598	1.5189	0.2140236	1.9039539	0.0531036	0.4724096
0.0673	1.7094	0.2710606	2.411355	0.0672556	0.5983058
0.0747	1.8974	0.333963	2.9709348	0.082863	0.7371492
0.0897	2.2784	0.4815531	4.2838963	0.1194831	1.0629216
0.1046	2.6568	0.6548188	5.825268	0.1624738	1.4453669
0.1196	3.0378	0.8560944	7.6158157	0.2124144	1.8896385
0.1345	3.4163	1.0826865	9.6315791	0.2686365	2.3897903
0.1494	3.7948	1.335852	11.883739	0.331452	2.9485969
0.1644	4.1758	1.6175759	14.389866	0.4013509	3.5704176
0.1793	4.5542	1.9240578	17.116418	0.4773978	4.2469308
0.1943	4.9352	2.2593375	20.099066	0.5605875	4.9869864
0.2092	5.3137	2.6192754	23.301073	0.6498954	5.7814694
0.2242	5.6947	3.0083602	26.762372	0.7464352	6.6402875
0.2391	6.0731	3.4215656	30.438238	0.8489596	7.5523446

Fig. 3-1

Fig. 3-2

3-17. INCONEL
TS = 100,000 psi

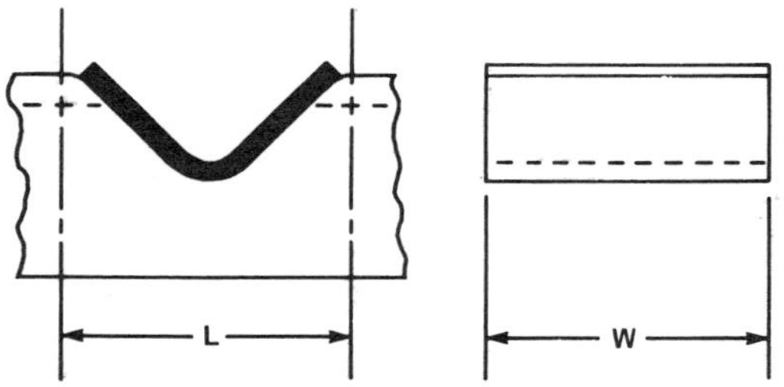

Bend Force = W/L times Force Factor

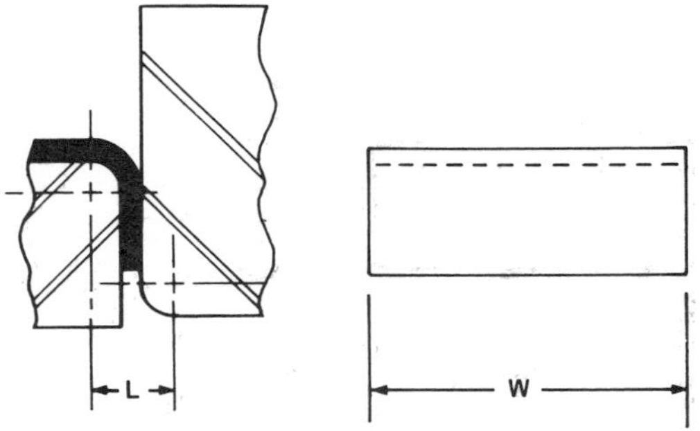

THICKNESS		V-BEND FORCE FACTORS		90° WIPE FORCE FACTORS	
inch	mm	To Obtain Tons	To Obtain kN	To Obtain Tons	To Obtain kN
0.0120	0.3048	0.009576	0.085188	0.002376	0.0211368
0.0135	0.3429	0.012103	0.1076682	0.003003	0.0267146
0.0149	0.3785	0.014763	0.1313316	0.003663	0.032586
0.0164	0.4166	0.017822	0.1585445	0.004422	0.0393381
0.0179	0.4547	0.02128	0.1893068	0.00528	0.0469709
0.0209	0.5309	0.028994	0.2579306	0.007194	0.0639978
0.0239	0.6071	0.0379715	0.3377944	0.0094215	0.0838136
0.0269	0.6833	0.048146	0.4283068	0.011946	0.1062716
0.0299	0.7595	0.059451	0.528876	0.014751	0.1312248
0.0329	0.8357	0.071953	0.6400938	0.017853	0.1588202
0.0359	0.9119	0.085652	0.7619601	0.021252	0.1890577
0.0418	1.0617	0.1161755	1.0334972	0.0288255	0.2564316
0.0478	1.2141	0.1519525	1.3517694	0.0377025	0.3354014
0.0538	1.3665	0.192451	1.712044	0.047751	0.4247928
0.0598	1.5189	0.237804	2.1155043	0.059004	0.5248994
0.0673	1.7094	0.3011785	2.6792839	0.0747285	0.6647847
0.0747	1.8974	0.37107	3.3010387	0.09207	0.8190547
0.0897	2.2784	0.535059	4.7598848	0.132759	1.181024
0.1046	2.6568	0.7275765	6.4725205	0.1805265	1.6059637
0.1196	3.0378	0.951216	8.4620175	0.236016	2.0995983
0.1345	3.4163	1.202985	10.701754	0.298485	2.6553225
0.1494	3.7948	1.48428	13.204154	0.36828	3.2762188
0.1644	4.1758	1.7972955	15.98874	0.4459455	3.9671311
0.1793	4.5542	2.137842	19.018242	0.530442	4.718812
0.1943	4.9352	2.510375	22.332296	0.633875	5.541096
0.2092	5.3137	2.910306	25.890082	0.722106	6.4298549
0.2242	5.6947	3.3426225	29.735969	0.8293725	7.3780977
0.2391	6.0731	3.8017385	33.820265	0.9432885	8.3914944

Fig. 3-1

Fig. 3-2

3-18. INCONEL
TS = 115,000 psi

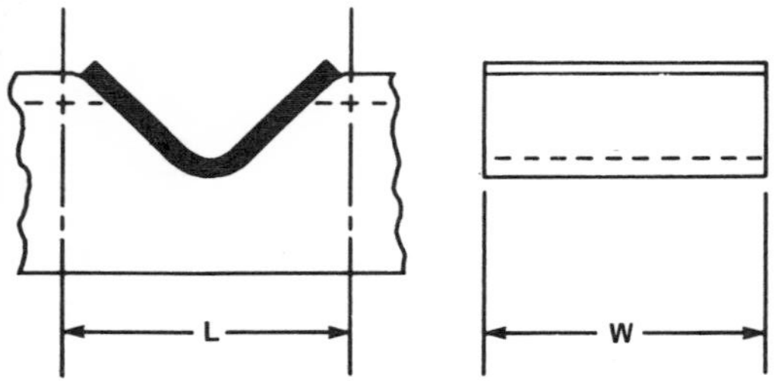

Bend Force = W/L times Force Factor

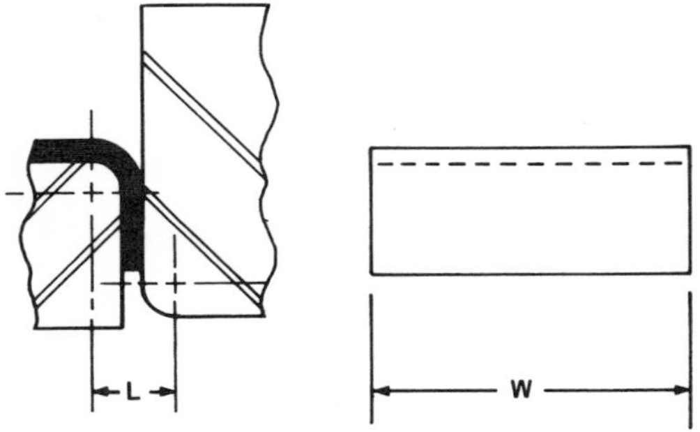

THICKNESS inch	mm	V-BEND FORCE FACTORS To Obtain Tons	To Obtain kN	90° WIPE FORCE FACTORS To Obtain Tons	To Obtain kN
0.0120	0.3048	0.0110124	0.0979663	0.0027324	0.0243074
0.0135	0.3429	0.0139184	0.123818	0.0034534	0.0307214
0.0149	0.3785	0.0169774	0.1510309	0.0042124	0.0374735
0.0164	0.4166	0.0204953	0.1823261	0.0050853	0.0452388
0.0179	0.4547	0.024472	0.2177029	0.006072	0.0540165
0.0209	0.5309	0.0333431	0.2966202	0.082731	0.0735974
0.0239	0.6071	0.0436672	0.3884634	0.0108347	0.0963854
0.0269	0.6833	0.0553679	0.4925528	0.0137379	0.1222123
0.0299	0.7595	0.0683686	0.608207	0.0169636	0.1509081
0.0329	0.8357	0.0827459	0.7461075	0.0205309	0.1826428
0.0359	0.9119	0.0984998	0.8762542	0.0244398	0.2174164
0.0418	1.0617	0.1336018	1.1885216	0.031493	0.2948961
0.0478	1.2141	0.1747453	1.5545341	0.0433578	0.3857109
0.0538	1.3665	0.2213186	1.9688502	0.0549136	0.4885113
0.0598	1.5189	0.2734746	2.43283	0.067854	0.6036291
0.0673	1.7094	0.3463552	3.0811758	0.0859377	0.7645017
0.0747	1.8974	0.4267305	3.7961945	0.1058805	0.9419129
0.0897	2.2784	0.6153178	5.4738671	0.1526728	1.3581772
0.1046	2.6568	0.8367129	7.4433979	0.2076054	1.8468576
0.1196	3.0378	1.0938984	9.7313201	0.2714184	2.414538
0.1345	3.4163	1.3834237	12.307017	0.3432577	3.0536204
0.1494	3.7948	1.706922	15.184778	0.423522	3.7676517
0.1644	4.1758	2.0668898	18.387051	0.5128373	4.5622006
0.1793	4.5542	2.4585183	21.870978	0.6100083	5.4266338
0.1943	4.9352	2.8869312	25.682139	0.7163062	6.3722599
0.2092	5.3137	3.3468519	29.773594	0.8304219	7.3874332
0.2242	5.6947	3.8440158	34.196364	0.9537783	8.4848117
0.2391	6.0731	4.3719992	38.893304	1.0847817	9.650218

Fig. 3-1

Fig. 3-2

3–19. INCONEL
TS = 140,000 psi

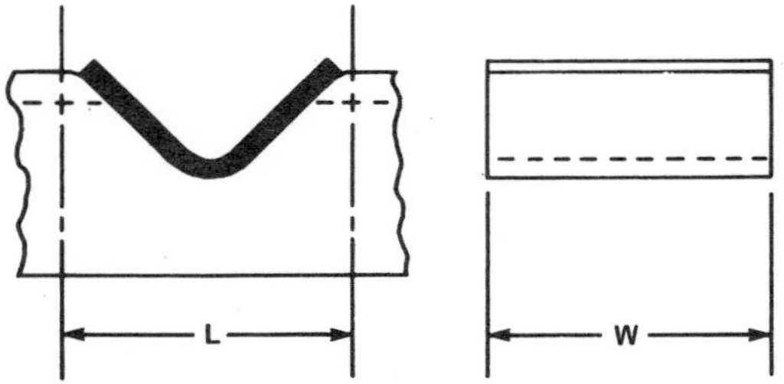

Fig. 3-1

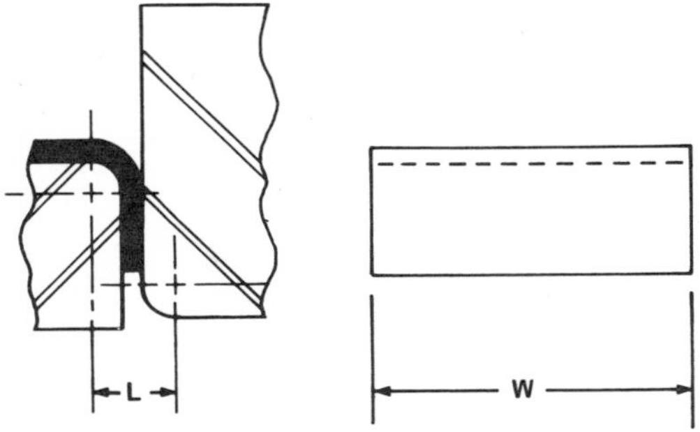

Fig. 3-2

Bend Force = W/L times Force Factor

THICKNESS *inch*	THICKNESS *mm*	V-BEND FORCE FACTORS *To Obtain Tons*	V-BEND FORCE FACTORS *To Obtain kN*	90° WIPE FORCE FACTORS *To Obtain Tons*	90° WIPE FORCE FACTORS *To Obtain kN*
0.0120	0.3048	0.0134064	0.1192633	0.0033264	0.0295916
0.0135	0.3429	0.0169442	0.1507356	0.0042042	0.0374005
0.0149	0.3785	0.0206682	0.1838643	0.0051282	0.0456204
0.0164	0.4166	0.0249508	0.2219623	0.0061908	0.0550733
0.0179	0.4547	0.029792	0.2650296	0.007392	0.0657592
0.0209	0.5309	0.0405916	0.3611028	0.0100716	0.0895969
0.0239	0.6071	0.0531601	0.4729122	0.0131901	0.1173391
0.0269	0.6833	0.0674044	0.5996295	0.0167244	0.1487802
0.0299	0.7595	0.0832314	0.7404265	0.0206514	0.1837148
0.0329	0.8357	0.1007342	0.8961314	0.0249942	0.2223484
0.0359	0.9119	0.1199128	1.0667442	0.0297528	0.2646809
0.0418	1.0617	0.1626457	1.4468961	0.0403557	0.3590043
0.0478	1.2141	0.2127335	1.8924772	0.0527835	0.469562
0.0538	1.3665	0.2694314	2.3968617	0.0668514	0.59471
0.0598	1.5189	0.3329256	2.9617061	0.0826056	0.7348594
0.0673	1.7094	0.4216499	3.7509975	0.1046199	0.9306986
0.0747	1.8974	0.519498	4.6214542	0.128898	1.1466766
0.0897	2.2784	0.7490826	6.6638388	0.1858626	1.6534336
0.1046	2,6568	1.0186071	9.0615287	0.2527371	2.2483492
0.1196	3.0378	1.3317024	11.846824	0.3304224	2.9394376
0.1345	3.4163	1.684179	14.982456	0.417879	3.7174515
0.1494	3.7948	2.077992	18.485815	0.515592	4.5867064
0.1644	4.1758	2.5162137	22.384237	0.6243237	5.5539836
0.1793	4.5542	2.9929788	26.625539	0.7426188	6.6063368
0.1943	4.9352	3.514525	31.265214	0.872025	7.7575344
0.2092	5.3137	4.0744284	36.246115	1.0109484	8.9933969
0.2242	5.6947	4.6796715	41.630357	1.1611215	10.329336
0.2391	6.0731	5.3224339	47.348371	1.3206039	11.748092

3–20. INCONEL
TS = 160,000 psi

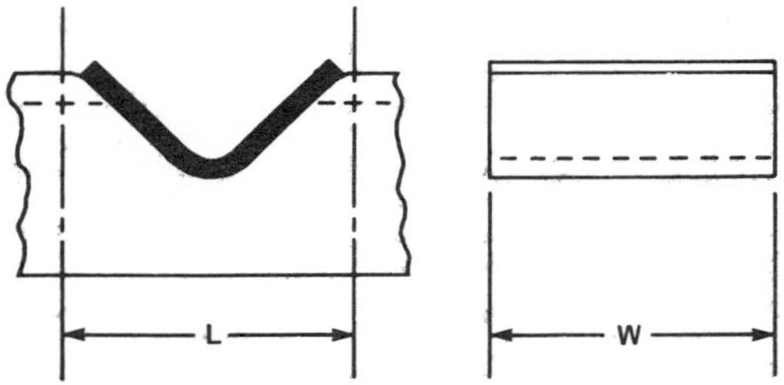

Fig. 3-1

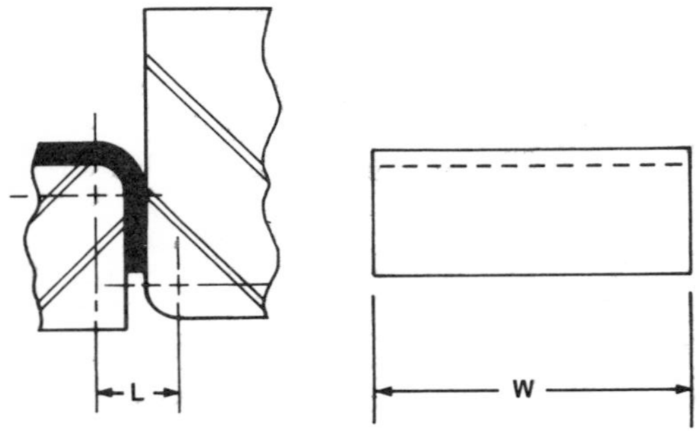

Fig. 3-2

Bend Force = W/L times Force Factor

THICKNESS *inch*	THICKNESS *mm*	V-BEND FORCE FACTORS *To Obtain Tons*	V-BEND FORCE FACTORS *To Obtain kN*	90° WIPE FORCE FACTORS *To Obtain Tons*	90° WIPE FORCE FACTORS *To Obtain kN*
0.0120	0.3048	0.0153216	0.1363009	0.0038016	0.033819
0.0135	0.3429	0.0193648	0.1722692	0.0048048	0.0427435
0.0149	0.3785	0.0236208	0.2101306	0.0058608	0.0521376
0.0164	0.4166	0.0285152	0.2536712	0.0070752	0.0629409
0.0179	0.4547	0.034048	0.302891	0.008448	0.0751534
0.0209	0.5309	0.0463904	0.4126889	0.0115104	0.1023965
0.0239	0.6071	0.0607544	0.5404711	0.0150744	0.1341018
0.0269	0.6833	0.0770336	0.6852909	0.191136	0.1700345
0.0299	0.7595	0.0951216	0.8462017	0.0236016	0.2099598
0.0329	0.8357	0.1151248	1.0241502	0.0285648	0.2541124
0.0359	0.9119	0.1370432	1.2191363	0.0340032	0.3024924
0.0418	1.0617	0.1858808	1.6535955	0.0461208	0.4102906
0.0478	1.2141	0.243124	2.1628311	0.060324	0.5366423
0.0538	1.3665	0.3079216	2.7392705	0.0764016	0.6796686
0.0598	1.5189	0.3804864	3.384807	0.0944064	0.8398393
0.0673	1.7094	0.4818856	4.2868542	0.1195656	1.0636555
0.0747	1.8974	0.593712	5.2816619	0.147312	1.3104875
0.0897	2.2784	0.8560944	7.6158157	0.2124144	1.8896385
0.1046	2.6568	1.1641224	10.356032	0.2888424	2.5695419
0.1196	3.0378	1.5219456	13.539228	0.3776256	3.3593573
0.1345	3.4163	1.924776	17.122807	0.477576	4.248516
0.1494	3.7948	2.374848	21.126647	0.589248	5.2419502
0.1644	4.1758	2.8756728	25.581985	0.7135128	6.3474098
0.1793	4.5542	2.4205472	30.429187	0.8487072	7.5500992
0.1943	4.9352	4.0166	35.731673	0.9966	8.8657536
0.2092	5.3137	4.6564896	41.424131	1.1553696	10.278167
0.2242	5.6947	5.348196	47.577551	1.326996	11.804956
0.2391	6.0731	6.0827816	54.112425	1.5092616	13.426391

3-21. INCONEL
TS = 175,000 psi

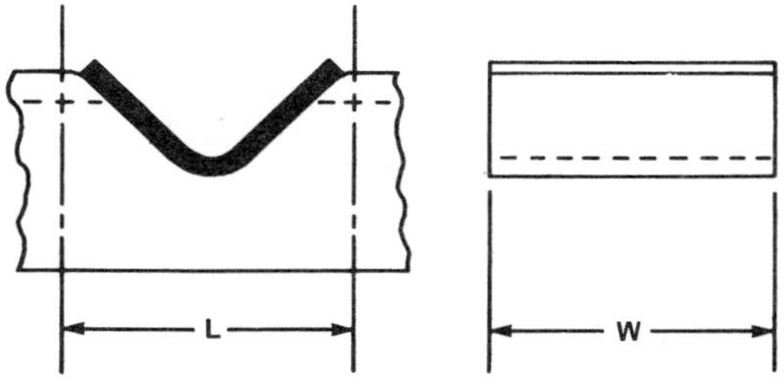

Bend Force = W/L times Force Factor

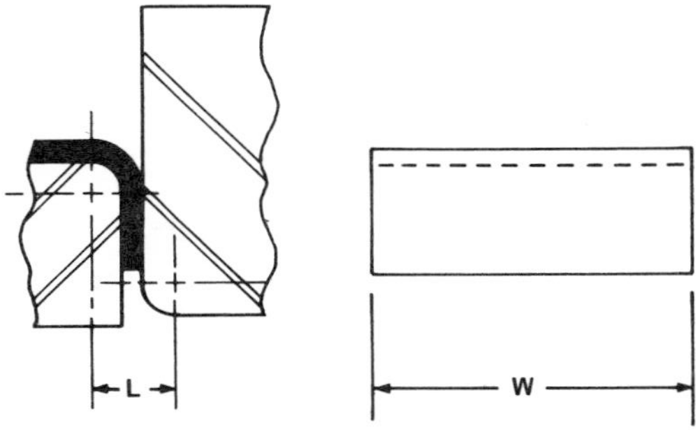

THICKNESS		V-BEND FORCE FACTORS		90° WIPE FORCE FACTORS	
inch	mm	To Obtain Tons	To Obtain kN	To Obtain Tons	To Obtain kN
0.0120	0.3048	0.016758	0.1490791	0.004158	0.0369895
0.0135	0.3429	0.0211802	0.188419	0.0052552	0.0467502
0.0149	0.3785	0.0258352	0.2298299	0.0064102	0.0570251
0.0164	0.4166	0.0311885	0.2774528	0.0077385	0.0688416
0.0179	0.4547	0.03724	0.331287	0.00924	0.082199
0.0209	0.5309	0.0507395	0.4513785	0.0125895	0.1119961
0.0239	0.6071	0.0664501	0.59114	0.0164876	0.1466736
0.0269	0.6833	0.0842555	0.7495369	0.0209055	0.1859753
0.0299	0.7595	0.1040392	0.9255327	0.0258142	0.2296431
0.0329	0.8357	0.1259177	1.1201638	0.0312427	0.277935
0.0359	0.9119	0.149891	1.3334303	0.037191	0.3308511
0.0418	1.0617	0.2033071	1.8086199	0.0504446	0.4487551
0.0478	1.2141	0.2659168	2.3655958	0.0659793	0.5869518
0.0538	1.3665	0.3367892	2.9960767	0.0835642	0.7433871
0.0598	1.5189	0.416157	3.7021326	0.103257	0.9135742
0.0673	1.7094	0.5270623	4.6887462	0.1307748	1.1633726
0.0747	1.8974	0.6493725	5.7768177	0.1611225	1.4333457
0.0897	2.2784	0.9363532	8.329798	0.2323282	2.0667916
0.1046	2.6568	1.2732588	11.32691	0.3159213	2.8104358
0.1196	3.0378	1.664628	14.80853	0.413028	3.674297
0.1345	3.4163	2.1052237	18.72807	0.5223487	4.646814
0.1494	3.7948	2.59749	23.107271	0.64449	5.733383
0.1644	4.1758	3.1452671	27.980296	0.7804046	6.9424793
0.1793	4.5542	3.7412235	33.281924	0.9282735	8.257921
0.1943	4.9352	4.3931562	39.081517	1.0900312	9.6969175
0.2092	5.3137	5.0930355	45.307643	1.2636855	11.241746
0.2242	5.6947	5.8495893	52.037946	1.4514018	12.91167
0.2391	6.0731	6.6530423	59.185464	1.6507548	14.685114

Fig. 3-1

Fig. 3-2

3–22. LEAD
TS = 3000 psi

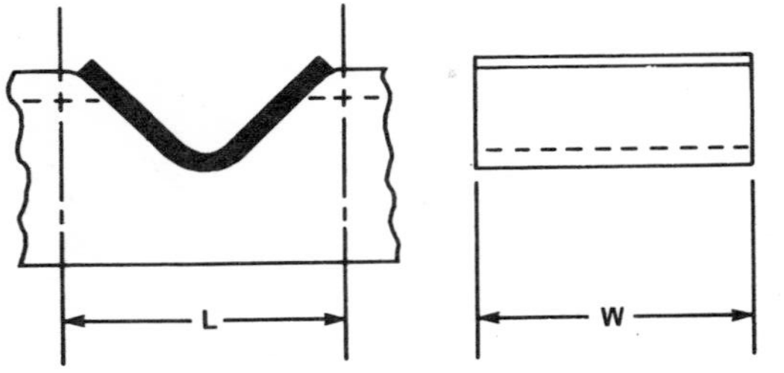

Fig. 3-1

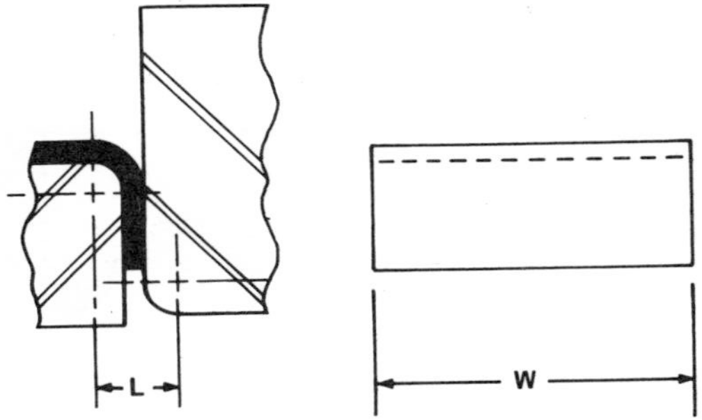

Fig. 3-2

Bend Force = W/L times Force Factor

THICKNESS *inch*	THICKNESS *mm*	V-BEND FORCE FACTORS *To Obtain Tons*	V-BEND FORCE FACTORS *To Obtain kN*	90° WIPE FORCE FACTORS *To Obtain Tons*	90° WIPE FORCE FACTORS *To Obtain kN*
0.0120	0.3048	0.0002872	0.0025549	0.0000712	0.0006333
0.0135	0.3429	0.000363	0.0032292	0.00009	0.0008006
0.0149	0.3785	0.0004428	0.0039391	0.0001098	0.0009767
0.0164	0.4166	0.0005346	0.0047558	0.0001326	0.0011796
0.0179	0.4547	0.0006384	0.0056792	0.0001584	0.0014091
0.0209	0.5309	0.0008698	0.0077377	0.0002158	0.0019197
0.0239	0.6071	0.0011391	0.0101334	0.0002826	0.002514
0.0269	0.6833	0.0014443	0.0128484	0.0003583	0.0031874
0.0299	0.7595	0.0017835	0.015866	0.0004425	0.0039364
0.0329	0.8357	0.0021585	0.019202	0.0005355	0.0047638
0.0359	0.9119	0.0025695	0.0228582	0.0006375	0.0056712
0.0418	1.0617	0.0034852	0.0310043	0.0008647	0.0076923
0.0478	1.2141	0.0045585	0.0405524	0.0011412	0.0010061
0.0538	1.3665	0.0057735	0.051361	0.0014325	0.0127435
0.0598	1.5189	0.0071341	0.0634649	0.0017701	0.0157468
0.0673	1.7094	0.0090353	0.080378	0.0022418	0.019943
0.0747	1.8974	0.0111321	0.0990311	0.0027621	0.0245716
0.0897	2.2784	0.0160517	0.1427959	0.0039827	0.03543
0.1046	2.6568	0.0218272	0.1941747	0.0054157	0.048178
0.1196	3.0378	0.0285364	0.2538598	0.0070804	0.0629872
0.1345	3.4163	0.0360895	0.3210521	0.0089454	0.0796592
0.1494	3.7948	0.0445284	0.3961246	0.0110484	0.0982865
0.1644	4.1758	0.0539188	0.4796616	0.0133783	0.1190133
0.1793	4.5542	0.0641352	0.5705467	0.0159132	0.1415638
0.1943	4.9352	0.0753112	0.6699684	0.0186862	0.1662324
0.2092	5.3137	0.0873091	0.7767017	0.0216631	0.1927149
0.2242	5.6947	0.1002786	0.8920784	0.0248811	0.2213422
0.2391	6.0731	0.1140521	1.0146074	0.0282986	0.2517443

3–23. MONEL (CAST)
TS = 75,000 psi

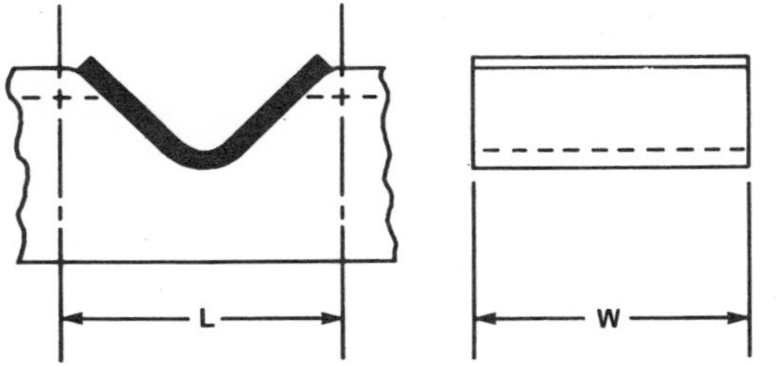

Fig. 3-1

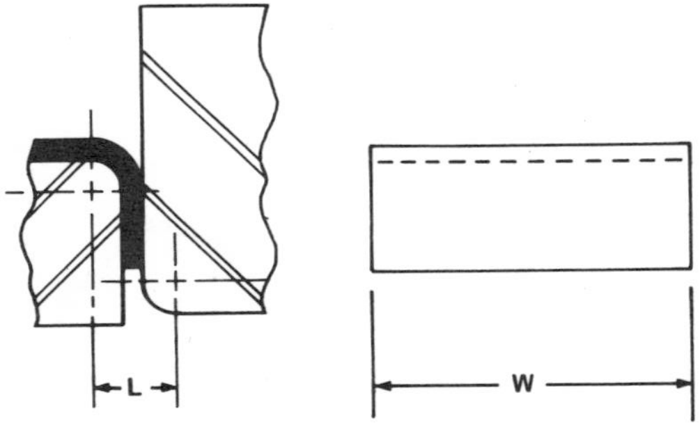

Fig. 3-2

Bend Force = W/L times Force Factor

THICKNESS inch	THICKNESS mm	V-BEND FORCE FACTORS To Obtain Tons	V-BEND FORCE FACTORS To Obtain kN	90° WIPE FORCE FACTORS To Obtain Tons	90° WIPE FORCE FACTORS To Obtain kN
0.0120	0.3048	0.007182	0.063891	0.001782	0.0158526
0.0135	0.3429	0.0090772	0.0807507	0.0022522	0.0200355
0.0149	0.3785	0.0110722	0.0984982	0.0027472	0.024439
0.0164	0.4166	0.0133665	0.1189083	0.0033165	0.0295035
0.0179	0.4547	0.01596	0.1419801	0.00396	0.0352281
0.0209	0.5309	0.0217455	0.1934479	0.0053955	0.0479983
0.0239	0.6071	0.0284786	0.2533456	0.0070661	0.06286
0.0269	0.6833	0.0361095	0.3212301	0.0089595	0.0797037
0.0299	0.7595	0.0445882	0.3966566	0.0110632	0.0984182
0.0329	0.8357	0.0539647	0.4800699	0.0133897	0.1191147
0.0359	0.9119	0.064239	0.5714701	0.015939	0.1417933
0.0418	1.0617	0.0871316	0.7751227	0.0216191	0.1923235
0.0478	1.2141	0.1139643	1.0138264	0.0282768	0.2515504
0.0538	1.3665	0.1443382	1.2840326	0.0358132	0.3185942
0.0598	1.5189	0.178353	1.5866282	0.044253	0.3936746
0.0673	1.7094	0.2258838	2.0094622	0.0560463	0.4985878
0.0747	1.8974	0.2783025	2.475779	0.0690525	0.614291
0.0897	2.2784	0.4012942	3.5699132	0.0995692	0.8857676
0.1046	2.6568	0.5456823	4.8543897	0.1353948	1.2044721
0.1196	3.0378	0.713412	6.3465131	0.177012	1.5746987
0.1345	3.4163	0.9022387	8.0263154	0.2238637	1.9914914
0.1494	3.7948	1.11321	9.9031161	0.27621	2.4571641
0.1644	4.1758	1.3479716	11.991555	0.3344591	2.9753481
0.1793	4.5542	1.6033815	14.263681	0.3978315	3.539109
0.1943	4.9352	1.8827812	16.749221	0.4671562	4.1558215
0.2092	5.3137	2.1827295	19.417561	0.5415795	4.8178912
0.2242	5.6947	2.5069668	22.301976	0.6220293	5.5335726
0.2391	6.0731	2.8513038	25.365198	0.7074663	6.2936202

3-24. MONEL (ROLLED)
TS = 95,000 psi

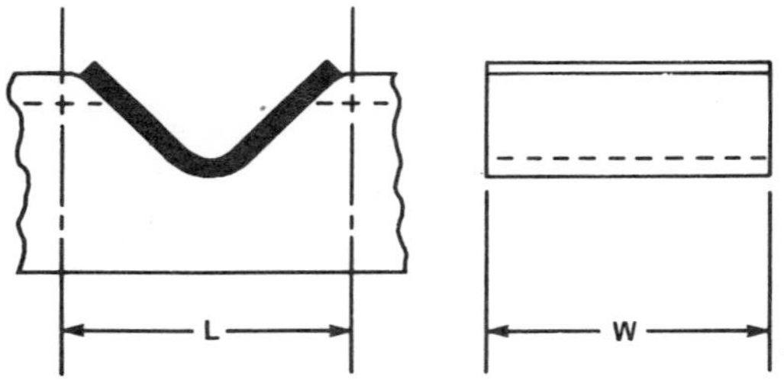

Bend Force = W/L times Force Factor

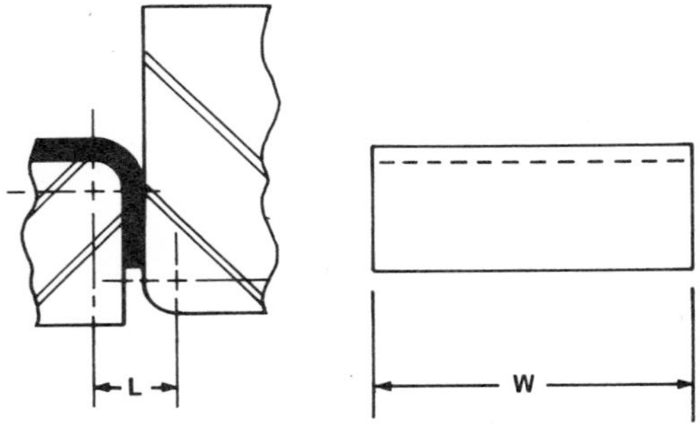

THICKNESS		V-BEND FORCE FACTORS		90° WIPE FORCE FACTORS	
inch	mm	To Obtain Tons	To Obtain kN	To Obtain Tons	To Obtain kN
0.0120	0.3048	0.0090972	0.0809286	0.0022572	0.02008
0.0135	0.3429	0.0114978	0.1022844	0.0028528	0.0253785
0.0149	0.3785	0.0140248	0.1247646	0.0034798	0.0309563
0.0164	0.4166	0.0169309	0.1506172	0.0042009	0.0373712
0.0179	0.4547	0.020216	0.1798415	0.005016	0.0446223
0.0209	0.5309	0.0275443	0.245034	0.0068343	0.0607979
0.0239	0.6071	0.0360729	0.3209045	0.0089504	0.0796227
0.0269	0.6833	0.0457387	0.4068914	0.0113487	0.100958
0.0299	0.7595	0.0564784	0.5024318	0.0140134	0.1246632
0.0329	0.8357	0.0683553	0.6080887	0.0169603	0.1508788
0.0359	0.9119	0.0813694	0.7238621	0.0201894	0.1796049
0.0418	1.0617	0.1103667	0.9818221	0.0273842	0.2436098
0.0478	1.2141	0.1443548	1.2841803	0.0358173	0.3186307
0.0538	1.3665	0.1828284	1.6264414	0.0453634	0.4035528
0.0598	1.5189	0.2259138	2.0097291	0.0560538	0.4986546
0.0673	1.7094	0.2861195	2.545319	0.070992	0.6315448
0.0747	1.8974	0.3525165	3.1359867	0.0874665	0.7781019
0.0897	2.2784	0.508306	4.5218901	0.126121	1.1219724
0.1046	2.6568	0.6911976	6.1488938	0.1715001	1.5256648
0.1196	3.0378	0.9036552	8.0389166	0.2242152	1.9946184
0.1345	3.4163	1.1428357	10.166666	0.2835607	2.5225559
0.1494	3.7948	1.410066	12.543947	0.349866	3.1124079
0.1644	4.1758	1.7074307	15.189303	0.4236482	3.7687743
0.1793	4.5542	2.0309499	18.06733	0.5039199	4.4828714
0.1943	4.9352	2.3848562	21.21568	0.5917312	5.2640407
0.2092	5.3137	2.7647907	24.595578	0.6860007	6.1026622
0.2242	5.6947	3.1754913	28.24917	0.7879038	7.0091922
0.2391	6.0731	3.6116515	32.129251	0.896124	7.9719191

Fig. 3-1

Fig. 3-2

3–25. SAE 4130
TS = 90,000 psi

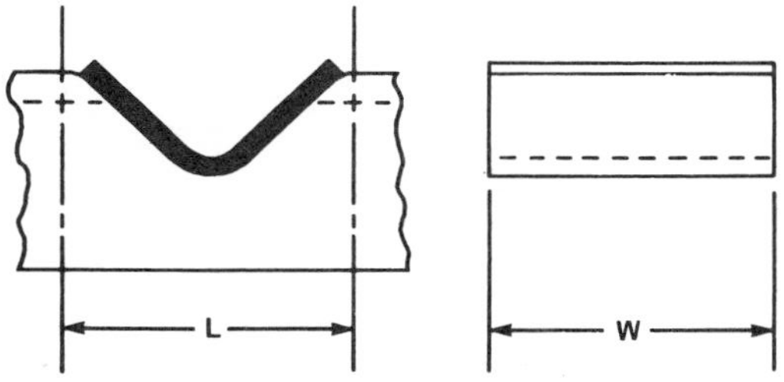

Fig. 3-1

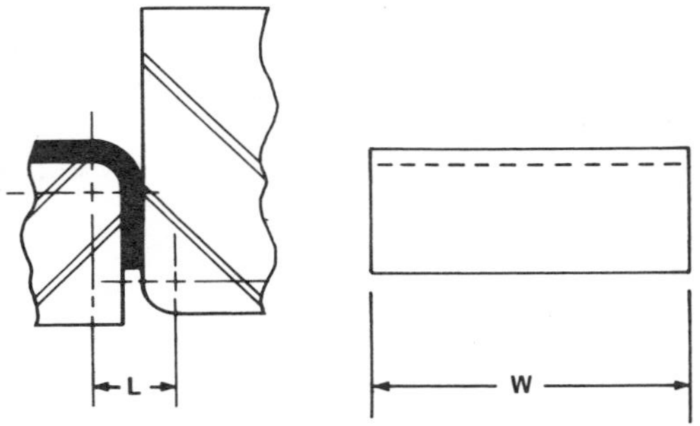

Fig. 3-2

Bend Force = W/L times Force Factor

THICKNESS inch	THICKNESS mm	V-BEND FORCE FACTORS To Obtain Tons	V-BEND FORCE FACTORS To Obtain kN	90° WIPE FORCE FACTORS To Obtain Tons	90° WIPE FORCE FACTORS To Obtain kN
0.0120	0.3048	0.0086184	0.0766692	0.0021384	0.0190232
0.0135	0.3429	0.0108927	0.0969014	0.0027027	0.0240432
0.0149	0.3785	0.0132867	0.1181984	0.0032967	0.0293274
0.0164	0.4166	0.0160398	0.14269	0.0039798	0.0354043
0.0179	0.4547	0.019152	0.1703761	0.004752	0.0422737
0.0209	0.5309	0.0260946	0.2321375	0.0064746	0.057598
0.0239	0.6071	0.0341743	0.3040145	0.0084793	0.0754318
0.0269	0.6833	0.0433314	0.3854761	0.0107514	0.0956444
0.0299	0.7595	0.0535059	0.4759884	0.0132759	0.1181024
0.0329	0.8357	0.0647577	0.5760844	0.0160677	0.1429382
0.0359	0.9119	0.0770868	0.6857641	0.0191268	0.170152
0.0418	1.0617	0.1045579	0.930147	0.0259429	0.230788
0.0478	1.2141	0.1367572	1.216592	0.0339322	0.3018608
0.0538	1.3665	0.1732059	1.5408396	0.0429759	0.3823136
0.0598	1.5189	0.2140236	1.9039539	0.0531036	0.4724096
0.0673	1.7094	0.2710606	2.411355	0.0672556	0.5983058
0.0747	1.8974	0.333963	2.9709348	0.082863	0.7371492
0.0897	2.2784	0.4815531	4.2838963	0.1194831	1.0629216
0.1046	2.6568	0.6548188	5.825268	0.1624738	1.4453669
0.1196	3.0378	0.8560944	7.6158157	0.2124144	1.8896385
0.1345	3.4163	1.0826865	9.6315791	0.2686365	2.3897903
0.1494	3.7948	1.335852	11.883739	0.331452	2.9485969
0.1644	4.1758	1.6175659	14.389866	0.4013509	3.5704176
0.1793	4.5542	1.9240578	17.116418	0.4773978	4.2469308
0.1943	4.9352	2.2593375	20.099066	0.5605875	4.9869864
0.2092	5.3137	2.6192754	23.301073	0.6498954	5.7814694
0.2242	5.6947	3.0083602	26.762372	0.7464352	6.6402875
0.2391	6.0731	3.4215646	30.438238	0.8489596	7.5523446

3-26. SAE 4130 TS = 100,000 psi

Bend Force = W/L times Force Factor

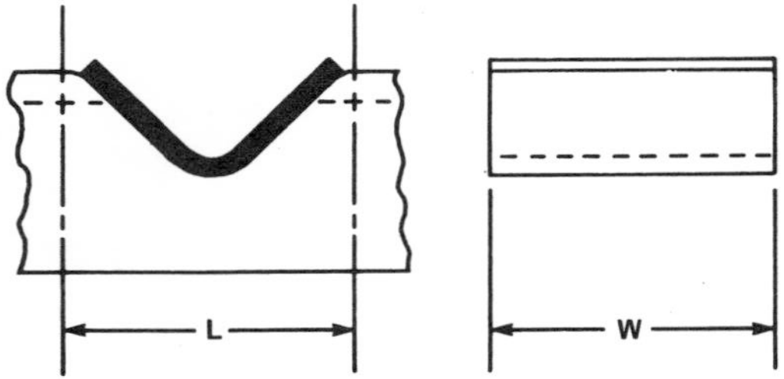

THICKNESS		V-BEND FORCE FACTORS		90° WIPE FORCE FACTORS	
inch	mm	To Obtain Tons	To Obtain kN	To Obtain Tons	To Obtain kN
0.0120	0.3048	0.009576	0.085188	0.002376	0.0211368
0.0135	0.3429	0.012103	0.1076682	0.003003	0.0267146
0.0149	0.3785	0.014763	0.1313316	0.003663	0.032586
0.0164	0.4166	0.017822	0.1585445	0.004422	0.0393381
0.0179	0.4547	0.02128	0.1893068	0.00528	0.0469708
0.0209	0.5309	0.028994	0.2579306	0.007194	0.0639978
0.0239	0.6071	0.0379715	0.3377944	0.0094215	0.0838136
0.0269	0.6833	0.048146	0.4283068	0.011946	0.1062716
0.0299	0.7595	0.059451	0.528876	0.014751	0.1312248
0.0329	0.8357	0.071953	0.6400938	0.017853	0.1588202
0.0359	0.9119	0.085652	0.7619601	0.021252	0.1890577
0.0418	1.0617	0.1161755	1.0334972	0.0288255	0.2564316
0.0478	1.2141	0.1519525	1.3517694	0.0377025	0.3354014
0.0538	1.3665	0.192451	1.712044	0.047751	0.4247928
0.0598	1.5189	0.237804	2.1155043	0.059004	0.5248995
0.0673	1.7094	0.3011785	2.6792839	0.0742285	0.6647847
0.0747	1.8974	0.37107	3.3010387	0.09207	0.8190547
0.0897	2.2784	0.535059	4.7598848	0.132759	1.181024
0.1046	2.6568	0.7275765	6.4725205	0.1805265	1.6059637
0.1196	3.0378	0.951216	8.4620175	0.236016	2.0995983
0.1345	3.4163	1.202985	10.701754	0.298485	2.6553225
0.1494	3.7948	1.48428	13.204154	0.36828	3.2762188
0.1644	4.1758	1.7972955	15.98874	0.4459455	3.9671311
0.1793	4.5542	2.137842	19.018242	0.530422	4.718812
0.1943	4.9352	2.510375	22.332296	0.622875	5.541096
0.2092	5.3137	2.910306	25.890082	0.722106	6.4238549
0.2242	5.6947	3.3426225	29.735969	0.8293725	7.3780977
0.2391	6.0731	3.8017385	33.820265	0.9432885	8.3914944

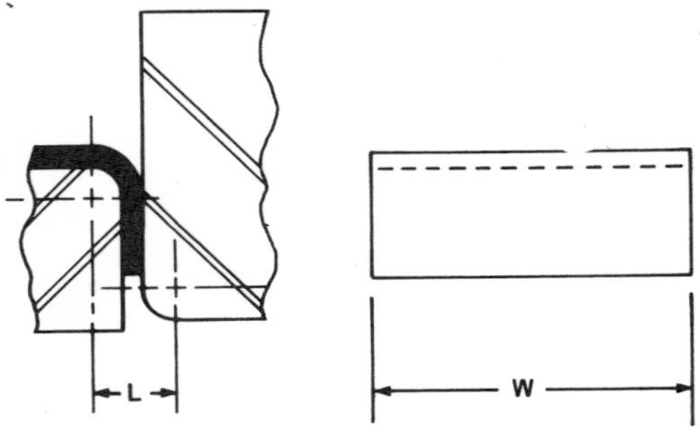

Fig. 3-1

Fig. 3-2

3–27. SAE 4130
TS = 125,000 psi

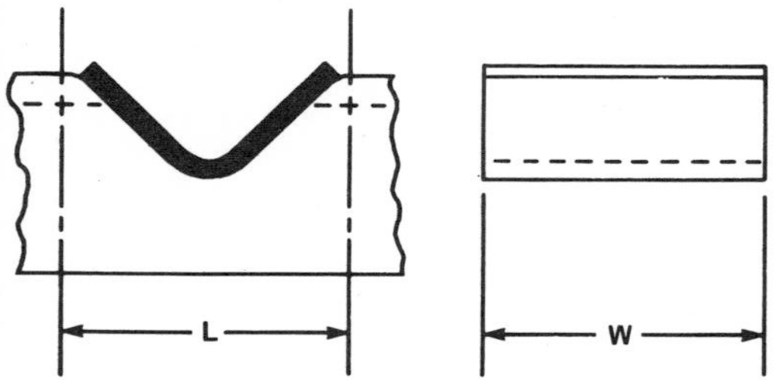

Fig. 3-1

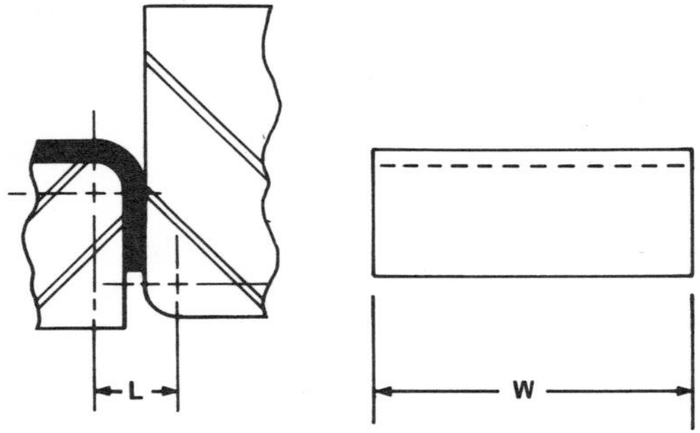

Fig. 3-2

Bend Force = W/L times Force Factor

THICKNESS *inch*	THICKNESS *mm*	V-BEND FORCE FACTORS *To Obtain Tons*	V-BEND FORCE FACTORS *To Obtain kN*	90° WIPE FORCE FACTORS *To Obtain Tons*	90° WIPE FORCE FACTORS *To Obtain kN*
0.0120	0.3048	0.01197	0.1064851	0.00297	0.0264211
0.0135	0.3429	0.0151287	0.1345849	0.0037537	0.0333929
0.0149	0.3785	0.0184537	0.1641641	0.0045787	0.0407321
0.0164	0.4166	0.0222775	0.1981806	0.0055275	0.0491726
0.0179	0.4547	0.0266	0.2366336	0.0066	0.0578136
0.0209	0.5309	0.0362425	0.3224132	0.0089925	0.0799972
0.0239	0.6071	0.0474643	0.4222424	0.0117768	0.0104759
0.0269	0.6833	0.0601825	0.5353835	0.0149325	0.1328395
0.0299	0.7595	0.0743137	0.6610946	0.0184387	0.1640306
0.0329	0.8357	0.0899412	0.8001169	0.0223162	0.1985249
0.0359	0.9119	0.107065	0.9524502	0.026565	0.2363222
0.0418	1.0617	0.1452193	1.2918708	0.0360318	0.3205388
0.0478	1.2141	0.1899406	1.6897115	0.0471281	0.4192515
0.0538	1.3665	0.2405637	2.1400546	0.0596887	0.5309906
0.0598	1.5189	0.297255	2.6443804	0.073755	0.6561244
0.0673	1.7094	0.3764731	3.3491046	0.0934106	0.8309806
0.0747	1.8974	0.4638375	4.1262984	0.1150875	1.0238184
0.0897	2.2784	0.6688237	5.9498556	0.1659487	1.4762796
0.1046	2.6568	0.9094706	8.0906504	0.2256581	2.0074544
0.1196	3.0378	1.18902	10.577521	0.29502	2.2644979
0.1345	3.4163	1.5307312	13.377192	0.3731062	3.3191527
0.1494	3.7948	1.85535	16.505193	0.46035	4.0952736
0.1644	4.1758	2.2466193	19.985925	0.5574318	4.9589132
0.1793	4.5542	2.6723025	23.772803	0.6630525	5.898515
0.1943	4.9352	3.1379687	27.915369	0.7785937	6.9263695
0.2092	5.3137	3.6378825	32.362602	0.9026325	8.0298187
0.2242	5.6947	4.1782781	37.169961	1.0367156	9.2226219
0.2391	6.0731	4.7521731	42.275331	1.1791106	10.489367

3–28. SAE 4130
TS = 150,000 psi

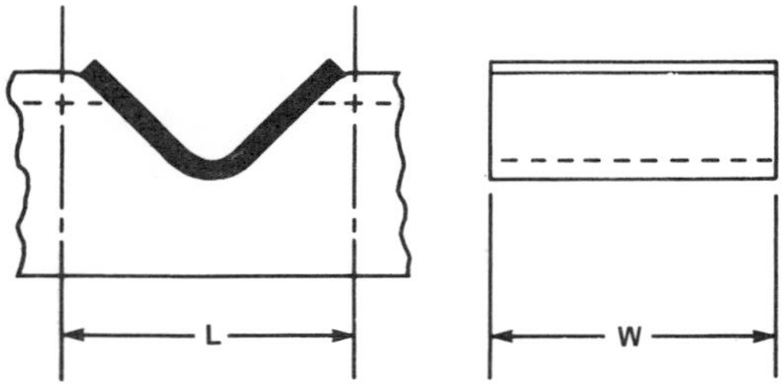

Bend Force = W/L times Force Factor

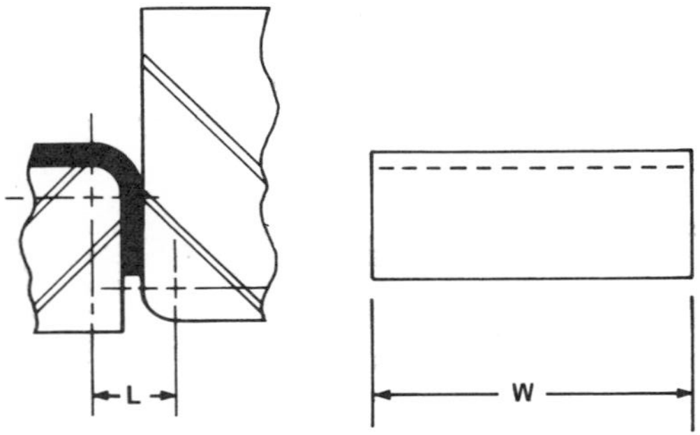

THICKNESS		V-BEND FORCE FACTORS		90° WIPE FORCE FACTORS	
inch	mm	To Obtain Tons	To Obtain kN	To Obtain Tons	To Obtain kN
0.0120	0.3048	0.014364	0.1277821	0.003564	0.1317053
0.0135	0.3429	0.0181545	0.1615024	0.0045045	0.040072
0.0149	0.3785	0.0221445	0.1969974	0.0054945	0.048879
0.0164	0.4166	0.026733	0.2378167	0.006633	0.0590071
0.0179	0.4547	0.03192	0.2839603	0.00792	0.0704563
0.0209	0.5309	0.043491	0.3868959	0.010791	0.0959967
0.0239	0.6071	0.0569572	0.5066912	0.0141322	0.12572
0.0269	0.6833	0.072219	0.6424602	0.017919	0.1594074
0.0299	0.7595	0.0891765	0.7933141	0.0221265	0.1968373
0.0329	0.8357	0.1079295	0.9601408	0.0267795	0.2382304
0.0359	0.9119	0.128478	1.1429402	0.031878	0.2835866
0.0418	1.0617	0.1742632	1.5502454	0.0432382	0.384647
0.0478	1.2141	0.2279287	2.0276537	0.0565537	0.5031017
0.0538	1.3665	0.2886765	2.5680661	0.0716265	0.6371893
0.0598	1.5189	0.356706	3.1732565	0.088506	0.7873493
0.0673	1.7094	0.4517677	4.0189254	0.1120927	0.9971766
0.0747	1.8974	0.556605	4.951558	0.138105	1.228582
0.0897	2.2784	0.8025885	7.1398272	0.1991385	1.771536
0.1046	2.6568	1.0913647	9.7087803	0.2707897	2.4089451
0.1196	3.0378	1.426824	12.693026	0.354024	3.1493975
0.1345	3.4163	1.8044775	16.052631	0.4477275	3.9829838
0.1494	3.7948	2.22642	19.806232	0.55242	4.9143283
0.1644	4.1758	2.6959432	23.98311	0.6689182	5.9506963
0.1793	4.5542	3.206763	28.527363	0.795663	7.078218
0.1943	4.9352	3.7655625	33.498444	0.9343125	8.311644
0.2092	5.3137	4.365459	38.835123	1.083159	9.3657824
0.2242	5.6947	5.0139337	44.603954	1.2440587	11.067146
0.2391	6.0731	5.7026077	50.730398	1.4149327	12.587241

Fig. 3-1

Fig. 3-2

3–29. SAE 4130
TS = 180,000 psi

Bend Force = W/L times Force Factor

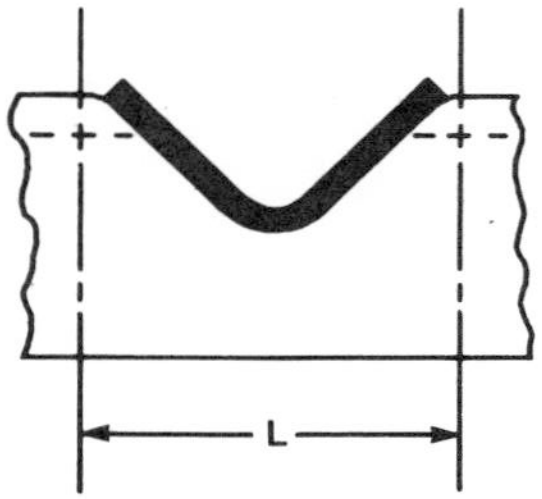

THICKNESS		V-BEND FORCE FACTORS		90° WIPE FORCE FACTORS	
inch	mm	To Obtain Tons	To Obtain kN	To Obtain Tons	To Obtain kN
0.0120	0.3048	0.0172368	0.1533385	0.0042768	0.0380464
0.0135	0.3429	0.0217854	0.1938029	0.0054054	0.0580864
0.0149	0.3785	0.0265734	0.2363969	0.0065934	0.0586548
0.0164	0.4166	0.0320796	0.2853801	0.0079596	0.0708086
0.0179	0.4547	0.038304	0.3407523	0.009504	0.0845475
0.0209	0.5309	0.0521892	0.4642751	0.0129492	0.115196
0.0239	0.6071	0.0683487	0.60803	0.0169587	0.1508645
0.0269	0.6833	0.0866628	0.7709522	0.0215028	0.1912889
0.0299	0.7595	0.1070118	0.9519769	0.0265518	0.2362048
0.0329	0.8357	0.1295154	1.1521689	0.0321354	0.2858765
0.0359	0.9119	0.1541736	1.3715283	0.0382536	0.340304
0.0418	1.0617	0.2091159	1.860295	0.0518859	0.4615769
0.0478	1.2141	0.2735145	2.4431849	0.0678645	0.6037225
0.0538	1.3665	0.3464118	3.0816793	0.0859518	0.7646272
0.0598	1.5189	0.4280472	3.8079078	0.1062072	0.9448192
0.0673	1.7094	0.5421213	4.822711	0.1345113	1.1966125
0.0747	1.8974	0.667926	5.9418696	0.165726	1.4742984
0.0897	2.2784	0.9631062	8.5677927	0.2389662	2.1258433
0.1046	2.6568	1.3096277	11.650536	0.3249477	2.8907347
0.1196	3.0378	1.7121888	15.231631	0.4248288	3.779277
0.1345	3.4163	2.165373	19.263158	0.537273	4.7795806
0.1494	3.7948	2.671704	23.767478	0.662904	5.8971939
0.1644	4.1758	3.2351319	28.779733	0.8027019	7.1408361
0.1793	4.5542	3.8481156	34.232836	0.9547956	8.4938616
0.1943	4.9352	4.518675	40.198132	1.121175	9.9739728
0.2092	5.3137	5.2385508	46.602147	1.2997908	11.562938
0.2242	5.6947	6.0167205	52.524745	1.4928705	13.280575
0.2391	6.0731	6.8431293	60.876478	1.6979193	15.10469

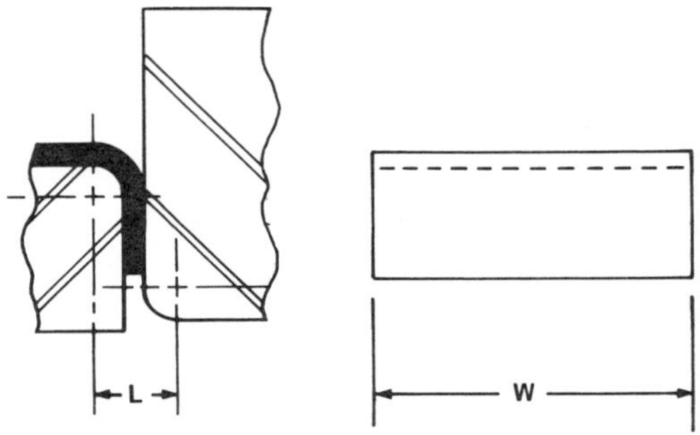

Fig. 3-1

Fig. 3-2

97

3–30. SAE 2330
TS = 105,000 psi

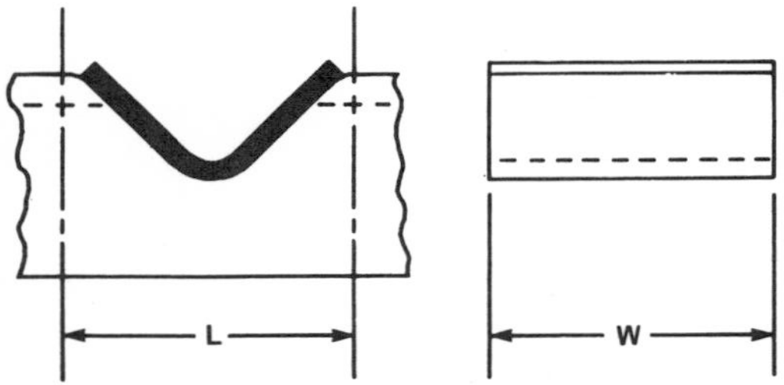

Bend Force = W/L times Force Factor

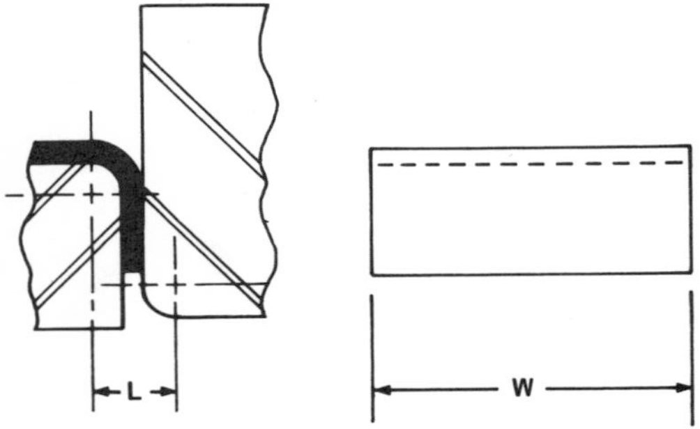

THICKNESS		V-BEND FORCE FACTORS		90° WIPE FORCE FACTORS	
inch	mm	To Obtain Tons	To Obtain kN	To Obtain Tons	To Obtain kN
0.0120	0.3048	0.0100548	0.0894475	0.0024948	0.0221937
0.0135	0.3429	0.0127081	0.1130512	0.0031531	0.0280499
0.0149	0.3785	0.0155011	0.1378977	0.0038461	0.0342149
0.0164	0.4166	0.0187131	0.1664717	0.0046431	0.041305
0.0179	0.4547	0.022344	0.1987722	0.005544	0.0493194
0.0209	0.5309	0.0304437	0.2708271	0.0075537	0.0671977
0.0239	0.6071	0.03987	0.3546835	0.0098925	0.0880036
0.0269	0.6833	0.0505533	0.4497221	0.0125433	0.1115851
0.0299	0.7595	0.0624235	0.5553194	0.0154885	0.1377856
0.0329	0.8357	0.0755506	0.6720981	0.0187456	0.1667608
0.0359	0.9119	0.0899346	0.8000582	0.0223146	0.1985106
0.0418	1.0617	0.1219842	1.0851714	0.0302667	0.2692525
0.0478	1.2141	0.1595011	1.4193576	0.0395876	0.3521712
0.0538	1.3665	0.2020735	1.7976458	0.0501385	0.446032
0.0598	1.5189	0.2496942	2.2212796	0.0619542	0.5511445
0.0673	1.7094	0.3162374	2.8132479	0.0784649	0.6980237
0.0747	1.8974	0.3896235	3.460906	0.0966735	0.8600074
0.0897	2.2784	0.5618119	4.9978786	0.1393969	1.240748
0.1046	2.6568	0.7639553	6.7961463	0.1895528	1.6862617
0.1196	3.0378	0.9987768	8.8851184	0.2478168	2.2045782
0.1345	3.4163	1.2631342	11.236841	0.3134092	2.7880882
0.1494	3.7948	1.558494	13.864362	0.386694	3.4400298
0.1644	4.1758	1.8871602	16.788177	0.4682427	4.165487
0.1793	4.5542	2.2447341	19.969154	0.5569641	4.9547526
0.1943	4.9352	2.6358937	23.44891	0.6540187	5.8181503
0.2092	5.3137	3.0558213	27.184586	0.7582113	6.7450477
0.2242	5.6947	3.5097536	31.222768	0.8708411	7.7470024
0.2391	6.0731	3.9918254	35.511278	0.9904529	8.8110689

Fig. 3-1

Fig. 3-2

3–31. SAE 3240 (HOT ROLLED, ANNEALED)
TS = 105,000 psi

Bend Force = W/L times Force Factor

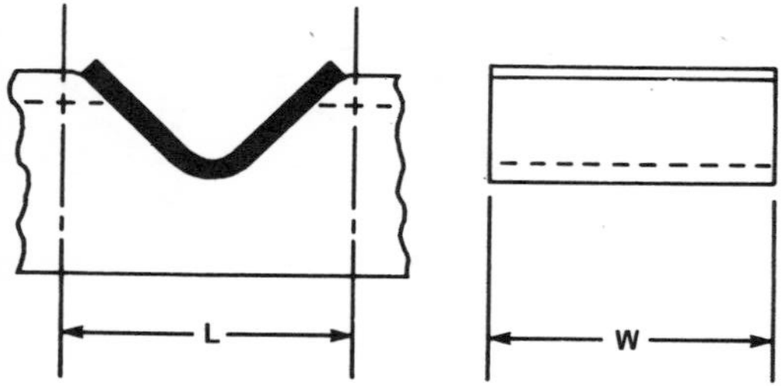

Fig. 3-1

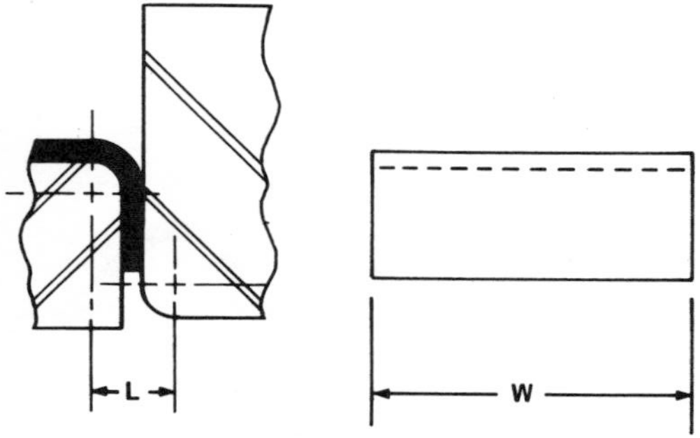

Fig. 3-2

THICKNESS *inch*	THICKNESS *mm*	V-BEND FORCE FACTORS *To Obtain Tons*	V-BEND FORCE FACTORS *To Obtain kN*	90° WIPE FORCE FACTORS *To Obtain Tons*	90° WIPE FORCE FACTORS *To Obtain kN*
0.0120	0.3048	0.0100548	0.894475	0.0024948	0.0221937
0.0135	0.3429	0.0127081	0.1130512	0.0031531	0.0380499
0.0149	0.3785	0.0155011	0.1378977	0.0038461	0.0342149
0.0164	0.4166	0.0187131	0.1664717	0.0046431	0.041305
0.0179	0.4547	0.022344	0.1987722	0.005544	0.0493194
0.0209	0.5309	0.0304437	0.2708271	0.0075537	0.0671977
0.0239	0.6071	0.03987	0.3546835	0.0098925	0.0880036
0.0269	0.6833	0.0505533	0.4497221	0.0125433	0.1115851
0.0299	0.7595	0.0624235	0.5553194	0.0154885	0.1377856
0.0329	0.8357	0.0755506	0.6720981	0.0187456	0.1667608
0.0359	0.9119	0.0899346	0.8000582	0.0223146	0.1985106
0.0418	1.0617	0.1219842	1.0851714	0.0302667	0.2692525
0.0478	1.2141	0.1595501	1.4193576	0.0395876	0.3521712
0.0538	1.3665	0.2020735	1.7976458	0.0501385	0.446032
0.0598	1.5189	0.2496942	2.2212796	0.0619542	0.5511445
0.0673	1.7094	0.3162374	2.8132479	0.0784649	0.6980237
0.0747	1.8974	0.3896235	3.4660906	0.0966735	0.8600074
0.0897	2.2784	0.5618119	4.9978786	0.1393969	1.2400748
0.1046	2.6568	0.7639553	6.7961463	0.1895528	1.6862617
0.1196	3.0378	0.9987768	8.8851184	0.2478168	2.2045782
0.1345	3.4163	1.2631342	11.236841	0.3134092	2.7880882
0.1494	3.7948	1.558494	13.864362	0.386694	3.4400298
0.1644	4.1758	1.8871602	16.788177	0.4682427	4.165487
0.1793	4.5542	2.2447341	19.969154	0.5569641	4.9547526
0.1943	4.9352	2.6358937	23.44891	0.6540187	5.8181503
0.2092	5.3137	3.0558213	27.184586	0.7582113	6.7450477
0.2242	5.6947	3.5097536	31.222768	0.8708411	7.7470024
0.2391	6.0731	3.9918254	35.511278	0.9904529	8.8110689

3-32. STEEL (0.10 CARBON)
TS = 60,000 psi

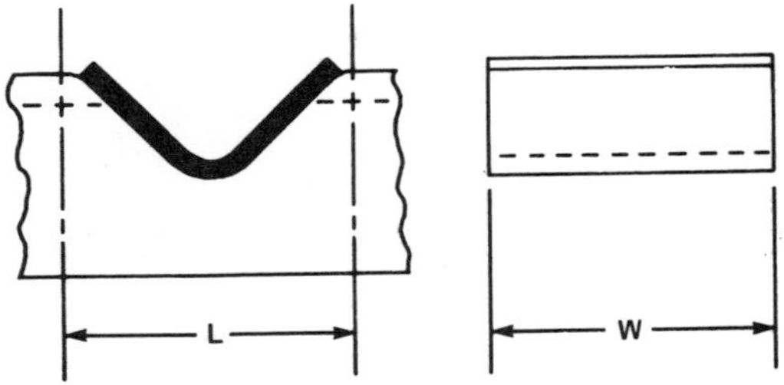

Bend Force = W/L times Force Factor

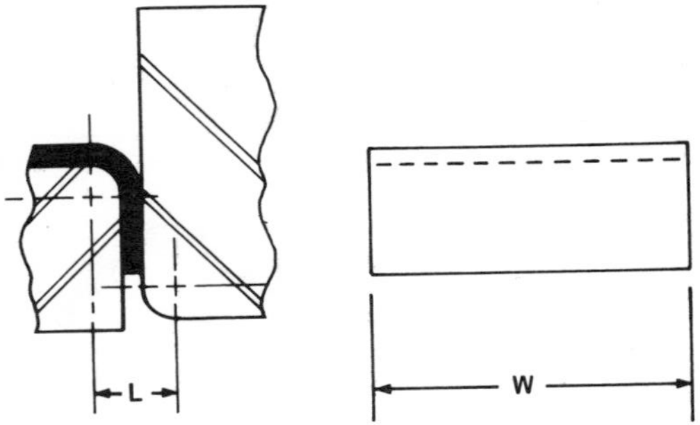

THICKNESS		V-BEND FORCE FACTORS		90° WIPE FORCE FACTORS	
inch	mm	To Obtain Tons	To Obtain kN	To Obtain Tons	To Obtain kN
0.0210	0.3048	0.0057456	0.0511128	0.0014256	0.0126821
0.0135	0.3429	0.0072618	0.0646009	0.0018018	0.0160288
0.0149	0.3785	0.0088578	0.0787989	0.0021978	0.0195516
0.0164	0.4166	0.0106932	0.0951267	0.0026532	0.0236028
0.0179	0.4547	0.012768	0.1135841	0.003168	0.0281825
0.0209	0.5309	0.0173964	0.1547583	0.0043164	0.0383986
0.0239	0.6071	0.0227829	0.2026766	0.0056529	0.0502881
0.0269	0.6833	0.028876	0.256984	0.0071676	0.0637629
0.0299	0.7595	0.0356706	0.3173256	0.0088506	0.0787349
0.0329	0.8357	0.431718	0.3840563	0.0107118	0.0952921
0.0359	0.9119	0.0513912	0.4571761	0.0127512	0.1134346
0.0418	1.0617	0.0697053	0.6200983	0.0172953	0.1538589
0.0478	1.2141	0.0911715	0.8110616	0.0226215	0.2012408
0.0538	1.3665	0.1154706	1.0272264	0.0286506	0.2548757
0.0598	1.5189	0.1426824	1.2693026	0.0354024	0.3149397
0.0673	1.7094	0.1807071	1.6075703	0.0448371	0.3998708
0.0747	1.8974	0.222642	1.9806232	0.055242	0.4914328
0.0897	2.2784	0.3210354	2.8559309	0.0796554	0.7086144
0.1046	2.6568	0.4365459	3.8835123	0.1083159	0.9635782
0.1196	3.0378	0.5707296	5.0772105	0.1416096	1.259759
0.1345	3.4163	0.721791	6.4210527	0.179091	1.5931935
0.1494	3.7948	0.890568	7.9924929	0.220968	1.9657313
0.1644	4.1758	1.0783773	9.5932444	0.2675673	2.3802787
0.1793	4.5542	1.2827052	11.410945	0.3182652	2.8312872
0.1943	4.9352	1.506225	13.399377	0.373725	3.3246576
0.2092	5.3137	1.7461836	15.534049	0.4332636	3.8543129
0.2242	5.6947	2.0055735	17.841581	0.4976235	4.4268586
0.2391	6.0731	2.2810431	20.292159	0.5659731	5.0348966

Fig. 3-1

Fig. 3-2

3-33. STEEL (0.25 CARBON) TS = 70,000 psi	Bend Force = W/L times Force Factor				
THICKNESS		V-BEND FORCE FACTORS		90° WIPE FORCE FACTORS	
inch	mm	To Obtain Tons	To Obtain kN	To Obtain Tons	To Obtain kN
0.0120	0.3048	0.0067032	0.0596316	0.0016635	0.0147984
0.0135	0.3429	0.0084721	0.0753678	0.0021021	0.0187002
0.0149	0.3785	0.0103341	0.0919321	0.0025641	0.0228102
0.0164	0.4166	0.0124754	0.1109811	0.0030954	0.0275366
0.0179	0.4547	0.014896	0.1325148	0.003696	0.0328796
0.0209	0.5309	0.020958	0.1805514	0.0050358	0.0447984
0.0239	0.6071	0.02658	0.2364556	0.006595	0.0586691
0.0269	0.6833	0.0337022	0.2998147	0.0083622	0.0743901
0.0299	0.7595	0.0416157	0.3702132	0.0103257	0.0918574
0.0329	0.8357	0.0503671	0.4480657	0.0124971	0.1111742
0.0359	0.9119	0.0599564	0.5333721	0.0148764	0.1323404
0.0418	1.0617	0.0813228	0.7234476	0.0201778	0.1795017
0.0478	1.2141	0.1063667	0.9462381	0.026917	0.2347805
0.0538	1.3665	0.1347157	1.1984308	0.0334257	0.297355
0.0598	1.5189	0.1664628	1.480853	0.0413028	0.3674297
0.0673	1.7094	0.2061699	1.8340874	0.0523099	0.4653488
0.0747	1.8974	0.259749	2.3107271	0.064449	0.5733383
0.0897	2.2784	0.3745413	3.3319194	0.0929313	0.8267168
0.1046	2.6568	0.5093035	4.5307639	0.1263685	1.1241741
0.1196	3.0378	0.6658512	5.9234122	0.1652112	1.4697188
0.1345	3.4163	0.8420895	7.4912281	0.2089395	1.8587257
0.1494	3.7948	1.038996	9.2429084	0.257796	2.2933532
0.1644	4.1758	1.2581068	11.192118	0.3121618	2.7769913
0.1793	4.5542	1.4964894	13.312769	0.3713094	3.3031684
0.1943	4.9352	1.7572625	15.632607	0.4360125	3.8787672
0.2092	5.3137	2.0372142	18.123047	0.5054742	4.4966984
0.2242	5.6947	2.3398357	20.815178	0.5805607	5.1646679
0.2391	6.0731	2.6612169	23.674185	0.6603019	5.8740457

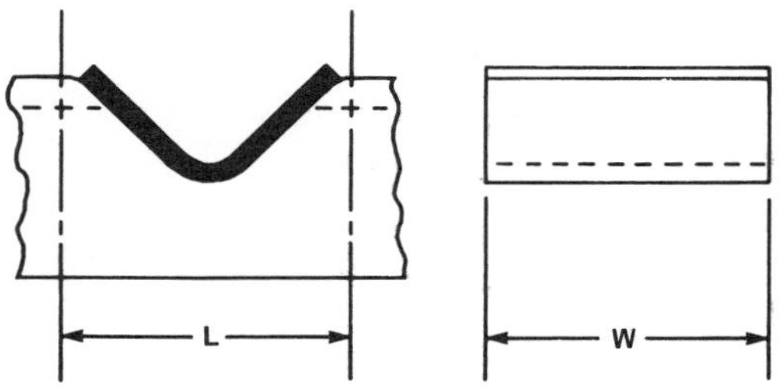

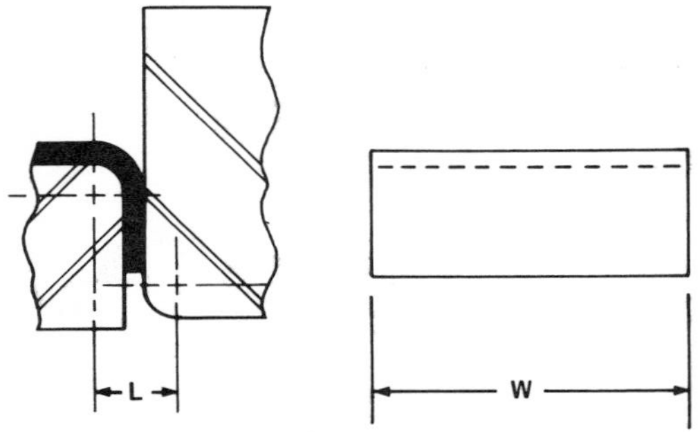

Fig. 3-1

Fig. 3-2

3–34. STEEL (0.5 CARBON)
TS = 95,000 psi

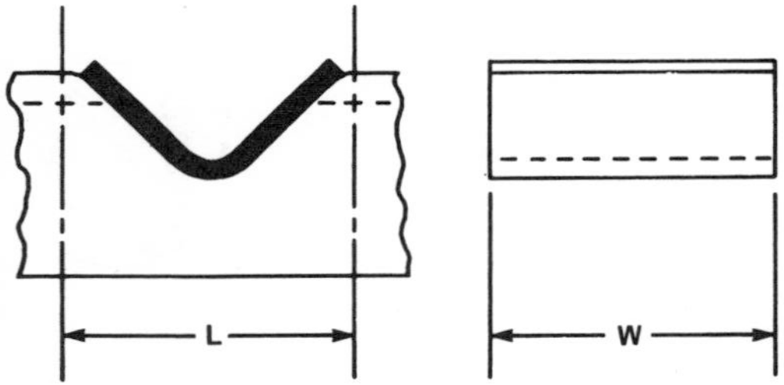

Fig. 3-1

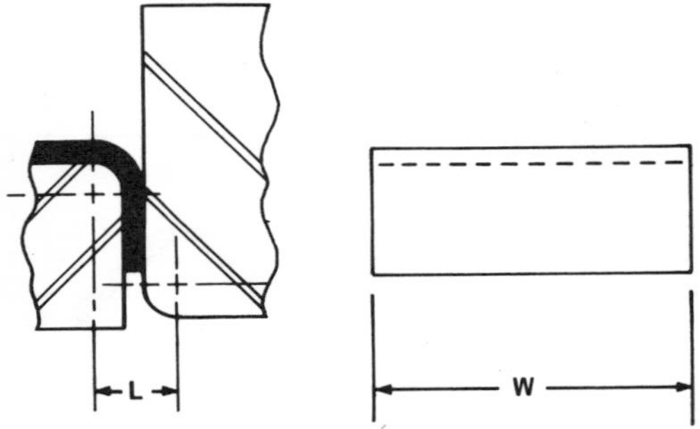

Fig. 3-2

Bend Force = W/L times Force Factor

THICKNESS inch	THICKNESS mm	V-BEND FORCE FACTORS To Obtain Tons	V-BEND FORCE FACTORS To Obtain kN	90° WIPE FORCE FACTORS To Obtain Tons	90° WIPE FORCE FACTORS To Obtain kN
0.0120	0.3048	0.0090972	0.0809286	0.0022572	0.02008
0.0135	0.3429	0.0114978	0.1022844	0.0028528	0.0253785
0.0149	0.3785	0.0140248	0.1247646	0.0034798	0.0309563
0.0164	0.4166	0.0169309	0.1506172	0.0042009	0.0373712
0.0179	0.4547	0.020216	0.1798415	0.005016	0.0446223
0.0209	0.5309	0.0275443	0.345034	0.0068343	0.0607979
0.0239	0.6071	0.0360729	0.3209045	0.0089504	0.0796227
0.0269	0.6833	0.0457387	0.4068914	0.0113487	0.100958
0.0299	0.7595	0.0564784	0.5024318	0.0140134	0.1246632
0.0329	0.8357	0.0683553	0.6080887	0.0169603	0.1508788
0.0359	0.9119	0.0813694	0.7238621	0.0201894	0.1796049
0.0418	1.0617	0.1103667	0.9818221	0.0273842	0.2436098
0.0478	1.2141	0.1443548	1.2841803	0.0358173	0.3186307
0.0538	1.3665	0.1828284	1.6264414	0.0453634	0.4035528
0.0598	1.5189	0.2259138	2.0097291	0.0560538	0.4986546
0.0673	1.7094	0.2861195	2.545319	0.070992	0.6315448
0.0747	1.8974	0.3525165	3.1359867	0.0874665	0.7781019
0.0897	2.2784	0.508306	4.5218901	0.126121	1.1219724
0.1046	2.6568	0.6911976	6.1488938	0.1715001	1.5256648
0.1196	3.0378	0.9036552	8.0390056	0.2242152	1.9946184
0.1345	3.4163	1.1428357	10.166666	0.2835607	2.5225559
0.1494	3.7948	1.410066	12.543947	0.349866	3.1124079
0.1644	4.1758	1.7074307	15.189303	0.4236482	3.7687742
0.1793	4.5542	2.0309499	18.06733	0.5039199	4.4828714
0.1943	4.9352	2.3848562	21.21568	0.5917312	5.2640407
0.2092	5.3137	2.7647907	24.595578	0.6860007	6.1026622
0.2242	5.6947	3.1754913	28.24917	0.7879038	7.0091922
0.2391	6.0731	3.6116515	32.129251	0.896124	7.9719191

3-35. STEEL, STAINLESS (LOW CARBON DRAWING)   TS = 80,000 psi

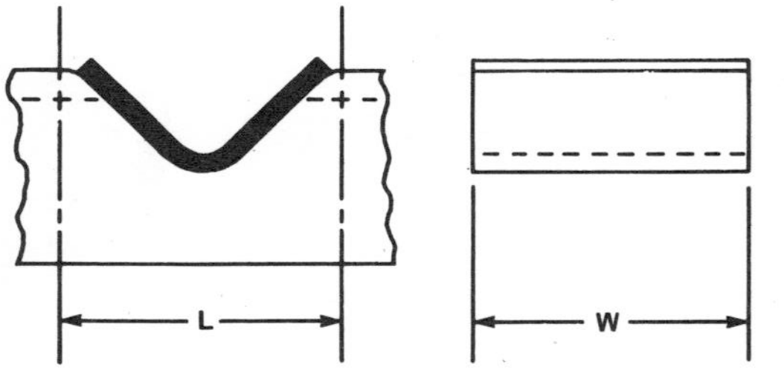

Bend Force = W/L times Force Factor

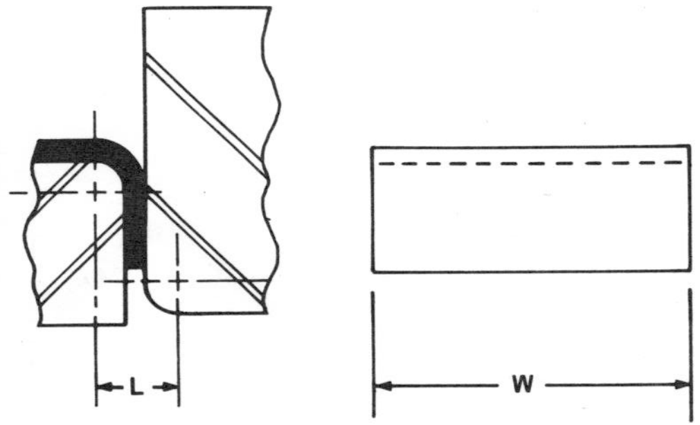

THICKNESS		V-BEND FORCE FACTORS		90° WIPE FORCE FACTORS	
inch	mm	To Obtain Tons	To Obtain kN	To Obtain Tons	To Obtain kN
0.0120	0.3048	0.0076608	0.0681504	0.0019008	0.0169095
0.0135	0.3429	0.0096824	0.0861346	0.0024024	0.0213717
0.0149	0.3785	0.0118104	0.1050653	0.0029304	0.0260689
0.0164	0.4166	0.0142576	0.1268356	0.0035376	0.0314704
0.0179	0.4547	0.017024	0.1514455	0.004224	0.0375767
0.0209	0.5309	0.0231952	0.2063444	0.0057552	0.0511982
0.0239	0.6071	0.0303772	0.2737477	0.0075372	0.0670509
0.0269	0.6833	0.0385168	0.3426454	0.0095568	0.0850172
0.0299	0.7595	0.0475608	0.4231008	0.0118008	0.1049799
0.0329	0.8357	0.0575624	0.5120751	0.0142824	0.1270562
0.0359	0.9119	0.0685216	0.6095681	0.0170016	0.1512462
0.0418	1.0617	0.0929404	0.8367977	0.0230604	0.2051453
0.0478	1.2141	0.121562	1.0814155	0.030162	0.2683211
0.0538	1.3665	0.1539608	1.3696352	0.0382008	0.3398343
0.0598	1.5189	0.1902432	1.6924035	0.0472032	0.4199196
0.0673	1.7094	0.2409428	2.1434271	0.0597828	0.5318277
0.0747	1.8974	0.296856	2.6408309	0.073656	0.6552437
0.0897	2.2784	0.4280472	3.8079078	0.1062072	0.9448192
0.1046	2.6568	0.5820612	5.1780164	0.1444212	1.2847709
0.1196	3.0378	0.7609728	6.769614	0.1888128	1.6796786
0.1345	3.4163	0.962388	8.5614036	0.238788	2.124258
0.1494	3.7948	1.187424	10.563323	0.294624	2.6209751
0.1644	4.1758	1.4378364	12.790992	0.3567564	3.1737049
0.1793	4.5542	1.7202736	15.214593	0.4243536	3.7750496
0.1943	4.9352	2.0083	17.865836	0.4983	4.4318768
0.2092	5.3137	2.3282448	20.712065	0.5776848	5.1390839
0.2242	5.6947	2.674098	23.788775	0.663498	5.9024782
0.2391	6.0731	3.0413908	27.056212	0.7546308	6.6131955

Fig. 3-1

Fig. 3-2

3-36. STEEL, STAINLESS (18-8)
TS = 95,000 psi

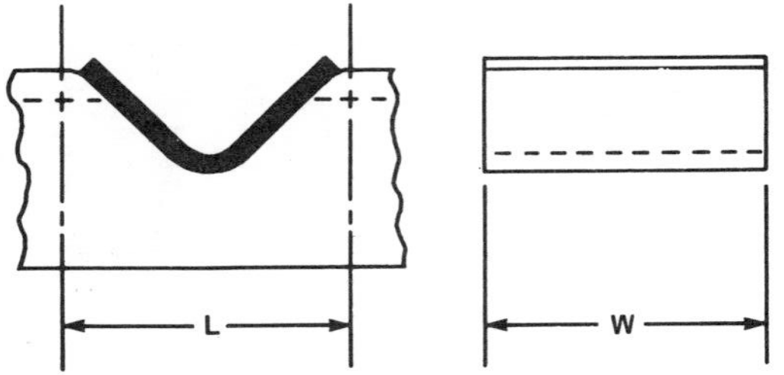

Bend Force = W/L times Force Factor

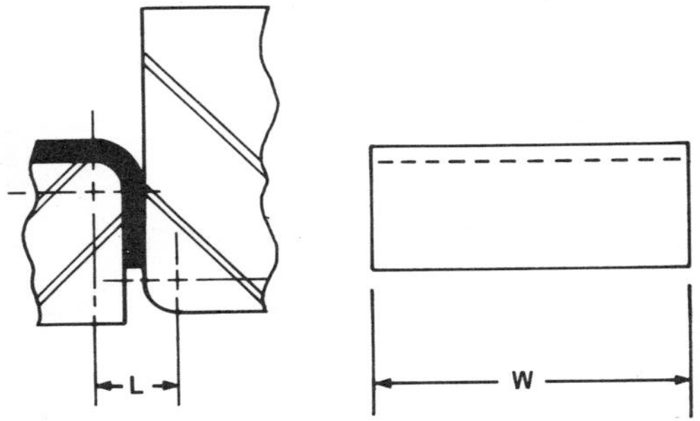

THICKNESS		V-BEND FORCE FACTORS		90° WIPE FORCE FACTORS	
inch	mm	To Obtain Tons	To Obtain kN	To Obtain Tons	To Obtain kN
0.0120	0.3048	0.0090972	0.0809286	0.0022572	0.02008
0.0135	0.3429	0.0114978	0.1022844	0.0028528	0.0253785
0.0149	0.3785	0.0140248	0.1247646	0.0034798	0.0309563
0.0164	0.4166	0.0169309	0.1506172	0.0042009	0.0373712
0.0179	0.4547	0.020216	0.1798415	0.005016	0.0446223
0.0209	0.5309	0.0275443	0.245034	0.0068343	0.0607979
0.0239	0.6071	0.0360729	0.3209045	0.0089504	0.0796227
0.0269	0.6833	0.0457387	0.4068914	0.0113487	0.11875
0.0299	0.7595	0.0564784	0.5024318	0.0140134	0.1246632
0.0329	0.8357	0.0683553	0.6080887	0.0169603	0.1508788
0.0359	0.9119	0.0813694	0.7238621	0.0201894	0.1796049
0.0481	1.0617	0.1103667	0.9818221	0.0273842	0.2436098
0.0478	1.2141	0.1443548	1.2841803	0.0358173	0.3186307
0.0538	1.3665	0.1828284	1.6264414	0.0453634	0.4035528
0.0598	1.5189	0.2259138	2.0097291	0.0560538	0.4986546
0.0673	1.7094	0.2861195	2.545319	0.070992	0.6315448
0.0747	1.8974	0.3525165	3.1359867	0.0874665	0.7781019
0.0897	2.2784	0.508306	4.5218901	0.126121	1.1219724
0.1046	2.6568	0.6911976	6.1488938	0.1715001	1.5256648
0.1196	3.0378	0.9036552	8.0389166	0.2242152	1.9946184
0.1345	3.4163	1.1428357	10.166666	0.2835607	2.5525559
0.1494	3.7948	1.410066	12.543947	0.349866	3.1124079
0.1644	4.1758	1.7074307	15.189303	0.4236482	3.7687743
0.1793	4.5542	2.0309499	18.06733	0.5039199	4.4828714
0.1943	4.9352	2.3848562	21.21568	0.5917312	5.2640407
0.2092	5.3137	2.7647907	24.595578	0.6860007	6.1026622
0.2242	5.6947	3.1754913	28.24917	0.7879038	7.0091922
0.2391	6.0731	3.6116515	32.129251	0.896124	7.9719191

Fig. 3-1

Fig. 3-2

3–37. TIN
TS = 5000 psi

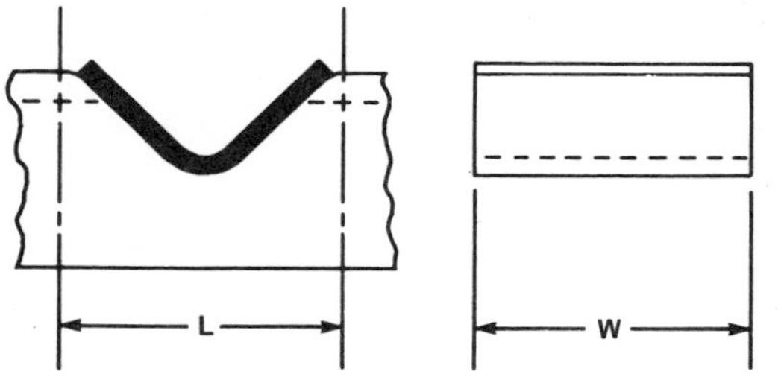

Fig. 3-1

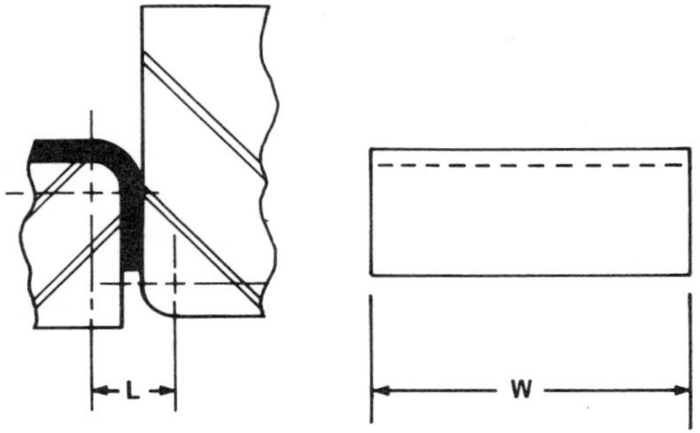

Fig. 3-2

Bend Force = W/L times Force Factor

THICKNESS inch	THICKNESS mm	V-BEND FORCE FACTORS To Obtain Tons	V-BEND FORCE FACTORS To Obtain kN	90° WIPE FORCE FACTORS To Obtain Tons	90° WIPE FORCE FACTORS To Obtain kN
0.0120	0.3048	0.0004788	0.0042594	0.0001188	0.0010568
0.0135	0.3429	0.0006051	0.0053829	0.0001501	0.0013352
0.0149	0.3785	0.0007381	0.0065661	0.0001831	0.0016288
0.0164	0.4166	0.0008911	0.0079272	0.0002211	0.0019669
0.0179	0.4547	0.001064	0.0094653	0.000264	0.0023485
0.0209	0.5309	0.0014497	0.0128965	0.0003597	0.0031998
0.0239	0.6071	0.0018985	0.016889	0.00471	0.00419
0.0269	0.6833	0.0024073	0.0214153	0.0005973	0.0053135
0.0299	0.7595	0.0029725	0.0264433	0.0007375	0.0065608
0.0329	0.8357	0.0035976	0.0320042	0.0008926	0.0079405
0.0359	0.9119	0.0024826	0.038098	0.0010626	0.0094528
0.0418	1.0617	0.0058087	0.0516741	0.0014412	0.0128209
0.0478	1.2141	0.0075976	0.0675882	0.0018851	0.1067698
0.0538	1.3665	0.0096225	0.0856017	0.0023875	0.0212392
0.0598	1.5189	0.0118902	0.1057752	0.0029502	0.0262449
0.0673	1.7094	0.0150589	0.1339639	0.0037364	0.033239
0.0747	1.8974	0.185535	0.1650519	0.0046035	0.0409527
0.0897	2.2784	0.0267529	0.2379937	0.0066379	0.0590507
0.1046	2.6568	0.0363788	0.3236258	0.0092063	0.0802979
0.1196	3.0378	0.0475608	0.4231008	0.0118008	0.1049799
0.1345	3.4163	0.0601492	0.5350872	0.0149242	0.1327656
0.1494	3.7948	0.074214	0.6602077	0.018414	0.1638109
0.1644	4.1758	0.0898647	0.7994363	0.0222972	0.1983558
0.1793	4.5542	0.1068921	0.9509121	0.0265221	0.2359406
0.1943	4.9352	0.1255187	1.1166143	0.0311437	0.2770543
0.2092	5.3137	0.1455153	1.2945041	0.0361053	0.3211927
0.2242	5.6947	0.1671311	1.4867982	0.0414686	0.3689046
0.2391	6.0731	0.1900869	1.691013	0.0471644	0.4195745

3-38. ZINC
TS = 24,000 psi

Bend Force = W/L times Force Factor

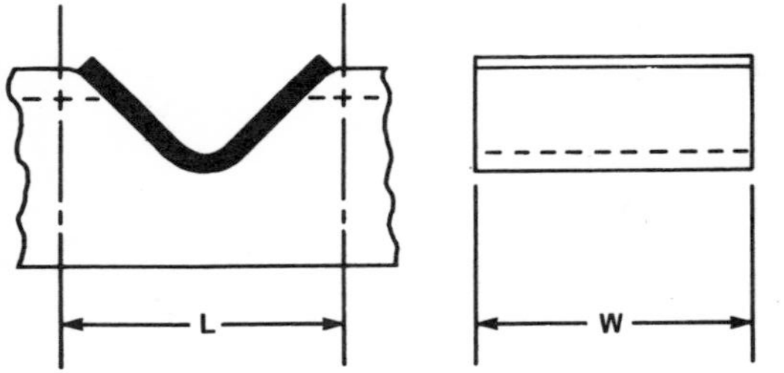

THICKNESS inch	mm	V-BEND FORCE FACTORS To Obtain Tons	To Obtain kN	90° WIPE FORCE FACTORS To Obtain Tons	To Obtain kN
0.0120	0.3048	0.0022982	0.0204447	0.0005702	0.0050724
0.0135	0.3429	0.0029047	0.0258402	0.0007207	0.0064113
0.0149	0.3785	0.0035431	0.0315194	0.0008791	0.0078204
0.0164	0.4166	0.0042772	0.0380499	0.0010612	0.0094404
0.0179	0.4547	0.0051072	0.0454336	0.0012672	0.011273
0.0209	0.5309	0.0069585	0.0619028	0.0017265	0.0153589
0.0239	0.6071	0.0091131	0.0810701	0.0022611	0.0201147
0.0269	0.6833	0.011555	0.1027932	0.002867	0.0255048
0.0299	0.7595	0.0142682	0.1269299	0.0035402	0.0314936
0.0329	0.8357	0.0172687	0.1536223	0.0042847	0.0381166
0.0359	0.9119	0.0205564	0.1828697	0.0051004	0.0453731
0.0418	1.0617	0.0278821	0.2480391	0.0069181	0.0615434
0.0478	1.2141	0.0364686	0.3244246	0.0090486	0.0894963
0.0538	1.3665	0.0461882	0.4108902	0.0114602	0.1019499
0.0598	1.5189	0.0570729	0.5077205	0.0141609	0.1259753
0.0673	1.7094	0.0722828	0.6430277	0.0179348	0.1595479
0.0747	1.8974	0.0890568	0.7922492	0.0220968	0.1965731
0.0897	2.2784	0.1284141	1.1423718	0.0318621	0.2834452
0.1046	2.6568	0.1746183	1.5534043	0.0443263	0.3854307
0.1196	3.0378	0.2282918	2.0308838	0.0566438	0.5039032
0.1345	3.4163	0.2887164	2.568421	0.716364	0.6372774
0.1494	3.7948	0.3562272	3.1689971	0.0883872	0.7862925
0.1644	4.1758	0.4313509	3.8372976	0.1070269	0.9521113
0.1793	4.5542	0.513082	4.5643774	0.127306	1.1325141
0.1943	4.9352	0.60249	5.359751	0.14949	1.329863
0.2092	5.3137	0.6984734	6.2136193	0.1733054	1.5417248
0.2242	5.6947	0.8022294	7.1366327	0.1990494	1.7707434
0.2391	6.0731	0.9124172	8.1168634	0.2263892	2.0139583

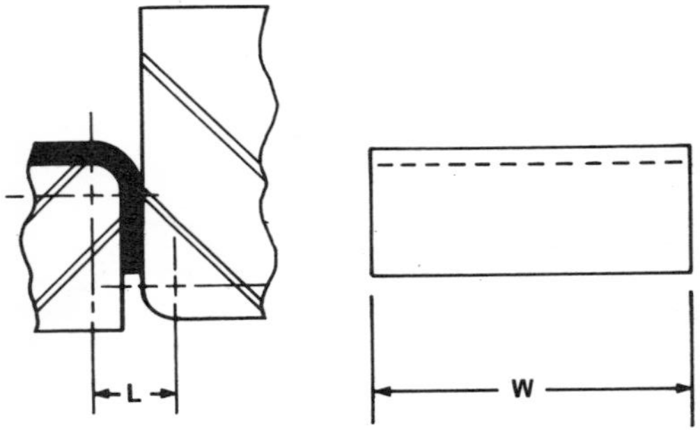

Fig. 3-1

Fig. 3-2

Draw Die Equations

THE DRAW DIE EQUATIONS

Figures 4–1 through 4–32 represent sectional views of standard cylindrical forms. The accompanying equations are developed on the basis of areas.

Since the draw operation is subject to numerous variables, the formulas accompanying these drawings should be used as a guide only. They are extremely well suited to the development of blanks for die engineering purposes, but they should not be relied upon too heavily in the die shop. In other words, the designer and diemaker alike should use them to lay out the initial blank in the process of blank development. These blanks should then be put through the various draw stages to determine whether corrections are needed.

It is of special importance that the blanking section of a progressive die remain the *last* station to be built. To rely on these equations—or any equations—in the blanking station of a close tolerance progressive die is to court disaster.

At the same time, it should be noted that the die engineer will find these equations extremely helpful in the design of blanking dies or blanking stations in progressive work. The rule to follow is *to not dimension* the blanking station. Leave that assignment for the men in the shop.

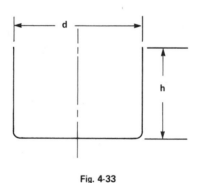

Fig. 4-33

Figure 4–33, shown above, represents the centerline of the basic drawn shell. Its equation is as follows:

$$D = \sqrt{d^2 + 4dh}$$

This equation is approximate and does not consider such factors as stretch and draw radii. The corners are sharp.

Table 4–1 provides answers to this equation in metric units.

Table 4–1A provides answer in standard inch units.

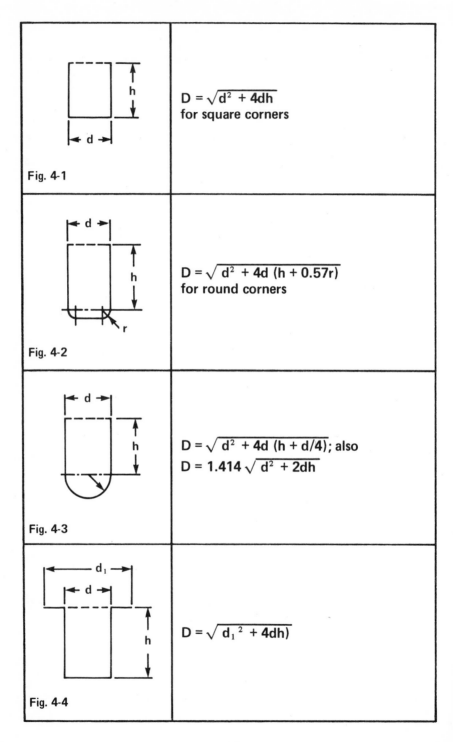

$D = \sqrt{d^2 + 4dh}$
for square corners

Fig. 4-1

$D = \sqrt{d^2 + 4d\,(h + 0.57r)}$
for round corners

Fig. 4-2

$D = \sqrt{d^2 + 4d\,(h + d/4)}$; also
$D = 1.414\sqrt{d^2 + 2dh}$

Fig. 4-3

$D = \sqrt{d_1{}^2 + 4dh)}$

Fig. 4-4

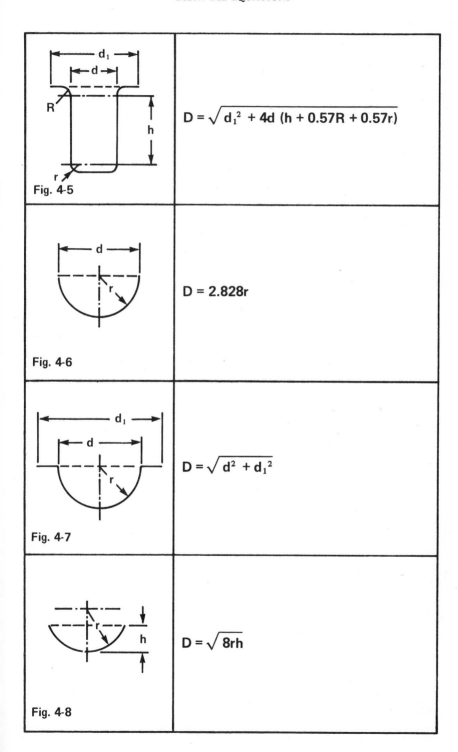

Fig. 4-5

$$D = \sqrt{d_1{}^2 + 4d\,(h + 0.57R + 0.57r)}$$

Fig. 4-6

$$D = 2.828r$$

Fig. 4-7

$$D = \sqrt{d^2 + d_1{}^2}$$

Fig. 4-8

$$D = \sqrt{8rh}$$

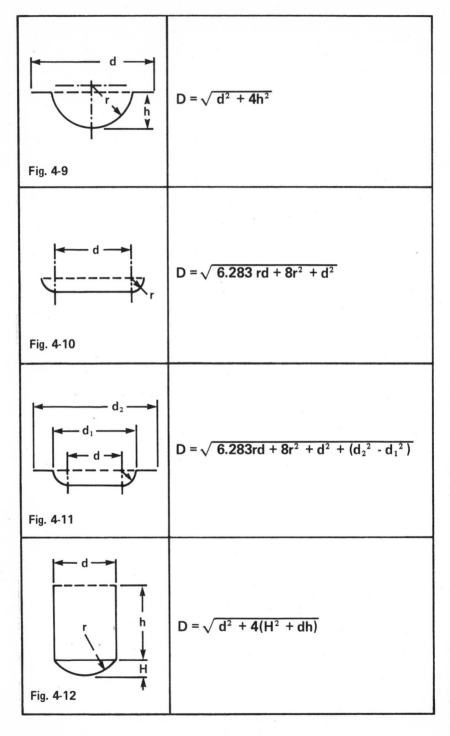

Fig. 4-9

$$D = \sqrt{d^2 + 4h^2}$$

Fig. 4-10

$$D = \sqrt{6.283\ rd + 8r^2 + d^2}$$

Fig. 4-11

$$D = \sqrt{6.283rd + 8r^2 + d^2 + (d_2{}^2 - d_1{}^2)}$$

Fig. 4-12

$$D = \sqrt{d^2 + 4(H^2 + dh)}$$

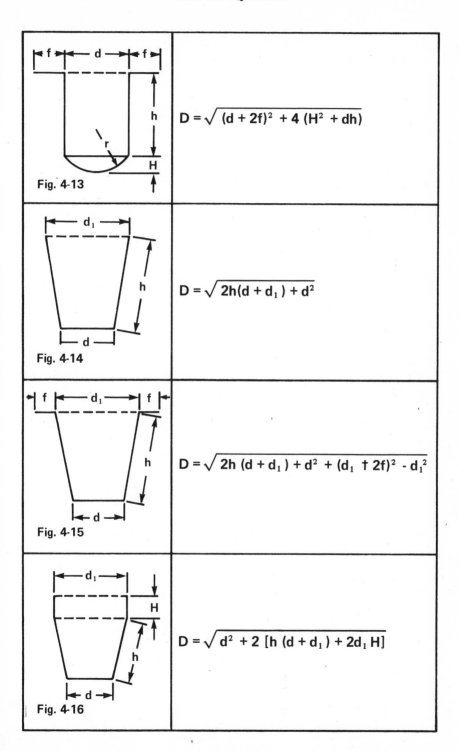

Fig. 4-13

$$D = \sqrt{(d + 2f)^2 + 4(H^2 + dh)}$$

Fig. 4-14

$$D = \sqrt{2h(d + d_1) + d^2}$$

Fig. 4-15

$$D = \sqrt{2h(d + d_1) + d^2 + (d_1 \dagger 2f)^2 - d_1^2}$$

Fig. 4-16

$$D = \sqrt{d^2 + 2[h(d + d_1) + 2d_1 H]}$$

111

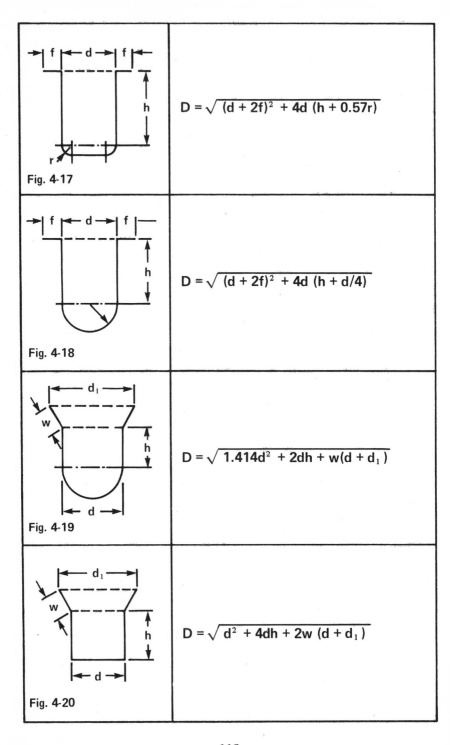

Fig. 4-17
$$D = \sqrt{(d + 2f)^2 + 4d(h + 0.57r)}$$

Fig. 4-18
$$D = \sqrt{(d + 2f)^2 + 4d(h + d/4)}$$

Fig. 4-19
$$D = \sqrt{1.414d^2 + 2dh + w(d + d_1)}$$

Fig. 4-20
$$D = \sqrt{d^2 + 4dh + 2w(d + d_1)}$$

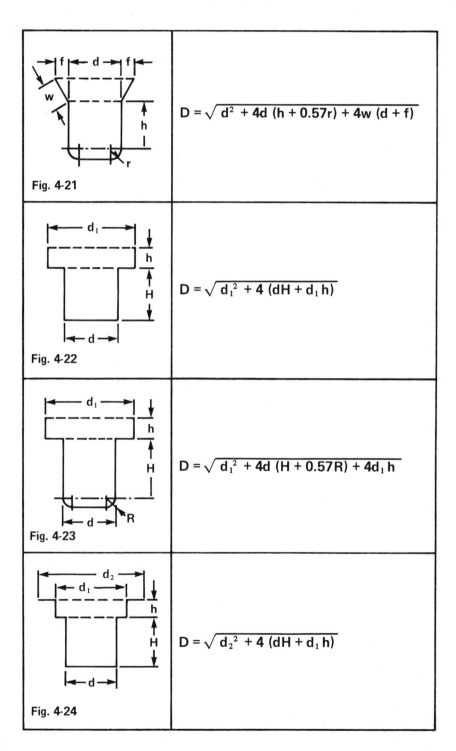

Fig. 4-21

$$D = \sqrt{d^2 + 4d\,(h + 0.57r) + 4w\,(d + f)}$$

Fig. 4-22

$$D = \sqrt{d_1^{\,2} + 4\,(dH + d_1 h)}$$

Fig. 4-23

$$D = \sqrt{d_1^{\,2} + 4d\,(H + 0.57R) + 4d_1 h}$$

Fig. 4-24

$$D = \sqrt{d_2^{\,2} + 4\,(dH + d_1 h)}$$

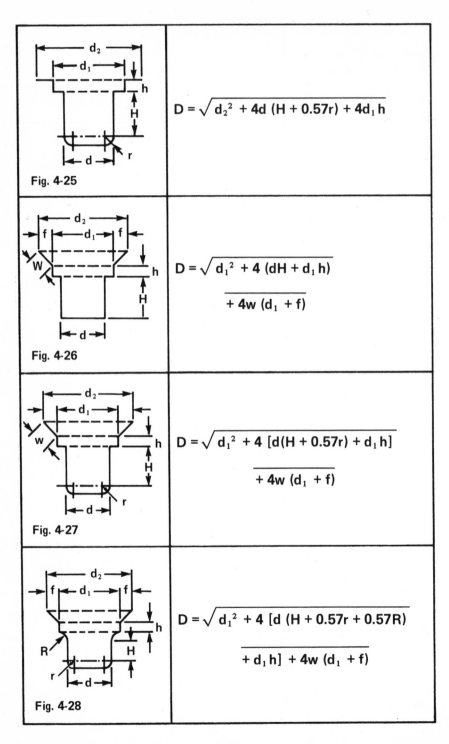

Fig. 4-25

$$D = \sqrt{d_2^2 + 4d\,(H + 0.57r) + 4d_1 h}$$

Fig. 4-26

$$D = \sqrt{d_1^2 + 4\,(dH + d_1 h)} \; \overline{+ 4w\,(d_1 + f)}$$

Fig. 4-27

$$D = \sqrt{d_1^2 + 4\,[d(H + 0.57r) + d_1 h]} \; \overline{+ 4w\,(d_1 + f)}$$

Fig. 4-28

$$D = \sqrt{d_1^2 + 4\,[d\,(H + 0.57r + 0.57R)} \; \overline{+ d_1 h] + 4w\,(d_1 + f)}$$

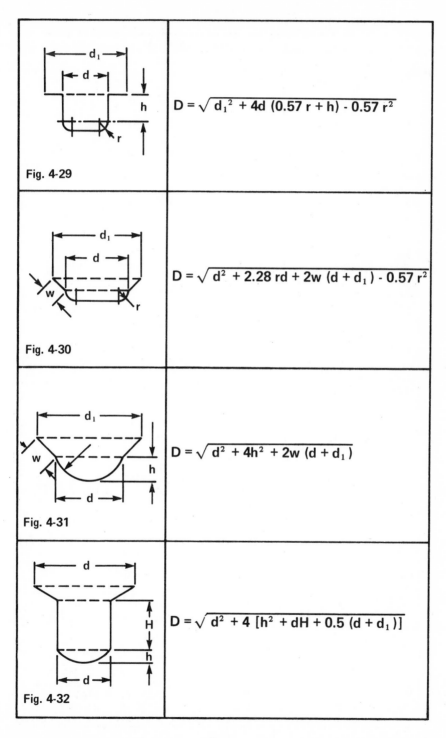

Fig. 4-29

$$D = \sqrt{d_1^2 + 4d\,(0.57\,r + h) - 0.57\,r^2}$$

Fig. 4-30

$$D = \sqrt{d^2 + 2.28\,rd + 2w\,(d + d_1) - 0.57\,r^2}$$

Fig. 4-31

$$D = \sqrt{d^2 + 4h^2 + 2w\,(d + d_1)}$$

Fig. 4-32

$$D = \sqrt{d^2 + 4\,[h^2 + dH + 0.5\,(d + d_1)]}$$

Table 4–1.   Metric Solutions for Diameter D in $D = \sqrt{d^2 + 4dh}$.

Shell Diam. (d)	Height of Shell (h)						
	10	15	20	25	30	35	40
6	16.61	19.90	22.72	25.22	27.50	29.60	31.56
9	21.00	24.92	28.30	31.32	34.07	36.62	39.00
12	24.98	29.39	33.23	36.66	39.80	42.71	45.43
15	28.72	33.54	37.75	41.54	45.00	48.22	51.23
18	32.31	37.47	42.00	46.09	49.84	53.33	56.60
21	35.79	41.24	46.05	50.41	54.42	58.15	61.65
24	39.19	44.90	49.96	54.55	58.79	62.74	66.45
27	42.54	48.47	53.75	58.56	63.00	67.15	71.06
30	45.83	51.96	57.45	62.45	67.08	71.41	75.50
33	49.08	55.40	61.07	66.25	71.06	75.56	79.81
36	52.31	58.79	64.62	69.97	74.94	79.60	84.00
39	55.51	62.14	68.12	73.63	78.75	83.55	88.10
42	58.69	65.45	71.58	77.23	82.49	87.43	92.11
45	61.85	68.74	75.00	80.78	86.17	91.24	96.05
48	64.99	72.00	78.38	94.29	89.80	94.99	99.92
51	68.12	75.24	81.74	87.76	93.39	98.70	103.74
54	71.25	78.46	85.06	91.19	96.93	102.35	107.50
57	74.36	81.66	88.37	94.60	100.44	105.97	111.22
60	77.46	84.85	91.65	97.98	103.92	109.54	114.89
63	80.55	88.03	94.92	101.34	107.37	113.09	118.53
66	83.64	91.19	98.16	104.67	110.80	116.60	122.13
69	86.72	94.35	101.40	107.99	114.20	120.09	125.70
72	89.80	97.49	104.61	111.28	117.58	123.55	129.24
75	92.87	100.62	107.82	114.56	120.93	126.98	132.76
78	95.94	103.75	111.01	117.83	124.27	130.40	136.25
81	99.00	106.87	114.20	121.08	127.60	133.79	139.72
84	102.06	109.98	117.37	124.33	130.90	137.17	143.16
87	105.11	113.09	120.54	127.55	134.20	140.53	146.59
90	108.17	116.19	123.69	130.77	137.48	143.87	150.00
93	111.22	119.29	126.84	133.97	140.74	147.20	153.39
96	114.26	122.38	129.98	137.17	144.00	150.52	156.77
99	117.30	125.46	133.12	140.36	147.24	153.82	160.13
102	120.35	128.55	136.25	143.54	150.48	157.11	163.47
107	125.42	133.67	141.45	148.83	155.85	162.57	169.02
110	128.45	136.75	144.57	151.99	159.06	165.83	172.34
115	133.51	141.86	149.75	157.24	164.39	171.25	177.83
120	138.56	146.97	154.92	162.48	169.71	176.64	183.30
125	143.61	152.07	160.08	167.71	175.00	182.00	188.74
130	148.66	157.16	165.23	172.92	180.28	187.35	194.16
135	153.70	162.25	170.37	178.12	185.54	192.68	199.56
140	158.75	167.33	175.50	183.30	190.79	197.99	204.94
145	163.78	172.41	180.62	188.48	196.02	203.29	210.30
150	168.82	177.48	185.74	192.65	201.25	208.57	215.64
155	173.85	182.55	190.85	198.81	206.46	213.83	220.96
160	178.89	187.62	195.96	203.96	211.66	219.09	226.27
165	183.92	192.68	201.06	209.11	216.85	224.33	231.57
170	188.94	197.74	206.16	214.24	222.04	229.56	236.85
175	193.97	202.79	211.25	219.37	227.21	234.79	242.13
180	199.00	207.85	216.33	224.50	232.38	240.00	247.39
185	204.02	212.90	221.42	229.62	237.54	245.20	252.64

Table 4–1. Metric Solutions for Diameter D in $D = \sqrt{d^2 + 4dh}$ *(Continued).*

Shell Diam. (d)	Height of Shell (h)						
	45	50	55	60	65	70	75
6	33.41	35.16	36.82	38.40	39.95	41.42	42.85
9	41.24	43.37	45.40	47.34	49.20	51.00	52.74
12	48.00	50.44	52.76	54.99	57.13	59.20	61.19
15	54.08	56.79	59.37	61.85	64.23	66.52	68.74
18	59.70	62.64	65.45	68.15	70.74	73.24	75.66
21	64.97	68.12	71.14	74.03	76.82	79.50	82.10
24	69.97	73.32	76.52	79.60	82.56	85.42	88.18
27	74.76	78.29	81.66	84.91	88.03	91.04	93.96
30	79.37	83.07	86.60	90.00	93.27	96.44	99.50
33	83.84	87.69	91.37	94.92	98.33	101.63	104.83
36	88.18	92.17	96.00	99.68	103.23	106.66	109.98
39	92.42	96.55	100.50	104.31	107.99	111.40	114.98
42	96.56	100.82	104.90	108.83	112.62	116.29	119.85
45	100.62	105.00	109.20	113.25	117.15	120.93	124.60
48	104.61	109.11	113.42	117.58	121.59	124.48	129.24
51	108.54	113.14	117.56	121.82	125.94	129.93	133.79
54	112.41	117.12	121.64	126.00	130.22	134.30	138.26
57	116.23	121.03	125.65	130.11	134.42	138.60	142.65
60	120.00	124.90	129.61	134.16	138.56	144.11	146.97
63	123.73	128.72	133.53	138.16	142.65	147.00	151.22
66	127.42	132.50	137.39	142.11	146.68	151.12	155.42
69	131.08	136.24	141.21	146.02	150.67	155.18	159.55
72	134.70	139.94	145.00	149.88	154.61	159.20	163.66
75	138.29	143.61	148.74	153.70	158.51	163.17	167.71
78	141.86	147.25	152.49	157.49	167.37	167.10	171.71
81	145.40	150.87	156.14	161.25	166.20	171.00	175.67
84	148.92	154.45	159.80	164.97	169.99	174.87	179.60
87	152.41	158.02	163.43	168.67	173.75	178.69	183.49
90	155.88	161.55	167.03	172.34	177.48	182.48	187.35
93	159.34	165.07	170.61	175.98	181.19	186.25	191.18
96	162.78	168.57	174.17	179.60	184.87	189.99	194.98
99	166.20	172.05	177.71	183.20	188.52	193.70	198.75
102	169.60	175.51	181.23	186.77	192.16	197.39	202.49
107	175.24	181.24	187.05	192.69	198.16	203.49	208.68
110	178.61	184.66	190.53	196.21	201.74	207.12	212.37
115	184.19	190.33	196.28	202.05	207.67	213.13	218.46
120	189.74	195.96	201.99	207.85	213.54	219.09	224.50
125	195.26	201.56	206.67	213.60	219.37	225.00	230.49
130	200.75	207.12	213.31	219.32	225.17	230.87	236.43
135	206.22	212.66	218.92	225.00	230.92	236.70	242.33
140	211.66	218.17	224.50	230.65	236.64	242.49	248.19
145	217.08	223.66	230.05	236.27	242.33	248.24	254.02
150	222.49	229.13	235.58	241.87	247.99	253.97	259.81
155	227.87	234.57	241.09	247.44	253.62	259.66	265.57
160	233.24	240.00	246.58	252.98	259.23	265.33	271.29
165	238.59	245.41	252.04	258.51	264.81	270.97	276.99
170	243.93	250.80	257.49	264.01	270.37	276.59	282.67
175	249.25	256.17	262.92	269.49	275.91	282.18	288.31
180	254.56	261.53	268.33	274.95	281.47	287.75	293.94
185	259.86	266.88	273.72	280.40	286.92	293.30	299.54

117

Table 4–1. Metric Solutions for Diameter D in $D = \sqrt{d^2 + 4dh}$ *(Continued).*

Shell Diam. (d)	Height of Shell (h)						
	80	*85*	*90*	*95*	*100*	*105*	*110*
6	44.23	45.56	46.86	48.12	49.36	50.56	51.73
9	54.42	56.04	57.63	59.17	60.67	62.14	63.47
12	63.12	64.99	66.81	68.59	70.31	72.00	73.65
15	70.89	72.97	75.00	76.97	78.90	80.78	82.61
18	78.00	80.27	82.00	84.64	86.74	88.79	90.80
21	84.62	87.07	89.45	91.77	94.03	96.23	98.39
24	90.86	93.47	96.00	98.47	100.88	103.23	105.53
27	96.79	99.54	102.22	104.83	107.37	109.86	112.29
30	102.47	105.36	108.17	110.91	113.58	116.29	118.74
33	107.93	110.94	113.88	116.74	119.54	122.27	124.94
36	113.21	116.34	119.40	122.38	125.28	128.12	130.90
39	118.33	121.58	124.74	127.83	130.85	133.79	136.68
42	123.30	126.66	129.94	133.13	136.25	139.30	142.28
45	128.16	131.62	135.00	138.29	141.51	144.65	147.73
48	132.91	136.47	139.94	143.33	146.64	149.88	153.05
51	137.55	141.21	144.78	148.26	151.66	154.99	158.24
54	142.11	145.86	149.52	153.09	156.58	159.99	163.33
57	146.59	150.43	154.17	157.83	161.40	164.89	168.31
60	151.00	154.92	158.92	158.75	166.13	169.71	173.21
63	155.34	159.34	163.25	167.06	170.79	174.44	178.01
66	159.61	163.69	167.68	171.37	175.37	179.10	182.75
69	163.83	167.99	172.05	176.01	179.89	183.69	187.41
72	168.00	172.23	176.36	180.40	184.35	188.22	192.00
75	172.12	176.42	180.62	184.73	188.75	192.68	196.53
78	176.19	180.57	184.84	189.01	193.09	197.09	201.01
81	180.22	184.66	189.00	193.24	197.39	201.45	205.43
84	184.22	188.72	193.12	197.42	201.63	205.76	209.80
87	188.17	192.74	197.20	201.57	205.84	210.02	214.12
90	192.09	196.72	201.25	205.67	210.00	214.24	218.40
93	195.98	200.67	205.25	209.74	214.12	281.42	222.64
96	199.84	204.59	209.23	213.77	218.21	222.57	226.84
99	203.67	208.47	213.17	217.76	222.26	226.67	231.00
102	207.47	212.33	217.08	221.73	226.28	230.75	235.13
107	213.75	218.70	223.54	228.27	232.91	237.46	241.92
110	217.49	222.49	227.38	232.16	236.85	241.45	245.97
115	223.66	228.75	233.72	238.59	243.36	248.04	252.64
120	229.78	234.95	240.00	244.95	249.80	254.56	259.23
125	235.85	241.09	246.22	251.25	256.17	261.01	265.75
130	241.87	247.18	252.39	257.49	262.49	267.39	272.21
135	247.84	253.23	258.51	263.68	268.75	273.72	278.61
140	253.77	259.23	264.58	269.81	274.95	280.00	284.96
145	259.66	265.19	270.60	275.91	281.11	286.23	291.25
150	265.52	271.11	276.59	281.96	287.23	292.40	297.49
155	271.34	276.99	282.53	287.97	293.30	298.54	303.69
160	277.13	282.84	288.44	293.94	299.33	304.63	309.84
165	282.89	288.66	294.32	299.87	305.33	310.68	315.95
170	288.62	294.45	300.17	305.78	311.29	316.70	322.02
175	294.32	300.21	305.98	311.65	317.21	322.68	328.06
180	300.00	305.94	311.77	317.49	323.11	328.63	334.07
185	305.66	311.65	317.53	323.30	328.98	334.55	340.04

Table 4–1. Metric Solutions for Diameter D in $D = \sqrt{d^2 + 4dh}$ *(Continued).*

Shell Diam. (d)	Height of Shell (h)						
	115	120	125	130	135	140	145
6	52.88	54.00	55.10	56.18	57.24	58.28	59.30
9	64.97	66.34	67.68	69.00	70.29	71.56	72.81
12	75.26	76.84	78.38	79.90	81.39	82.85	84.29
15	84.41	86.17	87.89	89.58	91.24	92.87	94.47
18	92.76	94.68	96.56	98.41	100.22	102.00	103.75
21	100.50	102.57	104.60	106.59	108.54	110.46	112.34
24	107.78	109.98	112.14	114.26	116.34	118.39	120.40
27	114.67	117.00	119.29	121.53	123.73	125.89	128.02
30	121.24	123.69	126.10	128.45	130.77	133.04	135.28
33	127.55	130.11	132.62	135.09	137.51	139.89	142.23
36	133.63	136.29	138.91	141.48	144.00	146.48	148.92
39	139.50	142.27	144.99	147.65	150.27	152.84	155.37
42	145.20	148.07	150.88	153.64	156.35	159.01	161.63
45	150.75	153.70	156.60	159.45	162.25	165.00	167.71
48	156.15	159.20	162.19	165.12	168.00	170.84	173.62
51	161.43	164.56	167.63	170.65	173.61	176.52	179.39
54	166.60	169.81	172.96	176.06	179.10	182.09	185.03
57	171.67	174.95	178.18	181.35	184.47	187.53	190.55
60	176.64	180.00	183.30	186.55	189.74	192.87	195.96
63	181.52	184.96	188.33	191.65	194.91	198.11	201.27
66	186.32	189.83	193.27	196.66	199.99	203.26	206.48
69	191.05	194.63	198.14	201.60	204.99	208.33	211.62
72	195.71	199.36	202.94	206.46	209.91	213.32	216.67
75	200.31	204.02	207.67	211.25	214.77	218.23	221.64
78	204.85	208.62	212.33	215.97	219.55	223.08	225.55
81	209.33	213.17	216.94	220.64	224.28	227.86	231.39
84	213.77	217.66	221.49	225.25	228.94	232.59	236.17
87	218.15	222.10	225.98	229.80	233.56	237.25	240.89
90	222.49	226.50	230.43	234.31	238.12	241.87	245.56
93	226.78	230.84	234.84	238.77	242.63	246.73	250.18
96	231.03	235.15	239.20	243.18	247.10	250.95	254.75
99	235.25	239.42	243.52	247.55	251.52	255.42	259.27
102	239.42	243.65	247.80	251.88	255.90	259.85	263.75
107	246.31	250.62	254.85	259.02	263.11	267.15	271.13
110	250.40	254.75	259.04	263.25	267.39	271.48	275.50
115	257.15	261.58	265.94	270.23	274.45	278.61	282.71
120	263.82	268.33	272.76	277.13	281.42	285.66	289.83
125	270.42	275.00	279.51	283.95	288.31	292.62	296.86
130	276.95	281.60	286.18	290.69	295.13	299.50	303.81
135	283.42	288.14	292.79	297.36	301.87	306.31	310.68
140	289.83	294.62	299.33	303.97	308.54	313.05	317.49
145	296.18	301.04	305.82	310.52	315.16	319.73	324.23
150	302.49	307.41	312.25	317.02	321.71	326.34	330.91
155	308.75	313.73	318.63	323.46	328.21	332.90	337.53
160	314.96	320.00	324.96	329.85	334.66	339.41	344.09
165	321.13	326.23	331.25	336.19	341.06	345.87	350.61
170	327.26	332.11	337.49	342.49	347.42	352.28	357.07
175	333.35	338.56	343.69	348.75	353.73	358.64	363.49
180	339.41	344.67	349.86	354.96	360.00	364.97	369.86
185	345.43	350.75	355.98	361.14	366.23	371.25	376.20

Table 4–1. Metric Solutions for Diameter D in $D = \sqrt{d^2 + 4dh}$ *(Continued)*.

Shell Diam. (d)	Height of Shell (h)						
	150	155	160	165	170	175	180
6	60.30	61.29	62.26	63.21	64.16	65.08	66.00
9	74.03	75.24	76.43	77.60	78.75	79.88	81.00
12	85.70	87.09	88.45	89.80	91.13	92.43	93.72
15	96.05	97.60	99.12	100.62	102.10	103.56	105.00
18	105.47	107.16	108.83	110.47	112.09	113.68	115.26
21	114.20	116.02	117.82	119.59	121.33	123.05	124.74
24	122.38	124.32	126.24	128.12	129.98	131.82	133.63
27	130.11	132.17	134.20	136.19	138.16	140.10	142.02
30	137.48	139.64	141.77	143.87	145.95	147.99	150.00
33	144.53	146.80	149.03	515.22	153.39	155.53	157.64
36	151.31	153.67	156.00	158.29	160.55	162.78	164.97
39	157.86	160.32	162.73	165.11	167.45	169.77	172.05
42	164.21	166.76	169.25	171.71	174.14	176.53	178.90
45	170.37	172.99	175.57	178.12	180.62	183.10	185.54
48	176.36	179.06	181.73	184.35	186.93	189.48	192.00
51	182.21	184.99	187.73	190.42	193.08	195.71	198.30
54	187.93	190.78	193.59	196.36	199.09	201.78	204.44
57	193.52	196.44	199.32	202.16	204.96	207.72	210.45
60	199.00	201.99	204.94	207.85	210.71	213.54	216.33
63	204.37	207.43	210.45	213.42	216.35	219.25	222.10
66	209.66	212.78	215.86	218.90	221.89	224.85	227.76
69	214.85	218.04	221.18	224.28	227.33	230.35	233.33
72	219.96	223.21	226.42	229.57	232.69	235.76	238.80
75	225.00	228.31	231.57	234.79	237.96	241.09	244.18
78	229.97	233.33	236.65	239.92	243.15	246.34	249.49
81	234.86	238.29	241.66	244.99	248.28	251.52	254.72
84	239.70	243.18	246.61	246.61	253.33	256.62	259.88
87	244.48	248.01	251.49	254.93	258.32	261.67	264.97
90	249.20	252.78	256.32	259.81	263.25	266.65	270.00
93	253.87	257.51	261.09	264.63	268.12	271.57	274.97
96	258.49	262.18	265.81	269.40	272.94	276.43	279.89
99	263.06	266.80	270.48	274.12	277.71	281.25	284.75
102	267.59	271.37	275.11	278.79	282.43	286.01	289.56
107	275.04	278.91	282.72	286.48	290.19	293.85	297.47
110	279.46	283.37	287.23	291.03	294.79	298.50	302.16
115	286.75	290.73	294.66	298.54	302.37	306.15	309.88
120	293.94	297.99	301.99	305.94	309.84	313.69	317.49
125	301.04	305.16	309.23	313.25	317.21	321.13	325.00
130	308.06	312.25	316.39	320.47	324.50	328.48	332.42
135	315.00	319.26	323.46	327.60	331.70	335.75	339.74
140	321.87	326.19	330.45	334.66	338.82	342.93	346.99
145	328.67	333.05	337.38	341.65	345.87	350.04	354.15
150	335.41	339.85	344.24	348.57	352.85	357.07	361.25
155	342.09	346.59	351.03	355.42	359.76	364.04	368.27
160	348.71	353.27	357.77	362.22	366.61	370.94	375.23
165	355.28	359.90	364.45	368.94	373.40	377.79	382.13
170	361.80	366.47	371.08	375.63	380.13	384.58	388.97
175	368.27	372.99	377.66	382.26	386.81	391.31	395.76
180	374.70	379.47	384.19	388.84	393.45	397.99	402.49
185	381.08	385.91	390.67	395.38	400.03	404.63	409.18

Table 4–1. Metric Solutions for Diameter D in $D = \sqrt{d^2 + 4dh}$ *(Continued).*

Shell Diam. (d)	Height of Shell (h)						
	185	*190*	*195*	*200*	*205*	*210*	*215*
6	66.90	67.79	68.67	69.54	70.40	71.25	72.08
9	82.10	83.19	84.27	85.33	86.38	87.41	88.44
12	94.99	96.25	97.49	98.71	99.92	101.11	102.29
15	106.42	107.82	109.20	110.57	111.92	113.25	114.56
18	116.81	118.34	119.85	121.34	122.82	124.27	125.71
21	126.42	128.07	129.70	131.30	132.89	134.47	136.02
24	135.41	137.17	138.91	140.63	142.32	144.00	145.66
27	143.91	145.77	147.61	149.43	151.22	153.00	154.75
30	151.99	153.95	155.88	157.80	159.69	161.55	163.40
33	159.72	161.77	163.80	165.80	167.78	169.73	171.67
36	167.14	169.28	171.39	173.48	175.54	177.58	179.60
39	174.30	176.52	178.72	180.89	183.03	185.15	187.25
42	181.23	183.53	185.81	188.05	190.27	192.47	194.64
45	187.95	190.33	192.68	195.00	197.29	199.56	201.80
48	194.48	196.94	199.36	201.75	204.12	206.46	208.77
51	200.85	203.37	205.87	208.33	210.76	213.17	215.55
54	207.07	209.66	212.22	214.75	217.25	219.72	222.16
57	213.14	215.80	218.42	221.02	223.58	226.12	228.62
60	219.09	221.81	224.50	227.16	229.78	232.38	234.95
63	224.92	227.70	230.45	233.17	235.86	238.51	241.14
66	230.64	233.49	236.30	239.07	241.82	244.53	247.22
69	236.26	239.17	242.04	244.87	247.67	250.44	253.18
72	241.79	244.75	247.68	250.57	253.42	256.24	259.04
75	247.23	250.25	253.23	256.17	259.08	261.96	264.81
78	252.59	255.66	258.70	261.69	264.66	267.59	270.49
81	257.88	261.00	264.09	267.13	270.15	273.13	276.08
84	263.09	266.26	269.40	272.50	275.56	278.60	281.60
87	268.23	271.46	274.65	277.79	280.91	283.99	287.03
90	273.31	276.59	279.82	283.02	286.18	289.31	292.40
93	278.33	281.65	284.94	288.18	291.39	294.57	297.71
96	283.29	286.66	293.28	296.54	299.76	302.95	306.10
99	288.20	291.62	298.33	301.63	304.90	308.12	311.32
102	293.06	296.52	303.32	306.67	309.97	313.25	316.49
107	301.05	304.58	311.53	314.94	318.32	321.67	324.98
110	305.78	309.35	316.39	319.84	323.26	326.65	330.00
115	313.57	317.21	324.38	327.91	331.40	334.85	338.27
120	321.25	324.96	332.26	335.86	339.41	342.93	346.41
125	328.82	332.60	340.04	343.69	347.31	350.89	354.44
130	336.30	340.15	347.71	351.43	355.11	358.75	362.35
135	343.69	347.60	355.28	359.06	362.80	366.50	370.17
140	351.00	354.96	362.77	366.61	370.41	374.17	377.89
145	358.22	362.25	370.17	374.07	377.92	381.74	385.52
150	365.38	369.46	377.49	381.44	385.36	389.23	393.06
155	372.46	376.60	384.74	388.75	392.71	396.64	400.53
160	379.47	383.67	391.92	395.98	400.00	403.98	407.92
165	386.43	390.67	399.03	403.14	407.22	411.25	415.24
170	393.32	397.62	406.08	410.24	414.37	418.45	422.49
175	400.16	404.51	413.07	417.28	421.46	425.59	429.68
180	406.94	411.34	420.00	424.26	428.49	432.67	436.81
185	413.67	418.12	426.88	431.19	435.46	439.69	443.87

Table 4–1. Metric Solutions for Diameter D in $D = \sqrt{d^2 + 4dh}$ (Continued).

Shell Diam. (d)	Height of Shell (h)						
	220	225	230	235	240	245	250
6	72.91	73.73	74.54	75.34	76.13	76.92	77.69
9	89.45	90.45	91.44	92.42	93.39	94.35	95.29
12	103.46	104.61	105.75	106.88	108.00	109.11	110.20
15	115.87	117.15	118.43	119.69	120.93	122.17	123.39
18	127.14	128.55	129.94	131.32	132.68	134.03	135.37
21	137.55	139.07	140.57	142.06	143.53	144.99	146.43
24	147.30	148.92	150.52	152.11	153.67	155.23	156.77
27	156.49	158.21	159.90	161.58	163.25	164.89	166.52
30	165.23	167.03	168.82	170.59	172.34	174.07	175.78
33	173.58	175.47	177.34	179.19	181.02	182.84	184.63
36	181.59	183.56	185.52	187.45	189.36	191.25	193.12
39	189.32	191.37	193.39	195.40	197.39	199.35	201.30
42	196.78	198.91	201.01	203.09	205.14	207.18	209.20
45	204.02	206.22	208.39	210.54	212.66	214.77	216.85
48	211.05	213.32	215.56	217.77	219.96	222.14	224.29
51	217.90	220.23	222.53	224.81	227.07	229.31	231.52
54	224.58	226.95	229.34	231.68	234.00	236.30	238.57
57	231.10	233.56	235.99	238.39	240.77	243.12	245.56
60	237.49	240.00	242.49	244.95	247.39	249.80	252.19
63	243.74	246.31	248.86	251.37	253.87	256.34	258.78
66	249.87	252.50	255.10	257.67	260.22	262.75	265.25
69	255.89	258.57	261.23	263.86	266.46	269.04	271.59
72	261.81	264.54	267.25	269.93	272.59	275.22	277.82
75	267.63	270.42	273.18	275.91	278.61	281.29	283.95
78	273.36	276.20	279.01	281.79	284.54	287.27	289.97
81	279.00	381.89	284.75	287.58	290.38	392.16	295.91
84	284.56	287.50	290.41	293.28	296.14	298.96	301.75
87	290.05	293.03	295.99	298.91	301.81	304.68	307.52
90	295.47	298.50	301.50	304.47	307.41	310.32	313.21
93	300.81	303.89	306.93	309.95	312.94	315.89	318.82
96	289.99	309.22	312.31	315.37	318.40	321.40	324.37
99	294.99	314.49	317.62	320.72	323.79	326.83	329.85
102	299.94	319.69	322.87	326.01	329.13	332.21	335.27
107	308.07	328.25	331.50	334.71	337.89	341.04	344.16
110	312.89	333.32	336.60	339.85	343.07	346.27	349.43
115	320.82	341.65	345.00	348.32	351.60	354.86	358.06
120	328.63	349.86	353.27	356.65	360.00	363.32	366.61
125	336.34	357.95	361.42	364.86	368.27	371.65	375.00
130	343.95	365.92	369.46	372.96	376.43	379.87	383.28
135	351.46	373.80	377.39	380.95	384.48	387.98	391.44
140	358.89	381.58	385.23	388.84	392.43	395.98	399.50
145	366.23	389.26	392.97	396.64	400.28	403.89	407.46
150	373.50	396.86	400.62	404.35	408.04	411.70	415.33
155	380.69	404.38	408.20	411.98	415.72	419.43	423.11
160	387.81	411.83	415.69	419.52	423.32	427.08	430.81
165	394.87	419.20	423.11	427.00	430.84	434.66	438.43
170	401.87	426.50	430.46	434.40	438.29	442.15	445.98
175	408.81	433.73	437.75	441.73	445.67	449.58	453.46
180	415.69	440.91	444.97	449.00	452.99	456.95	460.87
185	422.52	448.02	452.13	456.21	460.24	464.25	468.21

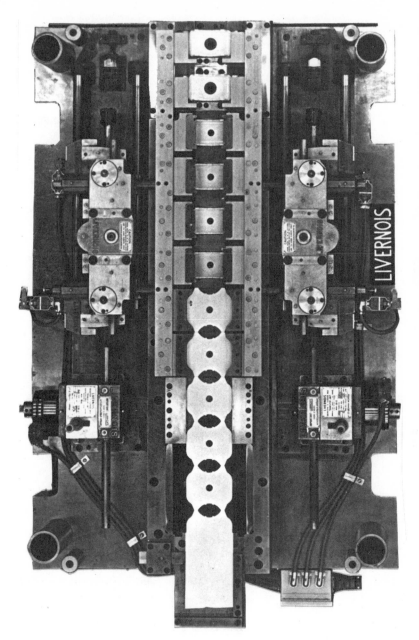

Half-progressive, half-transfer die. Photo courtesy Livernois Automation Co.

Table 4–1A. Inch Solutions for Diameter D in $D = \sqrt{d^2 + 4dh}$

Diameter of Shell	Height of Shell													
	1/2	5/8	3/4	7/8	1	1 1/8	1 1/4	1 3/8	1 1/2	1 5/8	1 3/4	1 7/8	2	2 1/4
1/4	.75	.83	.90	.97	1.03	1.09	1.15	1.20	1.25	1.30	1.34	1.39	1.43	1.52
3/8	.94	1.04	1.13	1.21	1.28	1.34	1.42	1.48	1.55	1.61	1.67	1.71	1.78	1.88
1/2	1.12	1.22	1.32	1.41	1.50	1.58	1.66	1.73	1.80	1.87	1.93	2.00	2.07	2.18
5/8	1.28	1.40	1.50	1.60	1.70	1.79	1.88	1.96	2.04	2.11	2.19	2.26	2.32	2.46
3/4	1.44	1.56	1.67	1.78	1.89	1.98	2.08	2.16	2.25	2.33	2.41	2.48	2.56	2.70
7/8	1.59	1.72	1.84	1.95	2.06	2.16	2.26	2.36	2.45	2.54	2.62	2.70	2.78	2.94
1	1.73	1.87	2.00	2.12	2.23	2.34	2.45	2.55	2.64	2.74	2.82	2.91	3.00	3.16
1 1/8	1.87	2.02	2.15	2.28	2.40	2.51	2.62	2.73	2.83	2.93	3.02	3.11	3.21	3.37
1 1/4	2.01	2.16	2.30	2.43	2.56	2.68	2.80	2.90	3.01	3.11	3.22	3.31	3.40	3.58
1 3/8	2.16	2.31	2.45	2.59	2.72	2.84	2.96	3.08	3.18	3.29	3.39	3.49	3.59	3.77
1 1/2	2.29	2.45	2.60	2.74	2.87	3.00	3.12	3.24	3.36	3.46	3.58	3.67	3.77	3.97
1 5/8	2.42	2.59	2.74	2.89	3.02	3.15	3.28	3.40	3.52	3.63	3.74	3.85	3.95	4.15
1 3/4	2.56	2.72	2.88	3.03	3.17	3.30	3.43	3.56	3.68	3.80	3.91	4.03	4.14	4.34
1 7/8	2.70	2.86	3.02	3.18	3.32	3.46	3.59	3.72	3.84	3.97	4.08	4.20	4.30	4.52
2	2.83	3.00	3.16	3.31	3.46	3.61	3.75	3.87	4.00	4.12	4.24	4.36	4.47	4.69
2 1/8	2.96	3.13	3.30	3.46	3.61	3.75	3.89	4.02	4.16	4.28	4.40	4.52	4.64	4.86
2 1/4	3.09	3.27	3.44	3.60	3.75	3.90	4.04	4.18	4.31	4.44	4.56	4.68	4.80	5.03
2 3/8	3.22	3.40	3.57	3.74	3.89	4.04	4.18	4.32	4.46	4.59	4.72	4.84	4.96	5.20
2 1/2	3.35	3.54	3.71	3.87	4.03	4.18	4.33	4.47	4.61	4.74	4.87	5.00	5.12	5.36
2 5/8	3.48	3.67	3.84	4.01	4.17	4.32	4.47	4.62	4.76	4.89	5.03	5.15	5.28	5.52
2 3/4	3.61	3.80	3.98	4.15	4.31	4.47	4.62	4.76	4.90	5.04	5.18	5.31	5.44	5.68
2 7/8	3.75	3.93	4.11	4.28	4.45	4.60	4.76	4.91	5.05	5.19	5.33	5.46	5.59	5.84
3	3.87	4.06	4.24	4.42	4.58	4.74	4.90	5.05	5.20	5.34	5.48	5.61	5.74	6.00
3 1/8	4.00	4.19	4.38	4.55	4.72	4.88	5.04	5.19	5.34	5.48	5.63	5.76	5.90	6.16
3 1/4	4.13	4.32	4.51	4.68	4.85	5.02	5.18	5.33	5.48	5.63	5.77	5.91	6.05	6.31
3 3/8	4.26	4.45	4.64	4.82	4.99	5.15	5.31	5.47	5.62	5.77	5.92	6.05	6.19	6.47
3 1/2	4.39	4.58	4.77	4.95	5.12	5.29	5.45	5.61	5.77	5.91	6.06	6.20	6.35	6.61
3 5/8	4.51	4.71	4.90	5.08	5.26	5.43	5.59	5.75	5.90	6.06	6.21	6.35	6.49	6.76
3 3/4	4.64	4.84	5.03	5.21	5.39	5.56	5.73	5.89	6.04	6.20	6.35	6.49	6.63	6.91
3 7/8	4.77	4.97	5.16	5.34	5.52	5.69	5.86	6.02	6.18	6.34	6.49	6.64	6.78	7.06
4	4.90	5.10	5.29	5.48	5.66	5.83	6.00	6.16	6.32	6.48	6.63	6.78	6.92	7.21

4 1/8	5.02	5.22	5.42	5.61	5.79	5.96	6.13	6.30	6.46	6.62	6.77	6.92	7.07	7.36
4 1/4	5.15	5.35	5.55	5.74	5.92	6.09	6.27	6.43	6.60	6.76	6.91	7.06	7.21	7.50
4 3/8	5.28	5.48	5.68	5.87	6.05	6.23	6.40	6.57	6.73	6.89	7.05	7.21	7.35	7.64
4 1/2	5.40	5.61	5.81	6.00	6.18	6.36	6.53	6.70	6.87	7.03	7.19	7.35	7.50	7.79
4 5/8	5.53	5.74	5.93	6.13	6.31	6.49	6.67	6.84	7.01	7.17	7.33	7.48	7.64	7.93
4 3/4	5.66	5.86	6.06	6.26	6.44	6.62	6.80	6.97	7.14	7.31	7.47	7.62	7.78	8.08
4 7/8	5.78	5.99	6.19	6.39	6.57	6.76	6.93	7.11	7.28	7.44	7.60	7.76	7.92	8.22
5	5.91	6.12	6.32	6.52	6.70	6.89	7.07	7.24	7.41	7.58	7.74	7.90	8.06	8.36
5 1/8	6.04	6.25	6.45	6.64	6.83	7.02	7.20	7.37	7.55	7.72	7.88	8.04	8.21	8.51
5 1/4	6.17	6.37	6.58	6.77	6.96	7.15	7.33	7.51	7.68	7.85	8.02	8.18	8.34	8.65
5 3/8	6.29	6.50	6.71	6.90	7.09	7.28	7.46	7.64	7.82	7.99	8.15	8.31	8.48	8.79
5 1/2	6.42	6.63	6.83	7.03	7.22	7.41	7.60	7.77	7.95	8.12	8.29	8.45	8.61	8.93
5 5/8	6.54	6.76	6.96	7.16	7.35	7.54	7.73	7.91	8.08	8.25	8.42	8.59	8.75	9.07
5 3/4	6.67	6.88	7.09	7.29	7.48	7.67	7.86	8.04	8.22	8.39	8.56	8.72	8.89	9.20
5 7/8	6.80	7.01	7.22	7.42	7.61	7.80	7.99	8.17	8.35	8.52	8.69	8.86	9.02	9.34
6	6.92	7.14	7.34	7.55	7.74	7.93	8.12	8.30	8.48	8.66	8.83	9.00	9.16	9.48
6 1/4	7.18	7.39	7.60	7.80	8.00	8.19	8.38	8.57	8.75	8.92	9.10	9.27	9.44	9.76
6 1/2	7.43	7.64	7.85	8.06	8.26	8.45	8.64	8.83	9.01	9.19	9.36	9.54	9.71	10.03
6 3/4	7.68	7.90	8.11	8.31	8.51	8.71	8.90	9.09	9.27	9.45	9.63	9.80	9.97	10.31
7	7.93	8.15	8.36	8.57	8.77	8.97	9.16	9.35	9.53	9.72	9.90	10.07	10.24	10.58
7 1/4	8.18	8.40	8.62	8.82	9.03	9.22	9.42	9.61	9.80	9.98	10.16	10.34	10.51	10.85
7 1/2	8.44	8.66	8.87	9.08	9.28	9.48	9.68	9.87	10.06	10.24	10.42	10.60	10.78	11.12
7 3/4	8.69	8.91	9.12	9.33	9.54	9.74	9.94	10.13	10.32	10.50	10.69	10.87	11.04	11.39
8	8.94	9.16	9.38	9.59	9.79	10.00	10.19	10.39	10.58	10.77	10.95	11.13	11.31	11.66
8 1/4	9.19	9.41	9.63	9.84	10.05	10.25	10.45	10.65	10.84	11.03	11.21	11.39	11.57	11.92
8 1/2	9.44	9.66	9.88	10.10	10.30	10.51	10.71	10.90	11.10	11.29	11.47	11.66	11.84	12.19
8 3/4	9.69	9.92	10.13	10.35	10.56	10.76	10.96	11.16	11.36	11.55	11.73	11.92	12.10	12.46
9	9.95	10.17	10.39	10.60	10.81	11.02	11.21	11.42	11.61	11.81	11.99	12.18	12.36	12.72
9 1/4	10.20	10.42	10.64	10.85	11.07	11.27	11.48	11.68	11.87	12.07	12.26	12.44	12.63	12.99
9 1/2	10.45	10.67	10.89	11.11	11.32	11.53	11.73	11.93	12.13	12.32	12.52	12.70	12.89	13.25
9 3/4	10.70	10.92	11.14	11.36	11.57	11.78	11.99	12.19	12.39	12.58	12.77	12.96	13.15	13.52
10	10.95	11.18	11.40	11.61	11.83	12.04	12.24	12.44	12.64	12.84	13.03	13.22	13.41	13.78
10 1/4	11.20	11.43	11.65	11.87	12.08	12.29	12.50	12.70	12.90	13.10	13.29	13.48	13.67	14.04
10 1/2	11.45	11.68	11.90	12.12	12.33	12.54	12.75	12.96	13.16	13.36	13.55	13.74	13.93	14.30
10 3/4	11.70	11.93	12.15	12.37	12.59	12.80	13.01	13.21	13.41	13.61	13.81	14.00	14.19	14.56
11	11.95	12.18	12.40	12.62	12.84	13.05	13.26	13.47	13.67	13.87	14.07	14.26	14.45	14.83

Table 4-1A. Inch Solutions for Diameter D in $D = \sqrt{d^2 + 4dh}$ (Continued).

Diameter of Shell	Height of Shell													
	2½	2¾	3	3¼	3½	3¾	4	4¼	4½	4¾	5	5¼	5½	5¾
¼	1.59	1.67	1.75	1.82	1.89	1.95	2.02	2.08	2.13	2.20	2.25	2.31	2.36	2.41
⅜	1.98	2.07	2.16	2.24	2.32	2.40	2.48	2.55	2.63	2.70	2.76	2.83	2.90	2.96
½	2.29	2.39	2.50	2.60	2.69	2.78	2.88	2.96	3.04	3.12	3.20	3.28	3.35	3.42
⅝	2.58	2.69	2.80	2.92	3.02	3.12	3.23	3.32	3.42	3.50	3.59	3.68	3.76	3.84
¾	2.84	2.96	3.09	3.21	3.32	3.43	3.54	3.65	3.75	3.85	3.94	4.03	4.13	4.22
⅞	3.08	3.22	3.38	3.50	3.63	3.75	3.84	3.95	4.06	4.17	4.27	4.38	4.47	4.57
1	3.31	3.46	3.61	3.74	3.87	4.00	4.13	4.24	4.35	4.46	4.58	4.69	4.79	4.89
1⅛	3.53	3.69	3.84	3.98	4.12	4.26	4.39	4.51	4.63	4.75	4.87	4.98	5.10	5.21
1¼	3.75	3.91	4.07	4.22	4.37	4.51	4.65	4.78	4.90	5.03	5.15	5.27	5.39	5.50
1⅜	3.95	4.12	4.28	4.44	4.59	4.74	4.88	5.02	5.16	5.29	5.42	5.54	5.67	5.79
1½	4.15	4.33	4.50	4.66	4.82	4.97	5.12	5.26	5.40	5.54	5.68	5.81	5.93	6.07
1⅝	4.34	4.53	4.70	4.87	5.03	5.20	5.35	5.50	5.64	5.78	5.92	6.06	6.20	6.33
1¾	4.54	4.73	4.90	5.08	5.25	5.42	5.57	5.72	5.88	6.02	6.17	6.31	6.45	6.58
1⅞	4.71	4.91	5.10	5.28	5.45	5.62	5.79	5.95	6.10	6.25	6.41	6.55	6.69	6.83
2	4.90	5.10	5.29	5.48	5.65	5.83	6.00	6.16	6.32	6.48	6.63	6.78	6.93	7.07
2⅛	5.08	5.28	5.48	5.67	5.85	6.03	6.21	6.38	6.54	6.70	6.86	7.01	7.16	7.31
2¼	5.25	5.46	5.66	5.86	6.05	6.23	6.41	6.58	6.75	6.91	7.08	7.23	7.39	7.54
2⅜	5.42	5.64	5.84	6.04	6.24	6.42	6.61	6.78	6.96	7.13	7.29	7.45	7.61	7.76
2½	5.59	5.81	6.02	6.22	6.42	6.61	6.80	6.98	7.16	7.33	7.50	7.66	7.82	7.98
2⅝	5.76	5.98	6.20	6.40	6.61	6.80	6.99	7.18	7.36	7.53	7.71	7.88	8.04	8.20
2¾	5.92	6.15	6.37	6.58	6.79	6.99	7.18	7.37	7.55	7.73	7.91	8.08	8.25	8.41
2⅞	6.08	6.32	6.54	6.76	6.96	7.17	7.37	7.56	7.75	7.93	8.11	8.29	8.46	8.62
3	6.25	6.48	6.71	6.93	7.14	7.35	7.55	7.75	7.94	8.12	8.30	8.48	8.66	8.83
3⅛	6.40	6.64	6.87	7.10	7.32	7.52	7.73	7.93	8.12	8.31	8.50	8.68	8.86	9.03
3¼	6.56	6.80	7.04	7.26	7.48	7.70	7.91	8.11	8.31	8.50	8.69	8.88	9.06	9.23
3⅜	6.72	6.96	7.20	7.43	7.66	7.87	8.08	8.29	8.49	8.69	8.88	9.07	9.25	9.43
3½	6.87	7.12	7.37	7.60	7.83	8.05	8.26	8.47	8.68	8.87	9.06	9.26	9.45	9.63
3⅝	7.03	7.28	7.52	7.76	7.99	8.21	8.43	8.65	8.85	9.06	9.25	9.45	9.64	9.82
3¾	7.18	7.43	7.68	7.92	8.16	8.38	8.60	8.82	9.03	9.23	9.44	9.63	9.82	10.01
3⅞	7.33	7.59	7.84	8.08	8.32	8.55	8.77	8.99	9.20	9.41	9.61	9.82	10.01	10.20
4	7.48	7.74	8.00	8.24	8.48	8.71	8.94	9.16	9.38	9.59	9.79	10.00	10.20	10.39

4 1/8	7.63	7.89	8.15	8.40	8.64	8.88	9.11	9.33	9.55	9.76	9.97	10.18	10.38	10.57
4 1/4	7.78	8.05	8.31	8.56	8.80	9.04	9.27	9.50	9.72	9.94	10.15	10.35	10.56	10.76
4 3/8	7.93	8.20	8.46	8.71	8.96	9.20	9.44	9.67	9.89	10.11	10.32	10.53	10.74	10.94
4 1/2	8.07	8.35	8.61	8.87	9.12	9.36	9.60	9.83	10.06	10.28	10.50	10.71	10.92	11.12
4 5/8	8.22	8.50	8.76	9.02	9.28	9.52	9.76	10.00	10.22	10.45	10.67	10.88	11.09	11.30
4 3/4	8.37	8.64	8.91	9.18	9.43	9.68	9.92	10.16	10.39	10.62	10.84	11.05	11.27	11.47
4 7/8	8.51	8.79	9.06	9.33	9.59	9.84	10.08	10.32	10.55	10.78	11.01	11.23	11.44	11.65
5	8.66	8.94	9.21	9.48	9.74	10.00	10.24	10.48	10.72	10.95	11.18	11.40	11.61	11.83
5 1/8	8.80	9.09	9.37	9.63	9.90	10.15	10.40	10.65	10.88	11.12	11.34	11.57	11.79	12.00
5 1/4	8.94	9.23	9.51	9.78	10.05	10.31	10.56	10.80	11.04	11.28	11.51	11.74	11.96	12.17
5 3/8	9.09	9.38	9.66	9.93	10.20	10.46	10.72	10.96	11.20	11.44	11.68	11.90	12.13	12.35
5 1/2	9.23	9.52	9.81	10.08	10.35	10.62	10.87	11.12	11.36	11.60	11.84	12.07	12.29	12.52
5 5/8	9.37	9.67	9.95	10.23	10.50	10.77	11.02	11.28	11.52	11.76	12.00	12.23	12.46	12.69
5 3/4	9.51	9.81	10.10	10.38	10.65	10.92	11.18	11.43	11.68	11.92	12.16	12.40	12.63	12.85
5 7/8	9.65	9.95	10.24	10.52	10.80	11.07	11.33	11.59	11.84	12.08	12.32	12.56	12.79	13.02
6	9.79	10.09	10.39	10.67	10.95	11.22	11.48	11.74	12.00	12.24	12.48	12.72	12.96	13.19
6 1/4	10.07	10.38	10.68	10.96	11.25	11.52	11.79	12.05	12.31	12.56	12.80	13.05	13.28	13.52
6 1/2	10.35	10.66	10.96	11.25	11.54	11.82	12.09	12.36	12.62	12.87	13.12	13.37	13.61	13.85
6 3/4	10.63	10.94	11.25	11.54	11.83	12.11	12.39	12.66	12.92	13.18	13.43	13.68	13.93	14.17
7	10.90	11.22	11.53	11.83	12.12	12.40	12.68	12.96	13.23	13.49	13.74	14.00	14.24	14.49
7 1/4	11.18	11.50	11.81	12.11	12.41	12.70	12.98	13.25	13.52	13.79	14.05	14.31	14.56	14.80
7 1/2	11.45	11.77	12.09	12.39	12.69	12.99	13.27	13.55	13.82	14.09	14.36	14.62	14.87	15.12
7 3/4	11.72	12.05	12.37	12.68	12.98	13.27	13.56	13.84	14.12	14.39	14.66	14.92	15.18	15.43
8	11.99	12.32	12.64	12.96	13.26	13.56	13.85	14.14	14.42	14.69	14.96	15.23	15.49	15.74
8 1/4	12.27	12.60	12.92	13.23	13.54	13.84	14.14	14.43	14.71	14.99	15.26	15.53	15.79	16.05
8 1/2	12.53	12.87	13.20	13.51	13.82	14.13	14.43	14.72	15.00	15.28	15.56	15.83	16.10	16.36
8 3/4	12.80	13.14	13.47	13.79	14.10	14.41	14.71	15.00	15.29	15.58	15.86	16.13	16.40	16.66
9	13.07	13.41	13.74	14.07	14.38	14.69	14.99	15.29	15.58	15.87	16.15	16.43	16.70	16.97
9 1/4	13.34	13.68	14.02	14.34	14.66	14.97	15.28	15.58	15.87	16.16	16.44	16.72	17.00	17.26
9 1/2	13.61	13.95	14.29	14.61	14.94	15.25	15.56	15.86	16.16	16.45	16.74	17.02	17.29	17.57
9 3/4	13.87	14.22	14.56	14.89	15.21	15.53	15.84	16.14	16.44	16.74	17.03	17.31	17.59	17.86
10	14.14	14.49	14.83	15.16	15.49	15.81	16.12	16.43	16.74	17.02	17.31	17.60	17.88	18.15
10 1/4	14.40	14.75	15.10	15.43	15.76	16.08	16.40	16.71	17.01	17.31	17.60	17.89	18.18	18.46
10 1/2	14.66	15.02	15.36	15.70	16.03	16.36	16.68	16.99	17.29	17.59	17.89	18.18	18.47	18.75
10 3/4	14.93	15.29	15.63	15.97	16.31	16.63	16.95	17.27	17.58	17.88	18.18	18.47	18.76	19.04
11	15.19	15.55	15.90	16.24	16.58	16.91	17.23	17.55	17.86	18.16	18.46	18.76	19.05	19.33

Table 4–1A. Inch Solutions for Diameter D in $D = \sqrt{d^2 + 4dh}$ (Continued).

Diameter of Shell	Height of Shell												
	6	6½	7	7½	8	8½	9	9½	10	10½	11	11½	12
1/4	2.46	2.56	2.66	2.75	2.83	2.93	3.01	3.09	3.17	3.25	3.33	3.40	3.48
3/8	3.03	3.15	3.27	3.38	3.48	3.59	3.70	3.80	3.90	3.98	4.08	4.17	4.26
1/2	3.50	3.64	3.77	3.90	4.03	4.15	4.27	4.39	4.50	4.61	4.71	4.82	4.93
5/8	3.92	4.08	4.23	4.38	4.52	4.65	4.78	4.91	5.04	5.16	5.28	5.39	5.51
3/4	4.30	4.48	4.64	4.80	4.96	5.10	5.25	5.39	5.53	5.66	5.79	5.92	6.05
7/8	4.66	4.84	5.03	5.19	5.36	5.52	5.68	5.83	5.98	6.12	6.26	6.40	6.53
1	5.00	5.19	5.39	5.57	5.74	5.92	6.08	6.24	6.40	6.56	6.71	6.86	7.00
1⅛	5.31	5.52	5.72	5.92	6.10	6.28	6.46	6.63	6.80	6.96	7.12	7.28	7.43
1¼	5.61	5.84	6.04	6.25	6.45	6.64	6.82	7.00	7.18	7.35	7.52	7.68	7.84
1⅜	5.90	6.13	6.35	6.57	6.78	6.97	7.16	7.35	7.54	7.73	7.89	8.07	8.24
1½	6.19	6.42	6.65	6.87	7.09	7.30	7.50	7.70	7.89	8.08	8.26	8.44	8.62
1⅝	6.45	6.70	6.94	7.17	7.39	7.61	7.82	8.02	8.22	8.42	8.61	8.80	8.98
1¾	6.71	6.97	7.22	7.46	7.69	7.91	8.13	8.34	8.55	8.75	8.95	9.14	9.33
1⅞	6.96	7.23	7.49	7.73	7.97	8.20	8.43	8.64	8.86	9.07	9.27	9.48	9.67
2	7.21	7.49	7.75	8.00	8.25	8.48	8.72	8.94	9.17	9.38	9.59	9.80	10.00
2⅛	7.45	7.73	8.00	8.26	8.52	8.76	9.00	9.23	9.46	9.68	9.90	10.11	10.32
2¼	7.68	7.97	8.25	8.52	8.78	9.03	9.28	9.52	9.75	9.98	10.21	10.42	10.63
2⅜	7.91	8.21	8.49	8.77	9.03	9.29	9.55	9.79	10.03	10.26	10.49	10.72	10.94
2½	8.14	8.44	8.73	9.01	9.29	9.55	9.81	10.06	10.31	10.55	10.78	11.01	11.24
2⅝	8.36	8.67	8.97	9.25	9.53	9.80	10.07	10.33	10.58	10.82	11.06	11.30	11.53
2¾	8.58	8.89	9.20	9.49	9.78	10.05	10.32	10.59	10.84	11.09	11.33	11.58	11.81
2⅞	8.79	9.11	9.42	9.72	10.01	10.29	10.57	10.84	11.11	11.35	11.61	11.85	12.09
3	9.00	9.33	9.64	9.95	10.25	10.53	10.82	11.09	11.36	11.62	11.87	12.12	12.37
3⅛	9.20	9.54	9.86	10.17	10.48	10.77	11.06	11.34	11.61	11.88	12.13	12.39	12.64
3¼	9.41	9.75	10.08	10.40	10.70	11.00	11.29	11.58	11.86	12.13	12.39	12.65	12.90
3⅜	9.61	9.96	10.29	10.61	10.93	11.23	11.53	11.82	12.10	12.37	12.64	12.91	13.17
3½	9.81	10.16	10.50	10.83	11.15	11.46	11.76	12.05	12.34	12.62	12.89	13.16	13.43
3⅝	10.00	10.36	10.71	11.04	11.36	11.68	11.98	12.28	12.57	12.86	13.14	13.41	13.68
3¾	10.20	10.56	10.91	11.25	11.58	11.90	12.21	12.51	12.80	13.09	13.37	13.65	13.93
3⅞	10.39	10.76	11.11	11.45	11.79	12.11	12.43	12.74	13.04	13.33	13.62	13.90	14.18
4	10.58	10.95	11.31	11.66	12.00	12.33	12.65	12.96	13.26	13.56	13.85	14.14	14.42

4⅛	10.76	11.14	11.51	11.86	12.20	12.54	12.86	13.18	13.49	13.79	14.09	14.38	14.66
4¼	10.95	11.33	11.71	12.06	12.41	12.75	13.07	13.40	13.72	14.02	14.32	14.61	14.90
4⅜	11.14	11.52	11.90	12.26	12.61	12.95	13.29	13.61	13.93	14.24	14.54	14.84	15.13
4½	11.32	11.71	12.09	12.45	12.81	13.16	13.50	13.82	14.15	14.45	14.77	15.07	15.37
4⅝	11.50	11.90	12.28	12.65	13.01	13.36	13.70	14.04	14.36	14.68	14.99	15.30	15.60
4¾	11.68	12.08	12.47	12.84	13.21	13.56	13.91	14.25	14.57	14.90	15.22	15.52	15.83
4⅞	11.86	12.26	12.65	13.03	13.41	13.76	14.11	14.45	14.79	15.11	15.43	15.74	16.05
5	12.04	12.45	12.84	13.23	13.60	13.96	14.32	14.66	15.00	15.33	15.65	15.97	16.28
5⅛	12.21	12.63	13.03	13.41	13.79	14.16	14.52	14.86	15.21	15.54	15.87	16.19	16.50
5¼	12.39	12.81	13.21	13.60	13.98	14.35	14.71	15.07	15.41	15.75	16.08	16.40	16.72
5⅜	12.56	12.98	13.39	13.79	14.17	14.54	14.91	15.27	15.61	15.95	16.29	16.61	16.93
5½	12.73	13.16	13.57	13.97	14.36	14.73	15.11	15.47	15.82	16.16	16.50	16.83	17.15
5⅝	12.90	13.33	13.75	14.15	14.54	14.93	15.30	15.66	16.02	16.36	16.70	17.04	17.36
5¾	13.07	13.51	13.93	14.33	14.73	15.11	15.49	15.86	16.21	16.57	16.91	17.25	17.58
5⅞	13.24	13.68	14.10	14.51	14.91	15.30	15.68	16.05	16.42	16.77	17.11	17.45	17.79
6	13.41	13.85	14.28	14.69	15.10	15.49	15.87	16.24	16.61	16.97	17.32	17.66	18.00
6¼	13.74	14.19	14.63	15.05	15.46	15.86	16.25	16.63	17.00	17.36	17.72	18.07	18.41
6½	14.08	14.53	14.97	15.40	15.82	16.22	16.62	17.00	17.38	17.75	18.11	18.47	18.82
6¾	14.40	14.86	15.31	15.75	16.17	16.58	16.98	17.38	17.76	18.14	18.50	18.87	19.22
7	14.73	15.19	15.65	16.09	16.52	16.94	17.34	17.74	18.13	18.52	18.89	19.26	19.62
7¼	15.05	15.52	15.98	16.43	16.86	17.29	17.70	18.11	18.51	18.89	19.27	19.64	20.01
7½	15.37	15.85	16.31	16.77	17.21	17.64	18.06	18.47	18.87	19.26	19.65	20.03	20.40
7¾	15.68	16.17	16.64	17.10	17.55	17.98	18.41	18.82	19.23	19.63	20.02	20.40	20.78
8	15.99	16.49	16.97	17.43	17.88	18.33	18.76	19.18	19.59	19.99	20.39	20.78	21.16
8¼	16.31	16.80	17.29	17.76	18.22	18.66	19.10	19.53	19.95	20.36	20.76	21.15	21.54
8½	16.62	17.12	17.61	18.09	18.55	19.00	19.44	19.88	20.30	20.71	21.11	21.51	21.91
8¾	16.92	17.43	17.93	18.41	18.88	19.34	19.78	20.22	20.65	21.07	21.48	21.88	22.28
9	17.23	17.74	18.24	18.73	19.20	19.67	20.12	20.56	21.00	21.42	21.84	22.24	22.64
9¼	17.53	18.05	18.56	19.05	19.53	20.00	20.45	20.90	21.34	21.77	22.19	22.60	23.00
9½	17.83	18.36	18.87	19.37	19.85	20.32	20.79	21.24	21.68	22.11	22.54	22.96	23.37
9¾	18.14	18.66	19.18	19.68	20.17	20.65	21.12	21.57	22.02	22.46	22.89	23.31	23.72
10	18.43	18.97	19.49	20.00	20.49	20.97	21.44	21.90	22.36	22.80	23.24	23.66	24.08
10¼	18.73	19.27	19.80	20.31	20.81	21.29	21.77	22.23	22.69	23.14	23.58	24.01	24.43
10½	19.03	19.57	20.10	20.62	21.12	21.61	22.09	22.56	23.02	23.47	23.92	24.35	24.78
10¾	19.32	19.87	20.40	20.93	21.43	21.93	22.41	22.89	23.35	23.81	24.25	24.69	25.13
11	19.62	20.17	20.71	21.23	21.74	22.24	22.73	23.21	23.68	24.14	24.59	25.04	25.47

$$D = \sqrt{d_1^2 + 6.28rd_1 + 8r^2 + 4d_2 H}$$

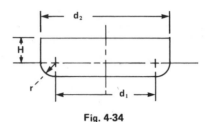

Fig. 4-34

A sectional view of a straight wall cylindrical shell is shown above. In the accompanying equation, D equals the diameter of the flat blank needed to produce the configuration shown in the sectional view. To assist diemakers and designers, Tables 4–2 through 4–9 provide values for D in millimetres. Tables 4–10 through 4–17 provide values for D in inches. The following index will prove helpful in finding the table you require for a specific problem.

$H = 0$ mm . . . . Use Table 4–2
$H = 10$ mm. Use Table 4–3
$H = 15$ mm. Use Table 4–4
$H = 20$ mm. Use Table 4–5
$H = 25$ mm. Use Table 4–6
$H = 30$ mm. Use Table 4–7
$H = 35$ mm. Use Table 4–8
$H = 40$ mm. Use Table 4–9

$H = 0$ inch . . . . .Use Table 4–10
$H = \frac{1}{4}$ inch . . . . .Use Table 4–11
$H = \frac{3}{8}$ inch . . . . .Use Table 4–12
$H = \frac{1}{2}$ inch . . . . .Use Table 4–13
$H = \frac{5}{8}$ inch . . . . .Use Table 4–14
$H = \frac{3}{4}$ inch . . . . .Use Table 4–15
$H = \frac{7}{8}$ inch . . . . .Use Table 4–16
$H = 1$ inch . . . . .Use Table 4–17

As an example of how to use these tables, let us assume a drawn sheet with an H value of 10 mm. The value of d_1 is 75, and the radius is 6. The diameter (D) of a flat blank to draw this part is found in Table 4–3, since all values given in this table are for H dimensions of 10. The solution can be readily found by going down the d_1 column to 75 and then over to the column representing a 6 mm radius. Diameter of the blank is 110.54 mm.

130

$$D = \sqrt{d_1^2 + 6.28rd_1 + 8r^2 + 4d_2 H}$$

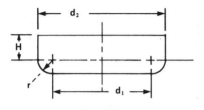

Fig. 4-34

In contrast, if one were to find the value of D by using the formula, the following steps would be necessary:

$$D = \sqrt{d_1^2 + 6.28rd_1 + 8r^2 + 4d_2 H}$$
$$D = \sqrt{(75 \times 75) + (6.28 \times 6 \times 75) + (8 \times 6 \times 6) + (4 \times 87 \times 10)}$$
$$= \sqrt{5625 + 2826 + 288 + 3480}$$
$$= \sqrt{12{,}219}$$
$$= 110.539 \text{ mm}$$

Interpolation can be used if the specific values needed for d_1, or r, or H are not found in the table. For example, let us assume $H = 10$ mm, $r = 10$ mm and $d_1 = 77$ mm. The problem is that 77 is not found in the d_1 column. The fast solution is:

When $r = 10$ and $d_1 = 80$,. . . . . $D = 127.37$
When $r = 10$ and $d_1 = 75$,. . . . . $D = 122.21$

The difference is 5.16

The value of D for $d_1 = 77$ is $\frac{2}{5}$ of 5.16 added to 122.21. The value of D when $d_1 = 77$ is (2.064 + 122.21) or 124.27.

Interpolation in this manner can be used between the given values of r, just as it can between the given values of d_1. Similarly, it is possible to interpolate between these tables when a desired value of H (as an example $H = 18$) falls between the tables. The process followed is precisely the same as that followed above.

131

$$D = \sqrt{d_1^2 + 6.28rd_1 + 8r^2 + 4d_2 H}$$

Table 4–2. Solutions for $D = \sqrt{d_1^2 + 6.28rd_1 + 8r^2 + 4d_2 H}$ when $H = 0$ mm.

	Radius of Shell					
d_1	4	6	8	10	12	14
50	62.32	68.35	74.32	80.25	86.14	92.00
55	67.34	73.39	79.37	85.32	91.22	97.10
60	72.36	78.41	84.42	90.38	96.30	102.19
65	77.37	83.44	89.45	95.43	101.37	107.27
70	82.38	88.46	94.49	100.48	106.43	112.35
75	87.39	93.48	99.52	105.52	111.49	117.42
80	92.40	98.50	104.55	110.56	116.54	122.48
85	97.41	103.52	109.58	115.60	121.58	127.54
90	102.42	108.53	114.60	120.63	126.63	132.59
95	107.42	113.55	119.62	125.66	131.67	137.64
100	112.43	118.56	124.64	130.69	136.70	142.69
105	117.43	123.57	129.66	135.72	141.74	147.73
110	122.44	128.58	134.68	140.74	146.77	152.77
115	127.44	133.59	139.70	145.76	151.80	157.81
120	132.45	138.60	144.81	150.79	156.83	162.85
125	137.45	143.61	149.72	155.80	161.86	167.88
130	142.46	148.62	154.74	160.82	166.88	172.91
135	147.46	153.62	159.75	165.84	171.90	177.94
140	152.46	158.63	164.76	170.86	176.93	182.97
145	157.47	163.64	169.77	175.87	181.95	187.99
150	162.47	168.64	174.78	180.89	186.97	193.02
155	167.47	173.65	179.79	185.90	191.98	198.04
160	172.47	178.65	184.80	190.91	197.00	203.07
165	177.48	183.66	189.81	195.93	202.02	208.09
170	182.48	188.66	194.82	200.94	207.03	213.11
175	187.48	193.67	199.82	205.95	212.05	218.13
180	192.48	198.67	204.83	210.96	217.06	223.15
185	197.49	203.68	209.84	215.97	222.08	228.16
190	202.49	208.68	214.84	220.98	227.09	233.18
195	207.49	213.68	219.85	225.99	232.10	238.20
200	212.49	218.69	224.86	231.00	237.12	243.21
205	217.49	223.69	229.86	236.01	242.13	248.23
210	222.49	228.69	234.87	241.02	247.14	253.24
215	227.50	233.70	239.87	246.02	252.15	258.26
220	232.50	238.70	244.88	251.03	257.16	263.27
225	237.50	243.70	249.88	256.04	262.17	268.28
230	242.50	248.71	254.89	261.04	267.18	273.29
235	247.50	253.71	259.89	266.05	272.19	278.31
240	252.50	258.71	264.90	271.06	277.20	283.32
245	257.50	263.71	269.90	276.06	282.21	288.33
250	262.50	268.72	274.90	281.07	287.21	293.34

$$D = \sqrt{d_1^2 + 6.28rd_1 + 8r^2 + 4d_2 H}$$

Table 4–2. Solutions for $D = \sqrt{d_1^2 + 6.28rd_1 + 8r^2 + 4d_2 H}$ when $H = 0$ mm (Continued).

d_1	Radius of Shell					
	16	18	20	22	24	26
50	97.84	103.65	109.45	115.24	121.01	126.78
55	102.95	108.79	114.60	120.40	126.19	131.96
60	108.06	113.91	119.74	125.55	131.34	137.13
65	113.16	119.02	124.86	130.68	136.49	142.29
70	118.24	124.12	129.97	135.81	141.63	147.44
75	123.33	129.21	135.07	140.92	146.76	152.58
80	128.40	134.30	140.17	146.03	151.87	157.70
85	133.47	139.38	145.26	151.13	156.99	162.82
90	138.53	144.45	150.35	156.23	162.09	167.94
95	143.59	149.52	155.43	161.31	167.19	173.05
100	148.65	154.58	160.50	166.40	172.28	178.15
105	153.70	159.64	165.57	171.48	177.37	183.24
110	158.75	164.70	170.63	176.55	182.45	188.33
115	163.79	169.76	175.70	181.62	187.53	193.42
120	168.84	174.81	180.75	186.69	192.60	198.50
125	173.88	179.85	185.81	191.75	197.67	203.58
130	178.92	184.90	190.86	196.81	202.74	208.65
135	183.95	189.94	195.91	201.86	207.80	213.72
140	188.99	194.98	200.96	206.92	212.86	218.79
145	194.02	200.02	206.00	211.97	217.92	223.85
150	199.05	205.06	211.05	217.02	222.97	228.91
155	204.08	210.09	216.09	222.06	228.02	233.97
160	209.11	215.12	221.12	227.11	233.07	239.03
165	214.13	220.16	226.16	232.15	238.12	244.08
170	219.16	225.19	231.20	237.19	243.17	249.13
175	224.18	230.22	236.23	242.23	248.21	254.18
180	229.20	235.24	241.26	247.27	253.25	259.23
185	234.23	240.27	246.30	252.30	258.30	264.27
190	239.25	245.30	251.32	257.34	263.33	269.32
195	244.27	250.32	256.35	262.37	268.37	274.36
200	249.29	255.34	261.38	267.40	273.41	279.40
205	254.31	260.37	266.41	272.43	278.44	284.44
210	259.32	265.39	271.43	277.46	283.48	289.48
215	264.34	270.41	276.46	282.49	288.51	294.51
220	269.36	275.43	281.48	287.52	293.54	299.55
225	274.37	280.45	286.51	292.55	298.57	304.58
230	279.39	285.47	291.53	297.57	303.60	309.62
235	284.40	290.49	296.55	302.60	308.63	314.65
240	289.42	295.50	301.57	307.62	313.66	319.68
245	294.43	300.52	306.59	312.64	318.68	324.71
250	299.45	305.54	311.61	317.67	323.71	329.74

$$D = \sqrt{d_1^2 + 6.28rd_1 + 8r^2 + 4d_2\,H}$$

Table 4–3. Solutions for $D = \sqrt{d_1^2 + 6.28rd_1 + 8r^2 + 4d_2\,H}$ when H = 10 mm.

	Radius of Shell					
d_1	4	6	8	10	12	14
50	78.77	84.57	90.35	96.12	101.88	107.63
55	83.99	89.81	95.60	101.39	107.15	112.91
60	89.19	95.02	100.83	106.62	112.40	118.17
65	94.37	100.21	106.03	111.83	117.62	123.40
70	99.53	105.38	111.22	117.03	122.83	128.62
75	104.68	110.54	116.38	122.21	128.02	133.82
80	109.81	115.68	121.54	127.37	133.19	139.00
85	114.93	120.81	126.68	132.53	138.36	144.17
90	120.04	125.93	131.81	137.67	143.51	149.33
95	125.14	131.04	136.93	142.80	148.65	154.48
100	130.23	136.15	142.04	147.92	153.78	159.62
105	135.32	141.24	147.15	153.03	158.90	164.76
110	140.40	146.33	152.24	158.14	164.02	169.88
115	145.47	151.41	157.34	163.24	169.13	175.00
120	150.54	156.49	162.42	168.33	174.23	180.11
125	155.61	161.56	167.50	173.42	179.32	185.21
130	160.67	166.63	172.58	178.50	184.41	190.31
135	165.72	171.70	177.65	183.58	189.50	195.40
140	170.78	176.76	182.72	188.66	194.58	200.49
145	175.83	181.81	187.78	193.73	199.66	205.58
150	180.88	186.87	192.84	198.80	204.73	210.66
155	185.92	191.92	197.90	203.86	209.80	215.73
160	190.96	196.97	202.95	208.92	214.87	220.81
165	196.00	202.02	208.01	213.98	219.93	225.88
170	201.04	207.06	213.06	219.03	225.00	230.94
175	206.08	212.10	218.10	224.09	230.05	236.01
180	211.12	217.14	223.15	229.14	235.11	241.07
185	216.15	222.18	228.19	234.19	240.16	246.13
190	221.18	227.22	233.23	239.23	245.22	251.18
195	226.21	232.25	238.27	244.28	250.26	256.24
200	231.24	237.28	243.31	249.32	255.31	261.29
205	236.27	242.32	248.35	254.36	260.36	266.34
210	241.29	247.35	253.38	259.40	265.40	271.39
215	246.32	252.38	258.42	264.44	270.44	276.43
220	251.35	257.41	263.45	269.47	275.48	281.48
225	256.37	262.43	268.48	274.51	280.52	286.52
230	261.39	267.46	273.51	279.54	285.56	291.56
235	266.41	272.48	278.54	284.58	290.60	296.60
240	271.43	277.51	283.57	289.61	295.63	301.64
245	276.46	282.53	288.59	294.64	300.67	306.68
250	281.47	287.56	293.62	299.67	305.70	311.72

$$D = \sqrt{d_1^2 + 6.28rd_1 + 8r^2 + 4d_2 H}$$

Table 4–3. Solutions for $D = \sqrt{d_1^2 + 6.28rd_1 + 8r^2 + 4d_2 H}$ when $H = 10$ mm *(Continued)*.

	Radius of Shell					
d_1	*16*	*18*	*20*	*22*	*24*	*26*
50	113.37	119.10	124.82	130.54	136.25	141.96
55	118.66	124.40	130.13	135.85	141.57	147.29
60	123.92	129.67	135.41	141.44	146.87	152.59
65	129.17	134.92	140.67	146.42	152.15	157.88
70	134.49	140.16	145.92	151.67	157.41	163.15
75	139.60	145.38	151.15	156.90	162.66	168.40
80	144.80	150.58	156.36	162.13	167.89	173.64
85	149.98	155.77	161.56	167.33	173.10	178.86
90	155.15	160.95	166.75	172.53	178.31	184.07
95	160.31	166.12	171.92	177.71	183.50	189.27
100	165.46	171.28	177.09	182.89	188.68	194.46
105	170.60	176.43	182.24	188.05	193.85	199.64
110	175.73	181.57	187.39	193.21	199.02	204.81
115	180.85	186.70	192.53	198.36	204.17	209.98
120	185.97	191.82	197.67	203.50	209.32	215.13
125	191.08	196.94	202.79	208.63	214.46	220.28
130	196.19	202.06	207.91	213.76	219.59	225.42
135	201.29	207.17	213.03	218.88	224.72	230.56
140	206.39	212.27	218.14	224.00	229.85	235.68
145	211.48	217.37	223.24	229.11	234.96	240.81
150	216.56	222.46	228.34	234.21	240.07	245.93
155	221.65	227.55	233.44	239.32	245.18	251.04
160	226.73	232.63	238.53	244.41	250.29	256.15
165	231.80	237.72	243.62	249.51	255.39	261.26
170	236.87	242.79	248.70	254.60	260.48	266.36
175	241.94	247.87	253.78	259.68	265.57	273.29
180	247.01	252.94	258.86	264.77	270.66	276.55
185	252.07	258.01	263.93	269.85	275.75	281.64
190	257.14	263.08	269.01	274.92	280.83	286.72
195	262.20	268.14	274.07	280.00	285.91	291.81
200	267.25	273.20	279.14	285.07	290.98	296.89
205	272.31	278.26	284.21	290.14	296.06	301.97
210	277.36	283.32	289.27	295.20	301.13	307.05
215	282.41	288.38	294.33	300.27	306.20	312.12
220	287.46	293.43	299.39	305.33	311.27	317.19
225	292.51	298.48	304.44	310.39	316.33	322.26
230	297.55	303.53	309.50	315.45	321.39	327.33
235	302.60	308.58	314.55	320.51	326.45	332.39
240	307.64	313.63	319.60	325.56	331.51	337.45
245	312.68	318.67	324.65	330.61	336.57	342.52
250	317.72	323.72	329.70	335.67	341.63	347.57

$$D = \sqrt{d_1^2 + 6.28rd_1 + 8r^2 + 4d_2 H}$$

Table 4–4.   Solutions for $D = \sqrt{d_1^2 + 6.28rd_1 + 8r^2 + 4d_2 H}$ when $H = 15$ mm.

d_1	Radius of Shell					
	4	6	8	10	12	14
50	85.81	91.61	97.39	103.15	108.90	114.65
55	91.18	96.98	102.76	108.53	114.29	120.04
60	96.52	102.32	108.10	113.88	119.64	125.39
65	101.81	107.62	113.41	119.19	124.96	130.72
70	107.08	112.90	118.70	124.48	130.26	136.02
75	112.33	118.15	123.96	129.75	135.53	141.30
80	117.55	123.38	129.19	135.00	140.79	146.57
85	122.75	128.59	134.42	140.22	146.02	151.81
90	127.94	133.79	139.62	145.44	151.24	157.04
95	133.11	138.97	144.81	150.64	156.45	162.25
100	138.28	144.14	149.99	155.82	161.64	167.45
105	143.42	149.30	155.15	160.99	166.82	172.64
110	148.56	154.44	160.31	166.16	172.00	177.82
115	153.69	159.58	165.45	171.31	177.15	182.99
120	158.82	164.71	170.59	176.45	182.31	188.14
125	163.93	169.83	175.72	181.59	187.45	193.30
130	169.04	174.95	180.84	186.72	192.58	198.44
135	174.14	180.05	185.96	191.84	197.71	203.57
140	179.23	185.16	191.06	196.96	202.84	208.70
145	184.32	190.25	196.17	202.07	207.95	213.83
150	189.41	195.35	201.27	207.17	213.06	218.94
155	194.49	200.43	206.36	212.27	218.17	224.05
160	199.57	205.52	211.45	217.37	223.27	229.16
165	204.64	210.59	216.53	222.46	228.37	234.26
170	209.71	215.67	221.61	227.54	233.46	239.36
175	214.78	220.74	226.69	232.63	238.55	244.46
180	219.84	225.81	231.77	237.71	243.63	249.55
185	224.90	230.88	236.84	242.78	248.71	254.63
190	229.96	235.94	241.90	247.85	253.79	259.72
195	235.01	241.00	246.97	252.92	258.87	264.80
200	240.07	246.06	252.03	257.99	263.94	269.87
205	245.12	251.11	257.09	263.06	269.01	274.95
210	250.17	256.17	262.15	268.12	274.08	280.02
215	255.21	261.22	267.21	273.18	279.14	285.09
220	260.26	266.27	272.26	278.24	284.20	290.16
225	265.30	271.31	277.31	283.29	289.26	295.22
230	270.34	276.36	282.36	288.35	294.32	300.28
235	275.38	281.40	287.41	293.40	299.38	305.34
240	280.42	286.45	292.45	298.45	304.43	310.40
245	285.46	291.49	297.50	303.50	309.48	315.46
250	290.50	296.53	302.54	308.54	314.53	320.51

136

$$D = \sqrt{d_1^2 + 6.28rd_1 + 8r^2 + 4d_2 H}$$

Table 4–4. Solutions for $D = \sqrt{d_1^2 + 6.28rd_1 + 8r^2 + 4d_2 H}$ when $H = 15$ mm (Continued).

			Radius of Shell			
d_1	16	18	20	22	24	26
50	120.38	126.11	131.83	137.55	143.26	148.97
55	125.78	131.51	137.23	142.95	148.67	154.38
60	131.14	136.87	142.60	148.33	154.05	159.76
65	136.47	142.21	147.95	153.68	159.40	165.12
70	141.78	147.53	153.27	159.01	164.74	170.46
75	147.07	152.82	158.57	164.31	170.05	175.78
80	152.34	158.10	163.85	169.60	175.34	181.08
85	157.59	163.36	169.12	174.87	180.62	186.36
90	162.82	168.60	174.37	180.13	185.88	191.63
95	168.04	173.83	179.60	185.37	191.13	196.89
100	173.25	179.04	184.82	190.60	196.37	202.13
105	178.45	184.24	190.03	195.82	201.59	207.36
110	183.63	189.44	195.23	201.02	206.80	212.58
115	188.81	194.62	200.42	206.22	212.00	217.78
120	193.97	199.79	205.60	211.40	217.20	222.98
125	199.13	204.96	210.77	216.58	222.38	228.17
130	204.28	210.11	215.94	221.75	227.56	233.35
135	209.42	215.26	221.09	226.91	232.72	238.53
140	214.56	220.40	226.24	232.07	237.88	243.69
145	219.69	225.54	231.38	237.21	243.04	248.85
150	224.81	230.67	236.52	242.36	248.19	254.00
155	229.93	235.79	241.65	247.49	253.33	259.16
160	235.04	240.91	246.77	252.62	258.46	264.30
165	240.15	246.03	251.89	257.75	263.59	269.43
170	245.25	251.14	257.01	262.87	268.72	274.56
175	250.35	256.24	262.12	267.98	273.84	279.69
180	255.45	261.34	267.22	273.09	278.96	284.81
185	260.54	266.44	272.33	278.20	284.07	289.93
190	265.63	271.53	277.42	283.31	289.18	295.04
195	270.71	276.62	282.52	288.41	294.28	300.15
200	275.80	281.71	287.61	293.50	299.39	305.26
205	280.88	286.79	292.70	298.60	304.48	310.36
210	285.95	291.87	297.79	303.69	309.58	315.46
215	291.03	296.95	302.87	308.77	314.67	320.56
220	296.10	302.03	307.95	313.86	319.76	325.65
225	301.17	307.10	313.03	318.94	324.85	330.74
230	306.23	312.17	318.10	324.02	329.93	335.83
235	311.30	317.24	323.17	329.10	335.01	340.92
240	316.36	322.31	328.24	334.17	340.09	346.00
245	321.42	327.37	333.31	339.24	345.17	351.08
250	326.48	332.43	338.38	344.31	350.24	356.16

$$D = \sqrt{d_1^2 + 6.28rd_1 + 8r^2 + 4d_2\,H}$$

Table 4–5.   Solutions for $D = \sqrt{d_1^2 + 6.28rd_1 + 8r^2 + 4d_2\,H}$
when $H = 20$ **mm.**

	Radius of Shell					
d_1	4	6	8	10	12	14
50	92.33	98.14	103.94	109.73	115.50	121.26
55	97.85	103.66	109.45	115.23	121.00	126.76
60	103.32	109.13	114.92	120.70	126.47	132.22
65	108.75	114.55	120.34	126.12	131.89	137.65
70	114.13	119.94	125.73	131.51	137.29	143.05
75	119.49	125.30	131.09	136.88	142.65	148.41
80	124.81	130.62	136.42	142.21	147.99	153.76
85	130.11	135.93	141.73	147.52	153.31	159.08
90	135.38	141.21	147.02	152.81	158.60	164.38
95	140.64	146.47	152.28	158.09	163.88	169.66
100	145.88	151.71	157.53	163.34	169.14	174.93
105	151.10	156.94	162.76	168.58	174.38	180.18
110	156.30	162.15	167.98	173.80	179.62	185.42
115	161.50	167.35	173.19	179.02	184.83	190.64
120	166.68	172.54	178.38	184.22	190.04	195.85
125	171.85	177.72	183.57	189.41	195.24	201.05
130	177.01	182.88	188.74	194.59	200.42	206.25
135	182.17	188.04	193.91	199.76	205.60	211.43
140	187.31	193.19	199.06	204.92	210.77	216.60
145	192.45	198.33	204.21	210.07	215.93	221.77
150	197.58	203.47	209.35	215.22	221.08	226.93
155	202.70	208.60	214.49	220.36	226.23	232.08
160	207.82	213.72	219.61	225.50	231.36	237.22
165	212.93	218.84	224.74	230.62	236.50	242.36
170	218.03	223.95	229.85	235.75	241.63	247.50
175	223.13	229.06	234.97	240.86	246.75	252.62
180	228.23	234.16	240.07	245.98	251.87	257.75
185	233.32	239.26	245.18	251.08	256.98	262.87
190	238.41	244.35	·250.28	256.19	262.09	267.98
195	243.50	249.44	255.37	261.29	267.29	273.09
200	248.58	254.53	260.46	266.38	272.29	278.19
205	253.66	259.61	265.55	271.48	277.39	283.30
210	258.73	264.69	270.63	276.56	282.48	288.39
215	263.81	269.77	275.71	281.65	287.58	293.49
220	268.88	274.84	280.79	286.73	292.66	298.58
225	273.94	279.91	285.87	291.81	297.75	303.67
230	279.01	284.98	290.94	296.89	302.83	308.75
235	284.07	290.05	296.01	301.97	307.91	313.84
240	289.13	295.11	301.08	307.04	312.98	318.92
245	294.19	300.17	306.15	312.11	318.06	324.00
250	299.25	305.23	311.21	317.18	323.13	329.07

$$D = \sqrt{d_1^2 + 6.28rd_1 + 8r^2 + 4d_2 H}$$

Table 4–5. Solutions for $D = \sqrt{d_1^2 + 6.28rd_1 + 8r^2 + 4d_2 H}$
when $H = 20$ **mm** *(Continued)*.

d_1	Radius of Shell					
	16	18	20	22	24	26
50	126.62	132.76	138.49	144.22	149.95	155.67
55	132.51	138.25	143.99	149.72	155.44	161.16
60	137.97	143.72	149.45	155.18	160.91	166.63
65	143.40	149.15	154.88	160.62	166.34	172.06
70	148.80	154.55	160.29	166.02	171.75	177.48
75	154.17	159.92	165.67	171.40	177.14	182.86
80	159.52	165.27	171.02	176.76	182.50	188.23
85	164.84	170.60	176.35	182.10	187.84	193.58
90	170.15	175.91	181.67	187.42	193.17	198.90
95	175.44	181.21	186.97	192.72	198.47	204.22
100	180.71	186.48	192.25	198.01	203.76	209.51
105	185.97	191.75	197.52	203.28	209.04	214.80
110	191.21	196.99	202.77	208.54	214.31	220.07
115	196.44	202.23	208.01	213.79	219.56	225.32
120	201.66	207.45	213.24	219.02	224.80	230.57
125	206.86	212.67	218.46	224.25	230.03	235.80
130	212.06	217.87	223.67	229.46	235.25	241.03
135	217.25	223.06	228.87	234.67	240.46	246.24
140	222.43	228.25	234.06	239.86	245.66	251.45
145	227.60	233.43	239.24	245.05	250.85	256.65
150	232.77	238.60	244.42	250.23	256.04	261.84
155	237.92	243.76	249.59	255.41	261.22	267.02
160	243.07	248.91	254.75	260.57	266.39	272.20
165	248.22	254.06	259.90	265.73	271.55	277.37
170	253.36	259.21	265.05	270.89	276.71	282.53
175	258.49	264.35	270.19	276.03	281.87	287.69
180	263.62	269.48	275.33	281.18	287.01	292.85
185	268.74	274.61	280.47	286.32	292.16	297.99
190	273.86	279.73	285.59	291.45	297.30	303.14
195	278.97	284.85	290.72	296.58	302.43	308.27
200	284.08	289.97	295.84	301.70	307.56	313.41
205	289.19	295.08	300.95	306.82	312.68	318.54
210	294.29	300.68	306.07	311.94	317.80	323.66
215	299.39	305.29	311.17	317.05	322.92	328.78
220	304.49	310.39	316.28	322.16	328.03	333.90
225	309.58	315.49	321.38	327.27	333.14	339.01
230	314.67	320.58	326.48	332.37	338.25	344.13
235	319.76	325.67	331.57	337.47	343.35	349.23
240	324.84	330.76	336.67	342.56	348.45	354.34
245	329.93	335.84	341.76	347.66	353.55	359.44
250	335.00	340.93	346.84	352.75	358.65	364.54

$$D = \sqrt{d_1^2 + 6.28rd_1 + 8r^2 + 4d_2 H}$$

Table 4–6. Solutions for $D = \sqrt{d_1^2 + 6.28rd_1 + 8r^2 + 4d_2 H}$ when $H = 25$ mm.

d_1	Radius of Shell					
	4	*6*	*8*	*10*	*12*	*14*
50	98.41	104.27	110.11	115.93	121.74	127.53
55	104.09	109.93	115.76	121.57	127.36	133.15
60	109.71	115.54	121.35	127.15	132.94	138.72
65	115.26	121.09	126.89	132.69	138.48	144.25
70	120.77	126.59	132.40	138.19	143.97	149.74
75	126.24	132.06	137.86	143.65	149.43	155.20
80	131.67	137.49	143.29	149.08	154.86	160.63
85	137.07	142.88	148.69	154.48	160.26	166.03
90	142.44	148.25	154.06	159.85	165.63	171.41
95	147.78	153.60	159.40	165.20	170.99	176.76
100	153.10	158.92	164.73	170.53	176.32	182.10
105	158.40	164.22	170.04	175.84	181.63	187.42
110	163.68	169.51	175.32	181.13	186.93	192.72
115	168.94	174.77	180.60	186.41	192.21	198.00
120	174.19	180.03	185.85	191.67	197.47	203.27
125	179.42	185.26	191.09	196.91	202.72	208.53
130	184.64	190.49	196.32	202.15	207.96	213.77
135	189.85	195.70	201.54	207.37	213.19	219.00
140	195.05	200.91	206.75	212.35	218.41	224.22
145	200.24	206.10	211.95	217.79	223.62	229.44
150	205.42	211.28	217.14	222.98	228.81	234.64
155	210.59	216.46	222.32	228.16	234.00	239.83
160	215.75	221.62	227.49	233.34	239.19	245.02
165	220.90	226.78	232.65	238.51	244.36	250.20
170	226.05	231.93	237.81	243.67	249.53	255.37
175	231.19	237.08	242.96	248.83	254.69	260.54
180	236.33	242.22	248.10	253.98	259.84	265.69
185	241.45	247.35	253.24	259.12	264.99	270.85
190	246.58	252.48	258.37	264.26	270.13	275.99
195	251.70	257.61	263.50	269.39	275.27	281.14
200	256.81	262.72	268.63	274.52	280.40	286.27
205	261.92	267.84	273.74	279.64	285.53	291.40
210	267.03	272.95	278.86	284.76	290.65	296.53
215	272.13	278.05	283.97	289.87	295.77	301.66
220	277.23	283.16	289.08	294.98	300.88	306.77
225	282.32	288.26	294.18	300.09	306.00	311.89
230	287.41	293.35	299.28	305.20	311.10	317.00
235	292.50	298.44	304.37	310.30	316.21	322.11
240	297.58	303.53	309.47	315.39	321.31	327.21
245	302.67	308.62	314.56	320.49	326.40	332.32
250	307.75	313.70	319.62	325.58	331.50	337.41

$$D = \sqrt{d_1^2 + 6.28rd_1 + 8r^2 + 4d_2 H}$$

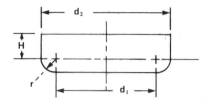

Table 4–6. Solutions for $D = \sqrt{d_1^2 + 6.28rd_1 + 8r^2 + 4d_2 H}$
when $H = 25$ **mm** *(Continued).*

	Radius of Shell					
d_1	*16*	*18*	*20*	*22*	*24*	*26*
50	133.31	139.08	144.84	150.60	156.35	162.09
55	138.92	144.69	150.44	156.19	161.93	167.67
60	144.49	150.25	156.00	161.75	167.48	173.22
65	150.01	155.77	161.52	167.26	173.00	178.73
70	155.50	161.26	167.01	172.75	178.49	184.22
75	160.96	166.72	172.47	178.21	183.95	189.68
80	166.39	172.15	177.90	183.64	189.38	195.12
85	171.80	177.55	183.31	189.05	194.79	200.53
90	177.18	182.94	188.69	194.44	200.18	205.92
95	182.53	188.30	194.05	199.81	205.55	211.29
100	187.87	193.64	199.40	205.15	210.90	216.65
105	193.19	198.96	204.73	210.48	216.24	221.99
110	198.50	204.27	210.04	215.80	221.56	227.31
115	203.78	209.56	215.33	221.10	226.86	232.62
120	209.06	214.84	220.62	226.39	232.15	237.91
125	214.32	220.11	225.89	231.66	237.43	243.19
130	219.57	225.36	231.14	236.92	242.70	248.46
135	224.81	230.60	236.39	242.17	247.95	253.72
140	230.03	235.83	241.63	247.42	253.20	258.97
145	235.25	241.06	246.85	252.65	258.43	264.21
150	240.46	246.27	252.07	257.87	263.66	269.44
155	245.66	251.47	257.28	263.08	268.88	274.67
160	250.85	256.67	262.48	268.29	274.09	279.88
165	256.03	261.86	267.67	273.48	279.29	285.09
170	261.21	267.04	272.86	278.67	284.48	290.29
175	266.38	272.21	278.04	283.86	289.67	295.48
180	271.54	277.38	283.21	289.03	294.85	300.66
185	267.70	282.54	288.38	294.21	300.03	305.84
190	281.85	287.70	293.54	299.37	305.20	311.02
195	287.00	292.85	298.69	304.53	310.36	316.18
200	292.14	297.99	303.84	309.68	315.52	321.35
205	297.27	303.13	308.99	314.83	320.67	326.50
210	302.41	308.27	314.13	319.98	325.82	331.66
215	307.53	313.40	319.26	325.12	330.96	336.81
220	312.66	318.53	324.39	330.25	336.10	341.95
225	317.78	323.65	329.52	335.38	341.24	347.09
230	322.89	328.77	334.65	340.51	346.37	352.22
235	328.00	333.89	339.77	345.64	351.50	357.36
240	333.11	339.00	344.88	350.77	356.62	362.48
245	338.22	344.11	350.00	355.87	361.74	367.61
250	343.32	349.22	355.11	360.99	366.86	372.73

$$D = \sqrt{d_1^2 + 6.28rd_1 + 8r^2 + 4d_2 H}$$

Table 4-7. Solutions for $D = \sqrt{d_1^2 + 6.28rd_1 + 8r^2 + 4d_2 H}$ when $H = 30$ mm.

	Radius of Shell					
d_1	4	6	8	10	12	14
50	104.13	110.05	115.95	121.82	127.67	133.51
55	109.98	115.87	121.74	127.59	133.42	139.24
60	115.74	121.61	127.46	133.30	139.12	144.92
65	121.43	127.29	133.12	138.95	144.76	150.56
70	127.07	132.91	138.74	144.55	150.36	156.15
75	132.65	138.49	144.31	150.12	155.91	161.70
80	138.19	144.02	149.84	155.64	161.43	167.22
85	143.69	149.52	155.33	161.13	166.92	172.70
90	149.16	154.98	160.79	166.59	172.38	178.16
95	154.59	160.41	166.22	172.02	177.81	183.59
100	160.00	165.82	171.63	177.43	183.22	189.00
105	165.38	171.20	177.01	182.81	188.60	194.38
110	170.74	176.56	182.37	188.17	193.96	199.75
115	176.07	181.90	187.71	193.51	199.31	205.09
120	181.39	187.22	193.03	198.84	204.63	210.42
125	186.69	192.52	198.34	204.14	209.95	215.74
130	191.97	197.80	203.63	209.44	215.24	221.04
135	197.24	203.08	208.90	214.72	220.52	226.32
140	202.50	208.33	214.16	219.98	225.79	231.60
145	207.74	213.58	219.41	225.24	231.05	236.86
150	212.97	218.81	224.65	230.48	236.30	242.11
155	218.19	224.04	229.88	235.71	241.53	247.35
160	223.40	229.25	235.10	240.93	246.76	252.58
165	228.60	234.46	240.31	246.14	251.97	257.80
170	233.79	239.65	245.51	251.35	257.18	263.01
175	238.97	244.84	250.70	256.54	262.38	268.21
180	244.15	250.02	255.88	261.73	267.58	273.41
185	249.32	255.19	261.06	266.91	272.76	278.60
190	254.48	260.36	266.23	272.09	277.94	283.78
195	259.64	265.52	271.39	277.26	283.11	288.96
200	264.79	270.67	276.55	282.42	288.28	294.13
205	269.93	275.82	281.70	287.57	293.44	299.29
210	275.07	280.96	286.85	292.73	298.59	304.45
215	280.20	286.10	291.99	297.87	303.74	309.61
220	285.33	291.23	297.13	303.01	308.89	314.75
225	290.46	296.36	302.26	308.15	314.03	319.90
230	295.58	301.49	307.39	313.28	319.16	325.04
235	300.69	306.61	312.51	318.41	324.29	330.17
240	305.81	311.72	317.63	323.53	329.42	335.30
245	310.91	316.84	322.75	328.65	334.54	340.43
250	316.02	321.94	327.86	333.77	339.66	345.55

$$D = \sqrt{d_1^2 + 6.28rd_1 + 8r^2 + 4d_2\,H}$$

Table 4–7. Solutions for $D = \sqrt{d_1^2 + 6.28rd_1 + 8r^2 + 4d_2\,H}$ when $H = 30$ mm (Continued).

d_1	Radius of Shell					
	16	18	20	22	24	26
50	139.33	145.13	150.93	156.72	162.49	168.26
55	145.05	150.84	156.63	162.41	168.17	173.94
60	150.72	156.51	162.28	168.05	173.81	179.57
65	156.35	162.13	167.90	173.66	179.42	185.17
70	161.93	167.70	173.47	179.23	184.98	190.73
75	167.48	173.25	179.01	184.77	190.52	196.26
80	172.99	178.76	184.52	190.28	196.02	201.77
85	178.48	184.24	190.00	195.76	201.50	207.25
90	183.93	189.70	195.46	201.21	206.96	212.70
95	189.36	195.13	200.89	206.65	212.39	218.14
100	194.77	200.54	206.31	212.06	217.81	223.55
105	200.16	205.93	211.69	217.45	223.20	228.95
110	205.53	211.30	217.06	222.82	228.58	234.33
115	210.87	216.65	222.42	228.18	233.94	239.69
120	216.21	221.98	227.75	233.52	239.28	245.03
125	221.52	227.30	233.08	238.85	244.61	250.37
130	226.83	232.61	238.39	244.16	249.92	255.68
135	232.12	237.90	243.68	249.46	255.23	260.99
140	237.39	243.18	248.97	254.74	260.52	266.28
145	242.66	248.45	254.24	260.02	265.80	271.57
150	247.91	253.71	259.50	265.28	271.06	276.84
155	253.15	258.96	264.75	270.54	276.32	282.10
160	258.39	264.19	270.00	275.79	281.57	287.35
165	263.61	269.42	275.23	281.02	286.81	292.60
170	268.83	274.64	280.45	286.25	292.05	297.83
175	274.04	279.86	285.67	291.47	297.27	303.06
180	279.24	285.06	290.87	296.68	302.49	308.28
185	284.43	290.26	296.08	301.89	307.69	313.50
190	289.62	295.45	301.27	307.09	312.90	318.70
195	294.80	300.63	306.46	312.28	318.09	323.90
200	299.97	305.81	311.64	317.46	323.28	329.10
205	305.14	310.98	316.82	322.65	328.47	334.28
210	310.30	316.62	321.99	327.82	333.65	339.47
215	315.46	321.31	327.15	332.99	338.82	344.64
220	320.61	326.47	332.31	338.15	343.99	349.81
225	325.76	331.62	337.47	343.31	349.15	354.98
230	330.91	336.77	342.62	348.47	354.31	360.14
235	336.04	341.91	347.77	353.62	359.46	365.30
240	341.18	347.05	352.91	358.76	364.61	370.45
245	346.31	352.18	358.05	363.90	369.76	375.60
250	351.44	357.31	363.18	369.04	374.90	380.75

$$D = \sqrt{d_1^2 + 6.28rd_1 + 8r^2 + 4d_2\,H}$$

Table 4–8. Solutions for $D = \sqrt{d_1^2 + 6.28rd_1 + 8r^2 + 4d_2\,H}$ when $H = 35$ mm.

	Radius of Shell					
d_1	4	6	8	10	12	14
50	109.56	115.55	121.51	127.44	133.34	139.23
55	115.56	121.51	127.44	133.34	139.22	145.08
60	121.47	127.39	133.29	139.17	145.03	150.87
65	127.30	133.20	139.07	144.94	150.78	156.61
70	133.07	138.94	144.81	150.65	156.48	162.30
75	138.77	144.63	150.48	156.32	162.14	167.95
80	144.42	150.27	156.11	161.94	167.75	173.56
85	150.03	155.87	161.70	167.52	173.33	179.13
90	155.59	161.43	167.25	173.07	178.87	184.66
95	161.12	166.95	172.77	178.58	184.38	190.17
100	166.61	172.44	178.26	184.07	189.86	195.65
105	172.08	177.90	183.72	189.52	195.32	201.11
110	177.51	183.34	189.15	194.96	200.75	206.54
115	182.93	188.75	194.56	200.37	206.16	211.95
120	188.31	194.14	199.95	205.76	211.55	217.34
125	193.68	199.51	205.32	211.13	216.93	222.72
130	199.03	204.86	210.67	216.48	222.28	228.07
135	204.36	210.19	216.01	221.82	227.62	233.41
140	209.68	215.51	221.33	227.14	232.94	238.74
145	214.98	220.81	226.63	232.45	238.25	244.05
150	220.26	226.10	231.92	237.74	243.55	249.35
155	225.54	231.37	237.20	243.02	248.83	254.64
160	230.80	236.64	242.47	248.29	254.11	259.91
165	236.05	241.89	247.72	253.55	259.37	265.18
170	241.28	247.13	252.97	258.80	264.62	270.43
175	246.51	252.36	258.20	264.04	269.86	275.68
180	251.73	257.59	263.43	269.27	275.09	280.92
185	256.94	262.80	268.65	274.49	280.32	286.14
190	262.15	268.01	273.86	279.70	285.54	291.36
195	267.34	273.20	279.06	284.91	290.74	296.58
200	272.53	278.40	284.25	290.10	295.95	301.78
205	277.71	283.58	289.44	295.29	301.14	306.98
210	282.88	288.76	294.62	300.48	306.33	312.17
215	288.05	293.93	299.80	305.66	311.51	317.36
220	293.21	299.09	304.97	310.83	316.69	322.54
225	298.37	304.25	310.13	316.00	321.86	326.34
230	303.52	309.41	315.29	321.16	327.02	332.88
235	308.67	314.56	320.44	326.32	332.18	338.04
240	313.81	319.70	325.59	331.47	337.34	343.20
245	318.95	324.85	330.74	336.62	342.49	348.36
250	324.08	329.98	335.87	341.76	347.64	353.51

$$D = \sqrt{d_1^2 + 6.28rd_1 + 8r^2 + 4d_2 H}$$

Table 4–8. **Solutions for** $D = \sqrt{d_1^2 + 6.28rd_1 + 8r^2 + 4d_2 H}$
when $H = 35$ **mm** *(Continued)*.

	Radius of Shell					
d_1	16	18	20	22	24	26
50	145.09	150.94	156.78	162.60	168.42	174.22
55	150.93	156.76	162.58	168.39	174.19	179.98
60	156.71	162.53	168.33	174.13	179.92	185.70
65	162.43	168.24	174.04	179.83	185.61	191.38
70	168.11	173.91	179.70	185.48	191.25	197.02
75	173.75	179.54	185.32	191.10	196.87	202.63
80	179.35	185.14	190.91	196.68	202.45	208.21
85	184.92	190.70	196.47	202.24	208.00	213.76
90	190.45	196.23	202.00	207.77	213.52	219.28
95	195.96	201.73	207.50	213.27	219.02	224.78
100	201.43	207.21	212.98	218.74	224.50	230.25
105	206.89	212.66	218.43	224.20	229.95	235.71
110	212.32	218.10	223.87	229.63	235.39	239.27
115	217.73	223.51	229.28	235.04	240.80	246.56
120	223.13	228.90	234.67	240.44	246.20	251.96
125	228.50	234.28	240.05	245.82	251.58	257.34
130	233.86	239.64	245.41	251.18	256.95	262.71
135	239.20	244.98	250.76	256.53	262.30	259.53
140	244.53	250.32	256.09	261.87	267.64	273.40
145	249.85	255.63	261.41	267.19	272.96	278.73
150	255.15	260.94	266.72	272.50	278.27	284.04
155	260.44	266.23	272.02	277.80	283.57	289.35
160	265.72	271.51	277.30	283.09	288.87	294.64
165	270.98	276.78	282.58	288.36	294.15	299.92
170	276.24	282.04	287.84	293.63	299.42	305.20
175	281.49	287.30	293.10	298.89	304.68	310.46
180	286.73	292.54	298.34	304.14	309.93	315.72
185	291.96	297.77	303.58	309.38	315.18	320.97
190	297.19	303.00	308.81	314.61	320.41	326.21
195	302.40	308.22	314.03	319.84	325.64	331.44
200	307.61	313.43	319.25	325.06	330.87	336.67
205	312.81	318.64	324.46	330.27	336.08	341.89
210	318.01	323.84	329.66	335.48	341.29	347.10
215	323.20	329.03	334.86	340.68	346.49	352.30
220	328.38	334.22	340.05	345.87	351.69	357.50
225	333.56	339.40	345.23	351.06	356.88	362.70
230	338.73	344.57	350.41	356.24	362.07	367.89
235	343.90	349.74	355.59	361.42	367.25	373.07
240	349.06	354.91	360.75	366.59	372.43	378.25
245	354.22	360.07	365.92	371.76	377.60	383.43
250	359.37	365.23	371.08	376.92	382.76	388.60

$$D = \sqrt{d_1^2 + 6.28rd_1 + 8r^2 + 4d_2\,H}$$

Table 4–9. Solutions for $D = \sqrt{d_1^2 + 6.28rd_1 + 8r^2 + 4d_2\,H}$ when $H = 40$ mm.

d_1	Radius of Shell					
	4	6	8	10	12	14
50	114.73	120.80	126.82	132.82	138.78	144.72
55	120.89	126.91	132.89	138.85	144.78	150.69
60	126.95	132.92	138.88	144.80	150.71	156.60
65	132.91	138.86	144.78	150.69	156.57	162.44
70	138.80	144.73	150.63	156.51	162.38	168.23
75	144.63	150.53	156.41	162.28	168.13	173.97
80	150.39	156.28	162.15	168.00	173.84	179.67
85	156.10	161.97	167.83	173.67	179.51	185.33
90	161.77	167.63	173.48	179.31	185.13	190.95
95	167.39	173.24	179.08	184.91	190.73	196.53
100	172.97	178.82	184.65	190.47	196.29	202.09
105	178.52	184.36	190.19	196.01	201.82	207.62
110	184.04	189.88	195.70	201.51	207.32	213.12
115	189.53	195.36	201.18	207.00	212.80	218.60
120	194.99	200.82	206.64	212.45	218.25	224.05
125	200.43	206.26	212.08	217.89	223.69	229.48
130	205.85	211.68	217.49	223.30	229.10	234.90
135	211.24	217.07	222.89	228.70	234.50	240.30
140	216.62	222.45	228.27	234.08	239.88	245.68
145	221.98	227.81	233.63	239.44	245.24	251.04
150	227.32	233.15	238.97	244.79	250.59	256.39
155	232.65	238.48	244.30	250.12	255.93	261.73
160	237.96	243.80	249.66	255.44	261.25	267.05
165	243.26	249.10	254.92	260.74	266.55	272.36
170	248.55	254.39	260.02	266.04	271.85	277.66
175	253.83	258.67	265.50	271.32	277.14	282.95
180	259.09	264.93	270.77	276.59	282.41	288.22
185	264.35	270.19	276.03	281.86	287.68	293.49
190	269.59	275.44	281.28	287.11	292.93	298.75
195	274.83	280.68	286.52	292.35	298.18	304.00
200	280.06	285.91	291.75	297.59	303.42	309.24
205	285.28	291.13	296.81	302.82	308.65	314.48
210	290.49	296.35	302.20	308.04	313.88	319.70
215	295.69	301.55	307.41	313.25	319.09	324.92
220	300.89	306.75	312.61	318.46	324.30	330.14
225	306.08	311.95	317.81	323.66	329.50	335.34
230	311.26	317.13	323.00	328.85	334.70	340.54
235	316.44	322.32	328.18	334.04	339.89	345.74
240	321.62	327.49	333.36	339.22	345.08	350.93
245	326.78	332.66	338.53	344.40	350.26	356.11
250	331.95	337.83	343.70	349.57	355.43	361.29

$$D = \sqrt{d_1^2 + 6.28rd_1 + 8r^2 + 4d_2\,H}$$

Table 4–9.   Solutions for $D = \sqrt{d_1^2 + 6.28rd_1 + 8r^2 + 4d_2\,H}$
when $H = 40$ mm (*Continued*).

	Radius of Shell					
d_1	16	18	20	22	24	26
50	150.64	156.54	162.42	168.29	174.14	179.98
55	156.59	162.46	168.32	174.17	180.01	185.83
60	162.47	168.33	174.17	180.00	185.83	191.64
65	168.30	174.14	179.97	185.79	191.60	197.40
70	174.07	179.90	185.72	191.53	197.33	203.12
75	179.80	185.62	191.43	197.23	203.02	208.80
80	185.49	191.30	197.10	202.89	208.68	214.45
85	191.14	196.94	202.73	208.52	214.30	220.07
90	196.75	202.55	208.34	214.12	219.89	225.66
95	202.33	208.12	213.91	219.69	225.46	231.22
100	207.88	213.67	219.45	225.23	231.00	236.76
105	213.41	219.19	224.97	230.75	236.51	242.28
110	218.91	224.69	230.47	236.24	242.01	247.77
115	224.38	230.17	235.94	241.71	247.48	253.24
120	229.84	235.62	241.40	247.17	252.93	258.69
125	235.27	241.05	246.83	252.60	258.37	264.13
130	240.69	246.47	252.25	258.02	263.78	269.54
135	246.08	251.87	257.65	263.42	269.18	274.95
140	251.47	257.25	263.03	268.80	274.57	280.33
145	256.83	262.62	268.40	274.17	279.94	285.71
150	262.18	267.97	273.75	279.53	285.30	291.07
155	267.52	273.31	279.09	284.87	290.65	296.41
160	272.85	278.64	284.42	290.20	295.98	301.75
165	278.16	283.95	289.74	295.52	301.30	307.07
170	283.46	289.26	295.05	300.83	306.61	312.39
175	288.75	294.55	300.34	306.13	311.91	317.69
180	294.03	299.83	305.63	311.42	317.20	322.98
185	299.30	305.11	310.90	316.70	322.48	328.27
190	304.56	310.37	316.17	321.97	327.76	333.54
195	309.82	315.63	321.43	327.23	333.02	338.81
200	315.06	320.87	326.68	332.48	338.28	344.07
205	320.30	326.11	331.92	337.73	343.53	349.32
210	325.53	331.35	337.16	342.97	348.77	354.57
215	330.75	336.57	342.39	348.20	354.00	359.80
220	335.97	341.79	347.61	353.42	359.23	365.03
225	341.18	347.00	352.82	358.64	364.45	370.26
230	346.38	352.21	358.03	363.85	369.67	375.48
235	351.58	357.41	363.24	369.06	374.88	380.69
240	356.77	362.60	368.43	374.26	380.08	385.90
245	361.95	367.79	373.63	379.46	385.28	391.10
250	367.13	372.98	378.81	384.65	390.47	396.29

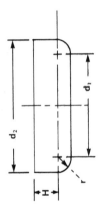

Table 4–10. Solutions for $D = \sqrt{d_1^2 + 6.28rd_1 + 8r^2 + 4d_2H}$ when $H = 0$ inch.

d_1						Radius of shell							
	1/4	5/16	3/8	7/16	1/2	9/16	5/8	11/16	3/4	13/16	7/8	15/16	1
2.0	2.764	2.951	3.136	3.321	3.504	3.687	3.870	4.052	4.233	4.414	4.595	4.776	4.956
2 1/8	2.890	3.077	3.263	3.447	3.632	3.815	3.998	4.180	4.362	4.543	4.724	4.905	5.085
2 1/4	3.016	3.201	3.389	3.574	3.759	3.942	4.125	4.308	4.490	4.672	4.853	5.034	5.215
2 3/8	3.142	3.329	3.516	3.701	3.886	4.070	4.253	4.436	4.618	4.800	4.982	5.163	5.344
2 1/2	3.267	3.455	3.642	3.828	4.012	4.197	4.380	4.563	4.746	4.928	5.110	5.292	5.473
2 5/8	3.393	3.581	3.768	3.954	4.139	4.324	4.508	4.691	4.874	5.056	5.238	5.420	5.601
2 3/4	3.519	3.707	3.894	4.080	4.266	4.451	4.635	4.818	5.002	5.184	5.366	5.548	5.730
2 7/8	3.644	3.833	4.020	4.207	4.392	4.577	4.762	4.946	5.129	5.312	5.494	5.677	5.858
3	3.770	3.958	4.146	4.333	4.519	4.704	4.889	5.073	5.256	5.440	5.622	5.805	5.987
3 1/8	3.895	4.084	4.272	4.459	4.645	4.831	5.016	5.200	5.384	5.567	5.750	5.933	6.115
3 1/4	4.020	4.210	4.398	4.585	4.771	4.957	5.142	5.327	5.511	5.694	5.877	6.060	6.243
3 3/8	4.146	4.335	4.524	4.711	4.898	5.084	5.269	5.454	5.638	5.822	6.005	6.188	6.371
3 1/2	4.271	4.461	4.650	4.837	5.024	5.210	5.396	5.581	5.765	5.949	6.133	6.316	6.498
3 5/8	4.397	4.587	4.775	4.963	5.150	5.336	5.522	5.707	5.892	6.076	6.260	6.443	6.626
3 3/4	4.522	4.712	4.901	5.089	5.276	5.463	5.648	5.834	6.019	6.203	6.387	6.570	6.754
3 7/8	4.648	4.838	5.027	5.215	5.402	5.589	5.775	5.960	6.145	6.330	6.514	6.698	6.881
4	4.773	4.963	5.152	5.341	5.528	5.715	5.901	6.087	6.272	6.457	6.641	6.825	7.009
4 1/8	4.898	5.088	5.278	5.466	5.654	5.841	6.028	6.213	6.399	6.584	6.768	6.952	7.136
4 1/4	5.024	5.214	5.403	5.592	5.780	5.967	6.154	6.340	6.525	6.710	6.894	7.079	7.263
4 3/8	5.149	5.339	5.529	5.718	5.906	6.093	6.280	6.466	6.652	6.837	7.022	7.206	7.390
4 1/2	5.274	5.465	5.654	5.843	6.032	6.219	6.406	6.592	6.778	6.964	7.149	7.333	7.517

4⅝	5.399	5.590	5.780	5.969	6.157	6.345	6.532	6.719	6.905	7.090	7.275	7.460	7.644
4¾	5.525	5.715	5.905	6.095	6.283	6.471	6.658	6.845	7.031	7.217	7.402	7.587	7.771
4⅞	5.650	5.841	6.031	6.220	6.409	6.597	6.784	6.971	7.157	7.343	7.529	7.714	7.898
5	5.775	5.966	6.156	6.346	6.535	6.723	6.910	7.097	7.284	7.470	7.655	7.840	8.025
5⅛	5.900	6.091	6.282	6.471	6.660	6.848	7.036	7.223	7.410	7.596	7.782	7.967	8.152
5¼	6.025	6.217	6.407	6.597	6.786	6.974	7.162	7.349	7.536	7.722	7.908	8.093	8.278
5⅜	6.151	6.342	6.533	6.722	6.912	7.100	7.288	7.475	7.662	7.848	8.034	8.220	8.405
5½	6.276	6.467	6.658	6.848	7.037	7.226	7.414	7.602	7.788	7.975	8.161	8.346	8.532
5⅝	6.401	6.592	6.783	6.973	7.163	7.351	7.539	7.727	7.914	8.101	8.287	8.473	8.658
5¾	6.526	6.718	6.909	7.099	7.288	7.477	7.665	7.853	8.040	8.227	8.413	8.599	8.785
5⅞	6.651	6.843	7.034	7.224	7.414	7.603	7.791	7.979	8.166	8.353	8.540	8.726	8.911
6	6.776	6.968	7.159	7.350	7.539	7.728	7.917	8.105	8.292	8.479	8.666	8.852	9.038
6⅛	6.901	7.093	7.284	7.475	7.664	7.854	8.042	8.230	8.418	8.605	8.791	8.978	9.164
6¼	7.027	7.219	7.410	7.600	7.790	7.979	8.168	8.356	8.544	8.731	8.918	9.104	9.290
6⅜	7.152	7.344	7.535	7.726	7.916	8.105	8.294	8.482	8.670	8.857	9.044	9.231	9.417
6½	7.277	7.469	7.660	7.851	8.041	8.231	8.420	8.608	8.796	8.983	9.170	9.357	9.543
6⅝	7.402	7.594	7.786	7.976	8.167	8.356	8.545	8.734	8.922	9.109	9.296	9.483	9.669
6¾	7.521	7.713	7.905	8.096	8.286	8.476	8.665	8.854	9.042	9.230	9.417	9.604	9.790
6⅞	7.652	7.845	8.036	8.227	8.417	8.607	8.796	8.985	9.173	9.361	9.548	9.735	9.922
7	7.778	7.970	8.161	8.352	8.543	8.733	8.922	9.111	9.299	9.487	9.674	9.861	10.048
7⅛	7.903	8.095	8.287	8.478	8.668	8.858	9.047	9.236	9.425	9.613	9.800	9.987	10.174
7¼	8.028	8.220	8.412	8.603	8.794	8.984	9.173	9.362	9.550	9.738	9.926	10.113	10.300
7⅜	8.153	8.345	8.537	8.728	8.919	9.109	9.299	9.488	9.676	9.864	10.052	10.239	10.426
7½	8.278	8.471	8.662	8.854	9.044	9.234	9.424	9.613	9.802	9.990	10.178	10.365	10.552
7⅝	8.403	8.596	8.788	8.979	9.170	9.360	9.550	9.739	9.927	10.116	10.304	10.491	10.678
7¾	8.528	8.721	8.913	9.104	9.295	9.485	9.675	9.864	10.053	10.241	10.429	10.617	10.804
7⅞	8.653	8.846	9.038	9.230	9.420	9.611	9.801	9.990	10.179	10.367	10.555	10.743	10.930
8	8.778	8.971	9.163	9.355	9.546	9.736	9.926	10.115	10.304	10.493	10.681	10.869	11.056
8⅛	8.903	9.096	9.288	9.480	9.671	9.861	10.051	10.241	10.430	10.619	10.807	10.995	11.182
8¼	9.029	9.221	9.414	9.605	9.796	9.987	10.177	10.336	10.556	10.744	10.933	11.121	11.308
8⅜	9.154	9.347	9.539	9.730	9.922	10.112	10.302	10.492	10.681	10.870	11.058	11.246	11.434
8½	9.279	9.472	9.664	9.856	10.047	10.238	10.428	10.617	10.807	10.996	11.184	11.372	11.560
8⅝	9.404	9.597	9.789	9.981	10.172	10.363	10.553	10.743	10.932	11.121	11.310	11.498	11.686
8¾	9.529	9.722	9.914	10.106	10.297	10.488	10.679	10.868	11.058	11.247	11.435	11.624	11.812
8⅞	9.654	9.847	10.040	10.231	10.423	10.614	10.804	10.994	11.183	11.372	11.561	11.749	11.937

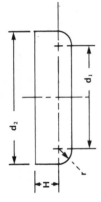

Table 4–11. Solutions for $D = \sqrt{d_1^2 + 6.28 r d_1 + 8 r^2 + 4 d_2 H}$ when $H = 1/4$ inch.

d_1	Radius of shell												
	1/4	5/16	3/8	7/16	1/2	9/16	5/8	11/16	3/4	13/16	7/8	15/16	1
2.0	3.184	3.366	3.548	3.728	3.909	4.089	4.269	4.449	4.628	4.807	4.986	5.165	5.344
2 1/8	3.313	3.495	3.677	3.858	4.039	4.219	4.400	4.580	4.759	4.939	5.118	5.297	5.476
2 1/4	3.442	3.623	3.806	3.988	4.169	4.349	4.530	4.710	4.890	5.070	5.249	5.428	5.607
2 3/8	3.570	3.753	3.935	4.117	4.298	4.479	4.660	4.840	5.020	5.200	5.380	5.559	5.739
2 1/2	3.698	3.881	4.064	4.246	4.427	4.608	4.789	4.970	5.150	5.330	5.510	5.690	5.869
2 5/8	3.826	4.009	4.192	4.374	4.556	4.738	4.919	5.100	5.280	5.460	5.640	5.820	6.000
2 3/4	3.954	4.137	4.320	4.503	4.685	4.867	5.048	5.229	5.410	5.590	5.771	5.951	6.130
2 7/8	4.081	4.265	4.448	4.631	4.813	4.995	5.177	5.358	5.539	5.720	5.900	6.080	6.261
3	4.208	4.392	4.576	4.759	4.942	5.124	5.306	5.487	5.668	5.849	6.030	6.210	6.391
3 1/8	4.336	4.520	4.704	4.887	5.070	5.252	5.434	5.616	5.797	5.978	6.159	6.340	6.520
3 1/4	4.463	4.647	4.831	5.015	5.198	5.380	5.563	5.744	5.926	6.107	6.288	6.469	6.650
3 3/8	4.590	4.774	4.959	5.142	5.326	5.509	5.691	5.873	6.055	6.236	6.418	6.599	6.779
3 1/2	4.716	4.902	5.086	5.270	5.453	5.636	5.819	6.001	6.183	6.365	6.547	6.728	6.909
3 5/8	4.843	5.029	5.213	5.397	5.581	5.764	5.947	6.130	6.312	6.494	6.675	6.857	7.038
3 3/4	4.970	5.155	5.340	5.524	5.708	5.892	6.075	6.258	6.440	6.622	6.804	6.985	7.167
3 7/8	5.097	5.282	5.467	5.652	5.836	6.020	6.203	6.386	6.568	6.750	6.932	7.114	7.296
4	5.223	5.409	5.594	5.779	5.963	6.147	6.330	6.514	6.696	6.879	7.061	7.243	7.424
4 1/8	5.349	5.536	5.721	5.906	6.090	6.274	6.458	6.641	6.824	7.007	7.189	7.371	7.553
4 1/4	5.476	5.662	5.848	6.033	6.218	6.402	6.586	6.769	6.952	7.135	7.317	7.499	7.681
4 3/8	5.602	5.789	5.974	6.160	6.345	6.529	6.713	6.896	7.080	7.263	7.445	7.628	7.810
4 1/2	5.728	5.915	6.101	6.286	6.471	6.656	6.840	7.024	7.207	7.390	7.573	7.756	7.938

4 5/8	5.855	6.041	6.228	6.413	6.598	6.783	6.967	7.151	7.335	7.518	7.701	7.884	8.066
4 3/4	5.981	6.168	6.354	6.540	6.725	6.910	7.095	7.279	7.462	7.646	7.829	8.012	8.194
4 7/8	6.107	6.294	6.481	6.666	6.852	7.037	7.221	7.406	7.590	7.773	7.956	8.139	8.322
5	6.233	6.420	6.607	6.793	6.979	7.164	7.348	7.533	7.717	7.901	8.084	8.267	8.450
5 1/8	6.359	6.546	6.733	6.919	7.105	7.290	7.475	7.660	7.844	8.028	8.211	8.395	8.578
5 1/4	6.485	6.672	6.859	7.046	7.232	7.417	7.602	7.787	7.971	8.155	8.339	8.522	8.705
5 3/8	6.611	6.799	6.986	7.172	7.358	7.544	7.729	7.914	8.098	8.282	8.466	8.650	8.833
5 1/2	6.737	6.925	7.112	7.298	7.485	7.670	7.856	8.041	8.225	8.410	8.593	8.777	8.960
5 5/8	6.863	7.051	7.238	7.425	7.611	7.797	7.982	8.167	8.352	8.537	8.721	8.904	9.088
5 3/4	6.989	7.176	7.364	7.551	7.737	7.923	8.109	8.294	8.479	8.664	8.848	9.032	9.215
5 7/8	7.114	7.303	7.490	7.677	7.864	8.050	8.236	8.421	8.606	8.791	8.975	9.159	9.343
6	7.240	7.428	7.616	7.803	7.990	8.176	8.362	8.548	8.733	8.917	9.102	9.286	9.470
6 1/8	7.366	7.554	7.742	7.929	8.116	8.302	8.488	8.674	8.859	9.044	9.228	9.413	9.597
6 1/4	7.492	7.680	7.868	8.055	8.242	8.429	8.615	8.801	8.986	9.171	9.356	9.540	9.724
6 3/8	7.617	7.806	7.994	8.182	8.369	8.555	8.741	8.927	9.113	9.298	9.483	9.667	9.851
6 1/2	7.743	7.932	8.120	8.308	8.495	8.681	8.868	9.054	9.239	9.425	9.610	9.794	9.978
6 5/8	7.869	8.058	8.246	8.434	8.621	8.808	8.994	9.180	9.366	9.551	9.736	9.921	10.105
6 3/4	7.988	8.177	8.366	8.554	8.741	8.928	9.115	9.301	9.487	9.673	9.858	10.043	10.228
6 7/8	8.120	8.309	8.497	8.685	8.873	9.060	9.247	9.433	9.619	9.804	9.990	10.175	10.359
7	8.246	8.435	8.623	8.811	8.999	9.186	9.373	9.559	9.745	9.931	10.116	10.301	10.486
7 1/8	8.371	8.560	8.749	8.937	9.125	9.312	9.499	9.686	9.872	10.057	10.243	10.428	10.613
7 1/4	8.497	8.686	8.875	9.063	9.251	9.438	9.625	9.812	9.998	10.184	10.370	10.555	10.740
7 3/8	8.622	8.812	9.000	9.189	9.377	9.564	9.751	9.938	10.124	10.310	10.496	10.681	10.867
7 1/2	8.748	8.937	9.126	9.315	9.503	9.690	9.877	10.064	10.251	10.437	10.623	10.808	10.993
7 5/8	8.873	9.063	9.252	9.440	9.629	9.816	10.003	10.190	10.377	10.563	10.749	10.935	11.120
7 3/4	8.999	9.188	9.378	9.566	9.754	9.942	10.130	10.316	10.503	10.689	10.875	11.061	11.246
7 7/8	9.124	9.314	9.503	9.692	9.880	10.068	10.255	10.443	10.629	10.816	11.002	11.188	11.373
8	9.250	9.440	9.629	9.818	10.006	10.194	10.381	10.569	10.755	10.942	11.128	11.314	11.500
8 1/8	9.375	9.565	9.754	9.943	10.132	10.320	10.507	10.695	10.882	11.068	11.254	11.440	11.626
8 1/4	9.501	9.691	9.880	10.069	10.258	10.446	10.665	10.821	11.008	11.233	11.383	11.567	11.753
8 3/8	9.626	9.816	10.006	10.195	10.383	10.572	10.759	10.947	11.134	11.321	11.507	11.693	11.879
8 1/2	9.752	9.942	10.131	10.320	10.509	10.697	10.885	11.073	11.260	11.447	11.633	11.819	12.005
8 5/8	9.877	10.067	10.257	10.446	10.635	10.823	11.011	11.199	11.386	11.573	11.759	11.946	12.132
8 3/4	10.003	10.193	10.382	10.572	10.760	10.949	11.137	11.325	11.512	11.699	11.886	12.072	12.258
8 7/8	10.128	10.318	10.508	10.697	10.886	11.075	11.263	11.451	11.638	11.825	12.012	12.198	12.385

Table 4-12. Solutions for $D = \sqrt{d_1^2 + 6.28rd_1 + 8r^2 + 4d_2H}$ when $H = 3/8$ inch.

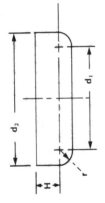

d_1						Radius of shell							
	1/4	5/16	3/8	7/16	1/2	9/16	5/8	11/16	3/4	13/16	7/8	15/16	1
2.0	3.375	3.556	3.736	3.921	4.096	4.276	4.455	4.634	4.814	4.992	5.171	5.350	5.528
2 1/8	3.506	3.687	3.867	4.048	4.228	4.408	4.587	4.767	4.946	5.125	5.304	5.483	5.661
2 1/4	3.636	3.816	3.998	4.179	4.359	4.539	4.719	4.899	5.078	5.257	5.436	5.615	5.794
2 3/8	3.766	3.948	4.129	4.310	4.490	4.670	4.850	5.030	5.210	5.389	5.568	5.747	5.926
2 1/2	3.896	4.077	4.259	4.440	4.621	4.801	4.981	5.161	5.341	5.520	5.700	5.879	6.058
2 5/8	4.025	4.207	4.389	4.570	4.751	4.932	5.112	5.292	5.472	5.652	5.831	6.011	6.190
2 3/4	4.154	4.336	4.518	4.700	4.881	5.062	5.242	5.423	5.603	5.783	5.962	6.142	6.321
2 7/8	4.283	4.465	4.648	4.829	5.011	5.192	5.372	5.553	5.733	5.913	6.093	6.273	6.452
3	4.411	4.594	4.777	4.958	5.140	5.321	5.502	5.683	5.863	6.044	6.224	6.404	6.583
3 1/8	4.540	4.723	4.905	5.088	5.269	5.451	5.632	5.813	5.994	6.174	6.354	6.534	6.714
3 1/4	4.668	4.851	5.034	5.216	5.398	5.580	5.761	5.942	6.123	6.304	6.484	6.664	6.844
3 3/8	4.796	4.979	5.163	5.345	5.527	5.709	5.891	6.072	6.253	6.434	6.614	6.795	6.975
3 1/2	4.924	5.108	5.291	5.474	5.656	5.838	6.020	6.201	6.382	6.563	6.744	6.925	7.105
3 5/8	5.052	5.236	5.419	5.602	5.785	5.967	6.149	6.330	6.512	6.693	6.874	7.054	7.235
3 3/4	5.179	5.363	5.547	5.730	5.913	6.095	6.281	6.459	6.641	6.822	7.003	7.184	7.365
3 7/8	5.307	5.491	5.675	5.858	6.041	6.224	6.406	6.588	6.770	6.951	7.132	7.313	7.494
4	5.434	5.619	5.803	5.986	6.169	6.352	6.535	6.717	6.899	7.080	7.262	7.443	7.624
4 1/8	5.561	5.746	5.930	6.114	6.297	6.480	6.663	6.845	7.027	7.209	7.391	7.572	7.753
4 1/4	5.689	5.873	6.058	6.242	6.425	6.608	6.791	6.974	7.156	7.338	7.519	7.701	7.882
4 3/8	5.816	6.001	6.185	6.369	6.553	6.736	6.919	7.102	7.284	7.466	7.648	7.830	8.011
4 1/2	5.943	6.128	6.313	6.497	6.681	6.864	7.047	7.230	7.412	7.595	7.777	7.958	8.140

$4^{5}/_{8}$	6.070	6.255	6.440	6.624	6.808	6.992	7.175	7.358	7.541	7.723	7.905	8.085	8.269
$4^{3}/_{4}$	6.196	6.382	6.567	6.751	6.936	7.119	7.303	7.486	7.669	7.851	8.034	8.216	8.397
$4^{7}/_{8}$	6.323	6.509	6.694	6.879	7.063	7.247	7.431	7.614	7.797	7.979	8.162	8.344	8.526
5	6.450	6.636	6.821	7.006	7.190	7.374	7.558	7.742	7.925	8.107	8.290	8.472	8.654
$5^{1}/_{8}$	6.576	6.762	6.948	7.133	7.318	7.502	7.686	7.869	8.052	8.235	8.418	8.601	8.783
$5^{1}/_{4}$	6.703	6.889	7.075	7.260	7.445	7.629	7.813	7.997	8.180	8.363	8.546	8.729	8.911
$5^{3}/_{8}$	6.830	7.016	7.201	7.387	7.572	7.756	7.940	8.124	8.308	8.491	8.674	8.857	9.039
$5^{1}/_{2}$	6.956	7.142	7.328	7.514	7.699	7.883	8.068	8.252	8.435	8.619	8.802	8.985	9.167
$5^{5}/_{8}$	7.082	7.269	7.455	7.640	7.826	8.010	8.195	8.379	8.563	8.746	8.931	9.113	9.295
$5^{3}/_{4}$	7.209	7.395	7.581	7.767	7.953	8.137	8.322	8.506	8.690	8.874	9.057	9.240	9.423
$5^{7}/_{8}$	7.335	7.522	7.708	7.894	8.079	8.264	8.449	8.633	8.818	9.001	9.185	9.368	9.551
6	7.461	7.648	7.835	8.021	8.206	8.391	8.576	8.761	8.945	9.129	9.312	9.496	9.679
$6^{1}/_{8}$	7.587	7.774	7.961	8.147	8.333	8.518	8.703	8.888	9.072	9.256	9.439	9.623	9.806
$6^{1}/_{4}$	7.714	7.901	8.087	8.274	8.459	8.645	8.830	9.015	9.199	9.383	9.567	9.751	9.934
$6^{3}/_{8}$	7.840	8.027	8.214	8.400	8.581	8.772	8.957	9.142	9.326	9.511	9.695	9.878	10.062
$6^{1}/_{2}$	7.966	8.153	8.340	8.527	8.713	8.898	9.084	9.269	9.453	9.638	9.822	10.006	10.189
$6^{5}/_{8}$	8.092	8.279	8.466	8.653	8.839	9.025	9.210	9.395	9.580	9.765	9.949	10.133	10.317
$6^{3}/_{4}$	8.212	8.400	8.587	8.774	8.960	9.146	9.332	9.517	9.702	9.887	10.071	10.255	10.439
$6^{7}/_{8}$	8.344	8.532	8.719	8.906	9.092	9.278	9.464	9.649	9.834	10.019	10.203	10.387	10.571
7	8.470	8.658	8.845	9.032	9.218	9.405	9.590	9.776	9.961	10.146	10.330	10.515	10.699
$7^{1}/_{8}$	8.596	8.784	8.971	9.158	9.345	9.531	9.717	9.902	10.088	10.273	10.457	10.642	10.826
$7^{1}/_{4}$	8.722	8.910	9.097	9.284	9.471	9.658	9.843	10.029	10.214	10.399	10.584	10.769	10.953
$7^{3}/_{8}$	8.848	9.036	9.223	9.411	9.597	9.784	9.970	10.156	10.341	10.526	10.711	10.896	11.080
$7^{1}/_{2}$	8.974	9.162	9.349	9.537	9.724	9.910	10.096	10.282	10.468	10.653	10.838	11.023	11.207
$7^{5}/_{8}$	9.099	9.288	9.476	9.663	9.850	10.037	10.223	10.409	10.594	10.780	10.965	11.150	11.334
$7^{3}/_{4}$	9.225	9.414	9.602	9.789	9.976	10.163	10.349	10.535	10.721	10.906	11.092	11.277	11.461
$7^{7}/_{8}$	9.351	9.539	9.728	9.915	10.102	10.289	10.476	10.662	10.848	11.033	11.218	11.403	11.588
8	9.477	9.665	9.853	10.041	10.228	10.415	10.602	10.788	10.974	11.160	11.345	11.530	11.715
$8^{1}/_{8}$	9.603	9.791	9.979	10.167	10.355	10.542	10.728	10.915	11.101	11.286	11.472	11.657	11.842
$8^{1}/_{4}$	9.728	9.917	10.105	10.293	10.481	10.668	10.854	11.041	11.227	11.413	11.598	11.784	11.969
$8^{3}/_{8}$	9.854	10.043	10.231	10.419	10.607	10.794	10.981	11.167	11.353	11.539	11.725	11.910	12.095
$8^{1}/_{2}$	9.980	10.169	10.357	10.545	10.733	10.920	11.107	11.293	11.480	11.666	11.851	12.037	12.222
$8^{5}/_{8}$	10.105	10.294	10.483	10.671	10.859	11.046	11.233	11.420	11.606	11.792	11.978	12.164	12.349
$8^{3}/_{4}$	10.231	10.420	10.609	10.797	10.985	11.172	11.359	11.546	11.732	11.919	12.105	12.290	12.475
$8^{7}/_{8}$	10.357	10.546	10.735	10.923	11.111	11.298	11.485	11.680	11.859	12.045	12.231	12.417	12.602

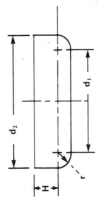

Table 4–13. Solutions for $D = \sqrt{d_1^2 + 6.28rd_1 + 8r^2 + 4d_2H}$ when $H = 1/2$ inch.

d_1	Radius of shell												
	1/4	5/16	3/8	7/16	1/2	9/16	5/8	11/16	3/4	13/16	7/8	15/16	1
2.0	3.555	3.736	3.916	4.096	4.276	4.455	4.634	4.813	4.992	5.171	5.349	5.528	5.706
2 1/8	3.688	3.869	4.049	4.229	4.409	4.588	4.768	4.947	5.126	5.305	5.483	5.662	5.840
2 1/4	3.820	4.000	4.182	4.362	4.542	4.721	4.901	5.080	5.259	5.438	5.617	5.796	5.974
2 3/8	3.952	4.133	4.314	4.494	4.674	4.854	5.034	5.213	5.392	5.571	5.750	5.929	6.108
2 1/2	4.084	4.265	4.446	4.626	4.806	4.986	5.166	5.346	5.525	5.704	5.883	6.062	6.241
2 5/8	4.214	4.396	4.577	4.758	4.938	5.118	5.298	5.478	5.657	5.837	6.016	6.195	6.374
2 3/4	4.345	4.527	4.708	4.889	5.069	5.250	5.430	5.610	5.789	5.969	6.148	6.327	6.506
2 7/8	4.475	4.657	4.839	5.020	5.200	5.381	5.561	5.741	5.921	6.101	6.280	6.459	6.639
3	4.605	4.787	4.969	5.150	5.331	5.512	5.692	5.872	6.052	6.232	6.412	6.591	6.771
3 1/8	4.735	4.917	5.099	5.280	5.462	5.642	5.823	6.003	6.183	6.363	6.543	6.723	6.902
3 1/4	4.865	5.047	5.229	5.410	5.592	5.773	5.953	6.134	6.314	6.494	6.674	6.854	7.034
3 3/8	4.994	5.176	5.359	5.540	5.722	5.903	6.084	6.265	6.445	6.625	6.805	6.985	7.165
3 1/2	5.123	5.306	5.488	5.670	5.851	6.033	6.214	6.395	6.575	6.756	6.936	7.116	7.296
3 5/8	5.252	5.435	5.617	5.799	5.981	6.163	6.344	6.525	6.706	6.886	7.066	7.247	7.427
3 3/4	5.380	5.563	5.746	5.928	6.110	6.292	6.473	6.655	6.835	7.016	7.197	7.377	7.557
3 7/8	5.509	5.692	5.875	6.058	6.240	6.421	6.603	6.784	6.965	7.146	7.327	7.507	7.688
4	5.637	5.821	6.004	6.186	6.369	6.551	6.732	6.914	7.095	7.276	7.457	7.637	7.818
4 1/8	5.766	5.949	6.132	6.315	6.498	6.680	6.862	7.043	7.225	7.406	7.587	7.767	7.948
4 1/4	5.894	6.077	6.261	6.444	6.626	6.809	6.991	7.172	7.354	7.535	7.716	7.897	8.078
4 3/8	6.022	6.205	6.389	6.572	6.755	6.937	7.120	7.301	7.483	7.665	7.846	8.027	8.028
4 1/2	6.149	6.333	6.517	6.700	6.883	7.066	7.248	7.430	7.612	7.794	7.975	8.156	8.337

4⅝	6.277	6.461	6.645	6.829	7.012	7.194	7.377	7.559	7.741	7.923	8.104	8.286	8.467
4¾	6.405	6.589	6.773	6.957	7.140	7.323	7.505	7.688	7.870	8.052	8.233	8.415	8.596
4⅞	6.532	6.717	6.901	7.085	7.268	7.451	7.633	7.816	7.999	8.181	8.362	8.544	8.725
5	6.660	6.844	7.029	7.212	7.396	7.579	7.762	7.945	8.127	8.309	8.491	8.673	8.854
5⅛	6.787	6.972	7.156	7.340	7.524	7.707	7.890	8.073	8.256	8.438	8.620	8.802	8.983
5¼	6.914	7.099	7.284	7.468	7.652	7.835	8.018	8.201	8.384	8.566	8.749	8.930	9.112
5⅜	7.041	7.226	7.411	7.595	7.779	7.963	8.146	8.329	8.512	8.695	8.877	9.059	9.241
5½	7.168	7.354	7.538	7.723	7.907	8.091	8.274	8.457	8.640	8.823	9.005	9.188	9.370
5⅝	7.295	7.481	7.666	7.850	8.035	8.218	8.402	8.585	8.768	8.951	9.134	9.316	9.498
5¾	7.422	7.608	7.793	7.978	8.162	8.346	8.530	8.713	8.896	9.079	9.262	9.444	9.627
5⅞	7.549	7.735	7.920	8.105	8.289	8.473	8.657	8.841	9.024	9.207	9.390	9.573	9.755
6	7.676	7.862	8.047	8.232	8.417	8.601	8.786	8.969	9.152	9.335	9.518	9.701	9.883
6⅛	7.803	7.988	8.174	8.359	8.544	8.728	8.912	9.096	9.279	9.463	9.646	9.829	10.011
6¼	7.929	8.115	8.301	8.486	8.671	8.856	9.040	9.224	9.407	9.591	9.774	9.957	10.140
6⅜	8.056	8.242	8.428	8.613	8.798	8.983	9.167	9.351	9.535	9.719	9.902	10.085	10.268
6½	8.183	8.369	8.555	8.740	8.925	9.110	9.295	9.479	9.663	9.846	10.030	10.213	10.396
6⅝	8.309	8.496	8.681	8.867	9.052	9.237	9.422	9.606	9.790	9.974	10.157	10.341	10.524
6¾	8.430	8.616	8.803	8.988	9.174	9.359	9.544	9.728	9.912	10.096	10.280	10.464	10.647
6⅞	8.562	8.749	8.935	9.121	9.306	9.491	9.676	9.861	10.045	10.229	10.412	10.596	10.779
7	8.688	8.875	9.061	9.247	9.433	9.618	9.803	9.988	10.172	10.356	10.540	10.724	10.907
7⅛	8.815	9.002	9.188	9.374	9.560	9.745	9.930	10.115	10.299	10.483	10.667	10.851	11.035
7¼	8.941	9.128	9.315	9.501	9.686	9.872	10.057	10.242	10.426	10.611	10.795	10.979	11.162
7⅜	9.068	9.254	9.441	9.627	9.813	9.999	10.184	10.369	10.554	10.738	10.922	11.106	11.290
7½	9.194	9.381	9.568	9.754	9.940	10.125	10.311	10.496	10.681	10.865	11.049	11.233	11.417
7⅝	9.320	9.507	9.694	9.880	10.066	10.252	10.438	10.623	10.808	10.992	11.177	11.361	11.545
7¾	9.446	9.633	9.820	10.007	10.193	10.379	10.564	10.750	10.935	11.119	11.304	11.488	11.672
7⅞	9.572	9.760	9.947	10.133	10.320	10.505	10.691	10.876	11.062	11.246	11.431	11.615	11.799
8	9.698	9.886	10.073	10.260	10.446	10.632	10.818	11.003	11.188	11.373	11.558	11.742	11.926
8⅛	9.825	10.012	10.199	10.386	10.573	10.759	10.944	11.130	11.315	11.500	11.685	11.869	12.054
8¼	9.951	10.138	10.326	10.512	10.699	10.885	11.071	11.257	11.442	11.627	11.812	11.996	12.181
8⅜	10.077	10.264	10.452	10.639	10.825	11.012	11.198	11.383	11.569	11.754	11.939	12.124	12.308
8½	10.203	10.390	10.578	10.765	10.952	11.138	11.324	11.510	11.696	11.923	12.107	12.291	12.435
8⅝	10.329	10.517	10.704	10.891	11.078	11.265	11.451	11.637	11.822	12.008	12.193	12.377	12.562
8¾	10.455	10.643	10.830	11.017	11.204	11.391	11.577	11.763	11.949	12.134	12.319	12.504	12.689
8⅞	10.581	10.769	10.956	11.144	11.331	11.517	11.704	11.890	12.075	12.261	12.446	12.631	12.816

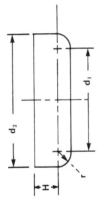

Table 4–14. Solutions for $D = \sqrt{d_1^2 + 6.28rd_1 + 8r^2 + 4d_2H}$ when $H = 5/8$ inch.

d_1	Radius of shell												
	1/4	5/16	3/8	7/16	1/2	9/16	5/8	11/16	3/4	13/16	7/8	15/16	1
2.0	3.727	3.907	4.088	4.268	4.447	4.627	4.806	4.985	5.164	5.343	5.522	5.700	5.879
$2^{1}/_8$	3.862	4.043	4.223	4.403	4.583	4.762	4.942	5.121	5.300	5.479	5.657	5.836	6.014
$2^{1}/_4$	3.996	4.176	4.357	4.537	4.717	4.897	5.076	5.256	5.435	5.614	5.792	5.971	6.150
$2^{3}/_8$	4.130	4.311	4.491	4.671	4.851	5.031	5.211	5.390	5.569	5.748	5.927	6.106	6.284
$2^{1}/_2$	4.263	4.444	4.625	4.805	4.985	5.165	5.344	5.524	5.703	5.882	6.061	6.240	6.419
$2^{5}/_8$	4.396	4.577	4.758	4.938	5.118	5.298	5.478	5.657	5.837	6.016	6.195	6.374	6.553
$2^{3}/_4$	4.528	4.709	4.890	5.071	5.251	5.431	5.611	5.790	5.970	6.149	6.328	6.507	6.686
$2^{7}/_8$	4.660	4.841	5.022	5.203	5.383	5.564	5.743	5.923	6.103	6.282	6.462	6.641	6.820
3	4.792	4.973	5.154	5.335	5.515	5.696	5.876	6.056	6.235	6.415	6.594	6.774	6.953
$3^{1}/_8$	4.923	5.104	5.286	5.467	5.647	5.828	6.008	6.188	6.368	6.547	6.727	6.906	7.085
$3^{1}/_4$	5.054	5.235	5.417	5.598	5.778	5.959	6.139	6.320	6.500	6.679	6.859	7.038	7.218
$3^{3}/_8$	5.184	5.366	5.548	5.729	5.910	6.090	6.271	6.451	6.631	6.811	6.991	7.171	7.350
$3^{1}/_2$	5.315	5.497	5.678	5.860	6.041	6.222	6.402	6.583	6.763	6.943	7.123	7.302	7.482
$3^{5}/_8$	5.445	5.627	5.809	5.990	6.171	6.352	6.533	6.714	6.894	7.074	7.254	7.434	7.614
$3^{3}/_4$	5.574	5.757	5.939	6.120	6.302	6.483	6.664	6.844	7.025	7.205	7.385	7.565	7.745
$3^{7}/_8$	5.704	5.887	6.069	6.251	6.432	6.613	6.794	6.975	7.156	7.336	7.516	7.696	7.876
4	5.834	6.016	6.198	6.380	6.562	6.743	6.925	7.106	7.286	7.467	7.647	7.827	8.007
$4^{1}/_8$	5.963	6.145	6.328	6.510	6.692	6.873	7.055	7.236	7.417	7.597	7.778	7.958	8.138
$4^{1}/_4$	6.092	6.275	6.457	6.640	6.822	7.003	7.185	7.366	7.547	7.728	7.908	8.089	8.269
$4^{3}/_8$	6.221	6.404	6.586	6.769	6.951	7.133	7.314	7.496	7.677	7.858	8.039	8.219	8.400
$4^{1}/_2$	6.349	6.533	6.716	6.898	7.080	7.262	7.444	7.625	7.807	7.988	8.169	8.349	8.530

4 5/8	6.478	6.661	6.844	7.027	7.209	7.392	7.573	7.755	7.936	8.118	8.299	8.480	8.660
4 3/4	6.607	6.790	6.973	7.156	7.338	7.521	7.703	7.884	8.066	8.247	8.428	8.609	8.790
4 7/8	6.735	6.918	7.102	7.285	7.467	7.650	7.832	8.014	8.195	8.377	8.558	8.739	8.920
5	6.863	7.047	7.230	7.413	7.596	7.779	7.961	8.143	8.325	8.506	8.688	8.869	9.050
5 1/8	6.991	7.175	7.358	7.542	7.725	7.907	8.090	8.272	8.454	8.636	8.817	8.998	9.180
5 1/4	7.119	7.303	7.487	7.670	7.853	8.036	8.219	8.401	8.583	8.765	8.946	9.128	9.309
5 3/8	7.247	7.431	7.615	7.798	7.982	8.164	8.347	8.530	8.712	8.894	9.075	9.257	9.438
5 1/2	7.375	7.559	7.743	7.927	8.110	8.293	8.476	8.658	8.841	9.023	9.205	9.386	9.568
5 5/8	7.502	7.687	7.871	8.055	8.238	8.421	8.604	8.787	8.969	9.151	9.333	9.515	9.697
5 3/4	7.630	7.814	7.999	8.183	8.366	8.549	8.733	8.915	9.098	9.280	9.462	9.644	9.826
5 7/8	7.757	7.942	8.126	8.310	8.494	8.678	8.861	9.044	9.226	9.409	9.591	9.773	9.955
6	7.885	8.070	8.254	8.438	8.622	8.806	8.989	9.172	9.355	9.537	9.720	9.902	10.084
6 1/8	8.012	8.197	8.381	8.566	8.750	8.933	9.117	9.300	9.483	9.665	9.848	10.030	10.212
6 1/4	8.139	8.325	8.509	8.694	8.878	9.061	9.245	9.428	9.611	9.794	9.977	10.159	10.341
6 3/8	8.267	8.452	8.637	8.821	9.005	9.189	9.373	9.556	9.739	9.922	10.105	10.287	10.470
6 1/2	8.394	8.579	8.764	8.949	9.133	9.317	9.501	9.684	9.867	10.050	10.233	10.416	10.598
6 5/8	8.521	8.706	8.891	9.076	9.260	9.445	9.628	9.812	9.995	10.178	10.361	10.544	10.727
6 3/4	8.642	8.828	9.013	9.198	9.383	9.567	9.751	9.935	10.118	10.302	10.485	10.668	10.850
6 7/8	8.775	8.960	9.146	9.331	9.515	9.670	9.884	10.068	10.251	10.434	10.618	10.800	10.983
7	8.902	9.087	9.273	9.458	9.643	9.827	10.011	10.195	10.369	10.562	10.745	10.928	11.111
7 1/8	9.029	9.214	9.400	9.585	9.770	9.954	10.139	10.323	10.507	10.690	10.873	11.056	11.239
7 1/4	9.155	9.341	9.527	9.712	9.897	10.082	10.266	10.450	10.634	10.818	11.001	11.184	11.367
7 3/8	9.282	9.468	9.654	9.839	10.024	10.209	10.394	10.578	10.762	10.945	11.129	11.312	11.495
7 1/2	9.409	9.595	9.781	9.966	10.151	10.336	10.521	10.705	10.889	11.073	11.257	11.440	11.623
7 5/8	9.535	9.722	9.908	10.093	10.278	10.463	10.648	10.832	11.017	11.201	11.384	11.568	11.751
7 3/4	9.662	9.848	10.034	10.220	10.405	10.590	10.775	10.960	11.144	11.328	11.512	11.695	11.879
7 7/8	9.789	9.985	10.161	10.347	10.532	10.718	10.902	11.087	11.271	11.456	11.639	11.823	12.007
8	9.915	10.102	10.288	10.477	10.659	10.845	11.030	11.214	11.399	11.583	11.767	11.951	12.134
8 1/8	10.042	10.228	10.415	10.600	10.786	10.972	11.157	11.341	11.526	11.710	11.894	12.078	12.262
8 1/4	10.168	10.355	10.541	10.727	10.913	11.098	11.284	11.468	11.653	11.838	12.022	12.206	12.389
8 3/8	10.295	10.481	10.668	10.854	11.040	11.225	11.411	11.596	11.780	11.965	12.149	12.333	12.517
8 1/2	10.421	10.608	10.794	10.981	11.166	11.352	11.537	11.723	11.907	12.092	12.276	12.460	12.644
8 5/8	10.547	10.734	10.921	11.107	11.293	11.479	11.664	11.849	12.034	12.219	12.404	12.588	12.772
8 3/4	10.674	10.861	11.047	11.234	11.420	11.606	11.791	11.976	12.161	12.346	12.531	12.715	12.899
8 7/8	10.800	10.987	11.174	11.360	11.546	11.732	11.918	12.103	12.288	12.473	12.658	12.842	13.026

Table 4-15. Solutions for $D = \sqrt{d_1^2 + 6.28rd_1 + 8r^2 + 4d_2H}$ when $H = 3/4$ inch.

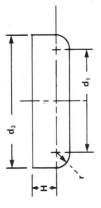

d_1	Radius of shell												
	1/4	5/16	3/8	7/16	1/2	9/16	5/8	11/16	3/4	13/16	7/8	15/16	1
2.0	3.891	4.072	4.253	4.433	4.613	4.793	4.972	5.152	5.331	5.510	5.689	5.868	6.046
2⅛	4.028	4.209	4.390	4.570	4.750	4.930	5.110	5.289	5.468	5.647	5.826	6.005	6.184
2¼	4.165	4.345	4.526	4.706	4.887	5.066	5.246	5.425	5.605	5.784	5.963	6.141	6.320
2⅜	4.301	4.481	4.662	4.842	5.022	5.202	5.382	5.561	5.740	5.919	6.099	6.277	6.456
2½	4.436	4.616	4.797	4.977	5.158	5.337	5.517	5.696	5.876	6.055	6.234	6.413	6.592
2⅝	4.570	4.751	4.932	5.112	5.292	5.472	5.652	5.831	6.011	6.190	6.369	6.548	6.727
2¾	4.704	4.885	5.066	5.246	5.427	5.607	5.786	5.966	6.145	6.325	6.504	6.683	6.862
2⅞	4.838	5.019	5.200	5.380	5.560	5.740	5.920	6.100	6.279	6.459	6.638	6.817	6.996
3	4.971	5.152	5.333	5.514	5.694	5.874	6.054	6.234	6.413	6.593	6.772	6.951	7.130
3⅛	5.104	5.285	5.466	5.647	5.827	6.007	6.187	6.367	6.547	6.726	6.906	7.085	7.264
3¼	5.236	5.417	5.598	5.779	5.960	6.140	6.320	6.500	6.680	6.859	7.039	7.218	7.397
3⅜	5.368	5.549	5.731	5.911	6.092	6.272	6.453	6.633	6.813	6.992	7.172	7.351	7.531
3½	5.500	5.681	5.862	6.043	6.224	6.405	6.585	6.765	6.945	7.125	7.305	7.484	7.664
3⅝	5.631	5.813	5.994	6.175	6.356	6.537	6.717	6.897	7.077	7.257	7.437	7.617	7.796
3¾	5.762	5.944	6.125	6.306	6.487	6.668	6.849	7.029	7.209	7.389	7.569	7.749	7.928
3⅞	5.893	6.075	6.256	6.438	6.619	6.800	6.980	7.161	7.341	7.521	7.701	7.881	8.061
4	6.023	6.205	6.387	6.569	6.750	6.931	7.112	7.292	7.473	7.653	7.833	8.013	8.193
4⅛	6.154	6.336	6.518	6.699	6.881	7.062	7.243	7.423	7.604	7.784	7.964	8.145	8.324
4¼	6.284	6.466	6.648	6.830	7.011	7.192	7.374	7.554	7.735	7.915	8.095	8.276	8.456
4⅜	6.414	6.596	6.778	6.960	7.142	7.323	7.504	7.685	7.866	8.046	8.227	8.407	8.587
4½	6.543	6.726	6.908	7.090	7.272	7.453	7.635	7.816	7.997	8.177	8.358	8.538	8.718

4 5/8	6.673	6.856	7.038	7.220	7.402	7.584	7.765	7.946	8.127	8.308	8.489	8.669	8.849
4 3/4	6.802	6.985	7.168	7.350	7.532	7.713	7.895	8.076	8.257	8.438	8.619	8.800	8.980
4 7/8	6.931	7.114	7.297	7.479	7.662	7.843	8.025	8.206	8.388	8.569	8.750	8.930	9.111
5	7.060	7.244	7.426	7.609	7.791	7.973	8.155	8.336	8.518	8.699	8.880	9.061	9.241
5 1/8	7.189	7.373	7.555	7.738	7.920	8.103	8.284	8.466	8.648	8.829	9.010	9.191	9.372
5 1/4	7.318	7.501	7.685	7.867	8.050	8.232	8.414	8.596	8.777	8.959	9.140	9.321	9.502
5 3/8	7.447	7.630	7.813	7.996	8.179	8.361	8.543	8.725	8.907	9.088	9.270	9.451	9.632
5 1/2	7.575	7.759	7.942	8.125	8.308	8.490	8.673	8.854	9.036	9.218	9.399	9.581	9.762
5 5/8	7.704	7.887	8.071	8.254	8.437	8.619	8.802	8.984	9.166	9.347	9.529	9.710	9.891
5 3/4	7.832	8.016	8.199	8.383	8.566	8.748	8.931	9.113	9.295	9.477	9.658	9.840	10.021
5 7/8	7.960	8.144	8.328	8.511	8.694	8.877	9.060	9.242	9.424	9.606	9.788	9.969	10.151
6	8.088	8.272	8.456	8.640	8.823	9.006	9.188	9.371	9.553	9.735	9.917	10.099	10.280
6 1/8	8.216	8.400	8.584	8.768	8.951	9.134	9.317	9.499	9.682	9.864	10.046	10.227	10.409
6 1/4	8.344	8.528	8.712	8.896	9.080	9.263	9.446	9.628	9.811	9.993	10.175	10.357	10.539
6 3/8	8.472	8.656	8.840	9.024	9.208	9.391	9.574	9.757	9.939	10.122	10.304	10.486	10.668
6 1/2	8.600	8.784	8.969	9.152	9.336	9.519	9.702	9.885	10.068	10.250	10.433	10.615	10.797
6 5/8	8.727	8.912	9.096	9.280	9.464	9.648	9.831	10.014	10.197	10.379	10.561	10.744	10.926
6 3/4	8.849	9.034	9.219	9.403	9.587	9.771	9.954	10.137	10.320	10.503	10.685	10.868	11.050
6 7/8	8.982	9.167	9.352	9.536	9.720	9.904	10.087	10.270	10.453	10.636	10.819	11.001	11.183
7	9.110	9.295	9.479	9.664	9.848	10.032	10.215	10.399	10.582	10.764	10.947	11.130	11.312
7 1/8	9.237	9.422	9.607	9.791	9.976	10.160	10.343	10.527	10.710	10.893	11.076	11.258	11.441
7 1/4	9.365	9.550	9.735	9.919	10.103	10.287	10.471	10.655	10.838	11.021	11.204	11.387	11.569
7 3/8	9.492	9.677	9.862	10.047	10.231	10.415	10.599	10.783	10.966	11.149	11.332	11.515	11.697
7 1/2	9.619	9.804	9.989	10.174	10.359	10.543	10.727	10.910	11.094	11.277	11.460	11.643	11.826
7 5/8	9.746	9.932	10.117	10.302	10.486	10.670	10.854	11.038	11.222	11.405	11.588	11.771	11.954
7 3/4	9.873	10.059	10.244	10.429	10.614	10.798	10.982	11.166	11.350	11.533	11.716	11.899	12.082
7 7/8	10.000	10.186	10.371	10.556	10.741	10.925	11.110	11.294	11.477	11.661	11.844	12.028	12.210
8	10.127	10.313	10.498	10.683	10.868	11.053	11.237	11.421	11.605	11.789	11.972	12.155	12.339
8 1/8	10.254	10.440	10.625	10.811	10.996	11.180	11.365	11.549	11.733	11.917	12.100	12.283	12.467
8 1/4	10.381	10.567	10.753	10.938	11.123	11.308	11.492	11.676	11.860	12.044	12.228	12.411	12.595
8 3/8	10.508	10.694	10.880	11.065	11.250	11.435	11.620	11.804	11.988	12.172	12.356	12.539	12.722
8 1/2	10.635	10.821	11.006	11.192	11.377	11.562	11.747	11.931	12.115	12.299	12.483	12.667	12.850
8 5/8	10.761	10.948	11.133	11.319	11.504	11.689	11.874	12.049	12.243	12.427	12.611	12.795	12.978
8 3/4	10.888	11.074	11.260	11.446	11.631	11.816	12.001	12.186	12.370	12.555	12.738	12.922	13.106
8 7/8	11.015	11.201	11.387	11.573	11.758	11.944	12.128	12.313	12.498	12.682	12.866	13.050	13.234

Table 4–16. Solutions for $D = \sqrt{d_1^2 + 6.28rd_1 + 8r^2 + 4d_2H}$ when $H = 7/8$ inch.

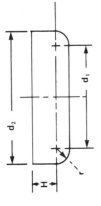

d_1	\multicolumn{13}{c}{Radius of shell}
	1/4	5/16	3/8	7/16	1/2	9/16	5/8	11/16	3/4	13/16	7/8	15/16	1
2.0	4.048	4.230	4.411	4.592	4.773	4.953	5.133	5.313	5.493	5.672	5.851	6.031	6.210
2 1/8	4.188	4.369	4.551	4.731	4.912	5.092	5.272	5.452	5.631	5.811	5.990	6.169	6.348
2 1/4	4.327	4.507	4.689	4.870	5.050	5.230	5.410	5.590	5.769	5.949	6.128	6.307	6.486
2 3/8	4.465	4.646	4.827	5.007	5.188	5.368	5.548	5.727	5.907	6.086	6.265	6.444	6.623
2 1/2	4.602	4.783	4.964	5.144	5.324	5.504	5.684	5.864	6.044	6.223	6.402	6.581	6.760
2 5/8	4.738	4.919	5.100	5.281	5.461	5.641	5.821	6.000	6.180	6.359	6.539	6.718	6.897
2 3/4	4.874	5.055	5.236	5.416	5.597	5.777	5.957	6.136	6.316	6.495	6.675	6.854	7.033
2 7/8	5.009	5.190	5.371	5.552	5.732	5.912	6.092	6.272	6.451	6.631	6.810	6.989	7.168
3	5.144	5.325	5.506	5.687	5.867	6.047	6.227	6.407	6.586	6.766	6.945	7.124	7.303
3 1/8	5.278	5.459	5.640	5.821	6.001	6.182	6.362	6.541	6.721	6.901	7.080	7.259	7.438
3 1/4	5.411	5.593	5.774	5.955	6.135	6.315	6.496	6.675	6.855	7.035	7.214	7.393	7.573
3 3/8	5.545	5.727	5.908	6.089	6.269	6.449	6.630	6.809	6.989	7.169	7.348	7.528	7.707
3 1/2	5.678	5.860	6.041	6.222	6.402	6.583	6.763	6.943	7.123	7.303	7.482	7.662	7.841
3 5/8	5.811	5.993	6.174	6.355	6.535	6.716	6.896	7.076	7.256	7.436	7.616	7.795	7.975
3 3/4	5.943	6.125	6.306	6.487	6.668	6.848	7.029	7.209	7.389	7.569	7.749	7.928	8.108
3 7/8	6.076	6.257	6.439	6.620	6.800	6.981	7.162	7.342	7.522	7.702	7.882	8.061	8.241
4	6.207	6.389	6.570	6.752	6.933	7.113	7.294	7.474	7.654	7.834	8.014	8.194	8.374
4 1/8	6.339	6.521	6.702	6.883	7.064	7.245	7.426	7.606	7.787	7.967	8.147	8.327	8.506
4 1/4	6.470	6.652	6.834	7.015	7.196	7.377	7.558	7.738	7.919	8.099	8.278	8.459	8.639
4 3/8	6.601	6.783	6.965	7.146	7.327	7.508	7.689	7.870	8.050	8.231	8.411	8.591	8.771
4 1/2	6.732	6.914	7.096	7.277	7.459	7.640	7.821	8.001	8.182	8.362	8.543	8.723	8.903

Size													
4 5/8	6.862	7.044	7.226	7.408	7.590	7.771	7.952	8.133	8.313	8.494	8.674	8.854	9.035
4 3/4	6.993	7.175	7.357	7.539	7.720	7.902	8.083	8.264	8.445	8.625	8.806	8.986	9.166
4 7/8	7.123	7.305	7.487	7.669	7.851	8.032	8.214	8.395	8.576	8.756	8.937	9.117	9.297
5	7.253	7.435	7.617	7.799	7.981	8.163	8.344	8.525	8.706	8.887	9.068	9.248	9.429
5 1/8	7.382	7.565	7.747	7.930	8.112	8.293	8.475	8.656	8.837	9.018	9.199	9.379	9.560
5 1/4	7.512	7.695	7.877	8.059	8.242	8.423	8.605	8.786	8.967	9.148	9.329	9.510	9.691
5 3/8	7.641	7.824	8.007	8.189	8.371	8.553	8.735	8.917	9.098	9.279	9.460	9.641	9.821
5 1/2	7.771	7.954	8.137	8.319	8.501	8.683	8.865	9.047	9.228	9.409	9.590	9.771	9.952
5 5/8	7.900	8.083	8.266	8.448	8.631	8.813	8.995	9.176	9.358	9.539	9.720	9.901	10.082
5 3/4	8.029	8.212	8.395	8.578	8.760	8.943	9.125	9.306	9.488	9.669	9.851	10.032	10.213
5 7/8	8.158	8.341	8.524	8.707	8.890	9.072	9.254	9.436	9.618	9.799	9.981	10.162	10.343
6	8.287	8.470	8.653	8.836	9.019	9.201	9.383	9.565	9.747	9.929	10.110	10.292	10.473
6 1/8	8.415	8.599	8.782	8.965	9.148	9.330	9.513	9.695	9.877	10.058	10.240	10.421	10.602
6 1/4	8.544	8.728	8.911	9.094	9.277	9.460	9.642	9.824	10.006	10.188	10.370	10.551	10.733
6 3/8	8.673	8.856	9.040	9.223	9.406	9.589	9.771	9.953	10.136	10.317	10.499	10.680	10.862
6 1/2	8.801	8.985	9.168	9.352	9.535	9.717	9.900	10.083	10.265	10.447	10.629	10.810	10.992
6 5/8	8.929	9.113	9.297	9.480	9.663	9.846	10.029	10.212	10.394	10.576	10.758	10.940	11.121
6 3/4	9.052	9.236	9.420	9.604	9.787	9.970	10.153	10.336	10.518	10.700	10.883	11.064	11.246
6 7/8	9.185	9.370	9.554	9.737	9.921	10.104	10.287	10.469	10.652	10.834	11.016	11.198	11.380
7	9.313	9.498	9.682	9.866	10.049	10.232	10.415	10.598	10.781	10.963	11.145	11.327	11.509
7 1/8	9.441	9.626	9.810	9.994	10.177	10.361	10.544	10.727	10.909	11.092	11.274	11.456	11.638
7 1/4	9.569	9.754	9.938	10.122	10.305	10.489	10.672	10.855	11.038	11.220	11.403	11.585	11.767
7 3/8	9.697	9.882	10.066	10.250	10.434	10.617	10.800	10.984	11.166	11.349	11.532	11.714	11.896
7 1/2	9.825	10.009	10.194	10.378	10.562	10.745	10.929	11.112	11.295	11.478	11.660	11.843	12.025
7 5/8	9.952	10.137	10.322	10.506	10.690	10.873	11.057	11.240	11.423	11.606	11.789	11.971	12.154
7 3/4	10.080	10.265	10.449	10.634	10.818	11.002	11.185	11.368	11.552	11.735	11.917	12.100	12.282
7 7/8	10.207	10.392	10.577	10.761	10.947	11.129	11.313	11.497	11.680	11.863	12.046	12.228	12.411
8	10.335	10.520	10.705	10.889	11.073	11.257	11.441	11.625	11.808	12.000	12.174	12.357	12.540
8 1/8	10.462	10.647	10.832	11.017	11.201	11.385	11.569	11.753	11.936	12.119	12.302	12.485	12.668
8 1/4	10.590	10.775	10.960	11.144	11.329	11.513	11.697	11.881	12.064	12.248	12.431	12.614	12.796
8 3/8	10.717	10.902	11.087	11.272	11.457	11.641	11.825	12.009	12.192	12.376	12.559	12.742	12.925
8 1/2	10.844	11.029	11.215	11.399	11.584	11.768	11.953	12.136	12.320	12.504	12.687	12.870	13.053
8 5/8	10.971	11.157	11.342	11.527	11.712	11.896	12.080	12.264	12.448	12.632	12.815	12.998	13.181
8 3/4	11.098	11.284	11.469	11.654	11.839	12.024	12.208	12.392	12.576	12.759	12.943	13.126	13.309
8 7/8	11.226	11.411	11.597	11.782	11.966	12.151	12.335	12.520	12.704	12.887	13.071	13.254	13.437

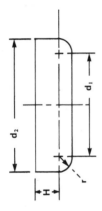

Table 4–17. Solutions for $D = \sqrt{d_1^2 + 6.28rd_1 + 8r^2 + 4d_2H}$ when $H = 1$ inch.

d_1	\multicolumn{13}{c}{Radius of shell}
	1/4	5/16	3/8	7/16	1/2	9/16	5/8	11/16	3/4	13/16	7/8	15/16	1
2.0	4.200	4.382	4.565	4.746	4.927	5.108	5.289	5.470	5.650	5.830	6.010	6.189	6.369
2 1/8	4.342	4.524	4.706	4.887	5.068	5.249	5.430	5.610	5.790	5.970	6.150	6.329	6.509
2 1/4	4.483	4.664	4.846	5.028	5.208	5.389	5.569	5.750	5.930	6.109	6.289	6.468	6.648
2 3/8	4.623	4.804	4.986	5.167	5.348	5.528	5.709	5.889	6.069	6.248	6.428	6.607	6.786
2 1/2	4.762	4.943	5.125	5.306	5.486	5.667	5.847	6.027	6.207	6.386	6.556	6.745	6.925
2 5/8	4.900	5.082	5.263	5.444	5.624	5.805	5.985	6.165	6.345	6.524	6.704	6.883	7.062
2 3/4	5.038	5.219	5.400	5.581	5.762	5.942	6.122	6.302	6.482	6.662	6.841	7.020	7.200
2 7/8	5.175	5.356	5.537	5.718	5.899	6.079	6.259	6.439	6.619	6.798	6.978	7.157	7.336
3	5.311	5.493	5.674	5.854	6.035	6.215	6.395	6.575	6.755	6.935	7.114	7.293	7.473
3 1/8	5.447	5.628	5.809	5.990	6.171	6.351	6.531	6.711	6.891	7.071	7.250	7.429	7.609
3 1/4	5.582	5.764	5.945	6.125	6.306	6.486	6.666	6.846	7.026	7.206	7.385	7.565	7.744
3 3/8	5.718	5.899	6.080	6.261	6.441	6.621	6.802	6.982	7.161	7.341	7.521	7.700	7.879
3 1/2	5.852	6.033	6.214	6.395	6.576	6.756	6.936	7.116	7.296	7.476	7.656	7.835	8.014
3 5/8	5.986	6.167	6.348	6.529	6.710	6.890	7.071	7.251	7.431	7.610	7.790	7.970	8.149
3 3/4	6.120	6.301	6.482	6.663	6.844	7.024	7.205	7.385	7.565	7.744	7.924	8.104	8.283
3 7/8	6.253	6.434	6.616	6.797	6.977	7.158	7.338	7.518	7.699	7.878	8.058	8.238	8.417
4	6.386	6.567	6.749	6.930	7.111	7.291	7.472	7.652	7.832	8.012	8.192	8.371	8.551
4 1/8	6.519	6.700	6.881	7.063	7.244	7.424	7.605	7.785	7.965	8.145	8.325	8.505	8.685
4 1/4	6.651	6.833	7.014	7.195	7.376	7.557	7.738	7.918	8.098	8.278	8.458	8.638	8.818
4 3/8	6.783	6.965	7.146	7.327	7.509	7.689	7.870	8.051	8.231	8.411	8.591	8.771	8.951
4 1/2	6.915	7.097	7.278	7.460	7.641	7.822	8.002	8.183	8.363	8.544	8.724	8.904	9.084

4 5/8	7.046	7.228	7.410	7.591	7.773	7.954	8.134	8.315	8.496	8.676	8.856	9.036	9.216
4 3/4	7.178	7.360	7.541	7.723	7.904	8.085	8.266	8.447	8.628	8.808	8.988	9.168	9.348
4 7/8	7.309	7.491	7.673	7.854	8.036	8.217	8.398	8.579	8.759	8.940	9.120	9.300	9.481
5	7.440	7.622	7.804	7.986	8.167	8.348	8.529	8.710	8.891	9.072	9.252	9.432	9.612
5 1/8	7.570	7.753	7.935	8.117	8.298	8.479	8.661	8.842	9.022	9.203	9.384	9.564	9.744
5 1/4	7.701	7.883	8.065	8.247	8.429	8.610	8.792	8.973	9.154	9.334	9.515	9.696	9.876
5 3/8	7.831	8.014	8.196	8.378	8.560	8.741	8.923	9.104	9.285	9.466	9.646	9.827	10.007
5 1/2	7.961	8.144	8.326	8.508	8.690	8.872	9.053	9.235	9.416	9.597	9.777	9.958	10.139
5 5/8	8.091	8.274	8.457	8.639	8.821	9.002	9.184	9.365	9.546	9.727	9.908	10.089	10.270
5 3/4	8.221	8.404	8.587	8.769	8.951	9.133	9.314	9.496	9.677	9.858	10.039	10.220	10.401
5 7/8	8.351	8.534	8.716	8.899	9.081	9.263	9.445	9.626	9.807	9.989	10.170	10.351	10.531
6	8.481	8.663	8.846	9.029	9.211	9.393	9.575	9.756	9.938	10.119	10.300	10.481	10.662
6 1/8	8.610	8.793	8.976	9.158	9.340	9.523	9.704	9.886	10.068	10.249	10.430	10.611	10.792
6 1/4	8.739	8.922	9.105	9.288	9.470	9.653	9.836	10.016	10.198	10.380	10.561	10.742	10.923
6 3/8	8.868	9.053	9.235	9.417	9.600	9.782	9.964	10.146	10.328	10.510	10.691	10.872	11.053
6 1/2	8.997	9.181	9.364	9.547	9.729	9.912	10.094	10.276	10.458	10.639	10.821	11.002	11.183
6 5/8	9.126	9.310	9.493	9.676	9.859	10.041	10.223	10.406	10.587	10.769	10.951	11.132	11.314
6 3/4	9.250	9.434	9.617	9.800	9.983	10.166	10.348	10.530	10.712	10.894	11.076	11.258	11.439
6 7/8	9.384	9.568	9.751	9.934	10.117	10.300	10.483	10.664	10.847	11.028	11.210	11.392	11.573
7	9.513	9.696	9.880	10.063	10.246	10.429	10.611	10.794	10.976	11.158	11.340	11.521	11.703
7 1/8	9.641	9.825	10.008	10.192	10.375	10.558	10.740	10.923	11.105	11.287	11.469	11.651	11.833
7 1/4	9.770	9.953	10.137	10.321	10.504	10.687	10.869	11.052	11.234	11.417	11.599	11.780	11.962
7 3/8	9.899	10.082	10.266	10.449	10.632	10.815	10.998	11.181	11.363	11.546	11.728	11.910	12.092
7 1/2	10.026	10.210	10.394	10.578	10.761	10.944	11.127	11.310	11.492	11.675	11.857	12.039	12.221
7 5/8	10.154	10.339	10.522	10.706	10.890	11.073	11.256	11.439	11.621	11.804	11.986	12.168	12.350
7 3/4	10.283	10.467	10.651	10.835	11.018	11.201	11.385	11.567	11.750	11.933	12.115	12.297	12.479
7 7/8	10.411	10.595	10.779	10.963	11.146	11.329	11.513	11.696	11.879	12.061	12.244	12.426	12.608
8	10.539	10.723	10.907	11.091	11.275	11.458	11.642	11.825	12.007	12.190	12.373	12.555	12.737
8 1/8	10.666	10.851	11.035	11.219	11.403	11.587	11.770	11.953	12.136	12.319	12.502	12.684	12.866
8 1/4	10.794	10.979	11.163	11.347	11.531	11.715	11.898	12.082	12.265	12.447	12.630	12.813	12.995
8 3/8	10.922	11.107	11.291	11.475	11.659	11.843	12.027	12.210	12.393	12.576	12.759	12.941	13.124
8 1/2	11.050	11.234	11.419	11.603	11.787	11.971	12.155	12.338	12.521	12.704	12.887	13.070	13.253
8 5/8	11.177	11.362	11.547	11.731	11.915	12.099	12.283	12.466	12.650	12.833	13.016	13.199	13.381
8 3/4	11.305	11.490	11.675	11.859	12.043	12.227	12.411	12.595	12.778	12.961	13.144	13.327	13.510
8 7/8	11.432	11.617	11.802	11.987	12.171	12.355	12.539	12.723	12.906	13.089	13.272	13.455	13.638

Transfer die for sequential draws. Photo courtesy Livernois Automation Co.

$$D = \sqrt{d_1^2 + 6.28rd_1 + 8r^2 + (d_3^2 - d_2^2)}$$

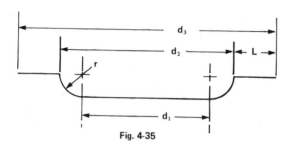

Fig. 4-35

A sectional view of a commonly encountered radial form is shown in *Figure* 4–35. In the accompanying equation, D equals the diameter of the flat blank needed to produce the configuration shown sectionally in *Figure* 4–35. Tables 4–18 through 4–26 provide values for D in millimetres. Tables 4–27 through 4–34 provide values for D in inches. The following index will prove helpful in finding the table you require for a specific problem.

Cases will arise when required values of d_1, r, and L do not coincide with the values given in these tables. When this happens, you can easily obtain a correct answer by interpolation.

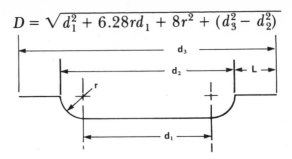

$$D = \sqrt{d_1^2 + 6.28rd_1 + 8r^2 + (d_3^2 - d_2^2)}$$

Table 4–18. Solutions for $D = \sqrt{d_1^2 + 6.28rd_1 + 8r^2 + (d_3^2 - d_2^2)}$ when $L = 10$ mm.

	Radius of Shell					
d_1	4	6	8	10	12	14
50	81.26	86.32	92.54	98.18	103.83	109.47
55	86.34	92.01	97.67	103.34	109.00	114.67
60	91.41	97.10	102.79	108.48	114.16	119.85
65	96.47	102.19	107.90	113.61	119.31	125.01
70	101.52	107.26	113.00	118.73	124.45	130.16
75	106.57	112.33	118.09	123.83	129.57	135.30
80	111.61	117.40	123.17	128.93	134.69	140.43
85	116.65	122.46	128.25	134.03	139.79	145.55
90	121.69	127.51	133.32	139.11	144.89	150.67
95	126.73	132.56	138.38	144.19	149.99	155.77
100	131.76	137.61	143.44	149.26	155.07	160.87
105	136.79	142.65	148.50	154.33	160.16	165.97
110	141.81	147.69	153.55	159.40	165.23	171.05
115	146.84	152.73	158.60	164.46	170.30	176.14
120	151.86	157.76	163.65	169.52	175.37	181.21
125	156.89	162.80	168.69	174.57	180.44	186.29
130	161.91	167.83	173.73	179.62	185.50	191.36
135	166.93	172.86	178.77	184.67	190.55	196.42
140	171.94	177.89	183.81	189.72	195.61	201.49
145	176.96	182.91	188.84	194.76	200.66	206.55
150	181.98	187.94	193.88	199.80	205.71	211.60
155	186.99	192.96	198.91	204.84	210.76	216.66
160	192.01	197.98	203.94	209.88	215.80	221.71
165	197.02	203.00	208.97	214.91	220.84	226.76
170	202.04	208.02	213.99	219.95	225.88	231.81
175	207.05	213.04	219.02	224.98	230.92	236.85
180	212.06	218.06	224.04	230.01	235.96	241.90
185	217.07	223.08	229.07	235.04	241.00	246.94
190	222.08	228.09	234.09	240.07	246.03	251.98
195	227.09	233.11	239.11	245.09	251.06	257.02
200	232.10	238.13	244.13	250.12	256.09	262.05
205	237.11	243.14	249.15	255.15	261.12	267.09
210	242.12	248.15	254.17	260.17	266.15	272.12
215	247.13	253.17	259.19	265.19	271.18	277.16
220	252.14	258.18	264.21	270.21	276.21	282.19
225	257.15	263.19	269.22	275.24	281.23	287.22
230	262.16	268.21	274.24	280.26	286.26	292.25
235	267.16	273.22	279.26	285.28	291.28	297.28
240	272.17	278.23	284.27	290.30	296.31	302.31
245	277.18	283.24	289.28	295.32	301.33	307.33
250	282.18	288.25	294.30	300.33	306.35	312.36

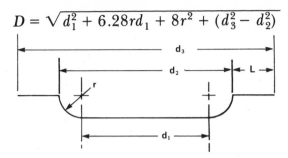

$$D = \sqrt{d_1^2 + 6.28rd_1 + 8r^2 + (d_3^2 - d_2^2)}$$

Table 4–18. Solutions for $D = \sqrt{d_1^2 + 6.28rd_1 + 8r^2 + (d_3^2 - d_2^2)}$ when $L = 10$ mm *(Continued)*.

	Radius of Shell					
d_1	16	18	20	22	24	26
50	115.12	120.76	126.41	132.06	137.71	143.36
55	120.33	125.99	131.65	137.32	142.98	148.64
60	125.52	131.20	136.88	142.55	148.23	153.90
65	130.71	136.40	142.09	147.77	153.46	159.14
70	135.87	141.58	147.28	152.98	158.68	164.37
75	141.03	146.75	152.46	158.17	163.88	169.58
80	146.17	151.91	157.63	163.35	169.07	174.79
85	151.31	157.05	162.79	168.52	174.25	179.98
90	156.43	162.19	167.94	173.68	179.42	185.16
95	161.55	167.32	173.08	178.84	184.58	190.33
100	166.66	172.44	178.21	183.98	189.74	195.49
105	171.77	177.56	183.34	189.11	194.88	200.64
110	176.86	182.66	188.46	194.24	200.02	205.79
115	181.96	187.77	193.57	199.36	205.15	210.93
120	187.04	192.86	198.68	204.48	210.27	216.06
125	192.13	197.96	203.78	209.59	215.39	221.19
130	179.21	203.04	208.87	214.69	220.50	226.31
135	202.28	208.13	213.96	219.79	225.61	231.42
140	207.35	213.21	219.05	224.89	230.71	236.53
145	212.42	218.28	224.14	229.98	235.81	241.64
150	217.49	223.36	229.22	235.07	240.91	246.74
155	222.55	228.43	234.29	240.15	246.00	251.84
160	227.61	233.49	239.37	245.23	251.08	256.93
165	232.66	238.56	244.44	250.31	256.17	262.02
170	237.72	243.62	249.50	255.38	261.25	267.11
175	242.77	248.67	254.57	260.45	266.32	272.19
180	247.82	253.73	259.63	265.52	271.40	277.27
185	252.87	258.78	264.69	270.59	276.47	282.35
190	257.91	263.84	269.75	275.65	281.54	287.42
195	262.96	268.89	274.80	280.71	286.61	292.49
200	268.00	273.93	279.86	285.77	291.67	297.56
205	273.04	278.98	284.91	290.83	296.73	302.63
210	278.08	284.03	289.96	295.88	301.81	307.70
215	283.12	289.07	295.01	300.93	306.85	312.76
220	288.16	294.11	300.05	305.99	311.91	317.82
225	293.19	299.15	305.10	311.04	316.96	322.88
230	298.23	304.19	310.14	316.08	322.01	327.94
235	303.26	309.23	315.18	321.13	327.07	332.99
240	308.29	314.26	320.22	326.18	332.12	338.05
245	313.32	319.30	325.26	331.22	337.16	343.10
250	318.35	324.33	330.30	336.26	342.21	348.15

$$D = \sqrt{d_1^2 + 6.28rd_1 + 8r^2 + (d_3^2 - d_2^2)}$$

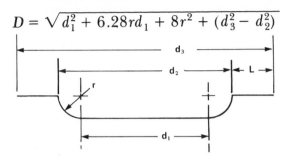

Table 4–19. Solutions for $D = \sqrt{d_1^2 + 6.28rd_1 + 8r^2 + (d_3^2 - d_2^2)}$ when $L = 15$ mm.

	Radius of Shell					
d_1	4	6	8	10	12	14
50	90.91	96.40	101.90	107.42	112.96	118.51
55	95.99	101.52	107.05	112.60	118.16	123.73
60	101.07	106.62	112.19	117.76	123.34	128.93
65	106.14	111.72	117.31	123.91	128.51	134.12
70	111.20	116.81	122.43	128.05	133.67	139.29
75	116.26	121.90	127.53	133.17	138.81	144.45
80	121.32	126.97	132.63	138.29	143.95	149.60
85	126.37	132.04	137.72	143.40	149.07	154.75
90	131.41	137.11	142.81	148.50	154.19	159.88
95	136.45	142.17	147.88	153.59	159.30	165.00
100	141.49	147.23	152.96	158.68	164.40	170.12
105	146.53	152.28	158.03	163.77	169.50	175.23
110	151.56	157.33	163.09	168.84	174.59	180.33
115	156.59	162.38	168.15	173.92	179.68	185.43
120	161.62	167.42	173.21	178.99	184.76	190.52
125	166.65	172.46	178.26	184.05	189.83	195.61
130	171.68	177.50	183.31	189.11	194.91	200.69
135	176.70	182.54	188.36	194.17	199.98	205.77
140	181.72	187.57	193.41	199.23	205.04	210.85
145	186.75	192.60	198.45	204.28	210.11	215.92
150	191.77	197.64	203.49	209.33	215.17	220.99
155	196.79	202.67	208.53	214.38	220.22	226.05
160	201.81	207.69	213.57	219.43	225.28	231.12
165	206.83	212.72	218.60	224.47	230.33	236.18
170	211.85	217.75	223.64	229.51	235.38	241.24
175	216.86	222.77	228.67	234.55	240.43	246.29
180	221.88	227.79	233.70	239.59	245.47	251.34
185	226.89	232.82	238.73	244.63	250.52	256.39
190	231.91	237.84	243.76	249.66	255.56	261.44
195	236.92	242.86	248.78	254.70	260.60	266.49
200	241.93	247.88	253.81	259.73	265.64	271.54
205	246.95	252.90	258.84	264.76	270.68	276.58
210	251.96	257.92	263.86	269.79	275.71	281.62
215	256.97	262.93	268.88	274.82	280.75	286.66
220	261.98	267.95	273.91	279.85	285.78	291.70
225	266.24	272.23	278.21	284.17	290.13	296.07
230	272.00	277.98	283.95	289.90	295.85	301.78
235	277.01	283.00	288.97	294.93	300.88	306.81
240	282.02	288.01	293.99	299.95	305.91	311.85
245	287.03	293.03	299.01	304.98	310.93	316.88
250	292.04	298.04	304.03	310.00	315.96	321.91

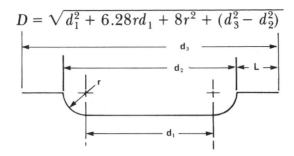

$$D = \sqrt{d_1^2 + 6.28rd_1 + 8r^2 + (d_3^2 - d_2^2)}$$

Table 4–19. Solutions for $D = \sqrt{d_1^2 + 6.28rd_1 + 8r^2 + (d_3^2 - d_2^2)}$
when $L = 15$ mm *(Continued)*.

	Radius of Shell					
d_1	16	18	20	22	24	26
50	124.06	129.63	135.20	140.78	146.40	151.96
55	129.30	134.89	140.47	146.07	151.67	157.27
60	134.52	140.12	145.73	151.33	156.94	162.56
65	139.73	145.34	150.96	156.58	162.20	167.83
70	144.92	150.55	156.18	161.81	167.45	173.08
75	150.10	155.74	161.38	167.03	172.68	178.32
80	155.26	160.92	166.58	172.23	177.89	183.55
85	160.42	166.09	171.76	177.43	183.10	188.76
90	165.56	171.25	176.93	182.61	188.29	193.97
95	170.70	176.40	182.09	187.78	193.47	199.16
100	175.83	181.54	187.24	192.95	198.65	204.34
105	180.95	186.67	192.39	198.10	203.81	209.52
110	186.07	191.80	197.52	203.25	208.97	214.68
115	191.18	196.92	202.65	208.39	214.12	219.84
120	196.28	202.03	207.78	213.52	219.26	224.99
125	201.38	207.14	212.90	218.65	224.39	230.14
130	206.47	212.24	218.01	223.77	229.52	235.28
135	211.56	217.34	223.12	228.89	234.65	240.41
140	216.65	222.44	228.22	234.00	239.77	245.53
145	221.73	227.53	233.32	239.10	244.88	250.66
150	226.80	232.61	238.41	244.20	250.00	255.77
155	231.88	237.69	243.50	249.30	255.10	260.89
160	236.95	242.77	248.59	254.40	260.20	265.99
165	242.02	247.85	253.67	259.49	265.30	271.10
170	247.08	252.92	258.75	264.57	270.39	276.20
175	252.14	257.99	263.83	269.66	275.48	281.30
180	257.20	263.06	268.90	274.74	280.57	286.39
185	262.26	268.12	273.97	279.82	285.65	291.48
190	267.32	273.18	279.04	284.89	290.73	296.57
195	272.37	278.24	284.11	289.96	295.81	301.65
200	277.42	283.30	289.17	295.03	300.89	306.73
205	282.47	288.36	294.23	300.10	305.96	311.81
210	287.52	293.41	299.29	305.16	311.03	316.89
215	292.57	298.46	304.35	310.23	316.10	321.96
220	297.61	303.51	309.41	315.29	321.16	327.03
225	302.00	307.91	313.82	319.72	325.61	331.50
230	307.70	313.61	319.51	325.41	331.29	337.17
235	312.74	318.66	324.56	330.46	336.35	342.23
240	317.78	323.70	329.61	335.52	341.41	347.15
245	322.82	328.74	334.66	340.57	346.47	352.36
250	327.85	333.78	339.71	345.62	251.52	357.42

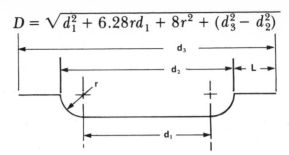

$$D = \sqrt{d_1^2 + 6.28rd_1 + 8r^2 + (d_3^2 - d_2^2)}$$

Table 4–20.   Solutions for $D = \sqrt{d_1^2 + 6.28rd_1 + 8r^2 + (d_3^2 - d_2^2)}$
when $L = 20$ **mm.**

	Radius of Shell					
d_1	4	6	8	10	12	14
50	100.62	105.98	111.37	116.79	122.23	127.69
55	105.71	111.11	116.53	121.98	127.44	132.92
60	110.79	116.23	121.68	127.15	132.64	138.14
65	115.87	121.34	126.81	132.31	137.82	143.35
70	120.94	126.43	131.94	137.46	142.99	148.53
75	126.00	131.53	137.06	142.60	148.15	153.71
80	131.06	136.61	142.17	147.73	153.30	158.88
85	136.12	141.69	147.27	152.85	158.44	164.03
90	141.17	146.76	152.36	157.96	163.57	169.18
95	146.22	151.83	157.45	163.07	168.69	174.31
100	151.26	156.89	162.53	168.17	173.80	179.44
105	156.30	161.95	167.61	173.26	178.91	184.57
110	161.34	167.01	172.68	178.35	184.02	189.68
115	166.38	172.06	177.75	183.43	189.11	194.79
120	171.41	177.11	182.81	188.51	194.20	199.90
125	176.45	182.16	187.87	193.58	199.29	205.00
130	181.48	187.21	192.93	198.66	204.37	210.09
135	186.51	192.25	197.99	203.72	209.45	215.18
140	191.53	197.29	203.04	208.79	214.53	220.27
145	196.56	202.33	208.09	213.85	219.60	225.35
150	201.58	207.36	213.14	218.91	224.67	230.43
155	206.61	212.40	218.18	223.96	229.73	235.50
160	211.63	217.43	223.23	229.02	234.80	240.57
165	216.65	222.46	228.27	234.07	239.86	245.64
170	221.67	227.49	233.31	239.12	244.91	250.71
175	226.69	232.52	238.35	244.16	249.97	255.77
180	231.71	237.55	243.38	249.21	255.02	260.83
185	236.73	242.58	248.42	254.25	260.07	265.89
190	241.75	247.60	253.45	259.29	265.12	270.95
195	246.76	252.63	258.48	264.33	270.17	276.00
200	251.78	257.65	263.51	269.37	275.22	281.06
205	256.79	262.67	268.54	274.41	280.26	286.11
210	261.81	267.70	273.57	279.44	285.30	291.15
215	266.82	272.72	278.60	284.48	290.34	296.20
220	271.84	277.74	283.63	289.51	295.38	301.25
225	276.85	282.76	288.65	294.54	300.42	306.29
230	281.86	287.77	293.68	299.57	305.46	311.34
235	286.87	292.79	298.70	304.60	310.49	316.38
240	291.88	297.81	303.73	309.63	315.53	321.42
245	296.90	302.83	308.75	314.66	320.56	326.46
250	301.91	307.84	313.77	319.69	325.59	331.49

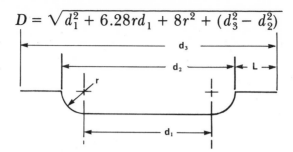

$$D = \sqrt{d_1^2 + 6.28rd_1 + 8r^2 + (d_3^2 - d_2^2)}$$

Table 4–20. Solutions for $H = \sqrt{d_1^2 + 6.28rd_1 + 8r^2 + (d_3^2 - d_2^2)}$ when $L = 20$ mm *(Continued).*

	Radius of Shell					
d_1	16	18	20	22	24	26
50	133.16	138.65	144.15	149.67	155.19	160.72
55	138.42	143.92	149.44	154.97	160.51	166.05
60	143.66	149.18	154.71	160.25	165.80	171.36
65	148.88	154.42	159.97	165.52	171.08	176.65
70	154.08	159.64	165.20	170.77	176.35	181.93
75	159.28	164.85	170.43	176.01	181.60	187.19
80	164.46	170.04	175.64	181.23	186.83	192.43
85	169.63	175.23	180.83	186.44	192.05	197.67
90	174.79	180.40	186.02	191.64	197.26	202.89
95	179.94	185.57	191.20	196.83	202.46	208.10
100	185.08	190.72	196.37	202.01	207.65	213.30
105	190.22	195.87	201.53	207.18	212.83	218.49
110	195.35	201.01	206.68	212.34	218.01	223.67
115	200.47	206.15	211.82	217.50	223.17	228.85
120	205.59	211.27	216.96	222.65	228.33	234.01
125	210.70	216.40	222.09	227.79	233.48	239.17
130	215.80	221.51	227.22	232.92	238.62	244.32
135	220.90	226.62	232.34	238.05	243.76	249.47
140	226.00	231.73	237.45	243.18	248.90	254.61
145	231.09	236.83	242.56	248.29	254.02	259.75
150	236.18	241.93	247.67	253.41	259.14	264.88
155	241.26	247.02	252.77	258.52	264.26	270.00
160	246.34	252.11	257.87	263.62	269.38	275.12
165	251.42	257.19	262.96	268.73	274.48	280.24
170	256.49	262.28	268.05	273.82	279.59	285.35
175	261.57	267.36	273.14	278.92	284.69	290.46
180	266.64	272.43	278.22	284.01	289.79	295.56
185	271.70	277.51	283.30	289.10	294.88	300.67
190	276.77	282.58	288.38	294.18	299.97	305.76
195	281.83	287.65	293.46	299.26	305.06	310.86
200	286.89	292.71	298.53	304.34	310.15	315.95
205	291.94	297.78	303.60	309.42	315.23	321.04
210	297.00	302.84	308.67	314.49	320.31	326.12
215	302.05	307.90	313.73	319.56	325.39	331.21
220	307.11	312.95	318.80	324.63	330.46	336.29
225	312.16	318.01	323.86	329.70	335.54	341.37
230	317.20	323.07	328.92	334.77	340.61	346.44
235	322.25	328.12	333.98	339.83	345.68	351.52
240	327.30	333.17	339.03	344.89	350.74	356.59
245	332.34	338.22	344.09	349.95	355.81	361.66
250	337.38	343.27	349.14	355.01	360.87	366.73

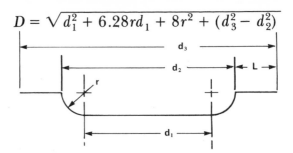

$$D = \sqrt{d_1^2 + 6.28rd_1 + 8r^2 + (d_3^2 - d_2^2)}$$

Table 4–21.   Solutions for $D = \sqrt{d_1^2 + 6.28rd_1 + 8r^2 + (d_3^2 - d_2^2)}$
when $L = 25$ **mm.**

	Radius of Shell					
d_1	4	6	8	10	12	14
50	110.38	115.64	120.93	126.25	131.61	136.98
55	115.48	120.77	126.10	131.45	136.83	142.23
60	120.56	125.89	131.25	136.63	142.03	147.46
65	125.64	131.00	136.39	141.80	147.23	152.67
70	130.71	136.11	141.52	146.96	152.40	157.87
75	135.78	141.21	146.65	152.10	157.57	163.06
80	140.85	146.30	151.76	157.24	162.73	168.23
85	145.90	151.38	156.87	162.37	167.88	173.40
90	150.96	156.46	161.97	167.49	173.02	178.55
95	156.01	161.53	167.06	172.60	178.15	183.70
100	161.06	166.60	172.15	177.71	183.27	188.84
105	166.10	171.67	177.23	182.81	188.39	193.97
110	171.15	176.73	182.31	187.90	193.50	199.10
115	176.19	181.79	187.39	192.99	198.60	204.22
120	181.22	186.84	192.46	198.08	203.70	209.33
125	186.26	191.89	197.53	203.16	208.80	214.44
130	191.29	196.94	202.59	208.24	213.89	219.54
135	196.33	201.99	207.65	213.31	218.98	224.64
140	201.36	207.03	212.71	218.38	224.06	229.73
145	206.39	212.08	217.77	223.45	229.14	234.82
150	211.41	217.12	222.82	228.52	234.21	239.91
155	216.44	222.16	227.87	233.58	239.29	244.99
160	221.47	227.19	232.92	238.64	244.36	250.07
165	226.49	232.23	237.96	243.69	249.42	255.15
170	231.51	237.26	243.01	248.75	254.49	260.22
175	236.54	242.30	248.05	253.80	259.55	265.29
180	241.56	247.33	253.09	258.85	264.61	270.36
185	246.58	252.36	258.13	263.90	269.66	275.42
190	251.60	257.39	263.17	268.95	274.72	280.49
195	256.62	262.41	268.20	273.99	279.77	285.55
200	261.63	267.44	273.24	279.03	284.82	290.61
205	266.65	272.47	278.27	284.08	289.87	295.66
210	271.67	277.49	283.31	289.12	294.92	300.72
215	276.68	282.51	288.34	294.15	299.97	305.77
220	281.70	287.54	293.37	299.19	305.01	310.82
225	286.71	292.56	298.40	304.23	310.05	315.87
230	291.73	297.58	303.43	309.26	315.09	320.92
235	296.74	302.60	308.45	314.30	320.14	325.97
240	301.76	307.62	313.48	319.33	325.17	331.01
245	306.77	312.64	318.51	324.36	330.21	336.06
250	311.78	317.66	323.53	329.39	335.25	341.10

172

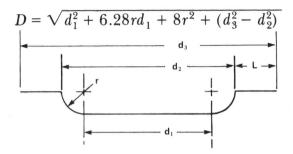

$$D = \sqrt{d_1^2 + 6.28rd_1 + 8r^2 + (d_3^2 - d_2^2)}$$

Table 4–21. Solutions for $D = \sqrt{d_1^2 + 6.28rd_1 + 8r^2 + (d_3^2 - d_2^2)}$ when $L = 25$ mm *(Continued)*.

	Radius of Shell					
d_1	16	18	20	22	24	26
50	142.38	147.80	153.23	158.68	164.15	169.62
55	147.65	153.08	158.53	164.00	169.48	174.97
60	152.89	158.35	163.82	169.30	174.79	180.29
65	158.13	163.60	169.08	174.58	180.08	185.60
70	163.35	168.83	174.33	179.84	185.36	190.89
75	168.55	174.05	179.57	185.09	190.62	196.16
80	173.74	179.26	184.79	190.33	195.87	201.42
85	178.92	184.46	190.00	195.55	201.11	206.67
90	184.10	189.65	195.20	200.76	206.33	211.90
95	189.26	194.82	200.39	205.97	211.55	217.13
100	194.41	199.99	205.57	211.16	216.75	222.34
105	199.56	205.15	210.74	216.34	221.94	227.55
110	204.70	210.30	215.91	221.52	227.13	232.74
115	209.83	215.45	221.06	226.68	232.31	237.93
120	214.95	220.58	226.21	231.84	237.48	243.11
125	220.07	225.71	231.35	237.00	242.64	248.28
130	225.19	230.84	236.49	242.14	247.79	253.45
135	230.30	235.96	241.62	247.28	252.94	258.60
140	235.40	241.08	246.75	252.42	258.09	263.76
145	240.50	246.19	251.87	257.55	263.22	268.90
150	245.60	251.29	256.98	262.67	268.36	274.04
155	250.69	256.39	262.09	267.79	273.49	279.18
160	255.78	261.49	267.20	272.91	278.61	284.31
165	260.87	266.59	272.30	278.02	283.73	289.44
170	265.95	271.68	277.40	283.12	288.84	294.56
175	271.03	276.77	282.50	288.23	293.95	299.68
180	276.11	281.85	287.59	293.33	299.06	304.79
185	281.18	286.93	292.68	298.42	304.16	309.90
190	286.25	292.01	297.77	303.52	309.26	315.01
195	291.32	297.09	302.85	308.61	314.36	320.11
200	296.38	302.16	307.93	313.69	319.46	325.21
205	301.45	307.23	313.01	318.78	324.55	330.31
210	306.51	312.30	318.08	323.86	329.63	335.41
215	311.57	317.37	323.15	328.94	334.72	340.50
220	316.63	322.43	328.23	334.02	339.80	345.59
225	321.68	327.49	333.29	339.09	344.88	350.67
230	326.74	332.55	338.36	344.16	349.96	355.76
235	331.79	337.61	343.43	349.23	355.04	360.84
240	336.84	342.67	348.49	354.30	360.11	365.92
245	341.89	347.72	353.55	359.37	365.18	370.99
250	346.94	352.78	358.61	364.43	370.25	376.07

$$D = \sqrt{d_1^2 + 6.28rd_1 + 8r^2 + (d_3^2 - d_2^2)}$$

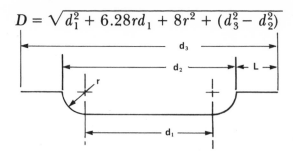

Table 4–22. Solutions for $D = \sqrt{d_1^2 + 6.28rd_1 + 8r^2 + (d_3^2 - d_2^2)}$ when $L = 30$ mm.

	Radius of Shell					
d_1	4	6	8	10	12	14
50	120.18	125.35	130.35	135.79	141.07	146.37
55	125.28	130.48	135.72	140.99	146.29	151.62
60	130.37	135.61	140.88	146.18	151.50	156.85
65	135.45	149.72	146.02	151.35	156.70	162.07
70	140.52	145.83	151.16	156.51	161.89	167.28
75	145.59	150.93	156.28	161.66	167.06	172.47
80	150.66	156.02	161.40	166.81	172.22	177.66
85	155.72	161.11	166.52	171.94	177.38	182.83
90	160.78	166.19	171.62	177.06	182.52	187.99
95	165.83	171.27	176.72	182.18	187.66	193.15
100	170.88	176.34	181.81	187.30	192.79	198.29
105	175.93	181.41	186.90	192.40	197.91	203.43
110	180.97	186.47	191.99	197.60	203.03	208.56
115	186.02	191.54	197.06	202.60	208.14	213.69
120	191.06	196.60	202.14	207.69	213.25	218.81
125	196.09	201.65	207.21	212.78	218.35	223.93
130	201.13	206.70	212.28	217.86	223.45	229.04
135	206.17	211.75	217.35	222.94	228.54	234.14
140	211.20	216.80	222.41	228.02	233.63	239.24
145	216.23	221.85	227.47	233.09	238.71	244.34
150	221.26	226.89	232.53	238.16	243.79	249.43
155	226.29	231.93	237.58	243.23	248.87	254.52
160	231.32	236.97	242.63	248.29	253.95	259.61
165	236.34	242.01	247.68	253.35	259.02	264.69
170	241.37	247.05	252.73	258.41	264.09	269.77
175	246.39	252.09	257.78	263.47	269.16	274.84
180	251.42	257.12	262.82	268.52	274.22	279.92
185	256.44	262.15	267.86	273.57	279.28	284.99
190	261.46	267.18	272.91	278.63	284.34	290.06
195	266.48	272.21	277.95	283.67	289.40	295.12
200	271.50	277.24	282.98	288.72	294.46	300.19
205	276.52	282.27	288.02	293.77	299.51	305.25
210	281.54	287.30	293.06	298.81	304.56	310.31
215	286.56	292.33	298.09	303.85	309.61	315.37
220	291.57	297.35	303.13	308.89	314.66	320.42
225	296.59	302.38	308.16	313.93	319.71	325.48
230	301.61	307.40	313.19	318.97	324.75	330.53
235	306.62	312.42	318.22	324.01	329.80	335.58
240	311.64	317.44	323.25	329.05	334.84	340.63
245	316.65	322.47	328.28	334.08	339.88	345.68
250	321.66	327.49	333.30	339.12	344.92	350.72

$$D = \sqrt{d_1^2 + 6.28rd_1 + 8r^2 + (d_3^2 - d_2^2)}$$

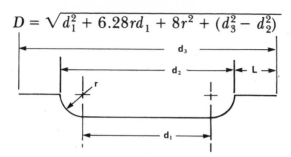

Table 4–22. Solutions for $D = \sqrt{d_1^2 + 6.28rd_1 + 8r^2 + (d_3^2 - d_2^2)}$ when $L = 30$ mm (Continued).

	Radius of Shell					
d_1	16	18	20	22	24	26
50	151.70	157.05	162.42	167.81	173.22	178.64
55	156.97	162.34	167.73	173.14	178.56	183.99
60	162.22	167.61	173.02	178.44	183.88	189.33
65	167.46	172.87	178.29	183.73	189.18	194.64
70	172.69	178.11	183.55	189.01	194.47	199.94
75	177.90	183.34	188.80	194.27	199.74	205.23
80	183.10	188.56	194.03	199.51	205.00	210.50
85	188.29	193.77	199.25	204.75	210.25	215.76
90	193.47	198.96	204.46	209.97	215.48	221.00
95	198.64	204.15	209.66	215.18	220.71	226.24
100	203.80	209.32	214.85	220.38	225.92	231.46
105	208.96	214.49	220.03	225.57	231.12	236.68
110	214.10	219.65	225.20	230.76	236.32	241.89
115	219.24	224.80	230.37	235.94	241.51	247.08
120	224.38	229.95	235.52	241.10	146.69	252.27
125	229.51	235.09	240.68	246.27	251.86	257.45
130	234.63	240.22	245.82	251.42	257.02	262.63
135	239.75	245.35	250.96	256.57	262.18	267.80
140	244.86	250.47	256.08	261.71	267.34	272.96
145	249.97	255.59	261.22	266.85	272.48	278.12
150	255.07	260.71	266.35	271.99	277.63	283.27
155	260.17	265.82	271.46	277.11	282.76	288.41
160	265.26	270.92	276.58	282.24	287.89	293.55
165	270.36	276.02	281.69	287.36	293.02	298.69
170	275.44	281.12	286.80	292.47	298.14	303.82
175	280.53	286.21	291.90	297.58	303.26	308.94
180	285.61	291.31	297.00	302.69	308.38	314.07
185	290.69	296.39	302.09	307.79	313.49	319.19
190	295.77	301.48	307.19	312.89	318.60	324.30
195	300.84	306.56	312.28	317.99	323.70	329.41
200	305.92	311.64	317.36	323.09	328.80	334.52
205	310.98	316.72	322.45	328.18	333.90	339.63
210	316.05	322.26	327.53	333.27	339.00	344.73
215	321.12	326.86	332.61	338.35	344.09	349.83
220	326.18	331.93	337.69	343.43	349.18	354.92
225	331.24	337.00	342.76	348.52	354.27	360.02
230	336.30	342.07	347.83	353.59	359.35	365.11
235	341.36	347.13	352.90	358.67	364.43	370.19
240	346.41	352.20	357.97	363.74	369.51	375.28
245	351.47	357.26	363.04	368.82	374.59	380.36
250	356.52	362.31	368.10	373.89	379.67	385.45

$$D = \sqrt{d_1^2 + 6.28rd_1 + 8r^2 + (d_3^2 - d_2^2)}$$

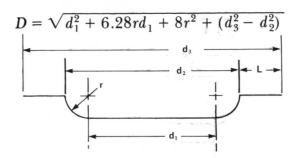

Table 4–23. Solutions for $D = \sqrt{d_1^2 + 6.28rd_1 + 8r^2 + (d_3^2 - d_2^2)}$ when $L = 35$ mm.

	Radius of Shell					
d_1	4	6	8	10	12	14
50	130.02	135.10	140.23	145.40	150.60	155.83
55	135.11	140.23	145.40	150.60	155.83	161.09
60	140.20	145.36	150.55	155.78	161.04	166.32
65	145.28	150.47	155.70	160.96	166.24	171.55
70	150.35	155.58	160.84	166.12	171.43	176.76
75	155.43	160.68	165.97	171.27	176.60	181.95
80	160.49	165.78	171.09	176.42	181.77	187.14
85	165.55	170.87	176.20	181.56	186.93	192.32
90	170.61	175.95	181.31	186.69	192.08	197.49
95	175.67	181.03	186.41	191.81	197.22	202.65
100	180.72	186.11	191.51	196.93	202.36	207.80
105	185.77	191.18	196.60	202.04	207.48	212.94
110	190.82	196.25	201.69	207.14	212.61	218.08
115	195.86	201.31	206.77	212.24	217.72	223.21
120	200.90	206.37	211.85	217.34	222.83	228.34
125	205.94	211.43	216.93	222.43	227.94	233.46
130	210.98	216.49	222.00	227.52	233.04	238.57
135	216.02	221.54	227.07	232.60	238.14	243.68
140	221.05	226.59	232.13	237.68	243.23	248.79
145	226.09	231.64	237.20	242.76	248.32	253.89
150	231.12	236.69	242.26	247.83	253.41	258.99
155	236.15	241.73	247.31	252.90	258.49	264.08
160	241.18	246.77	252.37	257.97	263.57	269.18
165	246.21	251.81	257.42	263.03	268.65	274.26
170	251.23	256.85	262.47	268.10	273.72	279.35
175	256.26	261.89	267.52	273.16	278.79	284.43
180	261.28	266.93	272.57	278.22	283.86	289.51
185	266.31	271.96	277.62	283.27	288.93	294.58
190	271.33	277.00	282.66	288.33	293.99	299.65
195	276.35	282.03	287.70	293.38	299.05	304.73
200	281.38	287.06	292.75	298.43	304.11	309.79
205	286.40	292.09	297.79	303.48	309.17	314.86
210	291.42	297.12	302.82	308.53	314.23	319.92
215	296.44	302.15	307.86	313.57	319.28	324.99
220	301.45	307.18	312.90	318.62	324.33	330.05
225	306.47	312.20	317.93	323.66	329.38	335.10
230	311.49	317.23	322.97	328.70	334.43	340.16
235	316.51	322.25	328.00	333.74	339.48	345.22
240	321.52	327.28	333.03	338.78	344.53	350.27
245	326.54	332.30	338.06	343.82	349.57	355.32
250	331.55	337.32	343.09	348.86	354.62	360.37

$$D = \sqrt{d_1^2 + 6.28rd_1 + 8r^2 + (d_3^2 - d_2^2)}$$

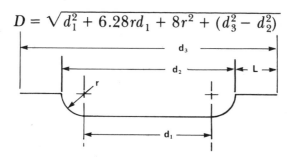

Table 4–23. Solutions for $D = \sqrt{d_1^2 + 6.28rd_1 + 8r^2 + (d_3^2 - d_2^2)}$ when $L = 35$ mm *(Continued).*

	Radius of Shell					
d_1	16	18	20	22	24	26
50	161.10	166.39	171.70	177.03	182.38	187.76
55	166.37	171.68	177.01	182.36	187.73	193.11
60	171.63	176.96	182.31	187.67	193.06	198.46
65	176.87	182.22	187.59	192.97	198.37	203.78
70	182.10	187.47	192.85	198.25	203.66	209.09
75	187.32	192.70	198.10	203.52	208.94	214.38
80	192.53	197.93	203.34	208.77	214.21	219.66
85	197.72	203.14	208.57	214.01	219.46	224.93
90	202.91	208.34	213.78	219.24	224.71	230.18
95	208.08	213.53	218.99	224.46	229.94	235.42
100	213.25	218.71	224.19	229.67	235.16	240.66
105	218.41	223.89	229.38	234.87	240.37	245.88
110	223.56	229.06	234.55	240.06	245.58	249.30
115	228.71	234.21	239.73	245.25	250.77	256.30
120	233.85	239.37	244.89	250.42	255.96	261.50
125	238.98	244.51	250.05	255.59	261.14	266.69
130	244.11	249.65	255.20	260.75	266.31	271.87
135	249.23	254.79	260.35	265.91	271.48	277.05
140	254.35	259.92	265.49	271.06	276.64	282.22
145	259.47	265.04	270.62	276.21	281.79	287.38
150	264.58	270.16	275.75	281.35	286.94	292.54
155	269.68	275.28	280.88	286.48	292.09	297.69
160	274.78	280.39	286.00	291.61	297.23	302.84
165	279.88	285.50	291.12	296.74	302.36	307.98
170	284.97	290.60	296.23	301.86	307.49	313.12
175	290.06	295.70	301.34	306.98	312.62	318.26
180	295.15	300.80	306.44	312.09	317.74	323.39
185	300.24	305.89	311.55	317.20	322.86	328.51
190	305.32	310.98	316.64	322.31	327.97	333.63
195	310.40	316.07	321.74	327.41	333.08	338.75
200	315.47	321.15	326.83	332.51	338.19	343.87
205	320.55	326.24	331.92	337.61	343.29	348.98
210	325.62	331.32	337.01	342.70	348.40	354.09
215	330.69	336.39	342.10	347.80	353.49	359.19
220	335.76	341.47	347.18	352.88	358.59	364.29
225	340.82	346.54	352.26	357.97	363.68	369.39
230	345.89	351.61	357.33	363.05	368.77	374.49
235	350.95	356.68	362.41	368.14	373.86	379.58
240	356.01	361.75	367.48	373.22	378.95	384.68
245	361.07	366.81	372.55	378.29	384.03	389.76
250	366.13	371.88	377.62	383.37	389.11	394.85

$$D = \sqrt{d_1^2 + 6.28rd_1 + 8r^2 + (d_3^2 - d_2^2)}$$

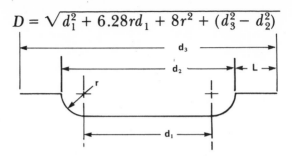

Table 4–24. Solutions for $D = \sqrt{d_1^2 + 6.28rd_1 + 8r^2 + (d_3^2 - d_2^2)}$ when $L = 40$ mm.

d_1	Radius of Shell					
	4	6	8	10	12	14
50	139.87	144.89	149.95	155.05	160.19	165.36
55	144.96	150.02	155.11	160.25	165.41	170.61
60	150.05	155.14	160.27	165.43	170.63	175.85
65	155.13	160.26	165.41	170.61	175.83	181.07
70	160.21	165.37	170.55	175.77	181.02	186.29
75	165.28	170.47	175.68	180.93	186.20	191.49
80	170.35	175.56	180.81	186.08	191.37	196.68
85	175.41	180.65	185.92	191.21	196.53	201.86
90	180.47	185.74	191.03	196.35	201.68	207.03
95	185.52	190.82	196.14	201.47	206.82	212.19
100	190.58	195.90	201.24	206.59	211.96	217.35
105	195.63	200.97	206.33	211.70	217.09	222.50
110	200.68	206.04	211.42	216.81	222.22	227.64
115	205.72	211.11	216.51	221.92	227.34	232.77
120	210.77	216.17	221.59	227.02	232.45	237.90
125	215.88	221.23	226.66	232.11	237.56	243.03
130	220.85	226.29	231.74	237.20	242.67	248.15
135	225.89	231.34	236.81	242.29	247.77	253.26
140	230.92	236.40	241.88	247.37	252.87	258.37
145	235.96	241.45	246.94	252.45	257.96	263.48
150	240.99	246.50	252.01	257.53	263.05	268.58
155	246.02	251.54	257.07	262.60	268.14	173.68
160	251.05	256.59	262.13	267.67	273.22	278.77
165	256.08	261.63	267.18	272.74	278.30	283.87
170	261.11	266.67	272.24	277.81	283.38	288.95
175	266.14	271.71	277.29	282.87	288.45	294.04
180	271.16	276.75	282.34	287.93	293.52	299.12
185	276.19	281.79	287.39	292.99	298.59	304.20
190	281.21	286.82	292.43	298.05	303.66	309.28
195	286.24	291.86	297.48	303.10	308.73	314.35
200	291.26	296.89	302.52	308.16	313.79	319.42
205	296.28	301.92	307.56	313.21	318.85	324.49
210	301.30	306.95	312.61	318.26	323.91	329.56
215	306.32	311.98	317.65	323.31	328.97	334.63
220	311.34	317.01	322.68	328.35	334.02	339.69
225	316.36	322.04	327.72	333.40	339.08	344.75
230	321.38	327.07	332.76	338.44	344.13	349.81
235	326.40	332.10	337.79	343.49	349.18	354.87
240	331.42	337.12	342.83	348.53	354.23	359.93
245	336.43	342.15	347.86	353.57	359.28	364.98
250	341.45	347.17	352.89	358.61	364.32	370.04

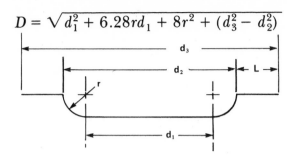

$$D = \sqrt{d_1^2 + 6.28rd_1 + 8r^2 + (d_3^2 - d_2^2)}$$

Table 4–24. Solutions for $D = \sqrt{d_1^2 + 6.28rd_1 + 8r^2 + (d_3^2 - d_2^2)}$ when $L = 40$ mm *(Continued)*.

			Radius of Shell			
d_1	16	18	20	22	24	26
50	170.56	175.80	181.05	186.33	191.64	196.96
55	175.84	181.09	186.37	191.67	196.98	202.32
60	181.10	186.37	191.67	196.98	202.31	207.67
65	186.34	191.64	196.95	202.28	207.63	212.99
70	191.58	196.89	202.22	207.56	212.93	218.31
75	196.80	202.13	207.47	212.84	218.21	223.60
80	202.01	207.35	212.72	218.09	223.49	228.89
85	207.20	212.57	217.95	223.34	228.74	234.16
90	212.39	217.77	223.17	228.57	233.99	239.42
95	217.57	222.97	228.38	233.80	239.23	244.67
100	222.75	228.16	233.58	239.01	244.46	249.91
105	227.91	233.34	238.77	244.22	249.68	255.14
110	233.07	238.51	243.96	249.42	254.89	260.36
115	238.22	243.67	249.14	254.61	260.09	265.58
120	243.36	248.83	254.31	259.79	265.28	270.78
125	248.50	253.98	259.47	264.97	270.47	275.98
130	253.63	259.13	264.63	270.13	275.65	281.17
135	258.76	264.27	269.78	275.30	280.82	286.35
140	263.88	269.40	274.93	280.45	285.99	291.53
145	269.00	274.53	280.07	285.60	291.15	296.70
150	274.12	279.66	285.20	290.75	296.30	301.86
155	279.23	284.78	290.33	295.89	301.45	307.02
160	284.33	289.89	295.46	301.03	306.60	312.17
165	289.43	295.01	300.58	306.16	311.74	317.32
170	294.53	300.11	305.70	311.29	316.88	322.47
175	299.63	305.22	310.81	316.41	322.01	327.61
180	304.72	310.32	315.92	321.53	327.14	332.74
185	309.81	315.42	321.03	326.64	332.26	337.88
190	314.90	320.51	326.13	331.76	337.38	343.00
195	319.98	325.61	331.24	336.87	342.50	348.13
200	325.06	330.70	336.33	341.97	347.61	353.25
205	330.14	335.78	341.43	347.07	352.72	358.36
210	335.21	340.87	346.52	352.17	357.83	363.48
215	340.29	345.95	351.61	357.27	362.93	368.59
220	345.36	351.03	356.70	362.36	368.03	373.70
225	350.43	356.11	361.78	367.45	373.13	378.80
230	355.50	361.18	366.86	372.54	378.22	383.90
235	360.56	366.25	371.94	377.63	383.32	389.00
240	365.63	371.32	377.02	382.71	388.41	394.10
245	370.69	376.39	382.10	387.80	393.50	399.19
250	375.75	381.46	387.17	392.88	398.58	404.29

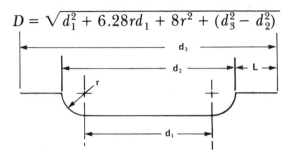

$$D = \sqrt{d_1^2 + 6.28rd_1 + 8r^2 + (d_3^2 - d_2^2)}$$

Table 4–25. Solutions for $D = \sqrt{d_1^2 + 6.28rd_1 + 8r^2 + (d_3^2 - d_2^2)}$ when $L = 45$ mm.

	Radius of Shell					
d_1	4	6	8	10	12	14
50	149.75	154.70	159.70	164.74	169.82	174.94
55	154.84	159.83	164.86	169.94	175.05	180.19
60	159.92	164.95	170.02	175.12	180.26	185.43
65	165.00	170.07	175.16	180.30	185.46	190.65
70	170.08	175.17	180.30	185.46	190.65	195.86
75	175.15	180.27	185.43	190.62	195.83	201.06
80	180.22	185.37	190.55	195.77	201.00	206.26
85	185.28	190.46	195.67	200.91	206.16	211.44
90	190.34	195.55	200.78	206.04	211.32	216.61
95	195.40	200.63	205.89	211.17	216.46	211.78
100	200.45	205.71	210.99	216.29	221.60	226.94
105	205.50	210.78	216.08	221.40	226.74	232.09
110	210.55	215.85	221.18	226.51	231.87	237.23
115	215.60	220.92	226.26	231.62	236.99	242.37
120	220.64	225.99	231.35	236.72	242.11	247.50
125	225.68	231.05	236.43	241.82	247.22	252.63
130	230.72	236.11	241.50	246.91	252.33	257.75
135	235.76	241.16	246.58	252.00	257.43	262.87
140	240.80	246.22	251.65	257.08	262.53	267.99
145	245.84	251.27	256.71	262.17	267.63	273.10
150	250.87	256.32	261.78	267.25	272.72	278.20
155	255.90	261.37	266.84	272.32	277.81	283.30
160	260.94	266.41	271.90	277.40	282.90	288.40
165	265.97	271.46	276.96	282.47	287.98	293.50
170	271.00	276.50	282.02	287.53	293.06	298.59
175	276.02	281.54	287.07	292.60	298.14	303.68
180	281.05	286.58	292.12	297.66	303.21	308.76
185	286.08	291.62	297.17	302.73	308.28	313.84
190	291.10	296.66	302.22	307.79	313.35	318.92
195	296.13	301.70	307.27	312.84	318.42	324.00
200	301.15	306.73	312.31	317.90	323.49	329.08
205	306.17	311.76	317.36	322.95	328.55	334.15
210	311.20	316.80	322.40	328.01	333.61	339.22
215	316.22	321.83	327.44	333.06	338.67	344.29
220	321.24	326.86	332.48	338.11	343.73	349.36
225	326.26	331.89	337.52	343.15	348.79	354.42
230	331.28	336.92	342.56	348.20	353.84	359.49
235	336.30	341.95	347.60	353.25	358.90	364.55
240	341.32	346.97	352.63	358.29	363.95	369.61
245	346.33	352.00	357.67	363.33	369.00	374.66
250	351.35	357.03	362.70	368.37	374.05	379.72

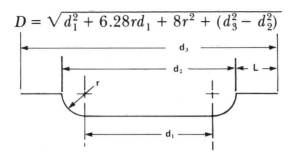

$$D = \sqrt{d_1^2 + 6.28rd_1 + 8r^2 + (d_3^2 - d_2^2)}$$

Table 4–25. Solutions for $D = \sqrt{d_1^2 + 6.28rd_1 + 8r^2 + (d_3^2 - d_2^2)}$ when $L = 45$ mm *(Continued)*.

	Radius of Shell					
d_1	16	18	20	22	24	26
50	180.09	185.27	190.47	195.70	200.96	206.23
55	185.36	190.56	195.79	201.04	206.31	211.60
60	190.62	195.84	201.09	206.35	211.64	216.94
65	195.87	201.11	206.37	211.65	216.96	222.28
70	201.10	206.12	211.64	216.94	222.26	227.59
75	206.32	211.60	216.90	222.21	227.55	232.89
80	211.53	216.83	222.14	227.47	232.82	238.18
85	216.73	222.05	227.38	232.72	238.08	243.46
90	221.93	227.26	232.60	237.96	243.34	248.72
95	227.11	232.46	237.82	243.19	248.58	253.98
100	232.28	237.65	243.02	248.41	253.81	259.22
105	237.45	242.83	248.22	253.62	259.03	264.46
110	242.61	248.00	253.41	258.82	264.25	269.68
115	247.77	253.17	258.59	264.02	269.45	274.90
120	252.91	258.33	263.77	269.20	274.65	280.11
125	258.06	263.49	268.93	274.38	279.84	285.31
130	263.19	268.64	274.09	279.56	285.03	290.51
135	268.32	273.78	279.25	284.73	290.21	295.70
140	273.45	278.92	284.40	289.89	295.38	300.88
145	278.57	284.06	289.55	295.04	300.55	306.05
150	283.69	289.19	294.69	300.19	305.71	311.22
155	288.80	294.31	299.82	305.34	310.86	316.39
160	293.91	299.43	304.95	310.48	316.01	321.55
165	299.02	304.55	310.08	315.62	321.16	326.70
170	304.12	309.66	315.20	320.75	326.30	331.85
175	309.22	314.77	320.32	325.88	331.43	337.00
180	314.32	319.87	325.44	331.00	336.57	342.14
185	319.41	324.98	330.55	336.12	341.70	347.27
190	324.50	330.08	335.65	341.24	346.82	352.41
195	329.59	335.17	340.76	346.35	351.94	357.54
200	334.67	340.26	345.86	351.46	357.06	362.66
205	339.75	345.36	350.96	356.57	362.17	367.78
210	344.83	350.44	356.06	361.67	367.29	372.90
215	349.91	355.53	361.15	366.77	372.39	378.02
220	354.98	360.61	366.24	371.87	377.50	383.13
225	360.06	365.69	371.33	376.97	382.60	388.24
230	365.13	370.77	376.41	382.06	387.70	393.35
235	370.20	375.85	381.50	387.15	392.80	398.45
240	375.26	380.92	386.58	392.24	397.90	403.55
245	308.33	385.99	391.66	397.32	402.99	408.65
250	385.39	391.07	396.74	402.41	408.08	413.75

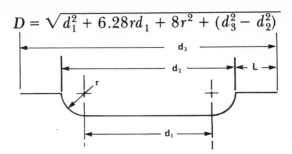

$$D = \sqrt{d_1^2 + 6.28rd_1 + 8r^2 + (d_3^2 - d_2^2)}$$

Table 4–26. Solutions for $D = \sqrt{d_1^2 + 6.28rd_1 + 8r^2 + (d_3^2 - d_2^2)}$ when $L = 50$ mm.

	Radius of Shell					
d_1	4	6	8	10	12	14
50	159.64	164.54	169.48	174.47	179.50	184.56
55	164.73	169.66	174.64	179.66	184.72	189.81
60	169.81	174.78	179.80	184.85	189.93	195.05
65	174.89	179.89	184.94	190.02	195.13	200.27
70	179.96	185.00	190.08	195.18	200.32	205.48
75	185.03	190.10	195.21	200.34	205.50	210.68
80	190.10	195.20	200.33	205.48	210.67	215.87
85	195.16	200.29	205.44	210.63	215.83	221.06
90	200.22	205.38	210.56	215.76	220.99	226.23
95	205.28	210.46	215.66	220.89	226.13	231.40
100	210.33	215.54	220.76	226.01	231.27	236.56
105	215.38	220.61	225.86	231.13	236.41	241.71
110	220.43	225.68	230.95	236.24	241.54	246.86
115	225.48	230.75	236.04	241.34	246.66	252.00
120	230.53	235.82	241.12	246.45	251.78	257.13
125	235.57	240.88	246.21	251.55	256.90	262.27
130	240.61	245.94	251.28	256.64	262.01	267.39
135	245.65	251.00	256.36	261.73	267.12	272.51
140	250.69	256.05	261.43	266.82	272.22	277.63
145	255.73	261.11	266.50	271.90	277.32	282.74
150	260.76	266.16	271.57	276.98	282.41	287.85
155	265.79	271.21	276.63	282.06	287.50	292.95
160	270.83	276.25	281.69	287.14	292.59	298.05
165	275.86	281.30	286.75	292.21	297.68	303.15
170	280.89	286.35	291.81	297.28	302.76	308.24
175	285.92	291.39	296.87	302.35	307.84	313.34
180	290.95	296.43	301.92	307.42	312.92	318.42
185	295.97	301.47	306.97	312.48	317.99	323.51
190	301.00	306.51	312.02	317.54	323.06	328.59
195	306.03	311.55	317.07	322.60	328.13	333.67
200	311.05	316.58	322.12	327.66	333.20	338.75
205	316.07	321.62	327.16	332.71	338.27	343.83
210	321.10	326.65	332.21	337.77	343.33	348.90
215	326.12	331.68	337.25	342.82	348.40	353.97
220	331.14	336.72	342.29	347.87	353.46	359.04
225	336.16	341.75	347.33	352.92	358.51	364.11
230	341.18	346.78	352.37	357.97	363.57	369.17
235	346.20	351.81	357.41	363.02	368.63	374.24
240	351.22	356.83	362.45	368.07	373.68	379.30
245	356.24	361.86	367.49	373.11	378.73	348.36
250	361.26	366.89	372.52	378.15	383.79	377.56

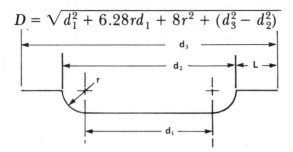

$$D = \sqrt{d_1^2 + 6.28rd_1 + 8r^2 + (d_3^2 - d_2^2)}$$

Table 4–26. Solutions for $D = \sqrt{d_1^2 + 6.28rd_1 + 8r^2 + (d_3^2 - d_2^2)}$ when $L = 50$ mm (Continued).

d_1	Radius of Shell					
	16	18	20	22	24	26
50	189.66	194.79	199.95	205.13	210.34	215.57
55	194.93	200.09	205.26	210.47	215.69	220.94
60	200.19	205.36	210.56	215.78	221.02	226.28
65	205.44	210.63	215.84	221.08	226.34	231.62
70	210.67	215.88	221.12	226.37	231.64	236.93
75	215.89	221.12	226.37	231.64	236.93	242.24
80	221.10	226.35	231.62	236.91	242.21	247.53
85	226.30	231.57	236.86	242.16	247.48	252.81
90	231.50	236.78	242.08	247.40	252.73	258.08
95	236.68	241.98	247.30	252.63	257.98	263.33
100	241.86	247.18	252.51	257.85	263.21	268.58
105	247.03	252.36	257.71	263.07	268.44	273.82
110	252.19	257.54	262.90	268.27	273.66	279.05
115	257.35	262.71	268.08	273.47	278.87	284.27
120	262.50	267.87	273.26	278.66	284.07	289.49
125	267.64	273.03	278.43	283.84	289.26	294.69
130	272.78	278.19	283.60	289.02	294.45	299.89
135	277.92	283.33	288.76	294.19	299.63	305.08
140	283.05	288.47	293.91	299.36	304.81	310.27
145	288.17	293.61	299.06	304.52	309.98	315.45
150	293.29	298.75	304.20	309.67	315.14	320.62
155	298.41	303.87	309.34	314.82	320.30	325.79
160	303.52	309.00	314.48	319.96	325.46	330.96
165	308.63	314.12	319.61	325.11	330.61	336.12
170	313.73	319.23	324.73	330.24	335.75	341.27
175	318.84	324.34	329.86	335.37	340.89	346.42
180	323.94	329.45	334.97	340.50	346.03	351.57
185	329.03	334.56	340.09	345.62	351.16	356.71
190	334.12	339.66	345.20	350.75	356.29	361.84
195	339.21	344.76	350.31	355.86	361.42	366.98
200	344.30	349.86	355.42	360.98	366.54	372.11
205	349.39	354.95	360.52	366.09	371.66	377.23
210	354.47	360.04	365.62	371.19	376.77	382.36
215	359.55	365.13	370.71	376.30	381.89	387.48
220	364.63	370.22	375.81	381.40	387.00	392.59
225	369.70	375.30	380.90	386.50	392.10	397.71
230	374.78	380.38	385.99	391.60	397.21	402.82
235	379.85	385.46	391.08	396.69	402.31	407.93
240	384.92	390.54	396.16	401.78	407.41	413.03
245	389.99	395.62	401.24	406.87	412.50	418.13
250	395.05	400.69	406.32	411.96	417.60	423.24

$$D = \sqrt{d_1^2 + 6.28rd_1 + 8r^2 + (d_3^2 - d_2^2)}$$

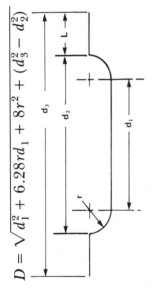

Table 4-27. Solutions for $D = \sqrt{d_1^2 + 6.28rd_1 + 8r^2 + (d_3^2 - d_2^2)}$ when $L = 1/4$ inch.

d_1	1/4	5/16	3/8	7/16	1/2	9/16	5/8	11/16	3/4	13/16	7/8	15/16	1
2	3.223	3.403	3.583	3.762	3.941	4.120	4.298	4.477	4.655	4.833	5.011	5.189	5.367
2 1/8	3.351	3.531	3.711	3.890	4.070	4.249	4.428	4.607	4.785	4.964	5.142	5.321	5.499
2 1/4	3.478	3.657	3.839	4.019	4.199	4.378	4.557	4.736	4.915	5.094	5.273	5.451	5.630
2 3/8	3.605	3.786	3.967	4.147	4.327	4.507	4.686	4.866	5.045	5.224	5.403	5.582	5.760
2 1/2	3.732	3.913	4.094	4.275	4.455	4.635	4.815	4.995	5.174	5.354	5.533	5.712	5.891
2 5/8	3.858	4.040	4.222	4.403	4.584	4.764	4.944	5.124	5.304	5.483	5.663	5.842	6.021
2 3/4	3.985	4.167	4.349	4.530	4.711	4.892	5.073	5.253	5.432	5.613	5.792	5.972	6.151
2 7/8	4.112	4.294	4.476	4.658	4.839	5.020	5.201	5.381	5.562	5.742	5.921	6.101	6.281
3	4.238	4.421	4.603	4.785	4.967	5.148	5.329	5.510	5.690	5.870	6.051	6.230	6.410
3 1/8	4.364	4.548	4.730	4.913	5.095	5.276	5.457	5.638	5.819	5.999	6.179	6.360	6.540
3 1/4	4.490	4.674	4.857	5.039	5.222	5.404	5.584	5.766	5.947	6.128	6.308	6.489	6.669
3 3/8	4.617	4.800	4.984	5.167	5.349	5.531	5.713	5.894	6.076	6.256	6.437	6.618	6.798
3 1/2	4.743	4.927	5.111	5.294	5.476	5.659	5.841	6.022	6.204	6.385	6.566	6.746	6.927
3 5/8	4.869	5.053	5.237	5.421	5.603	5.786	5.968	6.150	6.332	6.513	6.694	6.875	7.056
3 3/4	4.995	5.179	5.363	5.547	5.730	5.913	6.095	6.278	6.459	6.641	6.822	7.003	7.184
3 7/8	5.121	5.306	5.490	5.674	5.857	6.040	6.223	6.405	6.587	6.769	6.950	7.132	7.313
4	5.247	5.432	5.616	5.801	5.984	6.167	6.350	6.533	6.715	6.897	7.078	7.260	7.441
4 1/8	5.373	5.558	5.743	5.927	6.111	6.294	6.477	6.660	6.843	7.025	7.206	7.388	7.569
4 1/4	5.499	5.684	5.869	6.054	6.238	6.421	6.604	6.787	6.970	7.152	7.334	7.516	7.698
4 3/8	5.624	5.810	5.995	6.180	6.364	6.548	6.731	6.914	7.097	7.280	7.462	7.644	7.826

4½	5.750	5.936	6.122	6.306	6.491	6.675	6.858	7.042	7.225	7.407	7.590	7.772	7.954
4⅝	5.876	6.062	6.248	6.433	6.617	6.801	6.985	7.169	7.352	7.535	7.717	7.899	8.082
4¾	6.002	6.188	6.374	6.559	6.743	6.928	7.112	7.296	7.479	7.662	7.845	8.027	8.209
4⅞	6.127	6.314	6.500	6.685	6.870	7.055	7.239	7.423	7.606	7.789	7.972	8.155	8.337
5	6.253	6.440	6.626	6.811	6.996	7.181	7.365	7.549	7.733	7.916	8.099	8.282	8.465
5⅛	6.379	6.565	6.752	6.937	7.123	7.308	7.492	7.676	7.860	8.043	8.227	8.409	8.592
5¼	6.504	6.691	6.878	7.063	7.249	7.434	7.619	7.803	7.987	8.170	8.354	8.537	8.720
5⅜	6.630	6.817	7.003	7.190	7.375	7.560	7.745	7.930	8.114	8.297	8.481	8.664	8.847
5½	6.755	6.943	7.129	7.316	7.501	7.687	7.872	8.056	8.240	8.424	8.608	8.791	8.974
5⅝	6.881	7.068	7.255	7.442	7.628	7.813	7.998	8.183	8.367	8.551	8.735	8.918	9.102
5¾	7.006	7.194	7.381	7.567	7.754	7.939	8.124	8.309	8.494	8.678	8.862	9.046	9.229
5⅞	7.132	7.320	7.507	7.693	7.880	8.065	8.251	8.436	8.620	8.805	8.989	9.173	9.356
6	7.257	7.445	7.632	7.819	8.006	8.192	8.377	8.562	8.747	8.931	9.116	9.300	9.483
6⅛	7.383	7.571	7.758	7.945	8.131	8.317	8.503	8.688	8.873	9.058	9.242	9.426	9.610
6¼	7.508	7.696	7.884	8.071	8.258	8.444	8.630	8.815	9.000	9.185	9.369	9.553	9.737
6⅜	7.634	7.822	8.010	8.197	8.384	8.570	8.756	8.941	9.126	9.311	9.496	9.680	9.864
6½	7.759	7.947	8.135	8.323	8.509	8.696	8.882	9.068	9.253	9.438	9.623	9.807	9.991
6⅝	7.885	8.073	8.261	8.448	8.635	8.822	9.008	9.194	9.379	9.564	9.749	9.934	10.118
6¾	8.004	8.192	8.380	8.568	8.755	8.942	9.129	9.315	9.500	9.686	9.871	10.055	10.240
6⅞	8.135	8.324	8.512	8.700	8.887	9.074	9.260	9.446	9.632	9.817	10.002	10.187	10.371
7	8.261	8.449	8.638	8.825	9.013	9.200	9.386	9.572	9.758	9.944	10.129	10.314	10.498
7⅛	8.386	8.575	8.763	8.951	9.139	9.326	9.512	9.698	9.884	10.070	10.255	10.440	10.625
7¼	8.512	8.700	8.888	9.077	9.264	9.451	9.638	9.825	10.011	10.196	10.382	10.567	10.751
7⅜	8.637	8.826	9.014	9.202	9.390	9.577	9.764	9.951	10.137	10.322	10.508	10.693	10.878
7½	8.762	8.951	9.140	9.328	9.516	9.703	9.890	10.077	10.263	10.449	10.634	10.820	11.005
7⅝	8.887	9.077	9.265	9.454	9.642	9.829	10.016	10.203	10.389	10.575	10.761	10.946	11.131
7¾	9.013	9.202	9.391	9.579	9.767	9.955	10.142	10.329	10.515	10.701	10.887	11.072	11.258
7⅞	9.138	9.327	9.516	9.705	9.893	10.080	10.268	10.455	10.641	10.827	11.013	11.199	11.384
8	9.263	9.453	9.642	9.830	10.018	10.206	10.394	10.580	10.767	10.953	11.139	11.325	11.510
8⅛	9.389	9.578	9.767	9.956	10.144	10.332	10.519	10.706	10.893	11.079	11.266	11.451	11.637
8¼	9.514	9.704	9.893	10.081	10.270	10.458	10.645	10.832	11.019	11.206	11.392	11.578	11.763
8⅜	9.639	9.829	10.018	10.207	10.395	10.583	10.771	10.958	11.145	11.332	11.518	11.704	11.889
8½	9.764	9.954	10.144	10.332	10.521	10.709	10.897	11.084	11.271	11.458	11.644	11.830	12.016
8⅝	9.890	10.080	10.269	10.458	10.647	10.835	11.022	11.210	11.397	11.584	11.770	11.956	12.142
8¾	10.015	10.205	10.394	10.583	10.772	10.960	11.148	11.336	11.523	11.710	11.896	12.082	12.268
8⅞	10.140	10.330	10.520	10.709	10.898	11.086	11.274	11.461	11.649	11.836	12.022	12.209	12.395

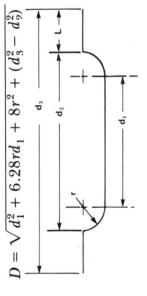

$$D = \sqrt{d_1^2 + 6.28rd_1 + 8r^2 + (d_3^2 - d_2^2)}$$

Table 4-28. Solutions for $D = \sqrt{d_1^2 + 6.28rd_1 + 8r^2 + (d_3^2 - d_2^2)}$ when $L = 1/2$ inch.

d_1	1/4	5/16	3/8	7/16	1/2	9/16	5/8	11/16	3/4	13/16	7/8	15/16	1
2	3.693	3.867	4.042	4.216	4.391	4.566	4.741	4.916	5.091	5.266	5.442	5.617	5.793
2 1/8	3.821	3.996	4.171	4.346	4.521	4.696	4.872	5.047	5.223	5.398	5.574	5.750	5.925
2 1/4	3.949	4.123	4.300	4.475	4.651	4.826	5.002	5.178	5.354	5.529	5.705	5.881	6.057
2 3/8	4.077	4.252	4.428	4.604	4.780	4.956	5.132	5.308	5.484	5.660	5.837	6.013	6.189
2 1/2	4.204	4.380	4.557	4.733	4.909	5.085	5.262	5.438	5.615	5.791	5.968	6.144	6.321
2 5/8	4.332	4.508	4.685	4.861	5.038	5.215	5.392	5.568	5.745	5.922	6.098	6.275	6.452
2 3/4	4.459	4.636	4.813	4.990	5.167	5.344	5.521	5.698	5.875	6.052	6.229	6.406	6.583
2 7/8	4.586	4.763	4.941	5.118	5.296	5.473	5.650	5.828	6.005	6.182	6.359	6.536	6.713
3	4.713	4.891	5.069	5.246	5.424	5.602	5.779	5.957	6.134	6.312	6.489	6.667	6.844
3 1/8	4.840	5.018	5.196	5.374	5.552	5.730	5.908	6.086	6.264	6.441	6.619	6.797	6.974
3 1/4	4.966	5.145	5.324	5.502	5.680	5.859	6.037	6.215	6.393	6.571	6.749	6.926	7.104
3 3/8	5.093	5.272	5.451	5.630	5.809	5.987	6.165	6.344	6.522	6.700	6.878	7.056	7.234
3 1/2	5.220	5.399	5.578	5.757	5.936	6.115	6.294	6.472	6.651	6.829	7.008	7.186	7.364
3 5/8	5.346	5.526	5.706	5.885	6.064	6.243	6.422	6.601	6.780	6.958	7.137	7.315	7.494
3 3/4	5.473	5.653	5.832	6.012	6.192	6.371	6.550	6.729	6.908	7.087	7.266	7.444	7.623
3 7/8	5.599	5.779	5.960	6.140	6.319	6.499	6.678	6.858	7.037	7.216	7.395	7.574	7.752
4	5.725	5.906	6.086	6.267	6.447	6.627	6.806	6.986	7.165	7.345	7.524	7.703	7.882
4 1/8	5.852	6.033	6.213	6.394	6.574	6.754	6.934	7.114	7.293	7.473	7.652	7.832	8.011
4 1/4	5.978	6.159	6.340	6.521	6.701	6.882	7.062	7.242	7.422	7.601	7.780	7.960	8.140
4 3/8	6.104	6.286	6.467	6.648	6.829	7.009	7.189	7.370	7.550	7.729	7.909	8.089	8.268

4½	6.230	6.412	6.593	6.775	6.956	7.136	7.317	7.497	7.678	7.858	8.038	8.217	8.397
4⅝	6.356	6.538	6.720	6.901	7.083	7.264	7.444	7.625	7.805	7.986	8.166	8.346	8.526
4¾	6.482	6.665	6.846	7.028	7.210	7.391	7.572	7.753	7.933	8.114	8.294	8.474	8.654
4⅞	6.608	6.791	6.973	7.155	7.336	7.518	7.699	7.880	8.061	8.241	8.422	8.602	8.782
5	6.734	6.917	7.099	7.281	7.463	7.645	7.826	8.007	8.188	8.369	8.550	8.730	8.911
5⅛	6.860	7.043	7.226	7.408	7.590	7.772	7.953	8.135	8.316	8.497	8.678	8.858	9.039
5¼	6.986	7.169	7.352	7.534	7.717	7.899	8.080	8.262	8.443	8.624	8.806	8.986	9.167
5⅜	7.112	7.295	7.478	7.661	7.843	8.026	8.207	8.389	8.571	8.752	8.933	9.114	9.295
5½	7.238	7.421	7.604	7.787	7.970	8.152	8.334	8.516	8.698	8.879	9.061	9.242	9.423
5⅝	7.364	7.547	7.731	7.914	8.097	8.279	8.461	8.643	8.825	9.007	9.188	9.370	9.551
5¾	7.489	7.673	7.857	8.040	8.223	8.406	8.588	8.770	8.952	9.134	9.316	9.497	9.678
5⅞	7.615	7.799	7.983	8.166	8.349	8.532	8.715	8.897	9.079	9.261	9.443	9.625	9.806
6	7.741	7.925	8.109	8.293	8.476	8.659	8.842	9.024	9.207	9.389	9.571	9.752	9.934
6⅛	7.866	8.051	8.235	8.419	8.602	8.785	8.968	9.151	9.333	9.515	9.697	9.879	10.061
6¼	7.992	8.177	8.361	8.545	8.729	8.912	9.095	9.278	9.460	9.643	9.825	10.007	10.189
6⅜	8.118	8.303	8.487	8.671	8.855	9.038	9.222	9.405	9.587	9.770	9.952	10.134	10.316
6½	8.243	8.428	8.613	8.797	8.981	9.165	9.348	9.531	9.714	9.897	10.079	10.262	10.444
6⅝	8.369	8.554	8.739	8.923	9.107	9.291	9.475	9.658	9.841	10.024	10.206	10.389	10.571
6¾	8.489	8.674	8.859	9.044	9.228	9.412	9.596	9.779	9.963	10.146	10.329	10.511	10.694
6⅞	8.620	8.806	8.991	9.175	9.360	9.544	9.728	9.911	10.094	10.277	10.460	10.643	10.825
7	8.746	8.931	9.116	9.301	9.486	9.670	9.854	10.038	10.221	10.404	10.587	10.770	10.953
7⅛	8.871	9.057	9.242	9.427	9.612	9.796	9.980	10.164	10.348	10.531	10.714	10.897	11.080
7¼	8.997	9.183	9.368	9.553	9.738	9.922	10.107	10.291	10.474	10.658	10.841	11.024	11.207
7⅜	9.122	9.308	9.494	9.679	9.864	10.049	10.233	10.417	10.601	10.784	10.968	11.151	11.334
7½	9.248	9.434	9.620	9.805	9.990	10.175	10.359	10.543	10.727	10.911	11.095	11.278	11.461
7⅝	9.373	9.560	9.745	9.931	10.116	10.301	10.485	10.670	10.854	11.038	11.221	11.405	11.588
7¾	9.499	9.685	9.871	10.057	10.242	10.427	10.612	10.796	10.980	11.164	11.348	11.531	11.715
7⅞	9.624	9.811	9.997	10.183	10.368	10.553	10.738	10.922	11.107	11.291	11.474	11.658	11.841
8	9.750	9.936	10.122	10.308	10.494	10.679	10.864	11.049	11.233	11.417	11.601	11.785	11.968
8⅛	9.875	10.062	10.248	10.434	10.620	10.805	10.990	11.175	11.359	11.544	11.728	11.911	12.095
8¼	10.001	10.187	10.374	10.560	10.746	10.931	11.116	11.301	11.486	11.670	11.854	12.038	12.222
8⅜	10.126	10.313	10.499	10.686	10.871	11.057	11.242	11.427	11.612	11.796	11.981	12.165	12.348
8½	10.252	10.438	10.625	10.811	10.997	11.183	11.368	11.553	11.738	11.923	12.107	12.291	12.475
8⅝	10.377	10.564	10.751	10.937	11.123	11.309	11.494	11.679	11.864	12.049	12.234	12.418	12.602
8¾	10.502	10.690	10.876	11.063	11.249	11.435	11.620	11.806	11.991	12.175	12.360	12.544	12.728
8⅞	10.628	10.815	11.002	11.188	11.375	11.561	11.746	11.932	12.117	12.302	12.486	12.671	12.855

$$D = \sqrt{d_1^2 + 6.28rd_1 + 8r^2 + (d_3^2 - d_2^2)}$$

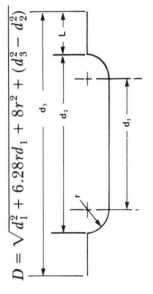

Table 4-29. Solutions for $D = \sqrt{d_1^2 + 6.28rd_1 + 8r^2 + (d_3^2 - d_2^2)}$ **when** $L = 3/4$ **inch.**

d_1	1/4	5/16	3/8	7/16	1/2	9/16	5/8	11/16	3/4	13/16	7/8	15/16	1
2	4.170	4.339	4.509	4.680	4.851	5.022	5.194	5.366	5.538	5.711	5.883	6.056	6.230
2 1/8	4.298	4.468	4.639	4.810	4.981	5.153	5.325	5.497	5.670	5.843	6.016	6.189	6.363
2 1/4	4.427	4.596	4.768	4.940	5.112	5.284	5.456	5.629	5.802	5.975	6.143	6.322	6.496
2 3/8	4.555	4.726	4.897	5.069	5.242	5.414	5.587	5.760	5.933	6.107	6.280	6.454	6.628
2 1/2	4.682	4.854	5.026	5.199	5.371	5.544	5.717	5.891	6.064	6.238	6.412	6.586	6.760
2 5/8	4.810	4.982	5.155	5.328	5.501	5.674	5.848	6.021	6.195	6.369	6.543	6.718	6.892
2 3/4	4.938	5.110	5.283	5.457	5.630	5.804	5.978	6.152	6.326	6.500	6.675	6.849	7.024
2 7/8	5.065	5.238	5.412	5.585	5.759	5.933	6.107	6.282	6.456	6.631	6.805	6.980	7.155
3	5.192	5.366	5.540	5.714	5.888	6.063	6.237	6.412	6.586	6.761	6.936	7.111	7.286
3 1/8	5.319	5.494	5.668	5.842	6.017	6.192	6.366	6.541	6.716	6.891	7.067	7.242	7.417
3 1/4	5.446	5.621	5.796	5.970	6.145	6.320	6.496	6.671	6.846	7.021	7.197	7.372	7.548
3 3/8	5.574	5.748	5.924	6.099	6.274	6.449	6.625	6.800	6.976	7.151	7.327	7.503	7.679
3 1/2	5.700	5.876	6.051	6.227	6.402	6.578	6.754	6.929	7.105	7.281	7.457	7.633	7.809
3 5/8	5.827	6.003	6.179	6.345	6.531	6.706	6.883	7.059	7.235	7.411	7.587	7.763	7.939
3 3/4	5.954	6.130	6.306	6.482	6.659	6.835	7.011	7.187	7.364	7.540	7.716	7.893	8.069
3 7/8	6.081	6.257	6.434	6.610	6.787	6.963	7.140	7.316	7.493	7.669	7.846	8.023	8.199
4	6.207	6.384	6.561	6.738	6.914	7.091	7.268	7.445	7.622	7.798	7.975	8.152	8.329
4 1/8	6.334	6.511	6.688	6.865	7.042	7.219	7.396	7.573	7.750	7.927	8.105	8.281	8.458
4 1/4	6.460	6.638	6.815	6.993	7.170	7.347	7.525	7.702	7.879	8.056	8.233	8.411	8.588
4 3/8	6.587	6.764	6.942	7.120	7.298	7.475	7.653	7.830	8.008	8.185	8.363	8.540	8.717

$4\frac{1}{2}$	6.713	6.891	7.069	7.247	7.425	7.603	7.781	7.958	8.136	8.314	8.491	8.669	8.846
$4\frac{5}{8}$	6.839	7.018	7.196	7.374	7.552	7.730	7.908	8.086	8.264	8.442	8.620	8.798	8.976
$4\frac{3}{4}$	6.966	7.144	7.323	7.501	7.680	7.858	8.036	8.214	8.393	8.571	8.749	8.927	9.105
$4\frac{7}{8}$	7.092	7.271	7.450	7.628	7.807	7.985	8.164	8.342	8.521	8.699	8.877	9.055	9.233
5	7.218	7.397	7.576	7.755	7.934	8.113	8.292	8.470	8.649	8.827	9.006	9.184	9.362
$5\frac{1}{8}$	7.344	7.524	7.707	7.882	8.061	8.240	8.419	8.598	8.777	8.955	9.134	9.312	9.491
$5\frac{1}{4}$	7.470	7.650	7.830	8.009	8.188	8.367	8.547	8.726	8.905	9.083	9.262	9.441	9.690
$5\frac{3}{8}$	7.596	7.776	7.956	8.136	8.315	8.495	8.674	8.853	9.032	9.211	9.390	9.569	9.748
$5\frac{1}{2}$	7.722	7.903	8.083	8.262	8.442	8.622	8.801	8.981	9.160	9.339	9.518	9.697	9.876
$5\frac{5}{8}$	7.848	8.029	8.209	8.389	8.569	8.749	8.929	9.108	9.288	9.467	9.646	9.825	10.005
$5\frac{3}{4}$	7.974	8.155	8.335	8.516	8.696	8.876	9.056	9.236	9.415	9.595	9.774	9.953	10.133
$5\frac{7}{8}$	8.100	8.281	8.462	8.642	8.823	9.003	9.183	9.363	9.543	9.722	9.902	10.081	10.261
6	8.226	8.407	8.588	8.769	8.949	9.130	9.310	9.490	9.670	9.850	10.030	10.209	10.389
$6\frac{1}{8}$	8.352	8.533	8.714	8.895	9.076	9.256	9.437	9.617	9.797	9.977	10.157	10.337	10.517
$6\frac{1}{4}$	8.478	8.659	8.841	9.022	9.203	9.383	9.564	9.744	9.925	10.105	10.285	10.465	10.645
$6\frac{3}{8}$	8.604	8.785	8.967	9.148	9.329	9.510	9.691	9.871	10.052	10.232	10.413	10.593	10.773
$6\frac{1}{2}$	8.730	8.911	9.093	9.274	9.456	9.637	9.818	9.998	10.179	10.360	10.540	10.720	10.900
$6\frac{5}{8}$	8.855	9.037	9.219	9.401	9.582	9.763	9.945	10.125	10.306	10.487	10.667	10.848	11.028
$6\frac{3}{4}$	8.976	9.158	9.340	9.522	9.704	9.885	10.066	10.248	10.429	10.609	10.790	10.971	11.151
$6\frac{7}{8}$	9.107	9.289	9.471	9.653	9.835	10.017	10.198	10.379	10.560	10.741	10.922	11.103	11.283
7	9.233	9.415	9.597	9.780	9.961	10.143	10.325	10.506	10.687	10.868	11.049	11.230	11.411
$7\frac{1}{8}$	9.358	9.541	9.723	9.906	10.088	10.270	10.451	10.633	10.814	10.996	11.177	11.358	11.538
$7\frac{1}{4}$	9.484	9.667	9.849	10.032	10.214	10.396	10.578	10.760	10.941	11.123	11.304	11.485	11.666
$7\frac{3}{8}$	9.610	9.793	9.975	10.158	10.340	10.523	10.705	10.886	11.068	11.250	11.431	11.612	11.793
$7\frac{1}{2}$	9.735	9.918	10.101	10.284	10.467	10.649	10.831	11.013	11.195	11.377	11.558	11.739	11.921
$7\frac{5}{8}$	9.861	10.044	10.227	10.410	10.593	10.775	10.958	11.140	11.322	11.503	11.685	11.867	12.048
$7\frac{3}{4}$	9.987	10.170	10.353	10.536	10.719	10.902	11.084	11.266	11.448	11.630	11.812	11.994	12.175
$7\frac{7}{8}$	10.112	10.296	10.479	10.662	10.845	11.028	11.210	11.393	11.575	11.757	11.939	12.121	12.302
8	10.238	10.421	10.605	10.788	10.971	11.154	11.337	11.519	11.702	11.884	12.066	12.248	12.429
$8\frac{1}{8}$	10.363	10.547	10.731	10.914	11.097	11.280	11.463	11.646	11.828	12.011	12.193	12.375	12.557
$8\frac{1}{4}$	10.489	10.673	10.857	11.040	11.224	11.407	11.590	11.772	11.955	12.137	12.320	12.502	12.684
$8\frac{3}{8}$	10.614	10.799	10.982	11.166	11.350	11.533	11.716	11.899	12.081	12.264	12.446	12.629	12.810
$8\frac{1}{2}$	10.740	10.924	11.108	11.292	11.476	11.659	11.842	12.025	12.208	12.391	12.573	12.755	12.938
$8\frac{5}{8}$	10.865	11.050	11.234	11.418	11.602	11.785	11.968	12.152	12.335	12.517	12.700	12.882	13.064
$8\frac{3}{4}$	10.991	11.175	11.360	11.544	11.728	11.911	12.095	12.278	12.461	12.644	12.826	13.009	13.191
$8\frac{7}{8}$	11.116	11.301	11.486	11.670	11.854	12.037	12.221	12.404	12.587	12.770	12.953	13.136	13.318

$$D = \sqrt{d_1^2 + 6.28rd_1 + 8r^2 + (d_3^2 - d_2^2)}$$

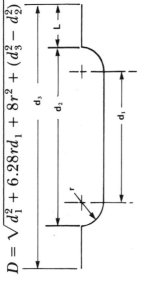

Table 4-30. Solutions for $D = \sqrt{d_1^2 + 6.28rd_1 + 8r^2 + (d_3^2 - d_2^2)}$ when $L = 1$ inch.

d_1	1/4	5/16	3/8	7/16	1/2	9/16	5/8	11/16	3/4	13/16	7/8	15/16	1
2	4.652	4.817	4.983	5.150	5.318	5.486	5.655	5.824	5.993	6.163	6.334	6.504	6.675
$2^1/8$	4.780	4.947	5.113	5.281	5.449	5.617	5.786	5.956	6.126	6.296	6.467	6.638	6.809
$2^1/4$	4.909	5.074	5.243	5.411	5.579	5.748	5.918	6.088	6.258	6.428	6.599	6.771	6.942
$2^3/8$	5.037	5.204	5.372	5.540	5.710	5.879	6.049	6.219	6.390	6.560	6.732	6.903	7.075
$2^1/2$	5.165	5.333	5.501	5.670	5.840	6.009	6.180	6.350	6.521	6.692	6.864	7.036	7.208
$2^5/8$	5.293	5.461	5.630	5.799	5.969	6.140	6.310	6.481	6.652	6.824	6.996	7.168	7.340
$2^3/4$	5.420	5.589	5.759	5.929	6.099	6.270	6.441	6.612	6.784	6.955	7.127	7.300	7.472
$2^7/8$	5.548	5.717	5.887	6.058	6.228	6.399	6.571	6.742	6.914	7.086	7.259	7.431	7.604
3	5.675	5.845	6.016	6.187	6.358	6.529	6.700	6.873	7.045	7.217	7.390	7.563	7.737
$3^1/8$	5.803	5.973	6.144	6.315	6.487	6.659	6.831	7.003	7.175	7.348	7.521	7.694	7.867
$3^1/4$	5.930	6.101	6.272	6.444	6.616	6.788	6.960	7.133	7.305	7.478	7.651	7.825	7.998
$3^3/8$	6.057	6.229	6.400	6.572	6.745	6.917	7.090	7.263	7.436	7.609	7.782	7.956	8.129
$3^1/2$	6.184	6.356	6.528	6.701	6.873	7.046	7.219	7.392	7.565	7.739	7.913	8.086	8.260
$3^5/8$	6.311	6.484	6.656	6.829	7.002	7.175	7.348	7.521	7.696	7.869	8.043	8.217	8.391
$3^3/4$	6.438	6.611	6.784	6.957	7.130	7.303	7.477	7.651	7.825	7.998	8.173	8.347	8.521
$3^7/8$	6.565	6.738	6.911	7.085	7.258	7.432	7.606	7.780	7.954	8.128	8.303	8.477	8.652
4	6.692	6.865	7.039	7.213	7.386	7.560	7.735	7.909	8.083	8.258	8.432	8.607	8.782
$4^1/8$	6.818	6.992	7.166	7.340	7.515	7.689	7.863	8.038	8.212	8.387	8.562	8.737	8.912
$4^1/4$	6.946	7.119	7.294	7.468	7.643	7.817	7.992	8.167	8.342	8.516	8.691	8.867	9.042
$4^3/8$	7.072	7.246	7.421	7.596	7.770	7.945	8.120	8.295	8.470	8.646	8.821	8.996	9.171

4½	7.198	7.373	7.548	7.723	7.898	8.173	8.249	8.424	8.599	8.775	8.950	9.126	9.301
4⅝	7.325	7.500	7.675	7.850	8.026	8.201	8.377	8.552	8.728	8.903	9.079	9.255	9.431
4¾	7.451	7.627	7.802	7.978	8.153	8.329	8.505	8.681	8.856	9.032	9.208	9.384	9.560
4⅞	7.578	7.753	7.929	8.105	8.281	8.457	8.633	8.809	8.985	9.161	9.337	9.513	9.689
5	7.704	7.880	8.056	8.232	8.408	8.585	8.760	8.937	9.113	9.289	9.466	9.642	9.818
5⅛	7.830	8.007	8.183	8.359	8.536	8.712	8.889	9.065	9.241	9.418	9.594	9.771	9.947
5¼	7.956	8.133	8.310	8.486	8.663	8.840	9.016	9.193	9.370	9.546	9.723	9.900	10.076
5⅜	8.083	8.260	8.436	8.613	8.790	8.967	9.144	9.321	9.498	9.675	9.851	10.028	10.205
5½	8.209	8.386	8.563	8.740	8.917	9.095	9.272	9.449	9.626	9.803	9.980	10.157	10.334
5⅝	8.335	8.512	8.690	8.867	9.045	9.222	9.399	9.576	9.754	9.931	10.108	10.285	10.463
5¾	8.461	8.639	8.816	8.994	9.172	9.349	9.527	9.704	9.882	10.059	10.236	10.414	10.591
5⅞	8.587	8.765	8.943	9.121	9.299	9.476	9.654	9.832	10.009	10.187	10.365	10.542	10.720
6	8.713	8.891	9.069	9.247	9.425	9.603	9.782	9.959	10.137	10.315	10.493	10.670	10.848
6⅛	8.839	9.017	9.196	9.374	9.552	9.730	9.908	10.086	10.264	10.442	10.620	10.798	10.976
6¼	8.965	9.144	9.322	9.501	9.679	9.858	10.036	10.214	10.392	10.570	10.749	10.927	11.105
6⅜	9.091	9.270	9.449	9.627	9.806	9.985	10.163	10.341	10.520	10.698	10.876	11.056	11.233
6½	9.217	9.396	9.575	9.754	9.933	10.111	10.290	10.469	10.647	10.826	11.004	11.183	11.361
6⅝	9.343	9.522	9.701	9.880	10.060	10.238	10.417	10.596	10.775	10.953	11.132	11.310	11.489
6¾	9.464	9.643	9.823	10.002	10.181	10.360	10.540	10.719	10.898	11.076	11.255	11.434	11.613
6⅞	9.595	9.774	9.954	10.133	10.313	10.492	10.671	10.850	11.029	11.208	11.387	11.566	11.745
7	9.721	9.900	10.080	10.260	10.439	10.619	10.798	10.977	11.157	11.336	11.515	11.694	11.873
7⅛	9.846	10.026	10.206	10.386	10.566	10.746	10.925	11.104	11.284	11.463	11.642	11.821	12.000
7¼	9.972	10.152	10.333	10.513	10.692	10.872	11.052	11.231	11.411	11.590	11.770	11.949	12.128
7⅜	10.098	10.278	10.459	10.639	10.819	10.999	11.179	11.358	11.538	11.718	11.897	12.077	12.256
7½	10.224	10.404	10.585	10.765	10.945	11.125	11.305	11.485	11.665	11.845	12.024	12.204	12.383
7⅝	10.349	10.530	10.711	10.891	11.072	11.252	11.432	11.612	11.792	11.972	12.152	12.331	12.511
7¾	10.475	10.656	10.837	11.018	11.198	11.379	11.559	11.739	11.919	12.099	12.279	12.459	12.639
7⅞	10.601	10.782	10.963	11.144	11.324	11.505	11.685	11.866	12.046	12.226	12.406	12.586	12.766
8	10.727	10.908	11.089	11.270	11.451	11.631	11.812	11.993	12.173	12.353	12.533	12.713	12.893
8⅛	10.852	11.034	11.215	11.396	11.577	11.758	11.939	12.119	12.300	12.480	12.660	12.841	13.021
8¼	10.978	11.160	11.341	11.522	11.703	11.884	12.065	12.246	12.427	12.607	12.788	12.968	13.148
8⅜	11.104	11.285	11.467	11.648	11.830	12.011	12.192	12.373	12.553	12.734	12.915	13.095	13.275
8½	11.229	11.411	11.593	11.774	11.956	12.137	12.318	12.499	12.680	12.861	13.042	13.222	13.403
8⅝	11.355	11.537	11.719	11.900	12.082	12.263	12.445	12.626	12.807	12.988	13.169	13.349	13.530
8¾	11.480	11.663	11.845	12.026	12.208	12.390	12.571	12.752	12.934	13.115	13.295	13.476	13.657
8⅞	11.606	11.788	11.970	12.152	12.334	12.516	12.697	12.879	13.060	13.241	13.422	13.603	13.784

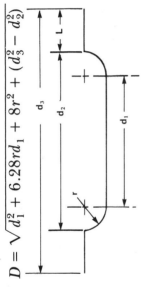

$$D = \sqrt{d_1^2 + 6.28rd_1 + 8r^2 + (d_3^2 - d_2^2)}$$

Table 4-31. Solutions for $D = \sqrt{d_1^2 + 6.28rd_1 + 8r^2 + (d_3^2 - d_2^2)}$ **when** $L = 1\,1/4$ **inch.**

d_1	1/4	5/16	3/8	7/16	1/2	9/16	5/8	11/16	3/4	13/16	7/8	15/16	1
2	5.137	5.299	5.462	5.626	5.791	5.956	6.122	6.288	6.455	6.623	6.791	6.959	7.128
2 1/8	5.266	5.428	5.592	5.756	5.921	6.087	6.254	6.420	6.588	6.756	6.924	7.093	7.262
2 1/4	5.394	5.557	5.722	5.887	6.052	6.218	6.385	6.552	6.720	6.888	7.057	7.226	7.395
2 3/8	5.522	5.686	5.851	6.016	6.183	6.349	6.516	6.684	6.852	7.021	7.190	7.359	7.529
2 1/2	5.650	5.815	5.980	6.146	6.313	6.480	6.647	6.815	6.984	7.153	7.322	7.492	7.662
2 5/8	5.778	5.943	6.109	6.276	6.443	6.610	6.778	6.947	7.115	7.285	7.454	7.624	7.794
2 3/4	5.906	6.072	6.238	6.405	6.573	6.740	6.909	7.078	7.247	7.416	7.586	7.756	7.927
2 7/8	6.034	6.200	6.367	6.534	6.702	6.870	7.039	7.208	7.378	7.548	7.718	7.888	8.059
3	6.161	6.328	6.495	6.663	6.832	7.000	7.169	7.339	7.509	7.679	7.849	8.020	8.191
3 1/8	6.289	6.456	6.624	6.792	6.961	7.130	7.299	7.469	7.639	7.810	7.980	8.151	8.323
3 1/4	6.416	6.584	6.752	6.921	7.090	7.259	7.429	7.599	7.770	7.940	8.111	8.283	8.454
3 3/8	6.543	6.712	6.880	7.049	7.219	7.389	7.559	7.729	7.900	8.071	8.242	8.414	8.586
3 1/2	6.670	6.839	7.008	7.178	7.348	7.518	7.688	7.859	8.030	8.202	8.373	8.545	8.717
3 5/8	6.798	6.967	7.136	7.306	7.477	7.647	7.818	7.989	8.160	8.332	8.504	8.675	8.848
3 3/4	6.925	7.094	7.264	7.434	7.605	7.776	7.947	8.118	8.290	8.462	8.634	8.806	8.978
3 7/8	7.052	7.222	7.392	7.563	7.734	7.905	8.076	8.248	8.420	8.592	8.764	8.936	9.109
4	7.178	7.349	7.520	7.691	7.862	8.033	8.205	8.377	8.549	8.722	8.894	9.067	9.240
4 1/8	7.305	7.476	7.647	7.819	7.990	8.162	8.334	8.506	8.679	8.851	9.024	9.197	9.370
4 1/4	7.432	7.603	7.775	7.946	8.118	8.290	8.463	8.635	8.808	8.981	9.153	9.327	9.500
4 3/8	7.559	7.730	7.902	8.074	8.246	8.419	8.591	8.764	8.937	9.110	9.283	9.457	9.630

4 1/2	7.685	7.857	8.030	8.202	8.374	8.547	8.720	8.893	9.066	9.239	9.413	9.586	9.760
4 5/8	7.812	7.984	8.157	8.329	8.502	8.675	8.848	9.022	9.195	9.369	9.542	9.716	9.890
4 3/4	7.939	8.111	8.284	8.457	8.630	8.803	8.977	9.150	9.324	9.498	9.672	9.846	10.020
4 7/8	8.065	8.238	8.411	8.584	8.758	8.931	9.105	9.279	9.453	9.627	9.801	9.975	10.149
5	8.191	8.365	8.538	8.712	8.885	9.059	9.233	9.407	9.581	9.755	9.930	10.104	10.279
5 1/8	8.318	8.491	8.665	8.839	9.013	9.187	9.361	9.535	9.710	9.884	10.059	10.233	10.408
5 1/4	8.444	8.618	8.792	8.966	9.140	9.315	9.489	9.664	9.838	10.013	10.188	10.362	10.537
5 3/8	8.571	8.745	8.919	9.093	9.268	9.442	9.617	9.792	9.967	10.141	10.316	10.491	10.666
5 1/2	8.697	8.871	9.046	9.220	9.395	9.570	9.745	9.920	10.095	10.270	10.445	10.620	10.795
5 5/8	8.823	8.998	9.173	9.348	9.523	9.698	9.873	10.048	10.223	10.398	10.574	10.749	10.924
5 3/4	8.949	9.124	9.299	9.475	9.650	9.825	10.000	10.176	10.351	10.527	10.702	10.878	11.053
5 7/8	9.076	9.251	9.426	9.602	9.777	9.952	10.128	10.303	10.479	10.655	10.830	11.006	11.182
6	9.202	9.377	9.553	9.728	9.904	10.080	10.255	10.431	10.607	10.783	10.959	11.135	11.311
6 1/8	9.328	9.503	9.679	9.855	10.031	10.207	10.383	10.559	10.735	10.911	11.087	11.263	11.439
6 1/4	9.454	9.630	9.806	9.982	10.158	10.334	10.510	10.687	10.863	11.039	11.215	11.391	11.568
6 3/8	9.580	9.756	9.932	10.109	10.285	10.461	10.638	10.814	10.991	11.167	11.343	11.520	11.696
6 1/2	9.706	9.882	10.059	10.235	10.412	10.589	10.765	10.942	11.118	11.295	11.471	11.648	11.825
6 5/8	9.832	10.009	10.185	10.362	10.539	10.716	10.892	11.069	11.246	11.423	11.599	11.776	11.953
6 3/4	9.953	10.130	10.307	10.484	10.661	10.838	11.015	11.192	11.369	11.546	11.723	11.900	12.077
6 7/8	10.084	10.261	10.438	10.615	10.793	10.970	11.147	11.324	11.501	11.678	11.855	12.032	12.209
7	10.210	10.387	10.565	10.742	10.919	11.097	11.275	11.451	11.628	11.806	11.983	12.160	12.337
7 1/8	10.336	10.513	10.691	10.868	11.046	11.223	11.401	11.578	11.756	11.933	12.111	12.288	12.465
7 1/4	10.462	10.639	10.817	10.995	11.173	11.350	11.528	11.706	11.883	12.061	12.238	12.416	12.593
7 3/8	10.587	10.765	10.943	11.121	11.299	11.477	11.655	11.833	12.010	12.188	12.366	12.544	12.721
7 1/2	10.713	10.892	11.070	11.248	11.426	11.604	11.782	11.960	12.138	12.316	12.494	12.671	12.849
7 5/8	10.839	11.018	11.196	11.374	11.552	11.731	11.909	12.087	12.265	12.443	12.621	12.799	12.977
7 3/4	10.965	11.144	11.322	11.501	11.679	11.857	12.036	12.214	12.392	12.570	12.748	12.927	13.105
7 7/8	11.091	11.270	11.448	11.627	11.805	11.984	12.162	12.341	12.519	12.698	12.876	13.054	13.232
8	11.217	11.395	11.574	11.753	11.932	12.111	12.289	12.468	12.646	12.825	13.003	13.182	13.360
8 1/8	11.342	11.521	11.700	11.879	12.058	12.237	12.416	12.595	12.773	12.952	13.131	13.309	13.488
8 1/4	11.468	11.647	11.827	12.006	12.185	12.364	12.543	12.722	12.900	13.079	13.258	13.437	13.615
8 3/8	11.594	11.773	11.953	12.132	12.311	12.490	12.669	12.848	13.027	13.206	13.385	13.564	13.743
8 1/2	11.719	11.899	12.079	12.258	12.437	12.617	12.796	12.975	13.154	13.333	13.512	13.691	13.870
8 5/8	11.845	12.025	12.205	12.384	12.564	12.743	12.923	13.102	13.281	13.460	13.639	13.819	13.998
8 3/4	11.971	12.151	12.331	12.510	12.690	12.870	13.049	13.229	13.408	13.587	13.767	13.946	14.125
8 7/8	12.096	12.277	12.457	12.636	12.816	12.996	13.176	13.355	13.535	13.714	13.894	14.073	14.252

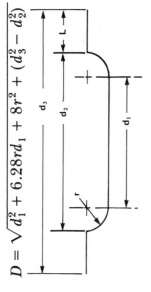

$$D = \sqrt{d_1^2 + 6.28rd_1 + 8r^2 + (d_3^2 - d_2^2)}$$

Table 4-32. Solutions for $D = \sqrt{d_1^2 + 6.28rd_1 + 8r^2 + (d_3^2 - d_2^2)}$ when $L = 1\,1/2$ inch.

d_1	1/4	5/16	3/8	7/16	1/2	9/16	5/8	11/16	3/4	13/16	7/8	15/16	1
2	5.625	5.784	5.944	6.105	6.267	6.430	6.594	6.758	6.922	7.088	7.254	7.420	7.587
2 1/8	5.753	5.913	6.074	6.236	6.398	6.562	6.725	6.890	7.055	7.221	7.387	7.554	7.721
2 1/4	5.882	6.042	6.204	6.366	6.529	6.693	6.857	7.022	7.188	7.354	7.520	7.687	7.854
2 3/8	6.010	6.171	6.333	6.496	6.660	6.824	6.988	7.154	7.320	7.486	7.653	7.820	7.988
2 1/2	6.138	6.300	6.462	6.626	6.790	6.954	7.120	7.285	7.452	7.618	7.785	7.953	8.121
2 5/8	6.266	6.428	6.592	6.755	6.920	7.085	7.250	7.417	7.583	7.750	7.918	8.086	8.254
2 3/4	6.394	6.557	6.720	6.885	7.050	7.215	7.381	7.548	7.715	7.882	8.050	8.218	8.387
2 7/8	6.522	6.685	6.849	7.014	7.179	7.345	7.512	7.679	7.846	8.014	8.182	8.350	8.519
3	6.649	6.813	6.978	7.143	7.309	7.475	7.642	7.809	7.977	8.145	8.313	8.482	8.651
3 1/8	6.777	6.941	7.106	7.272	7.438	7.605	7.772	7.940	8.108	8.276	8.445	8.614	8.783
3 1/4	6.904	7.069	7.235	7.401	7.567	7.735	7.902	8.070	8.238	8.407	8.576	8.745	8.915
3 3/8	7.031	7.197	7.363	7.530	7.697	7.864	8.032	8.200	8.369	8.538	8.707	8.876	9.046
3 1/2	7.159	7.325	7.491	7.658	7.836	7.993	8.162	8.330	8.499	8.668	8.838	9.008	9.178
3 5/8	7.286	7.452	7.619	7.785	7.954	8.123	8.291	8.460	8.629	8.799	8.969	9.139	9.309
3 3/4	7.413	7.580	7.747	7.915	8.083	8.252	8.421	8.590	8.759	8.929	9.099	9.269	9.440
3 7/8	7.540	7.707	7.875	8.043	8.212	8.381	8.550	8.719	8.889	9.059	9.230	9.400	9.571
4	7.667	7.835	8.003	8.171	8.340	8.509	8.679	8.849	9.019	9.189	9.360	9.531	9.702
4 1/8	7.794	7.962	8.130	8.299	8.469	8.638	8.808	8.978	9.148	9.319	9.490	9.661	9.832
4 1/4	7.921	8.089	8.258	8.427	8.597	8.767	8.937	9.107	9.278	9.449	9.619	9.791	9.963
4 3/8	8.047	8.216	8.386	8.555	8.725	8.895	9.066	9.236	9.407	9.578	9.750	9.921	10.093

4½	8.174	8.343	8.513	8.683	8.853	9.024	9.194	9.365	9.537	9.708	9.879	10.051	10.223
4⅝	8.301	8.471	8.640	8.811	8.981	9.152	9.323	9.494	9.663	9.837	10.009	10.181	10.353
4¾	8.427	8.597	8.768	8.938	9.109	9.280	9.452	9.623	9.795	9.966	10.138	10.311	10.483
4⅞	8.554	8.724	8.895	9.066	9.237	9.408	9.580	9.752	9.924	10.096	10.268	10.440	10.613
5	8.680	8.851	9.022	9.193	9.365	9.536	9.708	9.880	10.052	10.225	10.397	10.570	10.742
5⅛	8.807	8.978	9.149	9.321	9.493	9.664	9.837	10.009	10.181	10.354	10.526	10.699	10.872
5¼	8.933	9.105	9.276	9.448	9.620	9.792	9.965	10.137	10.310	10.482	10.655	10.828	11.001
5⅜	9.060	9.231	9.403	9.575	9.748	9.920	10.093	10.265	10.441	10.611	10.784	10.958	11.131
5½	9.186	9.358	9.530	9.703	9.875	10.048	10.221	10.394	10.567	10.740	10.913	11.087	11.260
5⅝	9.312	9.485	9.657	9.830	10.003	10.176	10.349	10.522	10.695	10.868	11.042	11.216	11.389
5¾	9.439	9.611	9.784	9.957	10.130	10.303	10.476	10.650	10.823	10.997	11.171	11.344	11.518
5⅞	9.565	9.738	9.911	10.084	10.257	10.431	10.604	10.778	10.952	11.125	11.299	11.473	11.647
6	9.691	9.864	10.038	10.211	10.385	10.558	10.732	10.906	11.080	11.254	11.428	11.602	11.776
6⅛	9.817	9.991	10.164	10.338	10.512	10.685	10.859	11.033	11.207	11.382	11.556	11.730	11.905
6¼	9.906	10.080	10.255	10.429	10.604	10.778	10.953	11.128	11.303	11.478	11.653	11.828	12.034
6⅜	10.032	10.207	10.382	10.556	10.731	10.906	11.081	11.256	11.431	11.606	11.781	11.988	12.162
6½	10.159	10.334	10.509	10.684	10.859	11.034	11.209	11.384	11.559	11.734	11.941	12.116	12.291
6⅝	10.286	10.461	10.636	10.811	10.986	11.161	11.337	11.512	11.687	11.894	12.069	12.244	12.420
6¾	10.407	10.583	10.758	10.933	11.109	11.284	11.460	11.636	11.843	12.018	12.193	12.369	12.544
6⅞	10.538	10.714	10.890	11.065	11.241	11.416	11.592	11.800	11.975	12.150	12.326	12.501	12.676
7	10.665	10.841	11.016	11.192	11.368	11.544	11.752	11.927	12.102	12.278	12.454	12.629	12.805
7⅛	10.791	10.967	11.143	11.319	11.495	11.703	11.879	12.054	12.230	12.406	12.581	12.757	12.933
7¼	10.918	11.094	11.270	11.446	11.655	11.830	12.006	12.182	12.358	12.533	12.709	12.885	13.061
7⅜	11.044	11.220	11.397	11.605	11.781	11.957	12.133	12.309	12.485	12.661	12.837	13.013	13.189
7½	11.170	11.347	11.556	11.732	11.908	12.084	12.260	12.436	12.612	12.789	12.965	13.141	13.317
7⅝	11.297	11.506	11.682	11.858	12.035	12.211	12.387	12.564	12.740	12.916	13.093	13.269	13.445
7¾	11.456	11.632	11.808	11.985	12.161	12.338	12.514	12.691	12.867	13.044	13.220	13.397	13.573
7⅞	11.581	11.758	11.935	12.111	12.288	12.465	12.641	12.818	12.994	13.171	13.348	13.524	13.701
8	11.707	11.884	12.061	12.238	12.415	12.591	12.768	12.945	13.122	13.299	13.475	13.652	13.829
8⅛	11.833	12.010	12.187	12.364	12.541	12.718	12.895	13.072	13.249	13.426	13.603	13.780	13.957
8¼	11.959	12.136	12.313	12.490	12.668	12.845	13.022	13.199	13.376	13.553	13.730	13.907	14.084
8⅜	12.085	12.262	12.439	12.617	12.794	12.971	13.149	13.326	13.503	13.680	13.858	14.035	14.212
8½	12.210	12.388	12.566	12.743	12.921	13.098	13.275	13.453	13.630	13.808	13.985	14.162	14.340
8⅝	12.336	12.514	12.692	12.869	13.047	13.225	13.402	13.580	13.757	13.935	14.112	14.290	14.467
8¾	12.462	12.640	12.818	12.996	13.173	13.351	13.529	13.707	13.884	14.062	14.240	14.417	14.595
8⅞	12.588	12.766	12.944	13.122	13.300	13.478	13.656	13.833	14.011	14.189	14.367	14.545	14.722

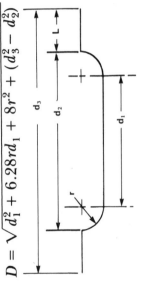

$$D = \sqrt{d_1^2 + 6.28rd_1 + 8r^2 + (d_3^2 - d_2^2)}$$

Table 4-33. Solutions for $D = \sqrt{d_1^2 + 6.28rd_1 + 8r^2 + (d_3^2 - d_2^2)}$ when $L = 1\,3/4$ inch.

d_1	1/4	5/16	3/8	7/16	1/2	9/16	5/8	11/16	3/4	13/16	7/8	15/16	1
2	6.115	6.271	6.429	6.588	6.748	6.908	7.069	7.231	7.394	7.557	7.721	7.885	8.050
2 1/8	6.243	6.401	6.559	6.718	6.879	7.039	7.201	7.364	7.527	7.690	7.854	8.019	8.192
2 1/4	6.371	6.529	6.689	6.848	7.009	7.171	7.333	7.496	7.659	7.823	7.988	8.160	8.318
2 3/8	6.500	6.658	6.818	6.978	7.140	7.302	7.464	7.627	7.791	7.956	8.128	8.286	8.452
2 1/2	6.628	6.787	6.947	7.108	7.270	7.432	7.595	7.759	7.923	8.095	8.253	8.419	8.585
2 5/8	6.756	6.915	7.076	7.238	7.400	7.563	7.726	7.890	8.063	8.220	8.385	8.551	8.718
2 3/4	6.883	7.044	7.205	7.367	7.530	7.693	7.857	8.029	8.186	8.352	8.518	8.684	8.851
2 7/8	7.011	7.172	7.334	7.496	7.660	7.823	7.995	8.152	8.318	8.483	8.650	8.816	8.983
3	7.139	7.300	7.463	7.626	7.789	7.961	8.118	8.283	8.449	8.615	8.781	8.948	9.115
3 1/8	7.266	7.428	7.591	7.755	7.926	8.083	8.248	8.414	8.580	8.746	8.913	9.080	9.247
3 1/4	7.394	7.556	7.719	7.891	8.048	8.213	8.378	8.544	8.710	8.877	9.044	9.211	9.379
3 3/8	7.521	7.684	7.856	8.012	8.177	8.342	8.508	8.674	8.841	9.008	9.175	9.343	9.511
3 1/2	7.648	7.820	7.976	8.141	8.306	8.472	8.638	8.804	8.971	9.139	9.306	9.474	9.643
3 5/8	7.783	7.940	8.104	8.269	8.435	8.601	8.767	8.934	9.102	9.269	9.437	9.605	9.774
3 3/4	7.902	8.067	8.232	8.398	8.564	8.730	8.897	9.064	9.232	9.400	9.568	9.736	9.905
3 7/8	8.030	8.195	8.360	8.526	8.692	8.859	9.026	9.194	9.362	9.530	9.698	9.867	10.036
4	8.157	8.322	8.488	8.654	8.821	8.988	9.156	9.323	9.492	9.660	9.829	9.998	10.167
4 1/8	8.284	8.449	8.616	8.782	8.950	9.117	9.285	9.453	9.621	9.790	9.959	10.128	10.298
4 1/4	8.410	8.577	8.743	8.910	9.078	9.246	9.414	9.582	9.751	9.920	10.089	10.259	10.428
4 3/8	8.537	8.704	8.871	9.038	9.206	9.374	9.543	9.711	9.880	10.050	10.219	10.389	10.559

4½	8.664	8.831	8.998	9.166	9.334	9.503	9.672	9.840	10.010	10.179	10.349	10.519	10.689
4⅝	8.791	8.958	9.126	9.294	9.463	9.631	9.800	9.969	10.139	10.309	10.479	10.649	10.819
4¾	8.917	9.085	9.253	9.422	9.591	9.760	9.929	10.098	10.268	10.438	10.608	10.779	10.950
4⅞	9.044	9.212	9.381	9.549	9.718	9.888	10.057	10.227	10.397	10.567	10.738	10.909	11.080
5	9.171	9.339	9.508	9.677	9.846	10.016	10.186	10.356	10.526	10.697	10.867	11.038	11.209
5⅛	9.297	9.466	9.635	9.804	9.974	10.144	10.314	10.484	10.655	10.826	10.997	11.168	11.339
5¼	9.424	9.593	9.762	9.932	10.102	10.272	10.442	10.613	10.784	10.955	11.126	11.297	11.469
5⅜	9.550	9.720	9.889	10.059	10.230	10.400	10.571	10.741	10.912	11.084	11.255	11.427	11.598
5½	9.677	9.846	10.016	10.187	10.357	10.528	10.699	10.870	11.041	11.212	11.384	11.556	11.728
5⅝	9.803	9.973	10.143	10.314	10.485	10.656	10.827	10.998	11.170	11.341	11.513	11.685	11.857
5¾	9.929	10.100	10.270	10.441	10.612	10.783	10.959	11.126	11.298	11.470	11.642	11.814	11.986
5⅞	10.056	10.226	10.397	10.568	10.740	10.911	11.083	11.254	11.426	11.598	11.771	11.943	12.116
6	10.182	10.353	10.524	10.695	10.867	11.039	11.210	11.382	11.555	11.727	11.899	12.072	12.245
6⅛	10.308	10.479	10.651	10.822	10.995	11.166	11.338	11.510	11.683	11.855	12.028	12.200	12.373
6¼	10.434	10.606	10.778	10.949	11.122	11.294	11.466	11.638	11.811	11.984	12.157	12.329	12.503
6⅜	10.561	10.732	10.904	11.076	11.249	11.421	11.594	11.766	11.939	12.112	12.285	12.458	12.631
6½	10.687	10.859	11.031	11.203	11.376	11.548	11.721	11.894	12.067	12.240	12.413	12.587	12.760
6⅝	10.813	10.985	11.158	11.330	11.503	11.676	11.849	12.022	12.195	12.368	12.542	12.715	12.889
6¾	10.934	11.107	11.280	11.453	11.626	11.799	11.972	12.145	12.319	12.492	12.666	12.840	13.014
6⅞	11.065	11.238	11.411	11.584	11.757	11.930	12.104	12.277	12.451	12.624	12.798	12.972	13.146
7	11.191	11.364	11.537	11.711	11.884	12.058	12.231	12.405	12.579	12.752	12.926	13.100	13.274
7⅛	11.317	11.490	11.664	11.837	12.011	12.185	12.358	12.532	12.706	12.880	13.054	13.229	13.403
7¼	11.443	11.617	11.790	11.964	12.138	12.312	12.486	12.660	12.834	13.008	13.182	13.357	13.531
7⅜	11.569	11.743	11.917	12.091	12.265	12.439	12.613	12.787	12.962	13.136	13.310	13.485	13.659
7½	11.695	11.869	12.043	12.217	12.392	12.566	12.740	12.915	13.089	13.264	13.438	13.613	13.788
7⅝	11.821	11.995	12.170	12.344	12.518	12.693	12.867	13.042	13.217	13.391	13.566	13.741	13.916
7¾	11.947	12.121	12.296	12.470	12.645	12.820	12.994	13.169	13.344	13.519	13.694	13.869	14.044
7⅞	12.073	12.248	12.422	12.597	12.772	12.947	13.122	13.297	13.472	13.647	13.822	13.997	14.172
8	12.199	12.374	12.549	12.723	12.898	13.073	13.249	13.424	13.599	13.774	13.949	14.125	14.300
8⅛	12.325	12.500	12.675	12.850	13.025	13.200	13.376	13.551	13.726	13.902	14.077	14.252	14.428
8¼	12.451	12.626	12.801	12.976	13.152	13.327	13.503	13.678	13.854	14.029	14.205	14.380	14.556
8⅜	12.576	12.752	12.927	13.103	13.278	13.454	13.629	13.805	13.981	14.156	14.332	14.508	14.684
8½	12.702	12.878	13.053	13.229	13.405	13.581	13.756	13.932	14.108	14.284	14.460	14.636	14.811
8⅝	12.828	13.004	13.180	13.355	13.531	13.707	13.883	14.059	14.235	14.411	14.587	14.763	14.939
8¾	12.954	13.130	13.306	13.482	13.658	13.834	14.010	14.186	14.362	14.538	14.715	14.891	15.067
8⅞	13.079	13.256	13.432	13.608	13.784	13.961	14.137	14.313	14.489	14.666	14.842	15.018	15.195

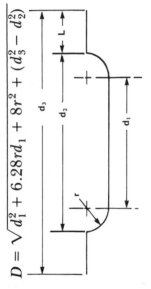

$$D = \sqrt{d_1^2 + 6.28rd_1 + 8r^2 + (d_3^2 - d_2^2)}$$

Table 4-34. Solutions for $D = \sqrt{d_1^2 + 6.28rd_1 + 8r^2 + (d_3^2 - d_2^2)}$ when $L = 2$ inches.

d_1	1/4	5/16	3/8	7/16	1/2	9/16	5/8	11/16	3/4	13/16	7/8	15/16	1
2	6.606	6.761	6.916	7.073	7.230	7.389	7.548	7.708	7.869	8.030	8.192	8.355	8.518
2⅛	6.734	6.890	7.046	7.203	7.361	7.520	7.680	7.840	8.002	8.163	8.326	8.489	8.652
2¼	6.861	7.018	7.175	7.333	7.493	7.651	7.811	7.972	8.134	8.296	8.459	8.622	8.786
2⅜	6.991	7.147	7.305	7.463	7.622	7.782	7.943	8.104	8.266	8.429	8.592	8.755	8.919
2½	7.119	7.276	7.434	7.593	7.752	7.913	8.074	8.236	8.398	8.561	8.724	8.888	9.053
2⅝	7.247	7.404	7.563	7.722	7.883	8.043	8.205	8.367	8.530	8.693	8.857	9.021	9.186
2¾	7.374	7.533	7.692	7.852	8.012	8.174	8.336	8.498	8.661	8.825	8.989	9.153	9.318
2⅞	7.502	7.661	7.821	7.981	8.142	8.304	8.466	8.629	8.792	8.956	9.121	9.286	9.451
3	7.630	7.789	7.949	8.110	8.272	8.434	8.597	8.760	8.924	9.088	9.253	9.418	9.583
3⅛	7.757	7.917	8.078	8.239	8.401	8.564	8.727	8.890	9.055	9.219	9.384	9.550	9.716
3¼	7.884	8.045	8.206	8.368	8.530	8.693	8.857	9.021	9.185	9.350	9.516	9.681	9.847
3⅜	8.012	8.173	8.335	8.497	8.660	8.823	8.987	9.151	9.316	9.481	9.647	9.813	9.979
3½	8.139	8.301	8.463	8.625	8.789	8.952	9.117	9.281	9.446	9.612	9.778	9.944	10.111
3⅝	8.266	8.428	8.591	8.754	8.918	9.082	9.246	9.411	9.577	9.743	9.909	10.075	10.242
3¾	8.393	8.556	8.719	8.882	9.046	9.211	9.376	9.541	9.707	9.873	10.040	10.206	10.374
3⅞	8.521	8.683	8.847	9.011	9.175	9.340	9.505	9.671	9.837	10.003	10.170	10.337	10.505
4	8.648	8.811	8.975	9.139	9.304	9.469	9.635	9.800	9.967	10.134	10.301	10.468	10.636
4⅛	8.775	8.938	9.102	9.267	9.432	9.598	9.764	9.930	10.097	10.264	10.431	10.599	10.767
4¼	8.901	9.066	9.230	9.395	9.561	9.727	9.893	10.059	10.226	10.394	10.561	10.729	10.897
4⅜	9.028	9.193	9.358	9.523	9.689	9.855	10.022	10.188	10.356	10.524	10.691	10.860	11.028

4½	9.155	9.320	9.485	9.651	9.817	9.984	10.151	10.318	10.485	10.653	10.821	10.990	11.158
4⅝	9.282	9.447	9.613	9.779	9.946	10.112	10.280	10.447	10.615	10.783	10.951	11.120	11.289
4¾	9.409	9.574	9.740	9.907	10.074	10.241	10.408	10.576	10.744	10.912	11.081	11.250	11.419
4⅞	9.535	9.701	9.868	10.034	10.202	10.369	10.537	10.705	10.873	11.042	11.211	11.380	11.549
5	9.662	9.828	9.995	10.162	10.330	10.497	10.665	10.834	11.002	11.171	11.340	11.510	11.679
5⅛	9.788	9.955	10.122	10.290	10.457	10.625	10.794	10.962	11.131	11.300	11.470	11.639	11.809
5¼	9.915	10.082	10.249	10.417	10.585	10.754	10.922	11.091	11.260	11.429	11.599	11.769	11.939
5⅜	10.041	10.209	10.377	10.545	10.713	10.882	11.050	11.220	11.389	11.558	11.728	11.898	12.068
5½	10.168	10.336	10.504	10.672	10.841	11.010	11.179	11.348	11.518	11.687	11.857	12.028	12.198
5⅝	10.294	10.462	10.631	10.799	10.968	11.137	11.307	11.476	11.646	11.816	11.986	12.157	12.327
5¾	10.421	10.589	10.758	10.927	11.096	11.265	11.435	11.605	11.775	11.945	12.115	12.286	12.457
5⅞	10.547	10.716	10.885	11.054	11.223	11.393	11.563	11.733	11.903	12.074	12.244	12.415	12.586
6	10.673	10.842	11.012	11.181	11.351	11.521	11.691	11.861	12.032	12.202	12.373	12.544	12.715
6⅛	10.800	10.969	11.138	11.308	11.478	11.648	11.818	11.989	12.160	12.331	12.502	12.673	12.844
6¼	10.926	11.095	11.265	11.435	11.606	11.776	11.947	12.117	12.288	12.459	12.631	12.802	12.974
6⅜	11.052	11.222	11.392	11.562	11.729	11.903	12.074	12.245	12.416	12.588	12.759	12.931	13.103
6½	11.178	11.348	11.519	11.689	11.860	12.031	12.202	12.373	12.545	12.716	12.888	13.059	13.231
6⅝	11.305	11.475	11.646	11.816	11.987	12.158	12.330	12.501	12.673	12.844	13.016	13.188	13.360
6¾	11.426	11.597	11.768	11.939	12.110	12.282	12.453	12.625	12.797	12.969	13.141	13.313	13.485
6⅞	11.557	11.728	11.899	12.070	12.241	12.413	12.585	12.757	12.929	13.101	13.273	13.445	13.618
7	11.683	11.854	12.025	12.197	12.369	12.540	12.712	12.884	13.056	13.229	13.401	13.574	13.746
7⅛	11.809	11.980	12.152	12.324	12.496	12.668	12.840	13.012	13.184	13.357	13.529	13.702	13.875
7¼	11.935	12.107	12.279	12.450	12.623	12.795	12.967	13.139	13.312	13.485	13.657	13.830	14.003
7⅜	12.061	12.233	12.405	12.577	12.749	12.922	13.094	13.267	13.440	13.613	13.786	13.959	14.132
7½	12.187	12.359	12.531	12.704	12.876	13.049	13.222	13.394	13.567	13.740	13.914	14.087	14.260
7⅝	12.313	12.485	12.658	12.831	13.003	13.176	13.349	13.522	13.695	13.868	14.042	14.215	14.388
7¾	12.439	12.612	12.784	12.957	13.130	13.303	13.476	13.649	13.823	13.996	14.169	14.343	14.517
7⅞	12.565	12.738	12.911	13.084	13.257	13.430	13.603	13.777	13.950	14.124	14.297	14.471	14.645
8	12.691	12.864	13.037	13.210	13.384	13.557	13.730	13.904	14.078	14.251	14.425	14.599	14.773
8⅛	12.817	12.990	13.163	13.337	13.510	13.684	13.858	14.031	14.205	14.379	14.553	14.727	14.901
8¼	12.943	13.116	13.290	13.463	13.637	13.811	13.985	14.158	14.333	14.507	14.681	14.855	15.029
8⅜	13.069	13.242	13.416	13.590	13.764	13.938	14.112	14.286	14.460	14.634	14.808	14.983	15.157
8½	13.195	13.368	13.542	13.716	13.890	14.064	14.239	14.413	14.587	14.762	14.936	15.110	15.285
8⅝	13.320	13.494	13.669	13.843	14.017	14.191	14.366	14.540	14.714	14.889	15.064	15.238	15.413
8¾	13.446	13.620	13.795	13.969	14.143	14.318	14.492	14.667	14.842	15.016	15.191	15.366	15.541
8⅞	13.572	13.746	13.921	14.095	14.270	14.445	14.619	14.794	14.969	15.144	15.319	15.494	15.668

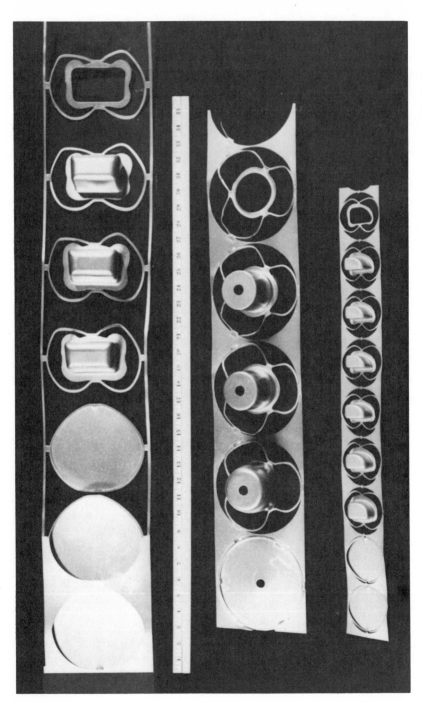

Examples of sequential draws. Photo courtesy Capitol Engineering

Sequential Drawing Operations

SEQUENTIAL DRAWS

The percentage reduction between successive draws depends largely on a material's modulus of strain hardening and its yield strength. Other factors influencing the percentage reduction include draw radii, variations in draw pressure, smoothness of the binder surface, and excessive punch-die tightness, a condition that can lead to ironing.

The critical figure is the *maximum percent reduction*. With this figure established, the intervening percentages of draw are not so critical. The Bliss Division of Gulf + Western suggests that successive reductions of 30, 25, 20 and 16 percent are feasible *for double action presses*. In single action presses, Bliss recommends that the series start at 25 percent.

These percentages are not additive. To illustrate how these percentages should be used, let us assume a 25–20–16 sequence for a 15-inch blank. In the first draw the shell diameter is 11.25 inches, which represents a 25 percent reduction.

In the second draw, the 11.25 shell is reduced 20 percent, or 2.25 inches, making shell diameter 9.00 inches. Now the 9.00 diameter can be reduced 16 percent to 7.56 inches. Thus the total reduction between the flat blank and the final draw is 49.6 percent.

The nomogram shown in *Figure* 5–1 provides a fast determination of successive diameters once the percent reductions have been established. In this example, three sequential draws are used to obtain a total reduction of 68 percent. The first draw, arbitrarily established as 40 percent takes a 10-inch blank down to a 6-inch shell. The next draw—established at 30 percent—reduces the shell to a diameter of 4.2 inches. In a final draw of 25 percent, the shell is brought to the required diameter of 3.18 inches. (See *Figure* 5–2 for a metric version of this nomogram.)

The thickness of metal is also a factor when laying out a draw sequence. The thinner the metal, the less the total reduction, and therefore the smaller the increments between successive draws. Tables 5–1 through 5–12 provide dimensions for successive draws in deep drawing stock. The percentage of reduction for each draw is specified according to initial workpiece thickness. These calculations presuppose an absence of ironing and uniform pressure throughout the draws.

REDUCTIONS IN DRAWING (Inches)

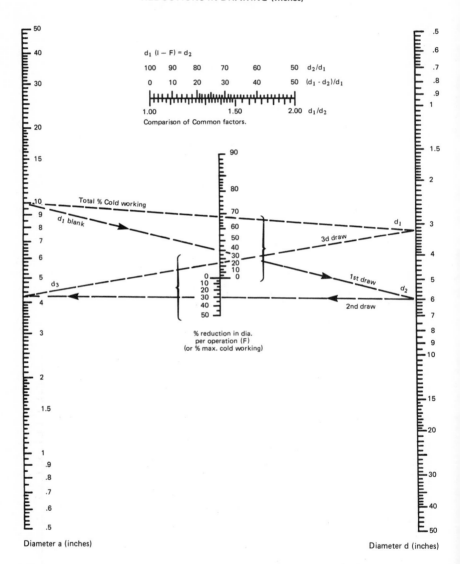

FIG. 5-1

REDUCTION IN DRAWING (METRIC)

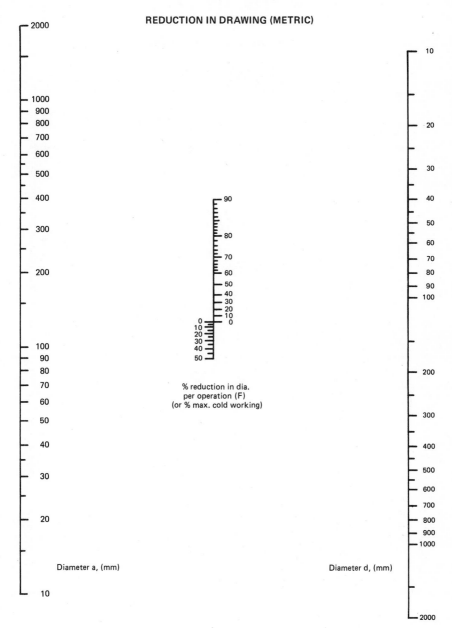

% reduction in dia.
per operation (F)
(or % max. cold working)

Diameter a, (mm)

Diameter d, (mm)

FIG. 5-2

Table 5–1. Deep Drawing Stock—0.010 inch (0.254 mm) Thick.

Blank Diameter		First Draw		Second Draw		Third Draw	
		27% Reduction		18% Reduction		17% Reduction	
D		*d*		*d_1*		*d_2*	
inch	mm	inch	mm	inch	mm	inch	mm
20.00	508	14.60	371	11.97	304	9.94	252
19.75	502	14.42	366	11.82	300	9.81	249
19.50	495	14.24	362	11.68	297	9.69	246
19.25	489	14.05	357	11.52	293	9.56	243
19.00	483	13.87	352	11.37	289	9.44	240
18.75	476	13.69	348	11.23	285	9.32	237
18.50	470	13.51	343	11.08	281	9.20	234
18.25	464	13.32	338	10.92	277	9.06	230
18.00	457	13.14	334	10.77	274	8.94	227
17.75	451	12.96	329	10.63	270	8.82	224
17.50	444	12.78	325	10.48	266	8.70	221
17.25	438	12.59	320	10.32	262	8.57	218
17.00	432	12.41	315	10.18	259	8.45	215
16.75	425	12.23	311	10.03	225	8.32	211
16.50	419	12.05	306	9.88	251	8.20	208
16.25	413	11.86	301	9.73	247	8.08	205
16.00	406	11.68	297	9.58	243	7.95	202
15.75	400	11.50	292	9.43	240	7.83	199
15.50	394	11.32	288	9.28	236	7.70	196
15.25	387	11.13	283	9.13	232	7.58	193
15.00	381	10.95	278	8.98	228	7.45	189
14.75	375	10.77	274	8.83	224	7.33	186
14.50	368	10.59	269	8.68	220	7.20	183
14.25	362	10.40	264	8.53	217	7.08	180
14.00	356	10.22	260	8.38	213	6.96	177
13.75	349	10.04	255	8.23	209	6.83	173
13.50	343	9.86	250	8.09	205	6.71	170
13.25	337	9.67	246	7.93	201	6.58	167
13.00	330	9.49	241	7.78	198	6.46	164
12.75	324	9.31	236	7.63	194	6.33	161
12.50	318	9.13	232	7.49	190	6.22	158
12.25	311	8.94	227	7.33	186	6.08	154
12.00	305	8.76	223	7.18	182	5.96	151
11.75	298	8.58	218	7.04	179	5.84	148
11.50	292	8.40	213	6.89	175	5.72	145

Table 5–1. Deep Drawing Stock—0.010 inch (0.254 mm) Thick (Continued).

Blank Diameter		First Draw		Second Draw		Third Draw	
		27% Reduction		18% Reduction		17% Reduction	
D		d		d_1		d_2	
inch	mm	inch	mm	inch	mm	inch	mm
11.25	286	8.21	209	6.73	171	5.59	142
11.00	279	8.03	204	6.58	167	5.46	139
10.75	273	7.85	199	6.44	164	5.35	136
10.50	267	7.67	195	6.29	160	5.22	133
10.25	260	7.48	190	6.13	156	5.09	129
10.00	254	7.30	185	5.99	152	4.97	126
9.75	248	7.12	181	5.84	148	4.85	123
9.50	241	6.94	176	5.69	145	4.72	120
9.25	235	6.75	171	5.54	141	4.60	117
9.00	229	6.57	167	5.39	137	4.47	114
8.75	222	6.39	162	5.24	133	4.35	110
8.50	216	6.21	158	5.09	129	4.22	107
8.25	210	6.02	153	4.94	125	4.10	104
8.00	203	5.84	148	4.79	122	3.98	101
7.75	197	5.66	144	4.64	118	3.85	98
7.50	191	5.48	139	4.49	114	3.73	95
7.25	184	5.29	134	4.34	110	3.60	91
7.00	178	5.11	130	4.19	106	3.48	88
6.75	171	4.93	125	4.04	103	3.35	85
6.50	165	4.75	121	3.90	99	3.24	82
6.25	159	4.56	116	3.74	95	3.10	79
6.00	152	4.38	111	3.59	91	2.98	76
5.75	146	4.20	107	3.44	87	2.86	73
5.50	140	4.02	102	3.30	84	2.74	70
5.25	133	3.83	97	3.14	80	2.61	66
5.00	127	3.65	93	2.99	76	2.48	63
4.75	121	3.47	88	2.85	72	2.37	60
4.50	114	3.29	84	2.70	69	2.24	57
4.25	108	3.10	79	2.54	65	2.11	54
4.00	102	2.92	74	2.39	61	1.98	50
3.75	95	2.74	70	2.25	57	1.87	47
3.50	89	2.56	65	2.10	53	1.74	44
3.25	83	2.37	60	1.94	49	1.61	41
3.00	76	2.19	56	1.80	46	1.49	38
2.75	70	2.01	51	1.65	42	1.40	36
2.50	64	1.83	46	1.50	38	1.25	32
2.00	51	1.46	37	1.20	30	1.00	25

Table 5–2. Deep Drawing Stock—0.015 inch (0.381 mm) Thick.

Blank Diameter		First Draw		Second Draw		Third Draw	
		32% Reduction		20% Reduction		19% Reduction	
D		d		d_1		d_2	
inch	mm	inch	mm	inch	mm	inch	mm
20.00	508	13.60	345	10.88	276	8.81	224
19.75	502	13.43	341	10.74	273	8.70	221
19.50	495	13.26	337	10.61	269	8.59	218
19.25	489	13.09	332	10.47	266	8.48	215
19.00	483	12.92	328	10.34	263	8.38	213
18.75	476	12.75	324	10.20	259	8.26	210
18.50	470	12.58	320	10.06	256	8.15	207
18.25	464	12.41	315	9.93	252	8.04	204
18.00	457	12.24	311	9.79	249	7.93	201
17.75	451	12.07	307	9.66	245	7.82	199
17.50	444	11.90	302	9.52	242	7.71	196
17.25	438	11.73	298	9.38	238	7.60	193
17.00	432	11.56	294	9.25	235	7.49	190
16.75	425	11.39	289	9.11	231	7.38	187
16.50	419	11.22	285	8.98	228	7.27	185
16.25	413	11.05	281	8.84	225	7.16	182
16.00	406	10.88	276	8.70	221	7.05	179
15.75	400	10.71	272	8.57	218	6.94	176
15.50	394	10.54	268	8.43	214	6.83	173
15.25	387	10.37	263	8.30	211	6.72	171
15.00	381	10.20	259	8.16	207	6.61	168
14.75	375	10.03	255	8.02	204	6.50	165
14.50	368	9.86	250	7.89	200	6.39	162
14.25	263	9.69	246	7.75	197	6.28	160
14.00	356	9.52	242	7.62	194	6.17	157
13.75	349	9.35	237	7.48	190	6.06	154
13.50	343	9.18	233	7.34	186	5.95	151
13.25	337	9.01	229	7.21	183	5.84	148
13.00	330	8.84	225	7.07	180	5.73	146
12.75	324	8.67	220	6.94	176	5.62	143
12.50	318	8.50	216	6.80	173	5.51	140
12.25	311	8.33	212	6.66	169	5.39	137
12.00	305	8.16	207	6.53	166	5.29	134
11.75	298	7.99	203	6.39	162	5.18	132
11.50	292	7.82	199	6.26	159	5.07	129

Table 5–2. Deep Drawing Stock—0.015 inch (0.381 mm) Thick *(Continued)*.

Blank Diameter		First Draw		Second Draw		Third Draw	
		32% Reduction		20% Reduction		19% Reduction	
D		d		d_1		d_2	
inch	mm	inch	mm	inch	mm	inch	mm
11.25	286	7.65	194	6.12	155	4.96	126
11.00	279	7.48	190	5.98	152	4.84	123
10.75	273	7.31	186	5.85	149	4.74	120
10.50	267	7.14	181	5.71	145	4.63	118
10.25	260	6.97	177	5.58	142	4.52	115
10.00	254	6.80	173	5.44	138	4.41	112
9.75	248	6.63	168	5.30	135	4.29	109
9.50	241	6.46	164	5.17	131	4.19	106
9.25	235	6.29	160	5.03	128	4.07	103
9.00	229	6.12	155	4.90	124	3.97	101
8.75	222	5.95	151	4.76	121	3.86	98
8.50	216	5.78	147	4.62	117	3.74	95
8.25	210	5.61	142	4.49	114	3.64	92
8.00	203	5.44	138	4.35	110	3.52	89
7.75	197	5.27	134	4.22	107	3.42	87
7.50	191	5.10	130	4.08	104	3.30	84
7.25	184	4.93	125	3.94	100	3.19	81
7.00	178	4.76	121	3.81	97	3.09	78
6.75	171	4.59	117	3.67	93	2.97	75
6.50	165	4.42	112	3.54	90	2.87	73
6.25	159	4.25	108	3.40	86	2.75	70
6.00	152	4.08	104	3.26	83	2.64	67
5.75	146	3.91	99	3.13	80	2.54	65
5.50	140	3.74	95	2.99	76	2.42	61
5.25	133	3.57	91	2.86	73	2.32	59
5.00	127	3.40	86	2.72	69	2.20	56
4.75	121	3.23	82	2.58	66	2.09	53
4.50	114	3.06	78	2.45	62	1.98	50
4.25	108	2.89	73	2.31	59	1.87	47
4.00	102	2.72	69	2.18	55	1.77	45
3.75	95	2.55	65	2.04	52	1.65	42
3.50	89	2.38	60	1.90	48	1.54	39
3.25	83	2.21	56	1.77	45	1.43	36
3.00	76	2.04	52	1.63	41	1.32	34
2.75	70	1.87	47	1.50	38	1.22	31
2.50	64	1.70	43	1.36	35	1.10	28
2.00	51	1.36	35	1.09	28	0.88	22

Table 5–3.   Deep Drawing Stock—0.020 inch (0.508 mm) Thick.

Blank Diameter		First Draw		Second Draw		Third Draw	
		35% Reduction		21% Reduction		20% Reduction	
D		d		d_1		d_2	
inch	mm	inch	mm	inch	mm	inch	mm
20.00	508	13.00	330	10.27	261	8.22	209
19.75	502	12.84	326	10.14	258	8.11	206
19.50	495	12.68	322	10.02	255	8.02	204
19.25	489	12.51	318	9.88	251	7.90	201
19.00	483	12.35	314	9.76	248	7.81	198
18.75	476	12.19	310	9.63	245	7.70	196
18.50	470	12.03	306	9.50	241	7.60	193
18.25	464	11.86	301	9.37	238	7.50	191
18.00	457	11.70	297	9.24	235	7.39	188
17.75	451	11.54	293	9.12	232	7.30	185
17.50	444	11.38	289	8.99	228	7.19	183
17.25	438	11.21	285	8.86	225	7.09	180
17.00	432	11.05	281	8.73	222	6.98	177
16.75	425	10.89	277	8.60	218	6.88	175
16.50	419	10.73	273	8.48	215	6.78	172
16.25	413	10.56	268	8.34	212	6.67	169
16.00	406	10.40	264	8.22	209	6.58	167
15.75	400	10.24	260	8.09	205	6.47	164
15.50	394	10.08	256	7.96	202	6.37	162
15.25	387	9.91	252	7.83	199	6.26	159
15.00	381	9.75	248	7.70	196	6.16	156
14.75	375	9.59	244	7.58	193	6.06	154
14.50	368	9.43	240	7.45	189	5.96	151
14.25	362	9.26	235	7.32	186	5.86	149
14.00	356	9.10	231	7.19	183	5.75	146
13.75	349	8.94	227	7.06	179	5.65	144
13.50	343	8.78	223	6.94	176	5.55	141
13.25	337	8.61	219	6.80	173	5.44	138
13.00	330	8.45	215	6.68	170	5.34	136
12.75	324	8.29	211	6.55	166	5.24	133
12.50	318	8.13	207	6.42	163	5.14	131
12.25	311	7.96	202	6.29	160	5.03	128
12.00	305	7.80	198	6.16	156	4.93	125
11.75	298	7.64	194	6.04	153	4.83	123
11.50	292	7.48	190	5.91	150	4.73	120

Table 5–3. Deep Drawing Stock—0.020 inch (0.508 mm) Thick (*Continued*).

Blank Diameter		First Draw		Second Draw		Third Draw	
		35% Reduction		*21% Reduction*		*20% Reduction*	
D		**d**		**d_1**		**d_2**	
inch	*mm*	*inch*	*mm*	*inch*	*mm*	*inch*	*mm*
11.25	286	7.31	186	5.77	147	4.62	117
11.00	279	7.15	182	5.65	144	4.52	115
10.75	273	6.99	178	5.52	140	4.42	112
10.50	267	6.83	173	5.40	137	4.32	110
10.25	260	6.66	169	5.26	134	4.21	107
10.00	254	6.50	165	5.14	131	4.11	104
9.75	248	6.34	161	5.01	127	4.01	102
9.50	241	6.18	157	4.88	124	3.90	99
9.25	235	6.01	153	4.75	121	3.80	97
9.00	229	5.85	149	4.62	117	3.70	94
8.75	222	5.69	145	4.50	114	3.60	91
8.50	216	5.53	140	4.37	111	3.50	89
8.25	210	5.36	136	4.23	107	3.38	86
8.00	203	5.20	132	4.11	104	3.29	84
7.75	197	5.04	128	3.98	101	3.18	81
7.50	191	4.88	124	3.86	98	3.09	78
7.25	184	4.71	120	3.72	94	2.98	76
7.00	178	4.55	116	3.59	91	2.87	73
6.75	171	4.39	112	3.47	88	2.78	71
6.50	165	4.23	107	3.34	85	2.67	68
6.25	159	4.06	103	3.21	82	2.57	65
6.00	152	3.90	99	3.08	78	2.46	62
5.75	146	3.74	95	2.95	75	2.36	60
5.50	140	3.58	91	2.83	72	2.26	57
5.25	133	3.41	87	2.69	68	2.15	55
5.00	127	3.25	83	2.57	65	2.06	52
4.75	121	3.09	78	2.44	62	1.95	50
4.50	114	2.93	74	2.31	59	1.85	47
4.25	108	2.76	70	2.18	55	1.74	44
4.00	102	2.60	66	2.05	52	1.64	42
3.75	95	2.44	62	1.93	49	1.54	39
3.50	89	2.28	58	1.80	46	1.44	37
3.25	83	2.11	54	1.67	42	1.34	34
3.00	76	1.95	50	1.54	39	1.23	31
2.75	70	1.79	45	1.41	36	1.13	29
2.50	64	1.63	41	1.29	33	1.03	26
2.00	51	1.30	33	1.03	26	0.82	21

Table 5–4.   Deep Drawing Stock—0.025 inch (0.635 mm) Thick.

Blank Diameter		First Draw		Second Draw		Third Draw	
		39% Reduction		*22% Reduction*		*21% Reduction*	
D		*d*		*d¹*		*d₂*	
inch	*mm*	*inch*	*mm*	*inch*	*mm*	*inch*	*mm*
20.00	508	12.20	310	9.52	242	7.52	191
19.75	502	12.05	306	9.40	239	7.43	189
19.50	495	11.90	302	9.28	236	7.33	186
19.25	489	11.74	298	9.16	233	7.24	184
19.00	483	11.59	294	9.04	230	7.14	181
18.75	476	11.44	291	8.92	227	7.05	179
18.50	470	11.29	287	8.81	224	6.96	177
18.25	464	11.13	283	8.68	220	6.86	174
18.00	457	10.98	279	8.56	217	6.76	172
17.75	451	10.83	275	8.45	215	6.68	170
17.50	444	10.68	271	8.33	212	6.58	167
17.25	438	10.52	267	8.21	209	6.49	165
17.00	432	10.37	263	8.09	205	6.39	162
16.75	425	10.22	260	7.97	202	6.30	160
16.50	419	10.07	256	7.85	199	6.20	157
16.25	413	9.91	252	7.73	196	6.11	155
16.00	406	9.76	248	7.61	193	6.01	153
15.75	400	9.61	244	7.50	191	5.93	151
15.50	394	9.46	240	7.38	187	5.83	148
15.25	387	9.30	236	7.25	184	5.73	146
15.00	381	9.15	232	7.14	181	5.64	143
14.75	375	9.00	229	7.02	178	5.55	141
14.50	368	8.85	225	6.90	175	5.45	138
14.25	362	8.69	221	6.78	172	5.36	136
14.00	356	8.54	217	6.66	169	5.26	134
13.75	349	8.39	213	6.54	166	5.17	131
13.50	343	8.24	209	6.43	163	5.08	129
13.25	337	8.08	205	6.30	160	4.98	126
13.00	330	7.93	201	6.19	157	4.89	124
12.75	324	7.78	198	6.07	154	4.80	122
12.50	318	7.63	194	5.95	151	4.70	119
12.25	311	7.47	190	5.83	148	4.61	117
12.00	305	7.32	186	5.71	145	4.51	115
11.75	298	7.17	182	5.59	142	4.42	112
11.50	292	7.02	178	5.48	139	4.33	110

Table 5–4. Deep Drawing Stock—0.025 inch (0.635 mm) Thick *(Continued).*

Blank Diameter		First Draw		Second Draw		Third Draw	
		39% Reduction		22% Reduction		21% Reduction	
D		d		d_1		d_2	
inch	mm	inch	mm	inch	mm	inch	mm
11.25	286	6.86	174	5.35	136	4.23	107
11.00	279	6.71	170	5.23	133	4.13	105
10.75	273	6.56	167	5.12	130	4.04	103
10.50	267	6.41	163	5.00	127	3.95	100
10.25	260	6.25	159	4.88	124	3.86	98
10.00	254	6.10	155	4.76	121	3.76	96
9.75	248	5.95	151	4.64	118	3.67	93
9.50	241	5.80	147	4.52	115	3.47	91
9.25	235	5.64	143	4.40	112	3.48	88
9.00	229	5.49	139	4.28	109	3.38	86
8.75	222	5.34	137	4.17	106	3.29	84
8.50	216	5.19	132	4.05	103	3.20	81
8.25	210	5.03	128	3.92	100	3.10	79
8.00	203	4.88	124	3.81	97	3.01	76
7.75	197	4.73	120	3.69	94	2.29	74
7.50	191	4.58	116	3.57	91	2.82	72
7.25	184	4.42	112	3.45	88	2.73	69
7.00	178	4.27	108	3.33	85	2.63	67
6.75	171	4.12	105	3.21	82	2.54	65
6.50	165	3.97	101	3.10	79	2.45	62
6.25	159	3.81	97	2.97	75	2.35	60
6.00	152	3.66	93	2.85	72	2.25	57
5.75	146	3.51	89	2.74	70	2.16	55
5.50	140	3.36	85	2.62	67	2.07	53
5.25	133	3.20	81	2.50	64	1.98	50
5.00	127	3.05	77	2.38	60	1.88	48
4.75	121	2.90	74	2.26	57	1.79	45
4.50	114	2.75	70	2.15	55	1.70	43
4.25	108	2.59	66	2.02	51	1.60	41
4.00	102	2.44	62	1.90	48	1.50	38
3.75	95	2.29	58	1.79	45	1.41	36
3.50	89	2.14	54	1.67	42	1.32	34
3.25	83	1.98	50	1.54	39	1.22	31
3.00	76	1.83	46	1.43	36	1.13	29
2.75	70	1.68	43	1.31	33	1.03	26
2.50	64	1.53	39	1.19	30	0.94	24
2.00	51	1.22	31	0.95	24	0.75	19

Table 5–5. Deep Drawing Stock—0.030 inch (0.762 mm) Thick.

Blank Diameter		First Draw		Second Draw		Third Draw	
		42% Reduction		23% Reduction		22% Reduction	
D		**d**		**d₁**		**d₂**	
inch	mm	inch	mm	inch	mm	inch	mm
20.00	508	11.60	295	8.93	227	6.97	177
19.75	502	11.46	291	8.82	224	6.88	175
19.50	495	11.31	287	8.71	221	6.79	172
19.25	489	11.17	284	8.60	218	6.71	170
19.00	483	11.02	280	8.49	216	6.62	168
18.75	476	10.88	276	8.38	213	6.54	166
18.50	470	10.73	273	8.26	210	6.44	164
18.25	464	10.59	269	8.15	207	6.36	162
18.00	457	10.44	265	8.04	204	6.27	159
17.75	451	10.30	262	7.93	201	6.19	157
17.50	444	10.15	258	7.82	199	6.10	155
17.25	438	10.01	254	7.71	196	6.01	153
17.00	432	9.86	250	7.59	193	5.92	150
16.75	425	9.72	247	7.48	190	5.83	148
16.50	419	9.57	243	7.37	187	5.75	146
16.25	413	9.43	240	7.26	184	5.66	144
16.00	406	9.28	236	7.15	182	5.58	142
15.75	400	9.14	232	7.04	179	5.49	139
15.50	394	8.99	228	6.92	176	5.40	137
15.25	387	8.85	225	6.81	173	5.31	135
15.00	381	8.70	221	6.70	170	5.23	133
14.75	375	8.56	217	6.59	167	5.14	131
14.50	368	8.41	214	6.48	165	5.05	128
14.25	362	8.27	210	6.37	162	4.97	126
14.00	356	8.12	206	6.25	159	4.88	124
13.75	349	7.98	203	6.14	156	4.79	122
13.50	343	7.83	199	6.03	153	4.70	119
13.25	337	7.69	195	5.92	150	4.62	117
13.00	330	7.54	192	5.81	148	4.53	115
12.75	324	7.40	188	5.70	145	4.45	113
12.50	318	7.25	184	5.58	142	4.35	110
12.25	311	7.11	181	5.47	139	4.27	108
12.00	305	6.96	177	5.40	137	4.21	107
11.75	298	6.82	173	5.25	133	4.10	104
11.50	292	6.67	169	5.14	131	4.01	102

**Table 5–5. Deep Drawing Stock—0.030 inch (0.762 mm)
Thick** *(Continued).*

Blank Diameter		First Draw		Second Draw		Third Draw	
		42% Reduction		23% Reduction		22% Reduction	
D		d		d_1		d_2	
inch	mm	inch	mm	inch	mm	inch	mm
11.25	286	6.53	166	5.03	128	3.92	100
11.00	279	6.38	162	4.91	125	3.83	97
10.75	273	6.24	158	4.80	122	3.74	95
10.50	267	6.09	155	4.69	119	3.66	93
10.25	260	5.95	151	4.58	116	3.47	91
10.00	254	5.80	147	4.47	114	3.49	89
9.75	248	5.66	144	4.36	111	3.40	86
9.50	241	5.51	140	4.24	108	3.31	84
9.25	235	5.37	136	4.13	105	3.22	82
9.00	229	5.22	133	4.02	102	3.14	80
8.75	222	5.08	129	3.91	99	3.05	77
8.50	216	4.93	125	3.80	96	2.96	75
8.25	210	4.79	122	3.69	94	2.88	73
8.00	203	4.64	118	3.57	91	2.78	71
7.75	197	4.50	114	3.47	88	2.71	69
7.50	191	4.35	110	3.35	85	2.61	66
7.25	184	4.21	107	3.24	82	2.53	64
7.00	178	4.06	103	3.13	80	2.44	62
6.75	171	3.92	100	3.02	77	2.36	60
6.50	165	3.77	96	2.90	74	2.26	57
6.25	159	3.63	92	2.80	71	2.18	55
6.00	152	3.48	88	2.68	68	2.09	53
5.75	146	3.34	85	2.57	65	2.00	51
5.50	140	3.19	81	2.46	62	1.92	49
5.25	133	3.05	77	2.35	60	1.83	46
5.00	127	2.90	74	2.23	57	1.74	44
4.75	121	2.76	70	2.13	54	1.66	42
4.50	114	2.61	66	2.01	51	1.57	40
4.25	108	2.47	63	1.90	48	1.48	38
4.00	102	2.32	59	1.79	45	1.40	36
3.75	95	2.18	55	1.68	43	1.31	33
3.50	89	2.03	52	1.56	40	1.22	31
3.25	83	1.89	48	1.46	37	1.14	29
3.00	76	1.74	44	1.34	34	1.05	27
2.75	70	1.60	41	1.23	31	0.96	24
2.50	64	1.45	37	1.12	28	0.87	22
2.00	51	1.16	29	0.89	23	0.69	18

Table 5–6. Deep Drawing Stock—0.035 inch (0.889 mm) Thick.

Blank Diameter		First Draw		Second Draw		Third Draw	
		44% Reduction		26% Reduction		24% Reduction	
D		d		d_1		d_2	
inch	mm	inch	mm	inch	mm	inch	mm
20.00	508	11.20	284	8.29	211	6.30	160
19.75	502	11.06	281	8.18	208	6.22	158
19.50	495	10.92	277	8.08	205	6.14	156
19.25	489	10.78	274	7.98	203	6.06	154
19.00	483	10.64	270	7.87	200	5.98	152
18.75	476	10.50	267	7.77	197	5.91	150
18.50	470	10.36	263	7.67	195	5.83	148
18.25	464	10.22	260	7.56	193	5.75	146
18.00	457	10.08	256	7.46	189	5.67	144
17.75	451	9.94	252	7.36	187	5.59	142
17.50	444	9.80	249	7.25	184	5.51	140
17.25	438	9.66	245	7.15	182	5.43	138
17.00	432	9.52	242	7.04	179	5.35	136
16.75	425	9.38	238	6.94	176	5.27	134
16.50	419	9.24	235	6.84	174	5.20	132
16.25	413	9.10	231	6.73	171	5.11	130
16.00	406	8.96	228	6.63	168	5.04	128
15.75	400	8.82	224	6.53	166	4.96	126
15.50	394	8.68	220	6.42	163	4.88	124
15.25	387	8.54	217	6.32	161	4.80	122
15.00	381	8.40	213	6.22	158	4.73	120
14.75	375	8.26	210	6.11	155	4.64	118
14.50	368	8.12	206	6.01	153	4.57	116
14.25	362	7.98	203	5.91	150	4.49	114
14.00	356	7.84	199	5.80	147	4.41	112
13.75	349	7.70	196	5.70	145	4.33	110
13.50	343	7.56	192	5.59	142	4.25	108
13.25	337	7.42	188	5.49	139	4.17	106
13.00	330	7.28	185	5.39	137	4.10	104
12.75	324	7.14	181	5.28	134	4.01	102
12.50	318	7.00	178	5.18	132	3.94	100
12.25	311	6.86	174	5.08	129	3.86	98
12.00	305	6.72	171	4.97	126	3.78	96
11.75	298	6.58	167	4.87	124	3.70	94
11.50	292	6.44	164	4.77	121	3.63	92

Table 5–6. Deep Drawing Stock—0.035 inch (0.889 mm) Thick *(Continued).*

Blank Diameter		First Draw		Second Draw		Third Draw	
		44% Reduction		26% Reduction		24% Reduction	
D		d		d_1		d_2	
inch	mm	inch	mm	inch	mm	inch	mm
11.25	286	6.30	160	4.66	118	3.54	90
11.00	279	6.16	156	4.56	116	3.47	88
10.75	273	6.02	153	4.45	113	3.38	86
10.50	267	5.88	149	4.35	110	3.31	84
10.25	260	5.74	146	4.25	108	3.23	82
10.00	254	5.60	142	4.14	105	3.15	80
9.75	248	5.46	139	4.04	103	3.07	78
9.50	241	5.32	135	3.94	100	2.99	76
9.25	235	5.18	132	3.83	97	2.91	74
9.00	229	5.04	128	3.73	95	2.83	72
8.75	222	4.90	124	3.63	92	2.76	70
8.50	216	4.76	121	3.52	89	2.68	68
8.25	210	4.62	117	3.42	87	2.60	66
8.00	203	4.48	114	3.32	84	2.52	64
7.75	197	4.34	110	3.21	82	2.44	62
7.50	191	4.20	107	3.11	80	2.36	60
7.25	184	4.06	103	3.00	76	2.28	58
7.00	178	3.92	100	2.90	74	2.20	56
6.75	171	3.78	96	2.80	71	2.13	54
6.50	165	3.65	92	2.69	68	2.04	52
6.25	159	3.50	89	2.59	66	1.97	50
6.00	152	3.36	85	2.49	63	1.89	48
5.75	146	3.22	82	2.38	60	1.81	46
5.50	140	3.08	78	2.28	58	1.73	44
5.25	133	2.94	75	2.18	55	1.66	42
5.00	127	2.80	71	2.07	53	1.57	40
4.75	121	2.66	68	1.97	50	1.50	38
4.50	114	2.52	64	1.86	47	1.41	36
4.25	108	2.38	60	1.76	45	1.34	34
4.00	102	2.24	57	1.66	42	1.26	32
3.75	95	2.10	53	1.55	39	1.18	30
3.50	89	1.96	50	1.45	37	1.10	28
3.25	83	1.82	46	1.35	34	1.03	26
3.00	76	1.68	43	1.24	31	0.94	24
2.75	70	1.54	39	1.14	29	0.87	22
2.50	64	1.40	36	1.04	26	0.79	20
2.00	51	1.12	28	0.83	21	0.63	16

Table 5-7.   Deep Drawing Stock—0.040 inch (1.016 mm) Thick.

Blank Diameter		First Draw		Second Draw		Third Draw	
		46% Reduction		28% Reduction		25% Reduction	
D		d		d_1		d_2	
inch	mm	inch	mm	inch	mm	inch	mm
20.00	508	10.80	274	7.78	198	5.84	148
19.75	502	10.67	271	7.68	195	5.76	146
19.50	495	10.53	267	7.58	193	5.69	145
19.25	489	10.40	264	7.49	190	5.62	143
19.00	483	10.26	261	7.39	188	5.54	141
18.75	476	10.13	257	7.29	185	5.47	139
18.50	470	9.99	254	7.19	183	5.39	137
18.25	464	9.86	250	7.10	180	5.33	135
18.00	457	9.72	247	7.00	178	5.25	133
17.75	451	9.59	244	6.90	175	5.18	132
17.50	444	9.45	240	6.80	173	5.10	130
17.25	438	9.32	237	6.71	170	5.03	128
17.00	432	9.18	233	6.61	168	4.96	126
16.75	425	9.05	230	6.52	166	4.89	124
16.50	419	8.91	226	6.42	163	4.82	122
16.25	413	8.76	223	6.31	160	4.73	120
16.00	406	8.64	219	6.22	158	4.67	119
15.75	400	8.51	216	6.13	156	4.60	117
15.50	394	8.37	213	6.03	153	4.52	115
15.25	387	8.24	209	5.93	151	4.45	113
15.00	381	8.10	206	5.83	148	4.37	111
14.75	375	7.97	202	5.74	146	4.31	109
14.50	368	7.83	199	5.64	143	4.23	107
14.25	362	7.70	196	5.54	141	4.16	106
14.00	356	7.56	192	5.44	138	4.08	104
13.75	349	7.43	189	5.35	136	4.01	102
13.50	343	7.29	185	5.25	133	3.94	100
13.25	337	7.16	182	5.16	131	3.87	98
13.00	330	7.02	178	5.05	128	3.79	96
12.75	324	6.89	175	4.96	126	3.72	94
12.50	318	6.75	171	4.86	123	3.65	93
12.25	311	6.62	168	4.77	121	3.58	91
12.00	305	6.48	165	4.67	119	3.50	89
11.75	298	6.35	161	4.57	116	3.43	87
11.50	292	6.21	158	4.47	114	3.35	85

Table 5–7. Deep Drawing Stock—0.040 inch (1.016 mm) Thick *(Continued)*.

Blank Diameter		First Draw		Second Draw		Third Draw	
		46% Reduction		28% Reduction		25% Reduction	
D		d		d_1		d_2	
inch	mm	inch	mm	inch	mm	inch	mm
11.25	286	6.08	154	4.38	111	3.29	84
11.00	279	5.94	151	4.28	109	3.21	82
10.75	273	5.81	148	4.18	106	3.14	80
10.50	267	5.67	144	4.08	104	3.06	78
10.25	260	5.54	141	3.99	101	2.99	76
10.00	254	5.40	137	3.89	99	2.92	74
9.75	248	5.27	134	3.79	96	2.84	72
9.50	241	5.13	130	3.69	94	2.77	70
9.25	235	5.00	127	3.60	91	2.70	69
9.00	229	4.86	123	3.50	89	2.63	67
8.75	222	4.73	120	3.41	87	2.56	65
8.50	216	4.59	117	3.30	84	2.48	63
8.25	210	4.46	113	3.21	82	2.41	61
8.00	203	4.32	110	3.11	79	2.33	59
7.75	197	4.19	106	3.02	77	2.27	58
7.50	191	4.05	103	2.92	74	2.19	56
7.25	184	3.92	100	2.82	72	2.12	54
7.00	178	3.78	96	2.72	69	2.04	52
6.75	171	3.65	93	2.63	67	1.97	50
6.50	165	3.51	89	2.53	64	1.90	48
6.25	159	3.38	86	2.43	62	1.82	46
6.00	152	3.24	82	2.33	59	1.75	44
5.75	146	3.11	79	2.24	57	1.68	43
5.50	140	2.97	75	2.14	54	1.61	41
5.25	133	2.84	72	2.04	52	1.53	39
5.00	127	2.70	69	1.94	49	1.46	37
4.75	121	2.57	65	1.85	47	1.39	35
4.50	114	2.43	62	1.75	44	1.31	33
4.25	108	2.30	58	1.66	42	1.25	32
4.00	102	2.16	55	1.56	40	1.17	30
3.75	95	2.03	52	1.46	37	1.10	28
3.50	89	1.89	48	1.36	35	1.02	26
3.25	83	1.76	45	1.27	32	0.95	24
3.00	76	1.62	41	1.17	30	0.88	22
2.75	70	1.49	38	1.07	27	0.80	20
2.50	64	1.35	34	0.97	25	0.73	19
2.00	51	1.08	27	0.78	20	0.59	15

Table 5–8.   Deep Drawing Stock—0.045 inch (1.143 mm) Thick.

Blank Diameter		First Draw		Second Draw		Third Draw	
		47% Reduction		*28% Reduction*		*25% Reduction*	
D		*d*		*d₁*		*d₂*	
inch	*mm*	*inch*	*mm*	*inch*	*mm*	*inch*	*mm*
20.00	508	10.60	269	7.63	194	5.72	145
19.75	502	10.47	266	7.54	192	5.66	144
19.50	495	10.34	263	7.44	189	5.58	142
19.25	489	10.20	259	7.34	186	5.51	140
19.00	483	10.07	256	7.25	184	5.44	138
18.75	476	9.94	252	7.16	182	5.37	136
18.50	470	9.81	249	7.06	179	5.30	135
18.25	464	9.67	246	6.96	177	5.22	133
18.00	457	9.54	242	6.87	174	5.15	131
17.75	451	9.41	239	6.78	172	5.09	129
17.50	444	9.28	236	6.68	170	5.01	127
17.25	438	9.14	232	6.58	167	4.94	125
17.00	432	9.01	229	6.49	165	4.87	124
16.75	425	8.88	226	6.39	162	4.79	122
16.50	419	8.75	222	6.30	160	4.73	120
16.25	413	8.61	219	6.20	157	4.65	118
16.00	406	8.48	215	6.11	155	4.58	116
15.75	400	8.35	212	6.01	153	4.51	115
15.50	394	8.22	209	5.92	150	4.44	113
15.25	387	8.08	205	5.82	148	4.37	111
15.00	381	7.95	202	5.72	145	4.29	109
14.75	375	7.82	199	5.63	143	4.22	107
14.50	368	7.69	195	5.54	141	4.15	105
14.25	362	7.55	192	5.44	138	4.08	104
14.00	356	7.42	188	5.34	136	4.01	102
13.75	349	7.29	185	5.25	133	3.94	100
13.50	343	7.16	182	5.16	131	3.87	98
13.25	337	7.02	178	5.05	128	3.79	96
13.00	330	6.89	175	4.96	126	3.72	94
12.75	324	6.76	172	4.87	124	3.65	93
12.50	318	6.63	168	4.77	121	3.58	91
12.25	311	6.49	165	4.67	119	3.50	89
12.00	305	6.36	162	4.58	116	3.44	87
11.75	298	6.23	158	4.49	114	3.37	86
11.50	292	6.10	155	4.39	112	3.29	84

Table 5–8. Deep Drawing Stock—0.045 inch (1.143 mm) Thick (*Continued*).

Blank Diameter		First Draw		Second Draw		Third Draw	
		47% Reduction		28% Reduction		25% Reduction	
D		d		d_1		d_2	
inch	mm	inch	mm	inch	mm	inch	mm
11.25	286	5.96	151	4.29	109	3.22	82
11.00	279	5.83	148	4.20	107	3.15	80
10.75	273	5.70	145	4.10	104	3.08	78
10.50	267	5.57	141	4.01	102	3.01	76
10.25	260	5.43	138	3.91	99	2.93	74
10.00	254	5.30	135	3.82	97	2.87	73
9.75	248	5.17	131	3.72	94	2.79	71
9.50	241	5.04	128	3.63	92	2.72	69
9.25	235	4.90	125	3.53	90	2.65	67
9.00	229	4.77	121	3.43	87	2.57	65
8.75	222	4.64	118	3.34	85	2.51	64
8.50	216	4.51	115	3.25	83	2.44	62
8.25	210	4.37	111	3.15	80	2.36	60
8.00	203	4.24	108	3.05	77	2.29	58
7.75	197	4.11	104	2.96	75	2.22	56
7.50	191	3.98	101	2.87	73	2.15	55
7.25	184	3.84	98	2.76	70	2.07	53
7.00	178	3.71	94	2.67	68	2.00	51
6.75	171	3.58	91	2.58	66	1.94	49
6.50	165	3.45	88	2.48	63	1.86	47
6.25	159	3.31	84	2.38	60	1.79	45
6.00	152	3.18	81	2.29	58	1.72	44
5.75	146	3.05	77	2.20	56	1.65	42
5.50	140	2.92	74	2.10	53	1.58	40
5.25	133	2.78	71	2.00	51	1.50	38
5.00	127	2.65	67	1.91	49	1.43	36
4.75	121	2.52	64	1.81	46	1.36	35
4.50	114	2.39	61	1.72	44	1.29	33
4.25	108	2.25	57	1.62	41	1.22	31
4.00	102	2.12	53	1.53	39	1.15	29
3.75	95	1.99	51	1.43	36	1.07	27
3.50	89	1.86	47	1.34	34	1.01	26
3.25	83	1.72	44	1.24	31	0.93	24
3.00	76	1.59	40	1.14	29	0.86	22
2.75	70	1.46	37	1.05	27	0.79	20
2.50	64	1.33	34	0.96	24	0.72	18
2.00	51	1.06	27	0.76	19	0.57	14

Table 5–9. Deep Drawing Stock—0.050 inch (1.270 mm) Thick.

Blank Diameter		First Draw		Second Draw		Third Draw	
		47% Reduction		29% Reduction		26% Reduction	
D		d		d_1		d_2	
inch	mm	inch	mm	inch	mm	inch	mm
20.00	508	10.60	269	7.53	191	5.57	141
19.75	502	10.47	266	7.43	189	5.50	140
19.50	495	10.34	263	7.34	186	5.43	138
19.25	489	10.20	259	7.24	184	5.36	136
19.00	483	10.07	256	7.15	182	5.29	134
18.75	476	9.94	252	7.06	179	5.22	133
18.50	470	9.81	249	6.97	177	5.16	131
18.25	464	9.67	246	6.87	174	5.08	129
18.00	457	9.54	242	6.77	172	5.01	127
17.75	451	9.41	239	6.68	170	4.94	125
17.50	444	9.28	236	6.59	167	4.88	124
17.25	438	9.14	232	6.49	165	4.80	122
17.00	432	9.01	229	6.40	163	4.74	120
16.75	425	8.88	226	6.30	160	4.66	118
16.50	419	8.75	222	6.21	158	4.60	117
16.25	413	8.61	219	6.11	155	4.52	115
16.00	406	8.48	215	6.02	153	4.45	113
15.75	400	8.35	212	5.93	151	4.39	112
15.50	394	8.22	209	5.84	148	4.32	110
15.25	387	8.08	205	5.74	146	4.25	108
15.00	381	7.95	202	5.64	143	4.17	106
14.75	375	7.82	199	5.55	141	4.11	104
14.50	368	7.69	195	5.50	140	4.07	103
14.25	362	7.55	192	5.36	136	3.97	101
14.00	356	7.42	188	5.27	134	3.90	99
13.75	349	7.29	185	5.18	132	3.83	97
13.50	343	7.16	182	5.08	129	3.76	96
13.25	337	7.02	178	4.98	126	3.69	94
13.00	330	6.89	175	4.89	124	3.62	92
12.75	324	6.76	172	4.80	122	3.55	90
12.50	318	6.63	168	4.71	120	3.49	89
12.25	311	6.49	165	4.61	117	3.41	87
12.00	305	6.36	162	4.52	115	3.34	85
11.75	298	6.23	158	4.42	112	3.27	83
11.50	292	6.10	155	4.33	110	3.20	81

Table 5–9. Deep Drawing Stock—0.050 inch (1.270 mm) Thick *(Continued).*

Blank Diameter		First Draw		Second Draw		Third Draw	
		47% Reduction		29% Reduction		26% Reduction	
D		*d*		*d₁*		*d₂*	
inch	mm	inch	mm	inch	mm	inch	mm
11.25	286	5.96	151	4.23	107	3.13	80
11.00	279	5.83	148	4.14	105	3.06	78
10.75	273	5.70	145	4.05	103	3.00	76
10.50	267	5.57	141	3.95	100	2.92	74
10.25	260	5.43	138	3.86	98	2.86	73
10.00	254	5.30	135	3.76	96	2.78	71
9.75	248	5.17	131	3.67	93	2.72	69
9.50	241	5.04	128	3.58	91	2.65	67
9.25	235	4.90	124	3.48	88	2.58	66
9.00	229	4.77	121	3.39	86	2.51	64
8.75	222	4.64	118	3.29	84	2.43	62
8.50	216	4.51	115	3.20	81	2.37	60
8.25	210	4.37	111	3.10	79	2.29	58
8.00	203	4.24	108	3.01	76	2.23	57
7.75	197	4.11	104	2.92	74	2.16	55
7.50	191	3.98	101	2.83	72	2.09	53
7.25	184	3.84	98	2.73	69	2.02	51
7.00	178	3.71	94	2.63	77	1.95	50
6.75	171	3.58	91	2.54	65	1.88	48
6.50	165	3.45	88	2.45	62	1.81	46
6.25	159	3.31	84	2.35	60	1.74	44
6.00	152	3.18	81	2.26	57	1.67	42
5.75	146	3.05	77	2.17	55	1.61	41
5.50	140	2.92	74	2.07	53	1.53	39
5.25	133	2.78	71	1.97	50	1.46	37
5.00	127	2.65	67	1.88	48	1.39	35
4.75	121	2.52	64	1.79	45	1.32	34
4.50	114	2.39	61	1.70	43	1.26	32
4.25	108	2.25	57	1.60	41	1.18	30
4.00	102	2.12	54	1.51	38	1.12	28
3.75	95	1.99	51	1.41	36	1.04	26
3.50	89	1.86	47	1.32	34	0.98	25
3.25	83	1.72	44	1.22	31	0.90	23
3.00	76	1.59	40	1.13	29	0.84	21
2.75	70	1.46	37	1.04	26	0.77	20
2.50	64	1.33	34	0.94	24	0.70	18
2.00	51	1.06	27	0.75	19	0.56	14

Table 5–10. Deep Drawing Stock—0.055 inch (1.397 mm) Thick.

Blank Diameter		First Draw		Second Draw		Third Draw	
		48% Reduction		29% Reduction		26% Reduction	
D		**d**		**d₁**		**d₂**	
inch	*mm*	*inch*	*mm*	*inch*	*mm*	*inch*	*mm*
20.00	508	10.40	264	7.38	187	5.46	139
19.75	502	10.27	261	7.29	185	5.39	137
19.50	495	10.14	258	7.20	183	5.33	135
19.25	489	10.01	254	7.11	181	5.26	134
19.00	483	9.88	251	7.01	178	5.19	132
18.75	476	9.75	248	6.92	176	5.12	130
18.50	470	9.62	244	6.83	173	5.05	128
18.25	464	9.49	241	6.74	171	4.99	127
18.00	457	9.36	238	6.65	169	4.92	125
17.75	451	9.23	234	6.55	166	4.85	123
17.50	444	9.10	231	6.46	164	4.78	121
17.25	438	8.97	228	6.37	162	4.71	120
17.00	432	8.84	225	6.28	160	4.65	118
16.75	425	8.71	221	6.18	157	4.57	116
16.50	419	8.58	218	6.09	155	4.51	115
16.25	413	8.45	215	6.00	152	4.44	113
16.00	406	8.32	211	5.90	150	4.37	111
15.75	400	8.19	208	5.81	148	4.30	109
15.50	394	8.06	205	5.72	145	4.23	107
15.25	387	7.93	201	5.63	143	4.17	106
15.00	381	7.80	198	5.54	141	4.10	104
14.75	375	7.67	195	5.45	138	4.03	102
14.50	368	7.54	192	5.35	136	3.96	101
14.25	362	7.41	188	5.26	134	3.89	98
14.00	356	7.28	185	5.17	131	3.83	97
13.75	349	7.15	182	5.08	129	3.76	96
13.50	343	7.02	178	4.98	126	3.69	94
13.25	337	6.89	175	4.89	124	3.62	92
13.00	330	6.76	172	4.80	122	3.55	90
12.75	324	6.63	168	4.71	120	3.49	89
12.50	318	6.50	165	4.62	117	3.42	87
12.25	311	6.37	162	4.52	115	3.35	85
12.00	305	6.24	158	4.43	113	3.28	83
11.75	298	6.11	155	4.34	110	3.21	82
11.50	292	5.98	152	4.25	108	3.15	80

Table 5–10. Deep Drawing Stock—0.055 inch (1.397 mm) Thick *(Continued)*.

Blank Diameter		First Draw		Second Draw		Third Draw	
		48% Reduction		29% Reduction		26% Reduction	
D		d		d_1		d_2	
inch	mm	inch	mm	inch	mm	inch	mm
11.25	286	5.85	149	4.15	105	3.07	78
11.00	279	5.72	145	4.06	103	3.00	76
10.75	273	5.59	142	3.97	101	2.94	75
10.50	267	5.46	139	3.88	99	2.87	73
10.25	260	5.33	135	3.78	96	2.80	71
10.00	254	5.20	132	3.69	94	2.73	69
9.75	248	5.07	129	3.60	91	2.66	68
9.50	241	4.94	125	3.51	89	2.60	66
9.25	235	4.81	122	3.42	87	2.53	64
9.00	229	4.68	119	3.32	84	2.56	62
8.75	222	4.55	116	3.23	82	2.39	61
8.50	216	4.42	112	3.14	80	2.32	59
8.25	210	4.29	109	3.05	77	2.26	57
8.00	203	4.16	106	2.95	75	2.18	55
7.75	197	4.03	102	2.10	53	1.55	39
7.50	191	3.90	99	2.03	52	1.50	38
7.25	184	3.77	96	1.96	50	1.45	37
7.00	178	3.64	92	1.89	48	1.40	36
6.75	171	3.51	89	1.83	46	1.35	34
6.50	165	3.38	86	1.76	45	1.30	33
6.25	159	3.25	83	1.69	43	1.25	32
6.00	152	3.12	79	1.62	41	1.20	30
5.75	146	2.99	76	1.55	39	1.15	29
5.50	140	2.86	73	1.49	38	1.10	28
5.25	133	2.73	69	1.42	36	1.05	27
5.00	127	2.60	66	1.35	34	1.00	25
4.75	121	2.47	63	1.28	33	0.95	24
4.50	114	2.34	59	1.22	31	0.90	23
4.25	108	2.21	56	1.15	29	0.85	22
4.00	102	2.08	53	1.08	27	0.80	20
3.75	95	1.95	50	1.01	26	0.75	19
3.50	89	1.82	46	0.95	24	0.70	18
3.25	83	1.69	43	0.88	22	0.65	17
3.00	76	1.56	40	0.81	21	0.60	15
2.75	70	1.43	36	0.74	19	0.55	14
2.50	64	1.30	33	0.68	17	0.50	13
2.00	51	1.04	26	0.54	14	0.40	10

223

Table 5–11.   Deep Drawing Stock—0.060 to 0.125 inch (1.524 to 3.175 mm) Thick.

Blank Diameter		First Draw		Second Draw		Third Draw	
		48% Reduction		30% Reduction		27% Reduction	
D		d		d_1		d_2	
inch	mm	inch	mm	inch	mm	inch	mm
20.00	508	10.40	264	7.28	185	5.31	135
19.75	502	10.27	261	7.19	183	5.25	133
19.50	495	10.14	258	7.10	180	5.18	132
19.25	489	10.01	254	7.01	178	5.12	130
19.00	483	9.88	251	6.92	176	5.05	128
18.75	476	9.75	248	6.83	173	4.99	127
18.50	470	9.62	244	6.73	171	4.91	125
18.25	464	9.49	241	6.64	169	4.85	123
18.00	457	9.36	238	6.55	166	4.78	121
17.75	451	9.23	234	6.46	164	4.72	120
17.50	444	9.10	231	6.37	162	4.65	.118
17.25	438	8.97	228	6.28	160	4.58	116
17.00	432	8.84	225	6.19	157	4.52	115
16.75	425	8.71	221	6.10	155	4.45	113
16.50	419	8.58	218	6.01	153	4.39	112
16.25	413	8.45	215	5.92	150	4.32	110
16.00	406	8.32	211	5.82	148	4.25	108
15.75	400	8.19	208	5.73	146	4.18	106
15.50	394	8.06	205	5.64	143	4.12	105
15.25	387	7.93	201	5.55	141	4.05	103
15.00	381	7.80	198	5.46	139	3.99	101
14.75	375	7.67	195	5.37	136	3.92	100
14.50	368	7.54	192	5.28	134	3.85	98
14.25	362	7.41	188	5.19	132	3.79	96
14.00	356	7.28	185	5.10	130	3.72	94
13.75	349	7.15	182	5.01	127	3.66	93
13.50	343	7.02	178	4.91	125	3.58	91
13.25	337	6.89	175	4.82	122	3.52	89
13.00	330	6.76	172	4.73	120	3.45	88
12.75	324	6.63	168	4.64	118	3.39	86
12.50	318	6.50	165	4.55	116	3.32	84
12.25	311	6.37	162	4.46	113	3.26	83
12.00	305	6.24	158	4.37	111	3.19	81
11.75	298	6.11	155	4.28	109	3.12	79
11.50	292	5.98	152	4.19	106	3.06	78

Table 5–11. Deep Drawing Stock—0.060 to 0.125 inch (1.524 to 3.175 mm) Thick *(Continued)*.

Blank Diameter		First Draw		Second Draw		Third Draw	
		48% Reduction		30% Reduction		27% Reduction	
D		d		d_1		d_2	
inch	mm	inch	mm	inch	mm	inch	mm
11.25	286	5.85	149	4.10	104	2.99	76
11.00	279	5.72	145	4.00	102	2.92	74
10.75	273	5.59	142	3.91	99	2.85	72
10.50	267	5.46	139	3.82	97	2.79	71
10.25	260	5.33	135	3.73	95	2.72	69
10.00	254	5.20	132	3.64	92	2.66	68
9.75	248	5.07	129	3.55	90	2.59	66
9.50	241	4.94	125	3.46	88	2.53	64
9.25	235	4.81	122	3.37	86	2.46	62
9.00	229	4.68	119	3.28	83	2.39	61
8.75	222	4.55	116	3.19	81	2.33	59
8.50	216	4.42	112	3.09	78	2.26	57
8.25	210	4.29	109	3.00	76	2.19	56
8.00	203	4.16	106	2.91	74	2.12	54
7.75	197	4.03	102	2.82	72	2.06	52
7.50	191	3.90	99	2.73	69	1.99	51
7.25	184	3.77	96	2.64	67	1.93	49
7.00	178	3.64	92	2.45	65	1.79	47
6.75	171	3.51	89	2.46	62	1.80	46
6.50	165	3.38	86	2.37	60	1.73	44
6.25	159	3.25	83	2.28	58	1.66	42
6.00	152	3.12	79	2.18	55	1.59	40
5.75	146	2.99	76	2.09	53	1.53	39
5.50	140	2.86	73	2.00	51	1.46	37
5.25	133	2.73	69	1.91	49	1.39	35
5.00	127	2.60	66	1.82	46	1.33	34
4.75	121	2.47	63	1.73	44	1.26	32
4.50	114	2.34	59	1.64	42	1.20	30
4.25	108	2.21	56	1.55	39	1.13	29
4.00	102	2.08	53	1.46	37	1.07	27
3.75	95	1.95	50	1.37	35	1.00	25
3.50	89	1.82	46	1.27	32	0.93	24
3.25	83	1.69	43	1.18	30	0.86	22
3.00	76	1.56	40	1.09	28	0.80	20
2.75	70	1.43	36	1.00	25	0.73	19
2.50	64	1.30	33	0.91	23	0.66	17
2.00	51	1.04	26	0.73	19	0.53	13

Table 5–12.   Deep Drawing Stock—0.125 to 0.250 inch (3.175 to 6.350 mm) Thick.

Blank Diameter		First Draw		Second Draw		Third Draw	
		47% Reduction		28% Reduction		26% Reduction	
D		d		d_1		d_2	
inch	mm	inch	mm	inch	mm	inch	mm
20.00	508	10.60	269	7.63	194	5.65	144
19.75	502	10.47	266	7.54	192	5.58	142
19.50	495	10.34	263	7.44	189	5.51	140
19.25	489	10.20	259	7.34	186	5.43	138
19.00	483	10.07	256	7.25	184	5.37	136
18.75	476	9.94	252	7.16	182	5.30	135
18.50	470	9.81	249	7.06	179	5.22	133
18.25	464	9.67	246	6.96	177	5.15	131
18.00	457	9.54	242	6.87	174	5.08	129
17.75	451	9.41	239	6.78	172	5.02	128
17.50	444	9.28	236	6.68	170	4.94	125
17.25	438	9.14	232	6.58	167	4.87	124
17.00	432	9.01	229	6.49	165	4.80	122
16.75	425	8.88	226	6.39	162	4.73	120
16.50	419	8.75	222	6.30	160	4.66	118
16.25	413	8.61	219	6.20	157	4.59	117
16.00	406	8.48	215	6.11	155	4.52	115
15.75	400	8.35	212	6.01	153	4.45	113
15.50	394	8.22	209	5.92	150	4.38	111
15.25	387	8.08	205	5.82	148	4.31	109
15.00	381	7.95	202	5.72	145	4.23	107
14.75	375	7.82	199	5.63	143	4.17	106
14.50	368	7.69	195	5.54	141	4.10	104
14.25	362	7.55	192	5.44	138	4.03	102
14.00	356	7.42	188	5.34	136	3.95	100
13.75	349	7.29	185	5.25	133	3.86	98
13.50	343	7.16	182	5.16	131	3.82	97
13.25	337	7.02	178	5.05	128	3.74	95
13.00	330	6.89	175	4.96	126	3.67	93
12.75	324	6.76	172	4.87	124	3.60	91
12.50	318	6.63	168	4.77	121	3.53	90
12.25	311	6.49	165	4.67	119	3.46	88
12.00	305	6.36	162	4.58	116	3.39	86
11.75	298	6.23	158	4.49	114	3.32	84
11.50	292	6.10	155	4.39	112	3.25	83

226

Table 5–12. Deep Drawing Stock—0.125 to 0.250 inch (3.175 to 6.350 mm) Thick *(Continued).*

Blank Diameter		First Draw		Second Draw		Third Draw	
		47% Reduction		28% Reduction		26% Reduction	
D		*d*		d_1		d_2	
inch	*mm*	*inch*	*mm*	*inch*	*mm*	*inch*	*mm*
11.25	286	5.96	151	4.29	109	3.17	81
11.00	279	5.83	148	4.20	107	3.11	79
10.75	273	5.70	145	4.10	104	3.03	77
10.50	267	5.57	141	4.01	102	2.97	75
10.25	260	5.43	138	3.91	99	2.89	73
10.00	254	5.30	135	3.82	97	2.83	72
9.75	248	5.17	131	3.72	94	2.75	70
9.50	241	5.04	128	3.63	92	2.69	68
9.25	235	4.90	124	3.53	90	2.61	66
9.00	229	4.77	121	3.43	87	2.54	65
8.75	222	4.64	118	3.34	85	2.47	63
8.50	216	4.51	115	3.25	83	2.41	61
8.25	210	4.37	111	3.15	80	2.33	59
8.00	203	4.24	108	3.05	77	2.26	57
7.75	197	4.11	104	2.96	75	2.19	56
7.50	191	3.98	101	2.87	73	2.12	54
7.25	184	3.84	98	2.76	70	2.04	52
7.00	178	3.71	94	2.67	68	1.98	50
6.75	171	3.58	91	2.58	66	1.91	49
6.50	165	3.45	88	2.48	63	1.84	47
6.25	159	3.31	84	2.38	60	1.76	45
6.00	152	3.18	81	2.29	58	1.69	43
5.75	146	3.05	77	2.20	56	1.63	41
5.50	140	2.92	74	2.10	53	1.55	39
5.25	133	2.78	71	2.00	51	1.48	38
5.00	127	2.65	67	1.91	49	1.41	36
4.75	121	2.52	64	1.81	46	1.34	34
4.50	114	2.39	61	1.72	44	1.27	32
4.25	108	2.25	57	1.62	41	1.20	30
4.00	102	2.12	54	1.53	39	1.13	29
3.75	95	1.99	51	1.43	36	1.06	27
3.50	89	1.86	47	1.34	34	0.99	25
3.25	83	1.72	44	1.24	31	0.92	23
3.00	76	1.59	40	1.14	29	0.84	21
2.75	70	1.46	37	1.05	27	0.78	20
2.50	64	1.33	34	0.96	24	0.71	18
2.00	51	1.06	27	0.76	19	0.56	14

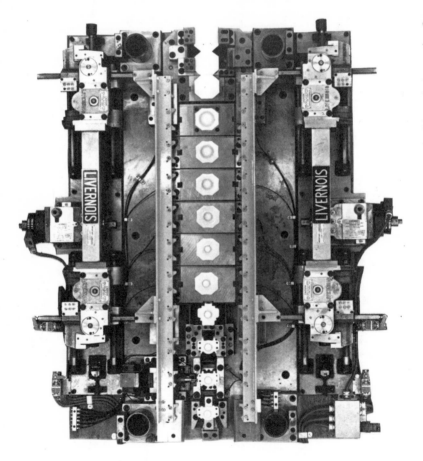

Twelve station transfer die. Photo courtesy Livernois Automation Co.

Sine Plate Settings

FIVE-INCH SINE BAR SETTINGS

The table in this section provides English and metric settings for a 5-inch sine bar for all angles from 0° to 54°. Should a 10-inch bar be used, the tabular figures given should be multiplied by 2.

Shown below is the correct design for a sine bar. It will be noted that this design lends itself to easy correction during the initial grinding. With continued use and the passage of time, the sine bar may "go out," which is to say that it may undergo varying degrees of distortion. Again, this design provides for easy, fast correction.

The holes through the sine bar lighten and strengthen the tool. They also provide a way to bolt the bar to an angle plate—a virtual necessity, since most sine bar work is done in conjuction with an angle plate.

Sine bar design is based on the basic sine function. That is, the sine of an angle equals the side opposite the angle divided by the hypotenuse. Thus,

$$\text{sine } \alpha = \frac{A}{5}$$

Since A is the gage block buildup required,

$$A = 5 \, (\text{sine } \alpha)$$

This table provides the values of A needed to set the bar to all angles through 54°.

A minor problem is presented in that many gage block sets do not provide for dimensions of less then 0.1000. As an example, the setting for 0° 2′ is 0.0029, a dimension beyond the capabilities of a standard gage block set.

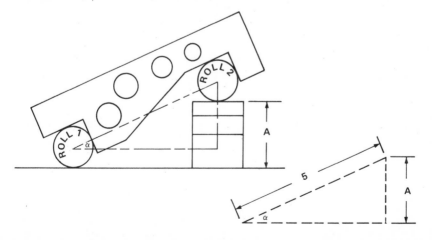

Sine Plate Settings

Min	0° Inch	0° mm	1° Inch	1° mm	2° Inch	2° mm	3° Inch	3° mm	4° Inch	4° mm
0	0.00000	0.000 00	0.08725	2.216 15	0.17450	4.432 30	0.26170	6.647 18	0.34880	8.859 52
1	.00145	.036 83	.08870	.252 98	.17595	.469 13	.26315	.684 01	.35025	.896 35
2	.00290	.073 66	.09015	.289 81	.17740	.505 96	.26460	.720 84	.35170	.933 18
3	.00435	.110 49	.09160	.326 64	.17885	.542 79	.26605	.757 67	.35315	.970 01
4	.00580	.147 32	.09310	.364 74	.18030	.579 62	.26750	.794 50	.35460	9.006 84
5	.00725	.184 15	.09455	2.401 57	.18175	4.616 45	.26895	6.831 33	.35605	9.043 67
6	.00875	.222 25	.09600	.438 40	.18320	.635 28	.27040	.868 16	.35750	.080 50
7	.01020	.259 08	.09745	.475 23	.18465	.690 11	.27185	.904 99	.35895	.117 33
8	.01165	.295 91	.09890	.512 06	.18615	.728 21	.27330	.941 82	.36040	.154 16
9	.01310	.332 74	.10035	.548 89	.18760	.765 04	.27475	.978 65	.36185	.190 99
10	.01455	.369 57	.10180	2.585 72	.18905	4.801 87	.27620	7.015 48	.36330	9.227 82
11	.01600	.406 40	.10325	.622 55	.19050	.838 70	.27765	.052 31	.36475	.264 65
12	.01745	.443 23	.10470	.659 38	.19195	.875 53	.27910	.089 14	.36620	.301 48
13	.01890	.480 06	.10615	.696 21	.19340	.912 36	.28055	.125 97	.36765	.338 31
14	.02035	.516 89	.10760	.733 04	.19485	.949 19	.28200	.162 80	.36910	.375 14
15	.02180	.553 72	.10905	2.769 87	.19630	4.986 02	.28345	7.199 63	.37055	9.411 97
16	.02325	.590 55	.11055	.807 97	.19775	5.022 85	.28490	.236 46	.37200	.448 80
17	.02475	.628 65	.11200	.844 80	.19920	.059 68	.28635	.273 29	.37345	.485 63
18	.02620	.665 48	.11345	.881 63	.20065	.096 51	.28780	.310 12	.37490	.522 46
19	.02765	.702 31	.11490	.918 46	.20210	.133 34	.28925	.346 95	.37635	.559 29
20	.02910	.739 14	.11635	2.955 29	.20355	5.170 17	.29070	7.383 78	.37780	9.596 12
21	.03055	.775 97	.11780	.992 12	.20500	.207 00	.29220	.421 88	.37925	.632 95
22	.03200	.812 80	.11925	3.028 95	.20645	.243 83	.29365	.458 71	.38070	.669 78
23	.03345	.849 63	.12070	.065 78	.20795	.281 93	.29510	.495 54	.38215	.706 61
24	.03490	.886 46	.12215	.102 61	.20940	.318 76	.29655	.532 37	.38360	.743 44
25	.03635	.923 29	.12360	3.139 44	.21085	5.355 59	.29800	7.569 20	.38505	9.780 27
26	.03780	.960 12	.12505	.176 27	.21230	.392 42	.29945	.606 03	.38650	.817 10
27	.03925	.996 95	.12650	.213 10	.21375	.529 25	.30090	.642 86	.38795	.853 93

28	.04070	1.033 78	.12800	.251 20	.21520	.466 08	.30235	.679 69	.38940	.890 76
29	.04220	.071 88	.12945	.288 03	.21665	.502 91	.30380	.716 52	.39085	.927 59
30	0.04365	1.108 71	0.13090	3.324 86	0.21810	5.539 74	0.30525	7.753 35	0.39230	9.964 42
31	.04510	.145 54	.13235	.361 69	.21955	.576 57	.30670	.790 18	.39375	10.001 25
32	.04655	.182 37	.13380	.398 52	.22100	.613 40	.30815	.827 01	.39520	.038 08
33	.04800	.219 20	.13525	.435 35	.22245	.650 23	.30960	.863 84	.29665	.074 91
34	.04945	.256 03	.13670	.472 18	.22390	.687 06	.31105	.900 67	.39810	.111 74
35	0.05090	1.292 86	0.13815	3.509 01	0.22535	5.723 89	0.31250	7.937 50	0.39955	10.148 57
36	.05235	.329 69	.13960	.545 84	.22680	.760 72	.31395	.974 33	.40100	.185 40
37	.05380	.366 52	.14105	.582 67	.22825	.797 55	.31540	8.011 16	.40245	.222 23
38	.05525	.403 35	.14250	.619 50	.22970	.834 38	.31685	.047 99	.40390	.259 06
39	.05670	.440 18	.14395	.656 33	.23115	.871 21	.31830	.084 82	.40535	.295 89
40	0.05820	1.478 28	0.14540	3.693 16	0.23265	5.909 31	0.31975	8.121 65	0.40680	10.332 72
41	.05965	.515 11	.14690	.731 26	.23410	.946 14	.32120	.158 48	.40825	.369 55
42	.06110	.551 94	.14835	.768 09	.23555	.982 97	.32265	.195 31	.40970	.406 38
43	.06255	.588 77	.14980	.804 92	.23700	6.019 80	.32410	.232 14	.41115	.443 21
44	.06400	.625 60	.15125	.841 75	.23845	.056 63	.32555	.268 97	.41260	.480 04
45	0.06545	1.662 43	0.15270	3.878 58	0.23990	6.093 46	0.32700	8.305 80	0.41405	10.516 87
46	.06690	.699 26	.15415	.915 41	.24135	.130 29	.32845	.342 63	.41550	.553 70
47	.06835	.736 09	.15560	.952 24	.24280	.167 12	.32990	.379 46	.46195	.590 53
48	.06980	.772 92	.15705	.989 07	.24425	.203 95	.33135	.416 29	.41840	.627 36
49	.07125	.809 75	.15850	4.025 90	.24570	.240 78	.33280	.453 12	.41985	.664 19
50	0.07270	1.846 58	0.15995	4.062 73	0.24715	6.277 61	0.33425	8.489 95	0.42130	10.701 02
51	.07415	.883 41	.16140	.099 56	.24860	.314 44	.33570	.526 78	.42275	.737 85
52	.07565	.921 51	.16285	.136 39	.25005	.351 27	.33715	.563 61	.42420	.774 68
53	.07710	.958 34	.16430	.173 22	.25150	.388 10	.33865	.601 71	.42565	.811 51
54	.07855	.995 17	.16580	.211 32	.25295	.424 93	.34010	.638 54	.42710	.848 34
55	0.08000	2.032 00	0.16725	4.248 15	0.25440	6.461 76	0.34155	8.675 37	0.42855	10.885 17
56	.08145	.068 83	.16870	.284 98	.25585	.498 59	.34300	.712 20	.43000	.922 00
57	.08290	.105 66	.17015	.321 81	.25730	.535 42	.34445	.749 03	.43145	.958 83
58	.08435	.142 49	.17160	.358 64	.25875	.572 25	.34590	.785 86	.43290	.995 66
59	.08580	.179 32	.17305	.395 47	.26028	.611 11	.34735	.822 69	.43435	11.032 49
60	0.08725	2.216 15	0.17450	4.432 30	0.26170	6.647 18	0.34880	8.859 52	0.43580	11.069 32

Sine Plate Settings (Continued).

Min	5° Inch	5° mm	6° Inch	6° mm	7° Inch	7° mm	8° Inch	8° mm	9° Inch	9° mm
0	0.43580	11.069 32	0.52265	13.275 31	0.60935	15.477 49	0.69585	17.674 59	0.78215	19.866 61
1	.43720	.104 88	.52410	.312 14	.61080	.514 32	.69730	.711 42	.78360	.903 44
2	.43865	.141 71	.52555	.348 97	.61225	.551 15	.69875	.748 25	.78505	.940 27
3	.44010	.178 54	.52700	.385 80	.61370	.587 98	.70020	.785 08	.78650	.977 10
4	.44155	.215 37	.52845	.422 63	.61510	.623 54	.70165	.821 91	.78790	20.012 66
5	0.44300	11.252 20	0.52985	13.458 19	0.61655	15.660 37	0.70305	17.857 47	0.78935	20.049 49
6	.44445	.289 03	.53130	.495 02	.61800	.697 20	.70450	.894 30	.79080	.086 32
7	.44590	.325 86	.53275	.531 85	.61945	.734 03	.70595	.931 13	.79225	.123 15
8	.44735	.362 69	.53420	.568 68	.62090	.770 86	.70740	.967 96	.79365	.158 71
9	.44880	.399 52	.53565	.605 76	.62235	.807 69	.70885	18.004 79	.79510	.195 54
10	0.45025	11.436 35	0.53710	13.642 34	0.62380	15.844 52	0.71025	18.040 35	0.79655	20.232 37
11	.45170	.473 18	.53855	.679 17	.62520	.880 08	.71170	.077 18	.79795	.267 93
12	.45315	.510 01	.54000	.716 00	.62665	.916 91	.71315	.114 01	.79940	.304 76
13	.45460	.546 84	.54145	.752 83	.62810	.953 74	.71460	.150 84	.80085	.341 59
14	.45605	.583 67	.54290	.789 66	.62955	.990 57	.71600	.186 40	.80230	.378 42
15	0.45750	11.620 50	0.54435	13.826 49	0.63100	16.027 40	0.71745	18.223 23	0.80370	20.413 98
16	.45895	.657 33	.54580	.863 32	.63245	.064 23	.71890	.260 06	.80515	.450 81
17	.46040	.694 16	.54725	.900 15	.63390	.101 06	.72035	.296 89	.80660	.487 64
18	.46185	.730 99	.54865	.935 71	.63530	.136 62	.72180	.333 72	.80800	.523 20
19	.46330	.767 82	.55010	.972 54	.63675	.173 45	.72320	.369 28	.80945	.560 03
20	0.46475	11.804 65	0.55155	14.009 37	0.63820	16.210 28	0.72465	18.406 11	0.81090	20.596 86
21	.46620	.841 48	.55300	.046 20	.63965	.247 11	.72610	.442 94	.81230	.632 42
22	.46765	.878 31	.55445	.083 03	.64110	.283 94	.72755	.479 77	.81375	.669 25
23	.46910	.915 14	.55590	.119 86	.64255	.320 77	.72900	.516 60	.81520	.706 08
24	.47055	.951 97	.55735	.156 69	.64400	.357 60	.73040	.552 16	.81665	.742 91
25	0.47200	11.988 80	0.55880	14.193 52	0.64540	16.393 16	0.73185	18.588 99	0.81805	20.778 47
26	.47345	12.025 63	.56025	.230 35	.64685	.429 99	.73330	.625 82	.81950	.815 30
27	.47490	.062 46	.56170	.267 18	.64830	.466 82	.73475	.662 65	.82095	.852 13

28	.47635	.099 29	.56315	.304 01	.64975	.503 65	.73615	.698 21	.82235	.887 69
29	.47780	.136 12	.56455	.339 57	.65120	.540 48	.73760	.735 04	.82380	.924 52
30	0.47925	12.172 95	0.56600	14.376 40	0.65265	16.577 31	0.73905	18.771 87	0.82525	20.961 35
31	.48070	.209 78	.56745	.413 23	.65405	.612 87	.74050	.808 70	.82665	.996 91
32	.48210	.245 34	.56890	.450 06	.65550	.649 70	.74190	.844 26	.82810	21.033 74
33	.48355	.282 17	.57035	.486 89	.65695	.686 53	.74335	.881 09	.82955	.070 57
34	.48500	.319 00	.57180	.523 72	.65840	.723 36	.74480	.917 92	.83100	.107 40
35	0.48645	12.355 83	0.57325	14.560 55	0.65985	16.760 19	0.74625	18.954 75	0.83240	21.142 96
36	.48790	.392 66	.57470	.597 38	.66130	.797 02	.74770	.991 58	.83385	.179 79
37	.48935	.429 49	.57615	.634 21	.66270	.832 58	.74910	19.027 14	.83530	.216 62
38	.49080	.466 32	.57760	.671 04	.66415	.869 41	.75055	.063 97	.83670	.252 18
39	.49225	.503 15	.57900	.706 60	.66560	.906 24	.75200	.100 80	.83815	.289 01
40	0.49370	12.539 98	0.58045	14.743 43	0.66705	16.943 07	0.75345	19.137 63	0.83960	21.325 84
41	.49515	.576 81	.58190	.780 26	.66850	.979 90	.75485	.173 19	.84100	.361 40
42	.49660	.613 64	.58335	.817 09	.66995	17.016 73	.75630	.210 02	.84245	.398 23
43	.49805	.650 47	.58480	.853 92	.67135	.052 29	.75775	.246 85	.84390	.435 06
44	.49950	.687 30	.58625	.890 75	.67280	.089 12	.75920	.283 68	.84530	.470 62
45	0.50095	12.724 13	0.58770	14.927 58	0.67425	17.125 95	0.76060	19.319 24	0.84675	21.507 45
46	.50240	.760 96	.58915	.964 41	.67570	.162 78	.76200	.354 80	.84820	.544 28
47	.50385	.797 79	.59060	15.001 24	.67715	.199 61	.76350	.392 90	.84960	.579 84
48	.50530	.834 62	.59200	.036 80	.67860	.236 44	.76495	.427 19	.85105	.616 67
49	.50675	.871 45	.59345	.073 63	.68000	.272 00	.76635	.465 29	.85250	.653 50
50	0.50820	12.908 28	0.59490	15.110 46	0.68145	17.308 83	0.76780	19.502 12	0.85390	21.689 06
51	.50960	.943 84	.59635	.147 29	.68290	.345 66	.76925	.538 95	.85535	.725 89
52	.51105	.980 67	.59780	.184 12	.68435	.382 49	.77070	.575 78	.85680	.762 72
53	.51250	13.017 50	.59925	.220 95	.68580	.419 32	.77210	.611 34	.85820	.798 28
54	.51395	.054 33	.60070	.257 78	.68720	.454 88	.77355	.648 17	.85965	.835 11
55	0.51540	13.091 16	0.60215	15.294 61	0.68865	17.491 71	0.77500	19.685 00	0.86110	21.871 94
56	.51685	.127 99	.60355	.330 17	.69010	.528 54	.77645	.721 83	.86250	.970 50
57	.51830	.164 82	.60500	.367 00	.69155	.565 37	.77785	.757 39	.86395	.944 33
58	.51975	.201 65	.60645	.403 83	.69300	.602 20	.77930	.794 22	.86540	.981 16
59	.52120	.238 48	.60790	.440 66	.69445	.639 03	.78075	.831 05	.86680	22.016 72
60	0.52265	13.275 31	0.60935	15.477 49	0.69585	17.674 59	0.78215	19.866 61	0.86825	22.053 55

Sine Plate Settings (Continued).

Min	10° Inch	10° mm	11° Inch	11° mm	12° Inch	12° mm	13° Inch	13° mm	14° Inch	14° mm
0	0.86825	22.053 55	0.95405	24.232 87	1.0395	26.403 30	1.1247	28.567 38	1.2096	30.723 84
1	.86965	.089 11	.95545	.268 43	.0410	.441 40	.1261	.602 94	.2110	.759 40
2	.87110	.125 94	.95690	.305 26	.0424	.476 96	.1276	.641 04	.2124	.794 96
3	.87255	.162 77	.95835	.342 09	.0438	.512 52	.1290	.676 60	.2138	.830 52
4	.87395	.198 33	.95975	.377 65	.0452	.548 08	.1304	.712 16	.2152	.866 08
5	.87540	22.235 16	.96120	24.414 48	.0466	26.583 64	.1318	28.747 72	.2166	30.901 64
6	.87685	.271 99	.96260	.450 04	.0481	.621 74	.1332	.783 28	.2181	.939 74
7	.87825	.307 55	.96405	.486 87	.0495	.657 30	.1346	.818 84	.2195	.975 30
8	.87970	.344 38	.96545	.522 43	.0509	.692 86	.1361	.856 94	.2209	31.010 86
9	.88115	.381 21	.96690	.559 26	.0523	.728 42	.1375	.892 50	.2223	.046 42
10	.88255	22.416 77	.96830	24.594 82	.0538	26.766 52	.1389	28.928 06	.2237	31.081 98
11	.88400	.453 60	.96975	.631 65	.0552	.802 08	.1403	.963 62	.2251	.117 54
12	.88540	.489 16	.97115	.667 21	.0566	.837 64	.1417	.999 18	.2265	.153 10
13	.88685	.525 99	.97260	.704 04	.0580	.873 20	.1431	29.034 74	.2279	.188 66
14	.88830	.562 82	.97405	.740 87	.0594	.908 76	.1446	.072 84	.2293	.224 22
15	.88970	22.598 38	.97545	24.776 43	.0609	26.946 86	.1460	29.108 40	.2307	31.259 78
16	.89115	.635 21	.97690	.813 26	.0623	.982 42	.1474	.143 96	.2322	.297 88
17	.89260	.672 04	.97830	.848 82	.0637	27.017 98	.1488	.179 52	.2336	.333 44
18	.89400	.707 60	.97975	.885 65	.0651	.053 54	.1502	.215 08	.2350	.369 00
19	.89545	.744 43	.98115	.921 21	.0665	.089 10	.1516	.250 64	.2364	.404 56
20	.89685	22.779 99	.98260	24.958 04	.0680	27.127 20	.1531	29.288 74	.2378	31.440 12
21	.89830	.816 82	.98400	.993 60	.0694	.162 76	.1545	.324 30	.2392	.475 68
22	.89975	.853 65	.98545	25.030 43	.0708	.198 32	.1559	.359 86	.2406	.511 24
23	.90115	.889 21	.98685	.065 99	.0722	.233 88	.1573	.395 42	.2420	.546 80
24	.90260	.926 04	.98830	.102 82	.0737	.271 98	.1587	.430 98	.2434	.582 36
25	.90405	22.962 87	.98970	25.138 38	.0751	27.307 54	.1601	29.466 54	.2448	31.617 92
26	.90545	.998 43	.99115	.175 21	.0765	.343 10	.1615	.502 10	.2462	.653 48
27	.90690	23.035 26	.99255	.210 77	.0779	.378 66	.1630	.540 20	.2477	.691 58

Min										
28	.727 14	.2491	.575 76	.1644	.414 22	.0793	.247 60	.99400	.070 82	.90830
29	.762 70	.2505	.611 32	.1658	.452 32	.0808	.283 16	.99540	.107 65	.90975
30	31.798 26	1.2519	29.646 88	1.1672	27.487 88	1.0822	25.319 99	0.99685	23.144 48	0.91120
31	.833 82	.2533	.682 44	.1686	.523 44	.0836	.355 55	.99825	.180 04	.91260
32	.869 38	.2547	.718 00	.1700	.559 00	.0850	.392 38	.99970	.216 87	.91405
33	.904 94	.2561	.753 56	.1714	.594 56	.0864	.427 94	1.0011	.252 43	.91545
34	.940 50	.2575	.791 66	.1729	.632 66	.0879	.466 04	.0026	.289 26	.91690
35	31.976 06	1.2589	29.827 22	1.1743	27.668 22	1.0893	25.499 06	1.0039	23.326 09	0.91835
36	32.011 62	.2603	.862 78	.1757	.703 78	.0907	.537 16	.0054	.361 65	.91975
37	.047 18	.2617	.898 34	.1771	.739 34	.0921	.572 72	.0068	.398 48	.92120
38	.082 74	.2631	.933 90	.1785	.774 90	.0935	.608 28	.0082	.434 04	.92260
39	.118 30	.2645	.969 46	.1799	.810 46	.0949	.643 84	.0096	.470 87	.92405
40	32.156 40	1.2660	30.005 02	1.1813	27.848 56	1.0964	25.679 40	1.0110	23.506 43	0.92545
41	.191 96	.2674	.043 12	.1828	.884 12	.0978	.717 50	.0125	.543 26	.92690
42	.227 52	.2688	.078 68	.1842	.919 68	.0992	.753 06	.0139	.580 09	.92835
43	.263 08	.2702	.114 24	.1856	.955 24	.1006	.788 62	.0153	.615 65	.92975
44	.298 64	.2716	.149 80	.1870	.990 80	.1020	.826 72	.0168	.652 48	.93120
45	32.334 20	1.2730	30.185 36	1.1884	28.028 90	1.1035	25.862 28	1.0182	23.688 04	0.93260
46	.369 76	.2744	.220 92	.1898	.064 46	.1049	.897 84	.0196	.724 87	.93405
47	.405 32	.2758	.256 48	.1912	.100 02	.1063	.933 40	.0210	.761 70	.93550
48	.440 88	.2772	.292 04	.1926	.135 58	.1077	.971 50	.0225	.797 26	.93690
49	.476 44	.2786	.330 14	.1941	.171 14	.1091	26.007 06	.0239	.834 09	.93835
50	32.512 00	1.2800	30.365 70	1.1955	28.209 24	1.1106	26.042 62	1.0253	23.869 65	0.93975
51	.547 56	.2814	.401 26	.1969	.244 80	.1120	.078 18	.0267	.906 48	.94120
52	.583 12	.2828	.436 82	.1983	.280 36	.1134	.113 74	.0281	.942 04	.94260
53	.618 68	.2842	.472 38	.1997	.315 92	.1148	.151 84	.0296	.978 87	.94405
54	.654 24	.2856	.507 94	.2011	.351 48	.1162	.187 40	.0310	24.015 70	.94550
55	32.689 80	1.2870	30.543 50	1.2025	28.287 04	1.1176	26.222 96	1.0324	24.051 26	0.94690
56	.725 36	.2884	.579 06	.2039	.425 14	.1191	.258 52	.0338	.088 09	.94835
57	.763 46	.2899	.617 16	.2054	.460 70	.1205	.296 62	.0353	.123 65	.94975
58	.799 02	.2913	.652 72	.2068	.496 26	.1219	.332 18	.0367	.160 48	.95120
59	.834 58	.2927	.688 28	.2082	.531 82	.1233	.367 74	.0381	.196 04	.95260
60	32.870 14	1.2941	30.723 84	1.2096	28.567 38	1.1247	26.403 30	0.0394	24.232 87	0.95405

Sine Plate Settings (Continued).

Min	15°		16°		17°		18°		19°	
	Inch	mm	Inch	mm	Inch	mm	Inch	mm	Inch	mm
0	1.2941	32.870 14	1.3782	35.006 28	1.4618	37.129 72	1.5451	39.245 54	1.6278	41.346 12
1	.2955	.905 70	.3796	.041 84	.4632	.165 28	.5464	.278 56	.6292	.381 68
2	.2969	.941 26	.3810	.077 40	.4646	.200 84	.5478	.314 12	.6306	.417 24
3	.2983	.976 82	.3824	.112 96	.4660	.236 40	.5492	.349 68	.6319	.450 26
4	.2997	33.012 38	.3838	.148 52	.4674	.271 96	.5506	.385 24	.6333	.485 82
5	1.3011	33.047 94	1.3852	35.184 08	1.4688	37.307 52	1.5520	39.420 80	1.6347	41.521 38
6	.3025	.083 50	.3865	.217 10	.4702	.343 08	.5534	.456 36	.6361	.556 94
7	.3039	.119 06	.3879	.252 66	.4716	.378 64	.5547	.489 38	.6374	.589 96
8	.3053	.154 62	.3893	.288 22	.4730	.414 20	.5561	.524 94	.6388	.625 52
9	.3067	.190 18	.3907	.323 78	.4743	.447 22	.5575	.560 50	.6402	.661 08
10	1.3081	33.225 74	1.3921	35.359 34	1.4757	37.482 78	1.5589	39.596 06	1.6416	41.696 64
11	.3095	.261 30	.3935	.394 90	.4771	.518 34	.5603	.631 62	.6429	.729 66
12	.3109	.296 86	.3949	.430 46	.4785	.553 90	.5616	.664 64	.6443	.765 22
13	.3123	.332 42	.3963	.466 02	.4799	.589 46	.5630	.700 20	.6457	.800 78
14	.3137	.367 98	.3977	.501 58	.4813	.625 02	.5644	.735 76	.6471	.836 34
15	1.3151	33.403 54	1.3991	35.537 14	1.4827	37.660 58	1.5658	39.771 32	1.6484	41.869 36
16	.3165	.439 10	.4005	.572 70	.4841	.696 14	.5672	.806 88	.6498	.904 92
17	.3179	.474 66	.4019	.608 26	.4855	.731 17	.5686	.842 44	.6512	.940 48
18	.3193	.510 22	.4033	.643 82	.4868	.764 72	.5699	.875 46	.6525	.973 50
19	.3207	.545 78	.4047	.679 38	.4882	.800 28	.5713	.911 02	.6539	42.009 06
20	1.3221	33.581 34	1.4061	35.714 94	1.4896	37.835 84	1.5727	39.946 58	1.6553	42.044 62
21	.3235	.616 90	.4075	.750 50	.4910	.871 40	.5741	.982 14	.6567	.080 18
22	.3250	.655 00	.4089	.786 06	.4924	.906 96	.5755	40.017 70	.6580	.113 20
23	.3264	.690 56	.4103	.821 62	.4938	.942 52	.5768	.050 72	.6594	.148 76
24	.3278	.726 12	.4117	.857 18	.4952	.978 08	.5782	.086 28	.6608	.184 32
25	1.3292	33.761 68	1.4131	35.892 74	1.4966	38.013 64	1.5796	40.121 84	1.6622	42.219 88
26	.3306	.797 24	.4145	.928 30	.4980	.049 20	.5810	.157 40	.6635	.252 90
27	.3320	.832 80	.4159	.963 86	.4993	.082 22	.5824	.192 96	.6649	.288 46

28	.3334	868 36	.4173	999 42	.5007	117 78	.5837	225 98	.6663	324 02
29	.3348	903 92	.4187	36.034 98	.5021	153 34	.5851	261 54	.6676	357 04
30	1.3362	33.939 48	1.4201	36.070 54	1.5035	38.188 90	1.5865	40.297 10	1.6690	42.392 60
31	.3376	.975 04	.4214	.103 56	.5049	.224 46	.5879	.332 66	.6704	.428 16
32	.3390	34.010 60	.4228	.139 12	.5063	.260 02	.5893	.368 22	.6718	.463 72
33	.3404	.046 16	.4242	.174 68	.5077	.295 58	.5906	.401 24	.6731	.496 74
34	.3418	.081 72	.4256	.210 24	.5091	.331 14	.5920	.436 80	.6745	.532 30
35	1.3432	34.117 28	1.4270	36.245 80	1.5104	38.364 16	1.5934	40.472 36	1.6759	42.567 86
36	.3446	.152 84	.4284	.281 36	.5118	.399 72	.5948	.507 92	.6772	.600 88
37	.3460	.188 40	.4298	.316 92	.5132	.435 28	.5961	.540 94	.6786	.636 44
38	.3474	.223 96	.4312	.352 48	.5146	.470 84	.5975	.576 50	.6800	.672 00
39	.3488	.259 52	.4326	.388 04	.5160	.506 40	.5989	.612 06	.6813	.705 02
40	1.3502	34.295 08	1.4340	36.423 60	1.5174	38.541 96	1.6003	40.647 62	1.6827	42.740 58
41	.3516	.330 64	.4354	.459 16	.5188	.577 52	.6017	.683 18	.6841	.776 14
42	.3530	.366 20	.4368	.494 72	.5201	.610 54	.6030	.716 20	.6855	.811 70
43	.3544	.401 76	.4382	.530 28	.5215	.646 10	.6044	.751 76	.6868	.844 72
44	.3558	.437 32	.4396	.565 84	.5229	.681 66	.6058	.787 32	.6882	.880 28
45	1.3572	34.472 88	1.4410	36.601 40	1.5243	38.717 22	1.6072	40.822 88	1.6896	42.915 84
46	.3586	.508 44	.4423	.634 42	.5257	.752 78	.6085	.855 90	.6909	.948 86
47	.3600	.544 00	.4437	.669 98	.5271	.788 34	.6099	.891 46	.6923	.984 42
48	.3614	.579 56	.4451	.705 54	.5285	.823 90	.6113	.927 02	.6937	43.019 78
49	.3628	.615 12	.4465	.741 10	.5298	.856 92	.6127	.962 58	.6950	.053 00
50	1.3642	34.650 68	1.4479	36.776 66	1.5312	38.892 48	1.6141	40.998 14	1.6964	43.088 56
51	.3656	.686 24	.4493	.812 22	.5326	.928 04	.6154	41.031 16	.6978	.124 12
52	.3670	.721 80	.4507	.847 78	.5340	.963 60	.6168	.066 72	.6991	.157 14
53	.3684	.757 36	.4521	.883 34	.5354	.999 16	.6182	.102 28	.7005	.192 70
54	.3698	.792 92	.4535	.918 90	.5368	39.034 72	.6196	.137 84	.7019	.228 26
55	1.3712	34.828 48	1.4549	36.954 46	1.5381	39.067 74	1.6209	41.170 86	1.7032	43.261 28
56	.3726	.864 04	.4563	.990 02	.5395	.103 30	.6223	.206 42	.7046	.296 84
57	.3740	.899 60	.4577	37.025 58	.5409	.138 86	.6237	.241 98	.7060	.332 40
58	.3754	.935 16	.4591	.061 14	.5423	.174 42	.6251	.277 54	.7073	.365 42
59	.3786	.970 72	.4604	.094 16	.5437	.209 98	.6264	.310 56	.7087	.400 98
60	1.3782	35.006 28	1.4618	37.129 72	1.5451	39.245 54	1.6278	41.346 12	1.7101	43.436 54

Sine Plate Settings (Continued).

Min	20° Inch	20° mm	21° Inch	21° mm	22° Inch	22° mm	23° Inch	23° mm	24° Inch	24° mm
0	1.7101	43.436 54	1.7918	45.511 72	1.8730	47.574 20	1.9536	49.621 44	2.0337	51.655 98
1	.7114	.469 56	.7932	.547 28	.8744	.609 76	.9550	.657 00	.0350	.689 00
2	.7128	.505 12	.7945	.580 30	.8757	.642 78	.9563	.690 02	.0363	.722 02
3	.7142	.540 68	.7959	.615 86	.8771	.678 34	.9576	.723 04	.0376	.755 04
4	.7155	.573 70	.7972	.648 88	.8784	.711 36	.9590	.758 60	.0390	.790 60
5	1.7169	43.609 26	1.7986	45.684 44	1.8797	47.744 38	1.9603	49.791 62	2.0403	51.823 62
6	.7183	.644 82	.8000	.720 00	.8811	.779 94	.9617	.827 18	.0416	.856 64
7	.7196	.677 84	.8013	.753 02	.8824	.812 96	.9630	.860 20	.0430	.892 20
8	.7210	.713 40	.8027	.788 58	.8838	.848 52	.9643	.893 22	.0443	.925 22
9	.7224	.748 96	.8040	.821 60	.8851	.881 54	.9657	.928 78	.0456	.958 24
10	1.7237	43.781 98	1.8054	45.857 16	1.8865	47.917 10	1.9670	49.961 80	2.0469	51.991 26
11	.7251	.817 54	.8067	.890 18	.8878	.950 12	.9683	.994 82	.0483	52.026 82
12	.7265	.853 10	.8081	.925 74	.8892	.985 68	.9697	50.030 38	.0496	.059 84
13	.7278	.886 12	.8094	.958 76	.8905	48.018 70	.9710	.063 40	.0509	.092 86
14	.7292	.921 68	.8108	.994 32	.8919	.054 26	.9724	.098 96	.0522	.125 88
15	1.7306	43.957 24	1.8122	46.029 88	1.8932	48.087 28	1.9737	50.131 98	2.0536	52.161 44
16	.7319	.990 26	.8135	.062 90	.8946	.122 84	.9750	.165 00	.0549	.194 46
17	.7333	44.025 82	.8149	.098 46	.8959	.155 86	.9764	.200 56	.0562	.227 48
18	.7347	.061 38	.8162	.131 48	.8973	.191 42	.9777	.233 58	.0575	.260 50
19	.7360	.094 40	.8176	.167 04	.8986	.224 44	.9790	.266 60	.0589	.296 06
20	1.7374	44.129 96	1.8189	46.200 06	1.8999	48.257 46	1.9804	50.302 16	2.0602	52.329 08
21	.7387	.162 98	.8203	.235 62	.9013	.293 02	.9817	.335 18	.0615	.362 10
22	.7401	.198 54	.8217	.271 18	.9026	.326 04	.9830	.368 20	.0628	.395 12
23	.7415	.234 10	.8230	.304 20	.9040	.361 60	.9844	.403 76	.0642	.430 68
24	.7428	.267 12	.8244	.339 76	.9053	.394 62	.9857	.436 78	.0655	.463 70
25	1.7442	44.302 68	1.8257	46.372 78	1.9067	48.430 18	1.9870	50.469 80	2.0668	52.496 72
26	.7456	.338 24	.8271	.408 34	.9080	.463 20	.9884	.505 36	.0681	.529 74
27	.7469	.371 26	.8284	.441 36	.9094	.498 76	.9897	.538 38	.0695	.565 30

Min										
28	.598 32	.0708	.573 94	.9911	.531 78	.9107	.476 92	.8298	.406 82	.7483
29	.631 34	.0721	.606 96	.9924	.564 80	.9120	.509 94	.8311	.439 84	.7496
30	52.664 36	2.0734	50.639 98	1.9937	48.600 36	1.9134	46.545 50	1.8325	44.475 40	1.7510
31	.699 92	.0748	.675 54	.9951	.633 38	.9147	.578 52	.8338	.510 96	.7524
32	.732 94	.0761	.708 56	.9964	.668 94	.9161	.614 08	.8352	.543 98	.7537
33	.765 96	.0774	.741 58	.9977	.701 96	.9174	.647 10	.8365	.579 54	.7551
34	.798 98	.0787	.777 14	.9991	.737 52	.9188	.682 66	.8379	.615 10	.7565
35	52.834 54	2.0801	50.810 16	2.0004	48.770 54	1.9201	46.715 68	1.8392	44.648 12	1.7578
36	.867 56	.0814	.843 18	.0017	.806 10	.9215	.751 24	.8406	.683 68	.7592
37	.900 58	.0827	.878 74	.0031	.839 12	.9228	.784 26	.8419	.716 70	.7605
38	.933 60	.0840	.911 76	.0044	.872 14	.9241	.819 82	.8433	.752 26	.7619
39	.966 62	.0853	.944 78	.0057	.907 70	.9255	.855 38	.8447	.787 82	.7633
40	53.002 18	2.0867	50.977 80	2.0070	48.940 72	1.9268	46.888 40	1.8460	44.820 84	1.7646
41	.035 20	.0880	51.013 36	.0084	.976 28	1.9282	.923 96	.8474	.856 40	.7660
42	.068 22	.0893	.046 38	.0097	49.009 30	.9295	.956 98	.8487	.889 42	.7673
43	.101 24	.0906	.079 40	.0110	.042 32	.9308	.992 54	.8501	.924 98	.7687
44	.136 80	.0920	.114 96	.0124	.077 88	.9322	47.025 56	.8514	.960 54	.7701
45	53.169 82	2.0933	51.147 98	2.0137	49.110 90	1.9335	47.061 12	1.8528	44.993 56	1.7714
46	.202 84	.0946	.181 10	.0150	.146 46	.9349	.094 14	.8541	45.029 12	.7728
47	.235 86	.0959	.216 56	.0164	.179 48	.9362	.129 70	.8555	.064 68	.7742
48	.268 88	.0972	.249 58	.0177	.215 04	.9376	.162 72	.8568	.097 70	.7755
49	.304 44	.0986	.282 60	.0190	.248 06	.9389	.198 28	.8582	.133 26	.7769
50	53.337 46	2.0999	51.318 16	2.0204	49.281 08	1.9402	47.231 30	1.8595	45.166 28	1.7782
51	.370 48	.1012	.351 18	.0217	.316 64	.9416	.266 86	.8609	.201 84	.7796
52	.403 50	.1025	.384 20	.0230	.349 66	.9429	.299 88	.9622	.234 86	.7809
53	.436 52	.1038	.419 76	.0244	.385 22	.9443	.335 44	.8636	.270 42	.7823
54	.472 08	.1052	.452 78	.0257	.418 24	.9456	.368 46	.8649	.305 98	.7837
55	53.505 10	2.1065	51.485 80	2.0270	49.451 26	1.9469	47.404 02	1.8663	45.339 00	1.7850
56	.538 12	.1078	.518 82	.0283	.486 82	.9483	.437 04	.8676	.374 56	.7864
57	.571 14	.1091	.554 38	.0297	.519 84	.9496	.472 60	.8690	.407 58	.7877
58	.604 16	.1104	.587 40	.0310	.555 40	.9510	.505 62	.8703	.443 14	.7891
59	.637 18	.1117	.620 42	.0323	.588 42	.9523	.541 18	.8717	.478 70	.7905
60	52.672 74	2.1131	51.655 98	2.0337	49.621 44	1.9536	47.574 20	1.8730	45.511 72	1.7918

PRESSWORKING AIDS FOR DESIGNERS AND DIEMAKERS

Sine Plate Settings (Continued).

Min	25° Inch	25° mm	26° Inch	26° mm	27° Inch	27° mm	28° Inch	28° mm	29° Inch	29° mm
0	2.1131	53.672 74	2.1918	55.671 72	2.2699	57.655 46	2.3473	59.621 42	2.4240	61.569 60
1	.1144	.705 76	.1931	.704 74	.2712	.688 48	.3486	.654 44	.4253	.602 62
2	.1157	.738 78	.1944	.737 76	.2725	.721 50	.3499	.687 46	.4266	.635 64
3	.1170	.771 80	.1958	.773 32	.2738	.754 52	.3512	.720 48	.4278	.666 12
4	.1183	.804 82	.1971	.806 34	.2751	.787 54	.3525	.753 50	.4291	.699 14
5	2.1197	53.840 38	2.1984	55.839 36	2.2764	57.820 56	2.3538	59.786 52	2.4304	61.732 16
6	.1210	.873 40	.1997	.872 38	.2777	.853 58	.3550	.817 00	.4317	.765 18
7	.1223	.906 42	.2010	.905 40	.2790	.886 60	.3563	.850 02	.4329	.795 66
8	.1236	.939 44	.2023	.938 42	.2803	.919 62	.3576	.883 04	.4342	.828 68
9	.1249	.972 46	.2036	.971 44	.2816	.952 64	.3589	.916 06	.4355	.861 70
10	2.1262	54.005 48	2.2049	56.004 46	2.2829	57.985 66	2.3602	59.949 08	2.4367	61.892 18
11	.1276	.041 04	.2062	.037 48	.2842	58.018 68	.3614	.979 56	.4380	.925 20
12	.1289	.074 06	.2075	.070 50	.2855	.051 70	.3627	60.012 58	.4393	.958 22
13	.1302	.107 08	.2088	.103 52	.2868	.084 72	.3640	.045 60	.4405	.988 70
14	.1315	.140 10	.2101	.136 54	.2881	.117 74	.3653	.078 62	.4418	62.021 72
15	2.1328	54.173 12	2.2114	56.169 56	2.2893	58.148 22	2.3666	60.111 64	2.4431	62.054 74
16	.1341	.206 14	.2127	.202 58	.2906	.181 24	.3679	.144 66	.4444	.087 76
17	.1354	.239 16	.2140	.235 60	.2919	.214 26	.3691	.175 14	.4456	.118 24
18	.1368	.274 72	.2153	.268 62	.2932	.247 28	.3704	.208 16	.4469	.151 26
19	.1381	.307 74	.2166	.301 64	.2945	.280 30	.3717	.241 18	.4482	.184 28
20	2.1394	54.340 76	2.2179	56.334 66	2.2958	58.313 32	2.3730	60.274 20	2.4494	62.214 76
21	.1407	.373 78	.2192	.367 68	.2971	.346 34	.3743	.307 22	.4507	.247 78
22	.1420	.406 80	.2205	.400 70	.2984	.379 36	.3755	.337 70	.4520	.280 80
23	.1433	.439 82	.2218	.433 72	.2997	.412 38	.3768	.370 72	.4532	.311 28
24	.1447	.475 38	.2232	.469 28	.3010	.445 40	.3781	.403 74	.4545	.344 30
25	2.1460	54.508 84	2.2245	56.502 30	2.3023	58.478 42	2.3794	60.436 76	2.4558	62.377 32
26	.1473	.541 42	.2258	.535 32	.3036	.511 44	.3807	.469 78	.4570	.407 80
27	.1486	.574 44	.2271	.568 34	.3048	.541 92	.3819	.500 26	.4583	.440 82

240

28	.1499	.607 46	.2284	.601 36	.3061	.574 94	.3832	.533 28	.4596	.473 84
29	.1512	.640 48	.2297	.634 38	.3074	.607 96	.3845	.566 30	.4608	.504 32
30	2.1525	54.673 50	2.2310	56.667 40	2.3087	58.640 98	2.3858	60.599 32	2.4621	62.537 34
31	.1538	.706 52	.2323	.700 42	.3100	.674 00	.3870	.629 80	.4634	.570 36
32	.1552	.742 08	.2336	.733 44	.3113	.707 02	.3883	.662 82	.4646	.600 84
33	.1565	.775 10	.2349	.766 46	.3126	.740 04	.3896	.695 84	.4659	.633 86
34	.1578	.808 12	.2362	.799 48	.3139	.773 06	.3909	.728 86	.4672	.666 88
35	2.1591	54.841 14	2.2375	56.832 50	2.3152	58.806 08	2.3922	60.761 88	2.4684	62.697 36
36	.1604	.874 16	.2388	.865 52	.3165	.839 10	.3934	.792 36	.4697	.730 38
37	.1617	.907 18	.2401	.898 54	.3177	.869 58	.3947	.825 38	.4709	.760 86
38	.1630	.940 20	.2414	.931 56	.3190	.902 60	.3960	.858 40	.4722	.793 88
39	.1643	.973 22	.2427	.964 58	.3203	.935 62	.3973	.891 42	.4735	.826 90
40	2.1656	55.006 24	2.2440	56.997 60	2.3216	58.968 64	2.3985	60.921 90	2.4747	62.857 38
41	.1670	.041 80	.2453	57.030 62	.3229	59.001 66	.3988	.929 52	.4760	.890 40
42	.1683	.074 82	.2466	.063 64	.3242	.034 68	.4011	.987 94	.4773	.923 42
43	.1696	.107 84	.2479	.096 66	.3255	.067 70	.4024	61.020 96	.4785	.953 90
44	.1709	.140 86	.2492	.129 68	.3268	.100 72	.4036	.051 44	.4798	.986 92
45	2.1722	55.173 88	2.2505	57.162 70	2.3280	59.131 20	2.4049	61.084 46	2.4811	63.019 94
46	.1735	.206 90	.2518	.195 72	.3293	.164 22	.4062	.117 48	.4823	.050 42
47	.1748	.239 92	.2531	.228 74	.3306	.197 24	.4075	.150 50	.4836	.083 44
48	.1761	.272 94	.2544	.261 76	.3319	.230 26	.4087	.180 98	.4848	.113 92
49	.1774	.305 96	.2557	.294 78	.3332	.263 28	.4100	.214 00	.4861	.146 94
50	2.1787	55.338 98	2.2570	57.327 80	2.3345	59.296 30	2.4113	61.247 03	2.4874	63.179 96
51	.1801	.374 54	.2583	.360 82	.3358	.329 32	.4126	.280 04	.4886	.210 44
52	.1814	.407 56	.2596	.393 84	.3371	.362 34	.4138	.310 52	.4899	.243 46
53	.1827	.440 58	.2609	.426 86	.3383	.392 82	.4151	.343 54	.4912	.276 48
54	.1840	.473 60	.2621	.457 34	.3396	.425 84	.4164	.376 56	.4924	.306 96
55	2.1853	55.506 62	2.2634	57.490 36	2.3409	59.458 86	2.4177	61.409 58	2.4937	63.339 98
56	.1866	.539 64	.2647	.523 38	.3422	.491 88	.4189	.440 06	.4949	.370 46
57	.1879	.572 66	.2660	.556 40	.3435	.524 90	.4202	.473 08	.4962	.403 48
58	.1892	.605 68	.2673	.589 42	.3448	.557 92	.4215	.506 10	.4975	.436 50
59	.1905	.638 70	.2686	.622 44	.3460	.588 40	.4228	.539 12	.4987	.466 98
60	2.1918	55.671 72	2.2699	57.655 46	2.3473	59.621 42	2.4240	61.569 60	2.5000	63.500 00

Sine Plate Settings (Continued).

Min	30° Inch	30° mm	31° Inch	31° mm	32° Inch	32° mm	33° Inch	33° mm	34° Inch	34° mm
0	2.5000	63.500 00	2.5752	65.410 08	2.6496	67.299 84	2.7232	69.169 28	2.7959	71.015 86
1	.5012	.530 48	.5764	.440 56	.6508	.330 32	.7244	.199 76	.7971	.046 34
2	.5025	.563 50	.5777	.473 58	.6520	.360 80	.7256	.230 24	.7984	.079 36
3	.5038	.596 52	.5789	.504 06	.6533	.393 82	.7268	.260 72	.7996	.109 84
4	.5050	.627 00	.5802	.537 08	.6545	.424 30	.7280	.291 20	.8008	.140 32
5	2.5063	63.660 02	2.5814	65.567 56	2.6557	67.454 78	2.7293	69.324 22	2.8020	71.170 80
6	.5075	.690 50	.5826	.598 04	.6570	.478 80	.7305	.354 70	.8032	.201 28
7	.5088	.723 52	.5839	.631 06	.6582	.518 28	.7317	.385 18	.8044	.231 76
8	.5100	.754 00	.5851	.661 54	.6594	.548 76	.7329	.415 66	.8056	.262 24
9	.5113	.787 02	.5864	.694 56	.6607	.581 78	.7341	.446 14	.8068	.292 72
10	2.5126	63.820 04	2.5876	65.725 04	2.6619	67.612 26	2.7354	69.479 16	2.8080	71.323 20
11	.5138	.850 52	.5889	.758 06	.6631	.642 74	.7366	.509 64	.8092	.353 68
12	.5151	.883 54	.5901	.788 54	.6644	.675 76	.7378	.540 12	.8104	.384 16
13	.5163	.914 02	.5914	.821 56	.6656	.706 24	.7390	.570 60	.8116	.414 64
14	.5176	.947 04	.5926	.852 04	.6668	.736 72	.7402	.601 08	.8128	.445 12
15	2.5188	63.977 52	2.5938	65.882 52	2.6680	67.767 20	2.7414	69.631 56	2.8140	71.475 60
16	.5201	64.010 54	.5951	.915 54	.6693	.800 22	.7427	.664 58	.8152	.506 08
17	.5214	.043 56	.5963	.946 02	.6705	.830 70	.7439	.695 06	.8164	.536 56
18	.5226	.074 04	.5976	.979 04	.6717	.861 18	.7451	.725 54	.8176	.567 04
19	.5239	.107 06	.5988	66.009 52	.6730	.894 20	.7463	.756 02	.8188	.597 52
20	2.5251	64.137 54	2.6001	66.042 54	2.6742	67.924 68	2.7475	69.786 50	2.8200	71.628 00
21	.5264	.170 56	.6013	.073 02	.6754	.955 16	.7487	.816 98	.8212	.658 48
22	.5276	.201 04	.6025	.103 50	.6767	.988 18	.7499	.847 46	.8224	.688 96
23	.5289	.234 06	.6038	.136 52	.6779	68.018 66	.7512	.880 48	.8236	.719 44
24	.5301	.264 54	.6050	.167 00	.6791	.049 14	.7524	.910 96	.8248	.749 92
25	2.5314	64.297 56	2.6063	66.200 02	2.6803	68.079 62	2.7536	69.941 44	2.8260	71.780 40
26	.5327	.330 58	.6075	.230 50	.6816	.112 64	.7548	.971 92	.8272	.810 88
27	.5339	.361 06	.6087	.260 98	.6828	.143 12	.7560	70.002 40	.8284	.841 36

28	.5352	.394 08	.6100	.294 00	.6840	.173 60	.7572	.032 88	.8296	.871 84
29	.5364	.424 56	.6112	.324 48	.6852	.204 08	.7584	.063 36	.8308	.902 32
30	2.5377	64.457 58	2.6125	66.357 50	2.6865	68.237 10	2.7597	70.096 38	2.8320	71.932 80
31	.5389	.488 06	.6137	.387 98	.6877	.267 58	.7609	.126 86	.8332	.963 28
32	.5402	.521 08	.6149	.418 46	.6889	.298 06	.7621	.157 34	.8344	.993 76
33	.5414	.551 56	.6162	.451 48	.6902	.331 08	.7633	.187 82	.8356	72.024 24
34	.5427	.584 58	.6174	.481 96	.6914	.361 56	.7645	.218 30	.8368	.054 72
35	2.5439	64.615 06	2.6187	66.514 98	2.6926	68.392 04	2.7657	70.248 78	2.8380	72.085 20
36	.5452	.648 08	.6199	.545 46	.6938	.422 52	.7669	.279 26	.8392	.115 68
37	.5464	.678 56	.6211	.575 94	.6951	.455 54	.7681	.309 74	.8404	.146 16
38	.5477	.711 58	.6224	.608 96	.6963	.486 02	.7694	.342 76	.8416	.176 64
39	.5489	.742 06	.6236	.639 44	.6975	.516 50	.7706	.373 24	.8428	.207 12
40	2.5502	64.775 08	2.6249	66.672 46	2.6987	68.546 98	2.7718	70.403 72	2.8440	72.237 60
41	.5514	.805 56	.6261	.702 94	.7000	.580 00	.7730	.434 20	.8452	.268 08
42	.5527	.838 58	.6273	.733 42	.7012	.610 48	.7742	.464 68	.8464	.298 56
43	.5539	.869 06	.6286	.766 44	.7024	.640 96	.7754	.495 16	.8476	.329 04
44	.5552	.902 08	.6298	.796 92	.7036	.671 44	.7766	.525 64	.8488	.359 52
45	2.5564	64.932 56	2.6310	66.827 40	2.7048	68.701 92	2.7778	70.556 12	2.8500	72.390 00
46	.5577	.965 58	.6323	.860 42	.7061	.734 94	.7790	.586 60	.8512	.420 48
47	.5589	.996 06	.6335	.890 90	.7073	.765 42	.7802	.617 08	.8523	.448 42
48	.5602	65.029 08	.6348	.923 92	.7085	.795 90	.7815	.650 10	.8535	.478 90
49	.5614	.059 56	.6360	.954 40	.7097	.826 38	.7827	.680 58	.8547	.509 38
50	2.5627	65.092 58	2.6372	66.984 88	2.7110	68.859 40	2.7839	70.711 06	2.8559	72.539 86
51	.5639	.123 06	.6385	67.017 90	.7122	.889 88	.7851	.741 54	.8571	.570 34
52	.5652	.156 08	.6397	.048 38	.7134	.920 36	.7863	.772 02	.8583	.600 82
53	.5665	.189 10	.6409	.078 86	.7146	.950 84	.7875	.802 50	.8595	.631 30
54	.5677	.219 58	.6422	.111 88	.7158	.981 32	.7887	.832 98	.8607	.661 78
55	2.5689	65.250 06	2.6434	67.142 36	2.7171	69.014 34	2.7899	70.863 46	2.8619	72.692 26
56	.5702	.283 08	.6446	.172 84	.7183	.044 82	.7911	.893 94	.8631	.722 74
57	.5714	.313 56	.6459	.205 86	.7195	.075 30	.7923	.924 42	.8643	.753 22
58	.5727	.346 58	.6471	.236 34	.7207	.105 78	.7935	.954 90	.8655	.783 70
59	.5739	.377 06	.6483	.266 82	.7220	.138 80	.7947	.985 38	.8667	.814 18
60	2.5752	65.410 08	2.6496	67.299 84	2.7232	69.169 28	2.7959	71.015 86	2.8679	72.844 66

Sine Plate Settings (Continued).

Min	35° Inch	35° mm	36° Inch	36° mm	37° Inch	37° mm	38° Inch	38° mm	39° Inch	39° mm
0	2.8679	72.844 66	2.9389	74.648 06	3.0091	76.431 14	3.0783	78.188 82	3.1466	79.923 64
1	.8690	.872 60	.9401	.678 54	.0102	.459 08	.0794	.216 76	.1477	.951 58
2	.8702	.903 08	.9413	.709 02	.0114	.489 56	.0806	.247 24	.1488	.979 52
3	.8714	.933 56	.9424	.736 96	.0125	.517 50	.0817	.275 18	.1500	80.010 00
4	.8726	.964 04	.9436	.767 44	.0137	.547 98	.0829	.305 66	.1511	.037 94
5	2.8738	72.994 52	2.9448	74.797 92	3.0149	76.578 46	3.0840	78.333 60	3.1522	80.065 88
6	.8750	73.025 00	.9460	.838 40	.0160	.606 40	.0852	.364 08	.1534	.096 36
7	.8762	.055 48	.9471	.856 34	.0172	.636 88	.0863	.392 02	.1545	.124 30
8	.8774	.085 96	.9483	.886 82	.0183	.664 82	.0874	.419 96	.1556	.152 24
9	.8786	.116 44	.9495	.917 30	.0195	.695 30	.0886	.450 44	.1567	.180 18
10	2.8798	73.146 92	2.9507	74.947 78	3.0207	76.725 78	3.0897	78.478 38	3.1579	30.210 66
11	.8809	.174 86	.9518	.975 72	.0218	.753 72	.0909	.508 86	.1590	.238 60
12	.8821	.205 34	.9530	75.006 20	.0230	.784 20	.0920	.536 80	.1601	.266 54
13	.8833	.235 82	.9542	.036 68	.0241	.812 14	.0932	.567 28	.1612	.294 48
14	.8845	.266 30	.9554	.067 16	.0253	.842 62	.0943	.595 22	.1624	.324 96
15	2.8857	73.296 78	2.9565	75.095 10	3.0264	76.870 56	3.0954	78.623 16	3.1635	80.352 90
16	.8869	.327 26	.9577	.125 58	.0276	.901 04	.0966	.653 64	.1646	.380 84
17	.8881	.357 74	.9589	.156 06	.0288	.931 52	.0977	.681 58	.1658	.411 32
18	.8893	.388 22	.9600	.184 00	.0299	.959 46	.0989	.712 06	.1669	.439 26
19	.8905	.418 70	.9612	.214 48	.0311	.989 94	.1000	.740 00	.1680	.467 20
20	2.8916	73.446 64	2.9624	75.244 64	3.0322	77.017 88	3.1012	78.770 48	3.1691	80.495 14
21	.8928	.477 12	.9636	.275 44	.0334	.048 36	.1023	.798 42	.1703	.525 62
22	.8940	.507 60	.9647	.303 38	.0345	.076 30	.1034	.826 36	.1714	.553 56
23	.8952	.538 08	.9659	.333 86	.0357	.106 78	.1046	.856 84	.1725	.581 50
24	.8964	.568 56	.9671	.364 34	.0369	.137 26	.1057	.884 78	.1736	.609 44
25	2.8976	73.599 04	2.9682	75.392 28	3.0380	77.165 20	3.1069	78.915 26	3.1748	80.639 92
26	.8988	.629 52	.9694	.422 76	.0392	.195 68	.1080	.943 20	.1759	.667 86
27	.8999	.657 46	.9706	.453 24	.0403	.223 62	.1091	.971 14	.1770	.695 58

28	.9011	.687 94	.9718	.483 72	.0415	.254 10	.1103	79.001 62	.1781	.723 74
29	.9023	.718 42	.9729	.511 66	.0426	.282 04	.1114	.029 56	.1792	.751 68
30	2.9035	73.748 90	2.9741	75.542 14	3.0438	77.312 52	3.1125	79.057 50	3.1804	80.782 16
31	.9047	.779 38	.9753	.572 62	.0449	.340 46	.1137	.087 98	.1815	.810 10
32	.9059	.809 86	.9764	.600 56	.0461	.370 94	.1148	.115 92	.1826	.838 04
33	.9070	.837 80	.9776	.631 04	.0472	.398 88	.1160	.146 40	.1837	.865 98
34	.9082	.868 28	.9788	.661 52	.0484	.429 36	.1171	.174 34	.1849	.896 46
35	2.9094	73.898 76	2.9799	75.689 46	3.0495	77.457 30	3.1182	79.202 28	3.1860	80.924 40
36	.9106	.929 24	.9811	.719 94	.0507	.487 78	.1194	.232 76	.1871	.952 34
37	.9118	.959 72	.9823	.750 42	.0519	.518 26	.1205	.260 70	.1882	.980 28
38	.9130	.990 20	.9834	.778 36	.0530	.546 20	.1216	.288 64	.1893	81.008 22
39	.9141	74.018 14	.9846	.808 84	.0542	.576 68	.1228	.319 12	.1905	.038 70
40	2.9153	74.048 62	2.9858	75.839 32	3.0553	77.604 62	3.1239	79.347 06	3.1916	81.066 64
41	.9165	.079 10	.9869	.867 26	.0565	.635 10	.1251	.377 54	.1927	.094 58
42	.9177	.109 58	.9881	.897 74	.0576	.663 04	.1262	.405 48	.1938	.122 52
43	.9189	.140 06	.9893	.928 22	.0588	.693 52	.1273	.433 42	.1949	.150 46
44	.9200	.168 00	.9904	.956 16	.0599	.721 46	.1285	.463 90	.1961	.180 94
45	2.9212	74.198 48	2.9916	75.986 64	3.0611	77.751 94	3.1296	79.491 84	3.1972	81.208 88
46	.9224	.228 96	.9928	76.017 12	.0622	.779 88	.1307	.519 78	.1983	.236 82
47	.9236	.259 44	.9939	.045 06	.0634	.810 36	.1319	.550 26	.1994	.264 76
48	.9248	.289 92	.9951	.075 54	.0645	.838 30	.1330	.578 20	.2005	.292 70
49	.9259	.317 86	.9963	.106 02	.0657	.868 78	.1341	.606 14	.2016	.320 64
50	2.9271	74.348 34	2.9974	76.133 96	3.0668	77.896 74	3.1353	79.636 62	3.2028	81.351 12
51	.9283	.378 82	.9986	.164 44	.0680	.927 20	.1364	.664 56	.2039	.379 06
52	.9295	.409 30	.9997	.192 38	.0691	.955 14	.1375	.692 50	.2050	.407 00
53	.9307	.439 78	3.0009	.222 86	.0703	.985 62	.1387	.722 98	.2061	.434 94
54	.9318	.467 72	.0021	.253 34	.0714	78.013 56	.1398	.750 92	.2072	.462 88
55	2.9330	74.498 20	3.0032	76.281 28	3.0725	78.041 50	3.1409	79.778 86	3.2083	81.490 82
56	.9342	.528 68	.0044	.311 76	.0737	.071 98	.1421	.809 34	.2095	.521 30
57	.9354	.559 16	.0056	.342 24	.0748	.099 92	.1432	.837 28	.2106	.549 24
58	.9365	.587 10	.0067	.370 18	.0760	.130 40	.1443	.865 22	.2117	.577 18
59	.9377	.617 58	.0079	.400 66	.0771	.158 34	.1454	.893 16	.2128	.605 12
60	2.9389	74.648 06	3.0091	76.431 14	3.0783	78.188 82	3.1466	79.923 64	3.2139	81.633 06

Sine Plate Settings (Continued).

Min	40° Inch	40° mm	41° Inch	41° mm	42° Inch	42° mm	43° Inch	43° mm	44° Inch	44° mm
0	3.2139	81.633 06	3.2803	83.319 62	3.3456	84.978 24	3.4100	86.614 00	3.4733	88.221 82
1	.2150	.661 00	.2814	.347 56	.3467	85.006 18	.4110	.639 40	.4743	.247 22
2	.2161	.688 94	.2825	.375 50	.3478	.034 12	.4121	.667 34	.4754	.275 16
3	.2173	.719 42	.2836	.403 44	.3489	.062 06	.4132	.695 28	.4764	.300 56
4	.2184	.747 36	.2847	.431 38	.3499	.087 46	.4142	.720 68	.4774	.325 96
5	3.2195	81.775 30	3.2858	83.459 32	3.3519	85.115 40	3.4153	86.748 62	3.4785	88.353 90
6	.2206	.803 24	.2869	.487 26	.3521	.143 34	.4163	.774 02	.4795	.379 30
7	.2217	.831 18	.2879	.512 66	.3532	.171 28	.4174	.801 96	.4806	.407 24
8	.2228	.859 12	.2890	.540 60	.3543	.199 22	.4185	.829 90	.4816	.432 64
9	.2239	.887 06	.2901	.568 54	.3553	.224 62	.4195	.855 30	.4827	.460 58
10	3.2250	81.915 00	3.2912	83.596 48	3.3564	85.252 56	3.4206	86.883 24	3.4837	88.485 98
11	.2262	.945 48	.2923	.624 42	.3575	.280 50	.4217	.911 18	.4848	.513 92
12	.2273	.973 42	.2934	.652 36	.3586	.308 44	.4227	.936 58	.4858	.539 32
13	.2284	82.001 36	.2945	.680 30	.3597	.336 38	.4238	.964 52	.4868	.564 72
14	.2295	.029 30	.2956	.708 24	.3607	.361 78	.4248	.989 92	.4879	.592 66
15	3.2306	82.057 24	3.2967	83.736 18	3.3618	85.389 72	3.4259	87.017 86	3.4889	88.618 06
16	.2317	.085 18	.2978	.764 12	.3629	.417 66	.4269	.043 26	.4900	.646 00
17	.2328	.113 12	.2989	.792 06	.3640	.445 60	.4280	.071 20	.4910	.671 40
18	.2339	.141 06	.3000	.820 00	.3650	.471 00	.4291	.099 14	.4921	.699 34
19	.2350	.169 00	.3011	.847 94	.3661	.498 94	.4301	.124 54	.4931	.724 74
20	3.2361	82.196 94	3.3022	83.875 88	3.3672	85.526 88	3.4312	87.152 48	3.4941	88.750 14
21	.2373	.227 42	.3033	.903 82	.3683	.554 82	.4322	.177 88	.4952	.778 08
22	.2384	.255 36	.3044	.931 76	.3693	.580 22	.4333	.205 82	.4962	.803 48
23	.2395	.283 30	.3054	.957 16	.3704	.608 16	.4344	.233 76	.4973	.831 42
24	.2406	.311 24	.3065	.985 10	.3715	.636 10	.4354	.259 16	.4983	.856 82
25	3.2417	82.339 18	3.3076	84.013 04	3.3726	85.664 04	3.4365	87.287 10	3.4993	88.882 22
26	.2428	.367 12	.3087	.040 98	.3736	.689 44	.4375	.312 50	.5004	.910 16
27	.2439	.395 06	.3098	.068 92	.3747	.717 38	.4386	.340 44	.5014	.935 56

28	.960 96	.5024	365 84	.4396	745 32	.3758	096 86	.3109	423 00	.2450
29	.988 90	.5035	393 78	.4407	773 26	.3769	124 80	.3120	450 94	.2461
30	89.014 30	3.5045	87.419 18	3.4417	85.798 66	3.3779	84.152 74	3.3131	82.478 88	3.2472
31	.042 24	.5056	.447 12	.4428	.826 60	.3790	.180 68	.3142	.506 82	.2483
32	.067 64	.5066	.475 06	.4439	.854 54	.3801	.208 62	.3153	.534 76	.2494
33	.093 04	.5076	.500 46	.4449	.879 94	.3811	.234 02	.3163	.562 70	.2505
34	.120 98	.5087	.528 40	.4460	.907 88	.3822	.261 96	.3174	.590 64	.2516
35	89.146 38	3.5097	87.553 80	3.4470	85.935 82	3.3833	84.289 90	3.3185	82.618 58	3.2527
36	.171 78	.5107	.581 74	.4481	.963 76	.3844	.317 84	.3196	.646 52	.2538
37	.199 72	.5118	.607 14	.4491	.989 16	.3854	.345 78	.3207	.677 00	.2550
38	.225 12	.5128	.635 08	.4502	86.017 10	.3865	.373 72	.3218	.704 94	.2561
39	.250 52	.5138	.660 48	.4512	.045 04	.3876	.401 66	.3229	.732 88	.2572
40	89.278 46	3.5149	87.688 42	3.4523	86.070 44	3.3886	84.429 60	3.3240	82.760 82	3.2583
41	.303 86	.5159	.713 82	.4533	.098 38	.3897	.455 00	.3250	.788 76	.2594
42	.329 26	.5169	.741 76	.4544	.126 32	.3908	.482 94	.3261	.816 70	.2605
43	.357 20	.5180	.767 16	.4554	.151 72	.3918	.510 88	.3272	.844 64	.2616
44	.382 60	.5190	.795 10	.4565	.179 66	.3929	.538 82	.3283	.872 58	.2627
45	89.408 00	3.5200	87.820 50	3.4575	86.207 60	3.3940	84.566 76	3.3294	82.900 52	3.2638
46	.435 94	.5211	.848 44	.4586	.233 00	.3950	.594 70	.3305	.928 46	.2649
47	.461 34	.5221	.873 84	.4596	.260 94	.3961	.622 64	.3316	.956 40	.2660
48	.486 74	.5231	.901 78	.4607	.288 88	.3972	.648 04	.3326	.984 34	.2671
49	.514 68	.5242	.927 18	.4617	.314 28	.3982	.675 98	.3337	83.012 28	.2682
50	89.540 08	3.5252	87.955 12	3.4628	86.342 22	3.3993	84.703 92	3.3348	83.040 22	3.2693
51	.565 48	.5262	.980 52	.4638	.370 16	.4004	.731 86	.3359	.068 16	.2704
52	.593 42	.5273	88.008 46	.4649	.395 56	.4014	.759 80	.3370	.096 10	.2715
53	.619 82	.5283	.033 86	.4659	.423 50	.4025	.787 74	.3381	.124 04	.2726
54	.644 22	.5293	.061 80	.4670	.451 44	.4036	.813 14	.3391	.151 98	.2737
55	89.672 16	3.5304	88.087 20	3.4680	86.476 84	3.4046	84.841 08	3.3402	83.179 92	3.2748
56	.697 56	.5314	.115 14	.4691	.504 78	.4057	.869 02	.3413	.207 86	.2759
57	.722 96	.5324	.140 54	.4701	.532 72	.4068	.896 96	.3424	.235 80	.2770
58	.750 90	.5335	.168 48	.4712	.558 12	.4078	.924 90	.3435	.263 74	.2781
59	.776 30	.5345	.193 88	.4722	.586 06	.4089	.950 30	.3445	.291 68	.2792
60	89.801 70	3.5355	88.221 82	3.4733	86.614 00	3.4100	84.978 24	3.3456	83.319 62	3.2803

Sine Plate Settings (Continued).

Min	45° Inch	45° mm	46° Inch	46° mm	47° Inch	47° mm	48° Inch	48° mm	49° Inch	49° mm
0	3.5355	89.801 70	3.5967	91.356 18	3.6567	92.880 18	3.7157	94.378 78	3.7735	95.846 90
1	.5365	.827 10	.5977	.381 58	.6577	.905 58	.7167	.404 18	.7745	.872 30
2	.5376	.855 04	.5987	.406 98	.6587	.930 98	.7176	.427 04	.7754	.895 16
3	.5386	.880 44	.5997	.432 38	.6597	.956 38	.7186	.452 44	.7764	.920 56
4	.5396	.905 84	.6007	.457 78	.6607	.981 78	.7196	.477 84	.7773	.943 42
5	.5406	89.931 24	.6017	91.483 18	.6617	93.007 18	.7206	94.503 24	.7783	95.968 82
6	.5417	.959 18	.6027	.508 58	.6627	.032 58	.7215	.526 10	.7792	.991 68
7	.5427	.984 58	.6037	.533 98	.6637	.057 98	.7225	.551 50	.7802	96.017 08
8	.5437	90.009 98	.6047	.559 38	.6647	.083 38	.7235	.576 90	.7811	.039 94
9	.5448	.037 92	.6058	.587 32	.6657	.108 78	.7244	.599 76	.7821	.065 34
10	.5458	90.063 32	.6068	91.612 72	.6666	93.131 64	.7254	94.625 16	.7830	96.088 20
11	.5468	.088 72	.6078	.638 12	.6676	.157 04	.7264	.650 56	.7840	.113 60
12	.5478	.114 12	.6088	.663 52	.6686	.182 44	.7274	.675 96	.7850	.139 00
13	.5489	.142 06	.6098	.688 92	.6696	.207 84	.7283	.698 82	.7859	.161 86
14	.5499	.167 46	.6108	.714 32	.6706	.233 24	.7293	.724 22	.7869	.187 26
15	.5509	90.192 86	.6118	91.739 72	.6716	93.258 64	.7303	94.749 62	.7878	96.210 12
16	.5519	.218 26	.6128	.765 12	.6726	.284 04	.7312	.772 48	.7887	.232 98
17	.5529	.243 66	.6138	.790 52	.6736	.309 44	.7322	.797 88	.7897	.258 38
18	.5540	.271 60	.6148	.815 92	.6745	.332 30	.7332	.823 28	.7906	.281 24
19	.5550	.297 00	.6158	.841 32	.6755	.357 70	.7341	.846 14	.7916	.306 64
20	.5560	90.322 40	.6168	91.866 72	.6765	93.383 10	.7351	94.871 54	.7925	96.329 50
21	.5570	.347 80	.6178	.892 12	.6775	.408 50	.7361	.896 94	.7935	.354 90
22	.5581	.375 74	.6188	.917 52	.6785	.433 90	.7370	.919 80	.7944	.377 76
23	.5591	.401 14	.6198	.942 92	.6795	.459 30	.7380	.945 20	.7954	.403 16
24	.5601	.426 54	.6208	.968 32	.6805	.484 70	.7390	.970 60	.7963	.426 02
25	.5611	90.451 94	.6218	91.993 72	.6814	93.507 56	.7399	94.993 46	.7973	96.451 42
26	.5621	.477 34	.6228	92.019 12	.6824	.532 96	.7409	95.018 86	.7982	.474 28
27	.5632	.505 28	.6238	.044 52	.6834	.558 36	.7419	.044 26	.7992	.499 68

28	.5642	.530 68	.6248	.069 92	.6844	.583 76	.7428	.067 12	.8001	.522 54
29	.5652	.556 08	.6258	.095 32	.6854	.609 16	.7438	.092 52	.8011	.547 94
30	3.5662	90.581 48	3.6268	92.120 72	3.6864	93.634 56	3.7448	95.117 92	3.8020	96.570 80
31	.5672	.606 88	.6278	.146 12	.6873	.657 42	.7457	.140 78	.8029	.593 66
32	.5683	.634 82	.6288	.171 52	.6883	.682 82	.7467	.166 18	.8039	.619 06
33	.5693	.660 22	.6298	.196 92	.6893	.708 22	.7476	.189 04	.8048	.641 92
34	.5703	.685 62	.6308	.222 32	.6903	.733 62	.7486	.214 44	.8058	.667 32
35	3.5713	90.711 02	3.6318	92.247 72	3.6913	92.759 02	3.7496	95.239 84	3.8067	96.690 18
36	.5723	.736 42	.6328	.273 12	.6923	.784 42	.7505	.262 70	.8077	.715 58
37	.5734	.764 36	.6338	.298 52	.6932	.807 28	.7515	.288 10	.8086	.738 44
38	.5744	.789 76	.6348	.323 92	.6942	.832 68	.7525	.313 50	.8096	.763 84
39	.5754	.815 16	.6358	.349 32	.6952	.858 08	.7534	.336 36	.8105	.786 70
40	3.5764	90.840 56	3.6368	92.374 72	3.6962	93.883 48	3.7544	95.361 76	3.8114	96.809 56
41	.5774	.865 96	.6378	.400 12	.6972	.908 88	.7553	.384 62	.8124	.834 96
42	.5784	.891 36	.6388	.425 52	.6981	.931 74	.7563	.410 02	.8133	.857 82
43	.5795	.919 30	.6398	.450 92	.6991	.957 14	.7573	.435 42	.8143	.883 22
44	.5805	.944 70	.6408	.476 32	.7001	.982 54	.7582	.458 28	.8152	.906 08
45	3.5815	90.970 10	3.6418	92.501 72	3.7011	94.007 94	3.7592	95.483 68	3.8161	96.928 94
46	.5825	.995 50	.6428	.527 12	.7020	.030 80	.7601	.506 54	.8171	.954 34
47	.5835	91.020 90	.6438	.552 52	.7030	.056 20	.7611	.531 94	.8180	.977 20
48	.5845	.046 30	.6448	.577 92	.7040	.081 60	.7620	.554 80	.8190	97.002 60
49	.5855	.071 70	.6458	.603 32	.7050	.107 00	.7630	.580 20	.8199	.025 46
50	3.5866	91.099 64	3.6468	92.628 72	3.7060	94.132 40	3.7640	95.605 60	3.8208	97.048 32
51	.5876	.125 04	.6478	.654 12	.7069	.155 26	.7649	.628 46	.8218	.073 72
52	.5886	.150 44	.6488	.679 52	.7079	.180 66	.7659	.653 86	.8227	.096 58
53	.5896	.175 84	.6498	.704 92	.7089	.206 06	.7668	.676 72	.8236	.119 44
54	.5906	.201 24	.6508	.730 32	.7099	.231 46	.7678	.702 12	.8246	.144 84
55	3.5916	91.226 64	3.6518	92.755 72	3.7108	94.254 32	3.7687	95.724 98	3.8255	97.167 70
56	.5926	.252 04	.6528	.781 12	.7118	.279 72	.7697	.750 38	.8265	.193 10
57	.5936	.277 44	.6538	.806 52	.7128	.305 12	.7707	.775 78	.8274	.215 96
58	.5947	.305 38	.6548	.831 92	.7138	.330 52	.7716	.798 64	.8283	.238 82
59	.5957	.330 78	.6558	.857 32	.7147	.353 38	.7726	.824 04	.8293	.264 22
60	3.5967	91.356 18	3.6567	92.880 18	3.7157	94.378 78	3.7735	95.846 90	3.8302	97.287 08

Sine Plate Settings (Continued).

Min	50° Inch	50° mm	51° Inch	51° mm	52° Inch	52° mm	53° Inch	53° mm	54° Inch	54° mm
0	3.8302	97.287 08	3.8857	98.696 78	3.9400	100.076 00	3.9932	101.427 28	4.0451	102.745 54
1	.8311	.309 94	.8866	.719 64	.9409	.098 86	.9940	.447 60	.0459	.765 86
2	.8321	.335 34	.8875	.742 50	.9418	.121 72	.9949	.470 46	.0468	.788 72
3	.8330	.358 20	.8884	.765 36	.9427	.144 58	.9958	.493 32	.0476	.809 04
4	.8339	.381 06	.8894	.790 76	.9436	.167 44	.9967	.516 18	.0485	.831 90
5	3.8349	97.406 46	3.8903	98.813 62	3.9445	100.190 30	3.9975	101.536 50	4.0493	102.852 22
6	.8358	.429 32	.8912	.836 48	.9454	.213 16	.9984	.559 36	.0502	.874 08
7	.8367	.452 18	.8921	.859 34	.9463	.236 02	.9993	.582 22	.0510	.895 40
8	.8377	.477 58	.8930	.882 20	.9472	.258 88	4.0001	.602 54	.0519	.918 26
9	.8386	.500 44	.8939	.905 06	.9481	.281 74	.0010	.625 40	.0527	.938 58
10	3.8395	97.523 30	3.8948	98.927 92	3.9490	100.304 60	4.0019	101.648 26	4.0536	102.961 44
11	.8405	.548 70	.8958	.953 32	.9499	.327 46	.0028	.671 12	.0544	.981 76
12	.8414	.571 56	.8967	.976 18	.9508	.350 32	.0036	.691 44	.0553	103.004 62
13	.8423	.594 42	.8976	.999 04	.9516	.370 64	.0045	.714 30	.0561	.024 94
14	.8433	.619 82	.8985	99.021 90	.9525	.393 50	.0054	.737 16	.0570	.047 80
15	3.8442	97.642 68	3.8994	99.044 76	3.9534	100.416 36	4.0062	101.757 48	4.0578	103.068 12
16	.8451	.665 54	.9003	.067 62	.9543	.439 22	.0071	.780 34	.0587	.090 98
17	.8460	.688 40	.9012	.090 48	.9552	.462 08	.0080	.803 20	.0595	.111 30
18	.8470	.713 80	.9021	.113 34	.9561	.484 94	.0089	.826 06	.0604	.134 16
19	.8479	.736 66	.9030	.136 20	.9570	.507 80	.0097	.846 38	.0612	.154 48
20	3.8488	97.759 52	3.9039	99.159 06	3.9579	100.530 66	4.0106	101.869 24	4.0621	103.177 34
21	.8498	.784 92	.9049	.184 46	.9588	.553 52	.0115	.892 10	.0629	.197 66
22	.8507	.807 78	.9058	.207 32	.9596	.573 84	.0123	.912 42	.0638	.220 52
23	.8516	.830 64	.9067	.230 18	.9605	.596 70	.0132	.935 28	.0646	.240 84
24	.8525	.853 50	.9076	.253 04	.9614	.619 56	.0141	.958 14	.0655	.263 70
25	3.8535	97.878 90	3.9085	99.275 90	3.9623	100.642 42	4.0149	101.978 46	4.0663	103.284 02
26	.8544	.901 76	.9094	.298 76	.9632	.665 28	.0158	102.001 32	.0672	.306 88
27	.8553	.924 62	.9103	.321 62	.9641	.688 14	.0167	.024 18	.0680	.327 20

28	.8562	.947 48	.9112	.344 84	.9650	.711 00	.0175	.044 50	.0689	.350 06
29	.8572	.972 88	.9121	.367 34	.9659	.733 86	.0184	.067 36	.0697	.370 38
30	3.8581	97.995 74	3.9130	99.390 20	3.9667	100.754 18	4.0193	102.090 22	4.0706	103.393 24
31	.8590	98.018 60	.9139	.413 06	.9676	.777 04	.0201	.110 54	.0714	.413 56
32	.8599	.041 46	.9148	.435 92	.9685	.799 90	.0210	.133 40	.0722	.433 88
33	.8609	.066 86	.9157	.458 78	.9694	.822 76	.0219	.156 26	.0731	.456 74
34	.8618	.089 72	.9166	.481 64	.9703	.845 62	.0227	.176 58	.0739	.477 06
35	3.8627	98.112 58	3.9175	99.504 50	3.9712	100.868 48	4.0236	103.199 44	4.0748	103.499 92
36	.8636	.135 44	.9184	.527 36	.9720	.888 80	.0244	.219 76	.0756	.520 24
37	.8646	.160 84	.9193	.550 22	.9729	.911 66	.0253	.242 62	.0765	.543 10
38	.8655	.183 70	.9202	.573 08	.9738	.934 52	.0262	.265 48	.0773	.563 42
39	.8664	.206 56	.9212	.598 48	.9747	.957 38	.0270	.285 80	.0781	.583 74
40	3.8673	98.229 42	3.9221	99.621 34	3.9756	100.980 24	4.0279	102.308 66	4.0790	103.606 60
41	.8683	.254 82	.9230	.644 20	.9765	101.003 10	.0288	.331 52	.0798	.626 92
42	.8692	.277 68	.9239	.667 06	.9773	.023 42	.0296	.351 84	.0807	.649 78
43	.8701	.300 54	.9248	.689 92	.9782	.046 28	.0305	.374 70	.0815	.670 10
44	.8710	.323 40	.9257	.712 78	.9791	.069 14	.0313	.395 02	.0823	.690 42
45	3.8719	98.346 26	3.9266	99.735 64	3.9800	101.092 00	4.0322	102.417 88	4.0832	103.713 28
46	.8729	.371 66	.9275	.758 50	.9809	.114 86	.0331	.440 74	.0840	.733 60
47	.8738	.394 52	.9284	.781 36	.9817	.135 18	.0339	.461 06	.0849	.756 46
48	.8747	.417 38	.9293	.804 22	.9826	.158 04	.0348	.483 92	.0857	.776 78
49	.8756	.440 24	.9302	.827 08	.9835	.180 90	.0356	.504 24	.0865	.797 10
50	3.8765	98.463 10	3.9311	99.849 94	3.9844	101.203 76	4.0365	102.527 10	4.0874	103.819 96
51	.8775	.488 50	.9320	.872 80	.9853	.226 62	.0374	.549 96	.0882	.840 28
52	.8784	.511 36	.9329	.895 66	.9861	.246 94	.0382	.570 28	.0891	.863 14
53	.8793	.534 22	.9338	.918 52	.9870	.269 80	.0391	.593 14	.0899	.883 46
54	.8802	.557 08	.9347	.941 38	.9879	.292 66	.0399	.613 46	.0907	.903 78
55	3.8811	98.579 94	3.9355	99.961 70	3.9888	101.315 52	4.0408	102.636 32	4.0916	103.926 64
56	.8820	.602 80	.9364	.984 56	.9896	.335 84	.0416	.656 64	.0924	.946 96
57	.8830	.628 20	.9373	100.007 42	.9905	.358 86	.0425	.679 50	.0932	.967 28
58	.8839	.651 06	.9382	.030 28	.9914	.381 56	.0433	.699 82	.0941	.990 14
59	.8848	.673 92	.9391	.053 14	.9923	.404 42	.0442	.722 68	.0949	104.010 46
60	3.8857	98.969 78	3.9400	100.076 00	3.9932	101.427 28	4.0451	102.745 54	4.0957	104.030 78

Sine Plate Settings (Continued).

Min	55° Inch	55° mm	56° Inch	56° mm
0	4.0957	104.030 78	4.1452	105.288 08
1	.0966	.053 64	.1460	.308 40
2	.0974	.073 96	.1468	.328 72
3	.0982	.094 28	.1476	.349 04
4	.0991	.117 14	.1484	.369 36
5	4.0999	104.137 46	4.1492	105.389 68
6	.1007	.157 78	.1500	.410 00
7	.1016	.180 64	.1508	.430 32
8	.1024	.200 96	.1517	.453 18
9	.1032	.221 28	.1525	.473 50
10	4.1041	104.244 14	4.1533	105.493 82
11	.1049	.264 46	.1541	.514 14
12	.1057	.284 78	.1549	.534 46
13	.1066	.307 64	.1557	.554 78
14	.1074	.327 96	.1565	.575 10
15	4.1082	104.348 28	4.1573	105.595 42
16	.1090	.368 60	.1581	.615 74
17	.1099	.391 46	.1589	.636 06
18	.1107	.411 78	.1597	.656 38
19	.1115	.432 21	.1606	.679 24
20	4.1124	104.454 96	4.1614	105.699 56
21	.1132	.475 28	.1622	.719 88
22	.1140	.495 60	.1630	.740 20
23	.1148	.515 92	.1638	.760 52
24	.1157	.538 78	.1646	.780 84
25	4.1165	104.559 10	4.1654	105.801 16
26	.1173	.579 42	.1662	.821 48
27	.1181	.599 74	.1670	.841 80

28	.1190	.622 60	.1678	.862 12
29	.1198	.642 92	.1686	.882 44
30	4.1206	104.663 24	4.1694	105.902 76
31	.1214	.683 56	.1702	.923 08
32	.1223	.706 42	.1710	.943 40
33	.1231	.726 74	.1718	.963 72
34	.1239	.747 06	.1726	.984 04
35	4.1247	104.767 38	4.1734	106.004 36
36	.1255	.787 70	.1742	.024 68
37	.1264	.810 56	.1750	.045 00
38	.1272	.830 88	.1758	.064 32
39	.1280	.851 20	.1766	.085 64
40	4.1288	104.871 52	4.1774	106.105 96
41	.1296	.891 84	.1782	.126 28
42	.1305	.914 70	.1790	.146 60
43	.1313	.935 02	.1798	.166 92
44	.1321	.955 34	.1806	.187 24
45	4.1329	104.975 66	4.1814	106.207 56
46	.1337	.995 98	.1822	.227 88
47	.1346	105.018 84	.1830	.248 20
48	.1354	.039 16	.1838	.268 52
49	.1362	.059 48	.1846	.288 84
50	4.1370	105.079 80	4.1854	106.309 16
51	.1378	.100 12	.1862	.329 48
52	.1386	.120 44	.1870	.349 80
53	.1395	.143 30	.1878	.370 12
54	.1403	.163 62	.1886	.390 44
55	4.1411	105.183 94	4.1894	106.410 76
56	.1419	.204 26	.1902	.431 08
57	.1427	.224 58	.1909	.448 86
58	.1435	.244 90	.1917	.469 18
59	.1443	.265 22	.1925	.478 95
60	4.1452	105.288 08	4.1933	106.509 82

Index